Heinrich Bullinger and the Covenant

HEINRYCHVS BVLLINGERVS
QVNDECIMI IAM NVNC LABVNTVR SYDERA LVSTRI,
HÆC ÆTAS, FORMAM PICTA TABELLA REFERT
NIL EGO VEL FORMAM VEL VITÆ TEMPORA SPECTO,
SED CHRISTVM, VITÆ QVI MIHI FORMA MEÆ EST.

Heinrich Bullinger and the Covenant:

THE OTHER REFORMED TRADITION

J. Wayne Baker

Ohio University Press
Athens, Ohio

© Copyright 1980 by J. Wayne Baker

Printed in the United States of America

Baker, J.   Wayne.
    Heinrich Bullinger and the covenant.

    Bibliography: p. 265
    Includes index.
        1. Covenants (Theology)—History of doctrines.
2. Bullinger, Heinrich, 1504-1575. I. Title.
BT155.B32   230'.42   80-14667
ISBN 0-8214-0554-3

FOR MY FATHER

Contents

ACKNOWLEDGMENTS

I WOULD like to give special thanks to H. O. Van Gilder, who first directed my attention to covenant theology; to Robert M. Kingdon, who taught me the craft of history and aroused my interest in Bullinger; and to James M. Kittelson, who guided me through the dissertation process.

I am grateful to the American Philosophical Society for a research grant that enabled me, in 1972, to spend the requisite time in the Zurich archival collections; to the University of Akron for research grants that helped to finance the research for this book; to the Department of History of the University of Akron for providing me with leaves of absence for research and writing; to Ulrich Helfenstein of the Staatsarchiv and Jean-Pierre Bodner of the Zentralbibliothek in Zurich, and their staffs, for their grace in aiding an archival neophyte; to Fritz Büsser and his incomparable staff, especially Ulrich Gäbler, at the Institut für Schweizerische Reformationsgeschichte in Zurich for their invaluable assistance in identifying Bullinger manuscripts in the Zurich archives and for providing me with a research desk at the Institut; and to Mrs. Garnette Dorsey and her staff for their untiring efforts in typing several drafts of the manuscript.

Several friends and colleagues have given much time and effort in reading various versions of this manuscript. I would like to express my gratitude to Robert M. Kingdon, James M. Kittelson, Ulrich Gäbler, Peggy K. Liss, Harry J. Ausmus, Phillip N. Bebb, and Jerald C. Brauer for their careful and thoughtful criticisms. I hope that they will agree that I have benefited from their efforts.

I must also thank the editors of the *Sixteenth Century Journal* for permission to use, in chapter 5, some material previously published in the *Journal* (5:1 [1974]); and the editor of the Theologischer Verlag Zurich for permission to use, in chapter 4 and the epilogue, brief portions of an essay published in *Heinrich Bullinger 1504–1575: Gesammelte Aufsätze zum 400. Todestag, volume 1: Leben und Werk* (1975).

This study began as a dissertation at the University of Iowa; portions of chapters 5 and 6 have been taken from that earlier version.

Prologue

HEINRICH BULLINGER was one of the makers of the Reformed tradition. It was Bullinger who preserved the Swiss Reformation after the death of Zwingli, and it was he who assured the essential theological unity of Reformed Protestantism with the First and Second Helvetic Confessions. During his forty-five-year tenure as leader of the Zurich church his importance in Reformed circles was unsurpassed, except perhaps by Calvin. Bullinger's influence was partly due to the many evangelical exiles, especially those from England and Italy, who went to Zurich. Mostly, however, this influence resulted from his voluminous writings and correspondence. He published a total of 119 works, not including titles that appeared posthumously or in later translations and editions.[1] His extant correspondence numbers more than twelve thousand pieces, letters to and from nearly every prominent ecclesiastical and political leader of his day. His works have been traced to almost every part of Europe, including Poland, Hungary, Romania, Italy, and Spain, and his books crossed the seas with the Dutch and English colonists.[2]

Bullinger's importance in the historical development of the Reformed tradition is thus indisputable. But the precise nature of his influence is largely yet to be determined. He is still among the least

known of the leading sixteenth-century reformers, especially among
English readers. Not only does Bullinger lack a biography in English,
but general histories of the Reformation contain very little information
about him. Invariably he is presented simply as Zwingli's successor and
alter ego. This paucity of knowledge about Bullinger and his thought
has made Bullinger the phantom figure of the Reformation. A short
biographical sketch will serve to place him within the context of the
early Reformation and to set the framework for the controversies that
had so much influence on the development of Reformed thought.

Bullinger was born on July 18, 1504, in Bremgarten, a town of about
eight hundred population, ten miles west of Zurich.[3] The Bullinger
family, among the oldest families of the town, had been in Bremgarten
at least since the first half of the fourteenth century. Heinrich's mother,
Anna Wiederkehr, was the daughter of the miller of Bremgarten, who
was also a councilman. His father, Heinrich the elder, was chaplain in
Bremgarten when Heinrich was born; he later became dean (*Dekan*).
Anna and Heinrich began living together as man and wife in 1495, and
although the marriage was not legalized until 1529, the relationship
was open and public from the beginning. In the eyes of the parish, if not
according to church law, they were husband and wife, and Heinrich
and his four older brothers, legitimate. Anna not only cared for the
home and the family but also for the poor and the sick of the parish.
The elder Heinrich was fully accepted both as parish priest and as husband and father. Such a living arrangement was not unusual, and
Heinrich's home life appears to have been normal.

When not yet five years old, Heinrich entered school, in March 1509.
The Latin school at Bremgarten was supported not by the church but
by the city, to prepare the sons of its more well-to-do citizens for the
university.[4] It had a late medieval curriculum that had not been
affected by humanism. Seven years later, in November 1516, Heinrich
left home to join his brother John at Emmerich, to continue his
schooling at the Latin school at the church of St. Martin. St. Martin's
school was "reformed," and thus Heinrich was introduced to humanist
studies and techniques. The reform consisted mostly of the use of new
books of instruction: modern grammars and pagan and early Christian
authors. Heinrich studied the Aldus edition of the Grammar of
Donatus and read from Pliny the Younger, Cicero, Vergil, Horace,
and Jerome.[5] In addition, he explored the elements of Greek and

logic.[6] Heinrich's father sent him to Emmerich because of this humanist "reform" and because his older brother was already there.[7] During his three-year stay at Emmerich, financial support from his father was scanty, apparently in order to teach the lessons of poverty to the young Heinrich. Like Luther earlier, Heinrich begged for his supper by singing.

In July 1519, Heinrich accompanied John to Cologne, where he studied under the arts faculty at the university. He took his instruction at Cologne's oldest and most famous bursa, the Bursa Montis, where he learned Aristotle in Thomistic form, the *via antiqua* rather than the Occamist *via moderna*, which Luther had received. Humanism had not affected the curriculum at Cologne, but, despite the conservatism at the university, two professors of the arts faculty, Johann Matthäus Phrissemius and Arnold von Wesel, were committed to the humanistic studies. Disenchanted with the traditional curriculum, Bullinger came under their influence in 1520. As he expressed it, "I therefore directed my mind to the more humane studies" (*ad humaniora studia*).[8] Under their direction, he read in Cicero, Plutarch, Vergil, Horace, Aristotle, Paul's letter to the Romans, Agricola, and Erasmus. In addition, he took advantage of the private lectures of Johann Caesarius and Jacob Sobius, humanists not associated with the university, reading Quintilian, Gellius, Macrobius, Pliny, Solon, and Homer. Also, under the tutelage of Arnold von Wesel and Caesarius, he improved his knowledge of Greek. Bullinger became Bachelor of Arts in November 1520.

The year 1520 was one of growing excitement in Cologne, as elsewhere in Germany. Luther's debate with Eck the previous year at Leipzig had made him the hero of the humanists, the defender of sound learning against the obscurantist scholastics. Then, during the year 1520, Luther published his three revolutionary tracts, in particular, *The Babylonian Captivity*. On October 10, the papal bull *Exsurge domine* was published against Luther, giving him a sixty-day grace period in which to recant. On November 15, the enraged theologians at Cologne burned Luther's books, just three days before Bullinger's first baccalaureate exam. Even though he remained aloof from the turmoil, Bullinger was hardly untouched by it. In fact, the book burning, plus the growing controversy about Luther at the university, ignited in Bullinger an interest in theology. Confessing ignorance of both the

papal and Lutheran teachings, he consulted a theologian, who directed
him to Lombard and Gratian. Then, turning to the church fathers, he
read in Chrysostum, Ambrose, Origen, and Augustine. At the same
time he studied Luther's crucial treatises of 1520. From this reading he
concluded, "Luther comes closer to the ancient theologians than do the
scholastics." Turning to a study of the New Testament itself, he soon
began "to abhor completely the papal teaching."[9] He also read
Melanchthon's *Loci communes* of 1521. By the time Bullinger became
Master in early 1522, he had embraced the evangelical understanding
of justification by faith, entirely through his own study.[10] He was not
yet eighteen years old.

Heinrich returned to his father's house in April 1522. Apparently the
elder Bullinger, although a Roman Catholic priest, did not react
strongly to his son's newly adopted Lutheran evangelical position, for
Heinrich continued his study of Luther's writings, as well as reading in
Athanasius, Lactantius, and Cyprian, throughout 1522. Then, in
January 1523, Wolfgang Joner, Abbot of the Cistercian Monastery at
Kappel, offered him the position of head teacher at the abbey school.
Bullinger accepted on the condition that he would have nothing to do
with the monk's life or the mass. Joner, already secretly inclined
toward the evangelical teaching, was only too happy to allow him such
religious freedom. On January 17, 1523 Bullinger became the
evangelical teacher of the Cistercian monks at Kappel.

Three important influences are evident during Bullinger's early
years. First, his knowledge of the classics was broader than might be
imagined from his writings. Although he was never really a humanist,
he had read widely in the Greek and Latin authors of antiquity. He was
also greatly influenced by the church fathers, particularly Jerome,
Chrysostum, and Augustine. The fathers continued to be of great
importance in the further development of his thought. Finally, Luther
exerted much influence on the early development of Bullinger's
theology. He had read many of Luther's works, and in the end it was
Luther who convinced him of the papal errors. In these early years and
the following years at Kappel and Bremgarten, Bullinger prized Luther
highly, even while disagreeing with him on the eucharist.

Bullinger began his teaching activities at Kappel on February 3,
immediately beginning a reform of the Latin school curriculum, using
both ancient and modern authors such as Vergil and Erasmus. But in

addition to his duties as teacher in the Latin school, he also taught the monks, introducing them to the *Paraclesis* and *Compendium* of Erasmus and the *Loci communes* of Melanchthon. Then, also in 1523 and 1524, he began to lecture on the New Testament, giving an exposition of Matthew and John. During his years at Kappel, he wrote Latin commentaries on most of the New Testament books, at the same time lecturing on them in German to the monks and others who wished to attend, a veritable "school of exposition," in which Bullinger preceded Zwingli by two years.[11] The result was the reform of the monastery, the mass being abolished on September 4, 1525 and the eucharist celebrated in the Reformed manner on March 29, 1526. Eventually many of the monks became Reformed ministers.

Late in 1523, Bullinger went to Zurich to meet Zwingli and Leo Jud. In his "Vita" of 1560, he wrote, "In the year 1523 I heard Huldreich Zwingli for the first time. . . . I was greatly encouraged by his firm, correct and scriptural teaching."[12] This does not mean, however, that Bullinger then became Zwingli's student any more than he had previously been bound to Luther and Melanchthon. Rather, he worked out his own point of view with some intellectual and spiritual freedom. Indeed, the single time Bullinger mentioned a theological matter in connection with Zwingli in his *Diarium*, he emphasized his own independence. In an entry dated September 12, 1524, he wrote that he had approached Zwingli about the eucharist: "I honestly set forth my opinion to him, which I had derived from a certain writing of the Waldensian brothers and from the books of Augustine." Zwingli then revealed that he had come to the same opinion, but he asked Bullinger not to publicize his teaching until the time was right.[13] Two months later Zwingli publicly expressed his teaching on the symbolic nature of the eucharist in his open letter to Alber.[14] But according to Bullinger's account, he had come to his own conclusion on the eucharist independently. Undoubtedly Zwingli exerted a considerable influence on Bullinger. The similarities in their thought are quite evident, and in later writings Bullinger several times acknowledged his debt to Zwingli. Nevertheless, their points of view were not always the same.

Bullinger's contacts with Zwingli increased during the next four years. On January 16, 1525, he attended the first disputation between the Reformed ministers and the Anabaptists, having been invited by the Zurich council at Zwingli's request. At the second (March 17 and 20) and third (November 6–8) disputations he acted as clerk. In 1527 he took five months' leave from Kappel, from mid-June through mid-November, to hear Zwingli preach and teach and to study Greek and Hebrew in Zurich. Then, in January of 1528, he accompanied Zwingli, as an official delegate from Zurich, to the disputation at Bern. In Bern for most of January, Bullinger there met Martin Bucer, Ambrosius Blarer, Berchtold Haller, and Guillaume Farel.

Bullinger's Kappel years were thus busy and fruitful. Not only had he lectured on most of the New Testament and consequently effected reform at the monastery, but he had also broadened his horizons through his contacts with Zwingli, in Zurich, and at the disputation at Bern. It was additionally a productive period for him as an author. In his *Diarium*, Bullinger listed seventy-two titles that he had authored between 1523 and 1528, including four published books.[15] Then, toward the end of the Kappel period, in June 1528, he agreed to serve part-time as pastor at Hausen am Albis, near Kappel. Bullinger preached his first sermon on June 21. Less than a year later, he left Kappel to become the reformer of his home parish, Bremgarten.

The elder Bullinger had embraced the Reformed teaching early in 1529. Although he was dismissed as a result, shortly thereafter the evangelical-minded group prevailed. Their request for a Reformed pastor brought Gervasius Shuler from Zurich, but many in Bremgarten wanted to hear the younger Heinrich Bullinger. On May 16, 1529 Bullinger preached in Bremgarten, so effectively that the altar was broken and the images removed from the church by the next day, and the council invited him to work as pastor with Shuler. Bullinger began his ministry at Bremgarten on June 1; by the end of June, the parish was committed to the Reformed teaching. That summer Bullinger was so engrossed in his new venture that he declined an invitation from Zwingli in August to accompany him to Marburg for the meeting with Luther on the eucharist.

In addition to his reforming activities, two significant events occurred in Bullinger's life during his Bremgarten period. First, on August 17, 1529, he married Anna Adlischwyler, a nun to whom he had become betrothed during his long visit to Zurich in 1527. Anna, the daughter of Hans Adlischwyler, was born about 1504 and died in 1564. She had entered the Dominican cloister in 1523; in 1527 she was one of the two remaining nuns in the cloister. There were eleven children, six sons and five daughters, from the marriage.[16]

Bullinger also experienced his first personal opposition from the Anabaptists while at Bremgarten. In 1530, Hans Pfistermeyer, from Aarau, appeared in the area and drew a crowd of three hundred to four hundred people at Bremgarten. This prompted Bullinger to write his first book against the Anabaptists in the summer of 1530, although it was not published until 1531. In January 1531, Bullinger participated in a disputation with the Anabaptists that dealt mainly with the problem of usury (*Zins*).[17]

Soon, however, even the problem of the Anabaptists was to be pushed into the background, with the defeat of Zurich by the Catholic states at Kappel in October 1531. Zwingli's foreign policy was nearly disastrous for the Reformation in Zurich: his death and the defeat threatened the entire Reformed structure. Bullinger was greatly affected by these events, for according to the Second Peace of Kappel (November 20) he, his father, and Shuler were exiled from Bremgarten. Bullinger immediately left for Zurich with his family.

The twenty-seven-year-old Bullinger arrived in Zurich on November 21, 1531. Within a few days, he had received three invitations to assume important pastoral positions, from Basel (November 27), Bern (December 6), and Zurich (December 9).[18] His future, however, was tied to Zurich; he became *Antistes*[19] of the Zurich church on December 13. Confronted with a divided council and a demoralized church, his performance during the first few months to a large extent determined the future form and the fate of the Zwinglian Reformation.

Zurich's foreign policy and expansionist activities within the Confederation under Zwingli threatened the entire program of reform in Zurich. Although according to the Second Peace of Kappel (November 20) Zurich was allowed to retain its Reformed faith, it had to abandon its proselytizing within the Confederation and give up its foreign alliances.[20] The internal consequences of the defeat held even more potential danger. Zurich had lost not only Zwingli but many other staunch defenders of the Reformation as well. Of the 514 who died in battle, there were 25 pastors, as well as 7 members of the small council and 19 from the great council. Those who replaced the fallen councilmen were either opponents or doubtful men. Secret Catholics began to emerge, and Reformed society seemed endangered.

The defeat also triggered opposition from the *Landschaft*, the country areas under Zurich rule. The Meilener Articles, demands submitted to the council by representatives of the *Landschaft* on November 28, were particularly important. The council should not go to war without the consent of the *Landschaft* and should submit all important questions to the people (*Landleute*). The political authority should be restored to the legal councils, and the secret council abolished. Finally, only peace-loving pastors, who would not berate the people for their godless lives but would only preach God's word, should be tolerated. The pastors were to be prohibited from involving themselves in political matters, either personally or from the pulpit. They should not criticize the council but should allow the civil authorities to rule as they saw fit.[21] The council acceded to these demands in an agreement on December 9,[22] the same day Bullinger was called to replace Zwingli. Quite clearly the council's decree would make impossible such power as Zwingli had wielded as leader of the Zurich church.

Even though Bullinger had opposed the Kappel War and had no apparent desire to involve himself in politics, the fourth article was unacceptable to him because it put conditions on the preaching of the gospel itself. On December 13, Bullinger replied to the council that he could not accept its offer without further clarification of the status of the preaching office. The essence of his reply was that the pastors must obey God alone in these matters. They would preach nothing against truth, honor, and oath, nor anything contrary to peace. He agreed that the pastors would no longer meddle in affairs properly under the authority of the magistracy. The crucial point for Bullinger was the freedom of the pulpit. The pastors must be allowed to fulfill their prophetic role, teaching God's will for man in society. Bullinger thus insisted on the absolute integrity of the preaching office. Although this reply caused considerable commotion and disagreement among the councilmen, they finally agreed in Bullinger's favor. The council would not put constraints on the preaching of God's word.[23]

Bullinger, then, successfully preserved the freedom of the pulpit in this initial test of his leadership. At the same time, however, it was evident that the magistracy would forcefully utilize its power in the future and that the pastors must remain within the bounds that they themselves had defined in this confrontation. Neither Bullinger nor any other pastor would again possess the power that Zwingli had exercised in the civil sphere. Zwingli was dead. Quite clearly there would be no new Zwinglis.

Bullinger's commitment to the freedom of the pulpit was soon matched by his support for magisterial authority. Although he denied the council's control over the clergy in their priestly functions, he firmly reasserted its power in matters of discipline. In May 1532, the council issued a mandate, the original draft of which had come from Bullinger's pen. First of all the mandate was an answer to rumors in the Confederation that Zurich was about to return to the Catholic fold. At the same time it reaffirmed the basic tenets and aims of Reformed society as it had existed before Zwingli's death. The mandate was an assertion from both Bullinger and the council that the Reformed structure had not crumbled despite the defeat and the resulting confusion in Zurich. The mandate renewed the morals legislation of previous years, particularly the Great Morals Mandate of 1530. It emphasized that the mass would not be tolerated. Any individuals who disobeyed in this matter would be exiled, and anyone involved in intrigue and plots to subvert Christian order would be punished in body and possessions. All must obey these laws concerning the Christian Reformation because they were bound to do so "by divine and civil duty."[24] This forceful mandate, sent to Zurich's allies to reassure them and read in every Zurich church, restored discipline and pacified the people. It was proof that Reformed society in Zurich had not expired along with Zwingli.

Bullinger's stance in regard to the relationship between the pastors and the magistracy was further clarified by two challenges in 1532. The first came from Leo Jud, a leading pastor and early associate of Zwingli. In a letter to Bullinger in March, Jud proposed a new method for discipline in Zurich—a purely ecclesiastical morals court with the power of excommunication. Bullinger rejected Jud's proposal, arguing vigorously for the continuation of magisterial discipline and against any ban from the eucharist.[25] Apparently Jud had been influenced by the Confession of the Bohemian-Moravian Brethren, just published in Zurich.[26] That Bullinger successfully met this challenge is evidenced by Jud's *Catechism* of January 1534: the section on the church gives conclusive proof that Bullinger had convinced Jud.[27]

The second attack, from the council, resulted in the magisterial encroachment on the wealth of the church. During the 1520s, the income from the secularized monasteries had been allotted to social services such as education and the care of the poor and the sick. In 1528 the council had wanted to appropriate any surplus for its own needs but instead had resorted to loans. The war, however, had increased the fiscal pressure, so the council tried again in 1532, arguing that the war had, after all, been fought for the sake of the church. Although Bullinger vigorously denied the right of the council to appropriate the surplus, he was overruled. On July 30, 1533 a new office, the *Obmannamt*, was created, the *Obmann* becoming overseer over all monastic property. Elected from the small council, he administered the surplus income, sometimes for church needs and at other times for civil needs.[28]

The relationship between the clergy and the civil authorities was more formally defined, also in 1532 (October 22), in a mandate from the council concerning the Synod, authored by Bullinger and Jud. The first section detailed the methods for the selection, examination, and ordination of pastors. Section 2 dealt with the task and life of the clergy. The third section defined the composition and role of the Synod. The membership included eight councilmen as well as all the pastors. There were two presidents: one pastor and one councilman. The Synod held the authority of censure over its clerical members. Article 9 of section 3 gave the Synod authority over the life and teachings of the clergy as outlined in the mandate. On the other hand, the Synod would not concern itself with civil matters. The pastors did not desire such power for themselves; nor did they wish to evade the authority of the lawful magistrate.[29]

Thus, less than a year after Bullinger's selection as *Antistes*, the relationship between the church and the civil government had been fully and finally defined. The church had no disciplinary power; that was completely in the hands of the magistracy. The council had established its ultimate control over ecclesiastical revenues. And the role of the clergy was clearly limited to the preaching of the word and other pastoral functions, under the control of the council.

Bullinger ministered to the needs of Zurich for the next forty-three years, as preacher, pastor, teacher, and author. His moderate nature, his courage in the face of outbreaks of the plague, his amicable relationships with the political leaders of Zurich,[30] and his implacable opposition to both the Anabaptists and the Catholics strengthened and confirmed his position throughout the years until his death on September 17, 1575.

Despite his irenic personality, Bullinger was involved in disagreement and conflict with other Protestant churches throughout his ministry at Zurich. His disagreements with the Lutherans and Anabaptists were public and often acrimonious. The specific theological quarrel between Zurich and the Lutherans was over the eucharist, but when responding to the Lutherans, especially Johannes Brenz, Bullinger felt compelled not only to uphold the orthodoxy of Zwinglianism but also to defend the Zurich Reformed church against the charge of radicalism.[31] Bullinger's lifelong antagonism toward the Anabaptists is well known if not fully understood.[32]

One of Bullinger's lifelong goals was agreement and cooperation among the Reformed churches. In 1536 he was a principal author of the First Helvetic Confession. Then, during the late 1540s, he and Calvin came to an agreement on the eucharist, as evidenced by the Consensus Tigurinus of 1549.[33] Finally, in the early 1560s, Bullinger authored the Second Helvetic Confession, a comprehensive affirmation of the Reformed faith, which became the most authoritative of all the Reformed confessions. After its publication in 1566, it was accepted not only by the Swiss Reformed churches but also by those in parts of Germany, France, and Eastern Europe as well, and was received as authoritative in England, Scotland, and Holland.[34] Nevertheless, despite these public affirmations of unity and Bullinger's indefatigable efforts to effect concord at least among the Reformed churches, there were issues on which he and the Genevans never agreed. Even though these disagreements were subdued and were seldom publicly aired, there was a sense in which Zurich and Geneva vied for leadership of the Reformed churches.

To a large extent Bullinger's differences with the Genevans, as well as the Anabaptists and Lutherans, stemmed from or were reinforced by his idea of the covenant and his view of Christian society, which was based on the covenant. The word "covenant" was, of course, used widely by the Protestant reformers, including Luther and Calvin. Covenant was simply one idiom among several, including predestination, by which the basic ideas of the Reformation, *sola fide* and *sola gratia*, could be expressed. Bullinger's idea of the covenant differed, however, from Luther's and Calvin's. His was a mutual or bilateral covenant, while theirs was a unilateral testament.[35] In fact, much of what has been called "covenant" theology in the sixteenth century was in reality a theology of testament. In general, testament (*testamentum*) has a double reference: to the Old and New Testament, a hermeneutical sense, and to the testament of God in terms of promise, a soteriological sense. When most sixteenth-century theologians used the term covenant (*foedus*), they meant testament in the soteriological sense. Christ was the Testator as well as the promised inheritance, and the elect, the heirs. The idea of covenant as a bilateral, mutual agreement was often missing. Bullinger, on the other hand, used both terms, *foedus* and *testamentum*, to refer to a mutual pact or covenant. Although *testamentum* also carried the meaning of last testament and promise for Bullinger, God's agreement with man included not only God's promises but also certain conditions that man was obligated to meet. Thus, for Bullinger, *testamentum* was the broader term of the two: it included both the idea of promise and the meaning of *foedus*, mutual agreement or pact.

Bullinger, then, used the terms interchangeably but not necessarily indiscriminately. Many reformers, such as Calvin and Olevianus, used them interchangeably and indiscriminately. Whether the word was *testamentum* or *foedus*, it meant a theology of testament, not a bilateral or mutual covenant. Bullinger, on the other hand, posited a conditional covenant, which included the idea of testament. This distinction between the Calvinistic theology of testament and Bullinger's notion of conditional covenant is crucial in understanding Bullinger and his influence on the early Reformed tradition.

Predestination was the second important matter of disagreement in Reformed Protestantism, and it was closely related to the issue of testament and covenant. The key Reformation principles of justification by faith alone through grace alone seemed endangered by the idea of a bilateral covenant. The Protestant logic appeared to be on the side of a theology of testament. Calvin's theology of testament within the confines of double predestination clearly avoided any weakening of the distinctive Protestant doctrine of justification. For Calvin, predestination implemented *sola fide* and protected *sola gratia*. Bullinger, while not avoiding the issue, did not attempt to solve the tensions, which he thought were also found in the Scripture, between conditional covenant and *sola gratia*. For Bullinger, the covenant was the exclusive vehicle through which God worked in history with His people. Bullinger held to a conditional covenant on the one hand and to *sola gratia* encased within a carefully stated doctrine of single predestination on the other hand. He interpreted both *sola fide* and *sola gratia* in convenantal terms, without falling into the semi-Pelagian stance that logic might have seemed to demand.

Community and discipline was the third issue dividing the Reformed churches. Bullinger's ideal was that of a covenanted Christian commonwealth under the complete authority of the Christian magistracy. Since God's covenant with His people was a single, eternal covenant, the norms for the Christian community were fully established in the Old Testament. Although the emphasis on community and on the Old Testament was not unique with Bullinger, the concept of magisterial discipline within the covenanted community was distinctively his. The notion of conditional covenant was the basic element of Bullinger's entire theory of Christian society. It was the Christian magistrate who enforced the conditions of the covenant in the Christian commonwealth, which meant that the civil government completely controlled discipline. Calvin and Beza, on the other hand, committed the powers of excommunication and church discipline into the hands of a consistory.[36]

Reformed Protestantism, then, has never been a unitary tradition. Rather, there has been a dual tradition from the beginning. One thrust, initiated by Zwingli, was fully defined and to a large extent created by Bullinger. The second thrust found its clearest early definition in the thought and church polity of Calvin. Most often this dual tradition has been ignored, and it has never been investigated in any depth.

This is a study of the origins of the first, the covenantal, tradition of Reformed Protestantism. The first chapter considers the beginnings of the covenant notion in the thought of Bullinger and Zwingli, as well as possible precedents in Christian thought prior to the Reformation. Chapter 2 discusses predestination and its relationship to the covenant in Bullinger's thought. The third and fourth chapters deal with Bullinger's reading of history in covenant terms, from Adam to his own day. The final two chapters examine Bullinger's application of this historical framework to his own society, i.e., his interpretation of community and his opposition to the Anabaptists in terms of the covenant. Three appendixes serve to present the larger setting within which Bullinger's covenant idea existed: the prevalence of testamental thought in the early Reformation; testament and predestination in Calvin's thought; and the fate of the convenantal Reformed tradition, in the latter sixteenth century, in its struggle with the Calvinistic notion of double predestination.

The sources of Reformed covenant thought have received only limited attention and Bullinger's role has never been adequately assessed. Indeed, despite a few older and several more recent works on the topic of the covenant, the sixteenth-century origins of the covenant idea remain shrouded in mystery. Most of these studies are inadequate not only with respect to origins but also in terms of defining the sixteenth-century usage of covenant and testament. Some of the older standard works demonstrate an awareness of the Zwinglian roots of the idea, but only recently has there been a thorough, systematic study of the covenant idea in Zwingli's thought. Jack Warren Cottrell's dissertation, "Covenant and Baptism in the Theology of Huldreich Zwingli,"[37] clearly demonstrates the shortcomings of previous assessments of Zwingli's role in the origins of Reformed covenant thought. But if Cottrell has for the most part clarified the development of the covenant idea in Zwingli's thought, Bullinger's role in the origins of the concept and his dependence on or independence from Zwingli have not yet been settled.

Diestel, in his book on the treatment of the Old Testament by Christian scholars, includes Zwingli in the discussion of the Reformation period; but Zwingli is only one among many in Diestel's general, rather disjointed, and rambling discourse. Bullinger is not mentioned at all.[38] Van t'Hooft, on the other hand, does not treat Zwingli in his study of the influence of Bullinger in the Netherlands, even though his narrower focus might seem to demand it. He presents Bullinger as the father of covenant theology without mentioning Zwingli's covenant thought.[39] Korff's was the first treatment of the origins of Reformed covenant thought. Following a brief reconstruction of Zwingli's idea of the covenant, Korff states that although Bullinger appropriated and developed Zwingli's ideas, Bullinger was nevertheless the first true covenant theologian and the pervasive influence on the origins and development of Dutch covenant theology.[40]

Gottlob Schrenk's study of Cocceius has been the most influential treatment of covenant thought. He devotes a chapter to the sixteenth-century origins of the covenant idea, with the assertion that Zwingli had renewed the biblical covenant emphasis. In his sketch of Zwingli's thought Schrenk emphasizes that Zwingli developed the Reformed idea of the unity and eternity of the covenant. Bullinger's role was that of systematizer and popularizer of Zwingli's idea, although Bullinger himself influenced Calvin, Melanchthon, Musculus and a whole group of Dutch theologians.[41] According to Schrenk, Bullinger's covenant thought was "minted" from Zwingli's major themes.[42] Finally among the older works, Ritschl devotes a chapter to the development of Reformed covenant theology, in which he briefly presents Zwingli as the originator and Bullinger as the developer of the covenant idea.[43]

Recently there has been a resurgence of interest in the sixteenth- and seventeenth-century ideas about the covenant.[44] Three articles in particular are important with respect to the origins and definition of covenant theology. Trinterud's provocative study raises more questions than it answers. He argues that English Puritanism was basically an indigenous movement, finding its origins in a late medieval Augustinian piety. The covenant idea, which became the framework for this Augustinian tradition, was borrowed by Tyndale and Frith from the Rhineland reformers. Trinterud gives precedence to Johannes Oecolampadius of Basel as the founder of the Reformed idea of the covenant in 1525, closely followed by Zwingli, Capito, and Cellarius. Bullinger finally finds his place in the third group. Trinterud, incidentally, sees each of these men as holding a bilateral idea of covenant.[45] Møller presents Zwingli and Bullinger as the source for Puritan covenant theology. Although the covenant was not prominent in Zwingli's thought, being basically a defense for infant baptism, according to Møller, it was the center of Bullinger's thought. Møller also contrasts the earlier Puritan covenant theology (a bilateral covenant influenced by Bullinger) and later Puritan covenant thought (in essence a theology of testament influenced by Calvin).[46] Hagen is more specifically concerned with the sixteenth-century origins of covenant theology. He treats the distinction between testament and covenant, tracing the development from the idea of testament to the idea of covenant in the thought of Luther, Melanchthon, Zwingli, and Bucer up to 1527. Arguing that Zwingli did not move from testament to covenant until late 1525, he mentions only briefly that Bullinger is considered to have been a covenant theologian in 1525.[47]

Thus much has been written on the covenant theology of the sixteenth and seventeenth centuries, but the origins of the idea are still somewhat obscure. Although Cottrell's study has clarified the development of Zwingli's thought, and Staedtke has included Bullinger's early covenant idea in his book on the young Bullinger,[48] no one has made a careful study of both Zwingli and Bullinger in the 1520s to determine precedence and to compare their covenant ideas.

CHAPTER ONE

The Zurich Origins of the
Covenant Idea in the 1520s

IT HAS been customary to locate the origins of Reformed covenant thought in Zurich. There are, however, two issues that have never been adequately explored. First, who was the father of covenant theology? Some see the beginnings of covenant thought in the use of the concept by the Anabaptists;[1] others credit Zwingli as the originator;[2] and at least one hints that Bullinger may have preceded Zwingli in developing the idea.[3] But, in determining precedence, more is involved than merely dating manuscripts and publications in which the term "covenant" appears. The search must also make use of the crucial distinction between bilateral covenant and unilateral testament—Bullinger's was a notion of bilateral covenant. Furthermore, the idea of the unity of the covenant will emerge as a salient feature. Bullinger insisted that there was only one covenant in human history. Finally, the corporate aspect is of import: Bullinger referred to "the people of God" in a corporate, inclusive sense. Therefore, along with the dating of publications and manuscripts, these three principal points of definition[4] will be accentuated in assessing precedence in the matter of the origins of the covenant idea in Zurich itself. The second, connected, unresolved issue has to do with the possibility of historical precedents in Christian thought prior to the Reformation. Was the Zurich covenant idea

1

original, or was it influenced by patristic sources or by medieval thought?

The answer to the first problem will emerge from a scrutiny of the development of Zwingli's and Bullinger's covenant ideas during the 1520s.

The notion of a covenant or testament as the basis for the relationship between God and believers was fairly common among Zwingli's contemporaries, but Zwingli was the first to develop the idea of covenant unity.[5] Zwingli's first clear statement of covenant unity came in November 1525. Although prior to that time he had referred to a covenant or testament of grace, to Christ as the pledge of grace, to a parallel between circumcision and baptism, and to the New Testament extending back into the Old in terms of promise and fulfillment, none of this was based on covenant unity, on the unity between the people of the two Testaments.[6] Even in his "Taufbüchlein"[7] of late May 1525 Zwingli's thought was still dominated by the distinction between the two Testaments. Contrast, not unity, was the motif. In the "Tauf-büchlein," the term "covenant" referred to man's pledge to rear his children to serve God.[8]

Zwingli's crucial writing in terms of covenant unity was his "Reply to Hubmaier"[9] of November 5, 1525.[10] Here was a clear case for his testamental unity, a covenant of grace that comprehended the entire sphere of salvation in all ages. To be in the covenant meant to be in the church, to be part of the people of God. The New Testament was the old covenant with Abraham—there was one people, one faith, one God. Zwingli even presented a table that compared the two Testaments in order to demonstrate their unity. There were, to be sure, differences: Abraham had only the promise, Christians, the reality; Abraham's covenant was made with a new people; the covenant signs were changed. Zwingli also excluded the Mosaic Law from the covenant. Thus he saw contrast between New Testament and Old Testament law, but unity of the New Testament with the Abrahamic covenant. Finally, Zwingli assigned a new significance to baptism: whereas baptism had been only a human pledge in the "Taufbüchlein," in the "Reply to Hubmaier" it became a sign of belonging to the covenant, to the people of God.[11]

On July 31, 1527, Zwingli published his "Refutation of the Tricks of the Anabaptists,"[12] usually referred to as his "Elenchus," where he most clearly stated his covenant idea. The new element here was that Zwingli commenced his discussion with Adam, with whom God first made the covenant, in the protevangelium (Gen. 3:15). This same covenant was subsequently renewed with Noah, with Abraham, and finally with the entire nation of Israel (Exod. 19:5), each renewal clarifying the contents of the covenant. Christ then renewed and fulfilled the covenant. There was thus one covenant, one people of God, one church from Adam to Zwingli's own day. Zwingli also made clear the relationship between election and the covenant in the "Elenchus." Although only the elect could be part of the people of God, no judgment could be made about an individual until he reached the age of faith. So all born under the covenant had to be considered elect until God demonstrated differently.[13]

The most important aspect of Zwingli's concept of covenant or testament was his idea of covenant unity, the second of the three essential points in defining covenant theology. Furthermore, he affirmed the corporate nature of the covenant. Finally, Zwingli's thought brings out an additional aspect of covenant theology: the unity of the Old and New Testament, at least in the soteriological sense, which is actually correlative to the unity of the testament or covenant.

How, then, did Bullinger relate to Zwingli on the covenant? Did he precede or follow Zwingli in developing the idea? Was he only a disciple and popularizer of Zwingli? Was his covenant idea identical with Zwingli's? The chronological problem depends to a large extent on the dating of two early manuscripts in which Bullinger developed his own covenant idea.

The first is an undated missive to Heinrich Simler of Bern, "Von dem Touff,"[14] in which Bullinger defended infant baptism on the basis of the covenant. Late 1524 or early 1525 was the first tentative date given for the letter,[15] which would give Bullinger precedence in the origins of the covenant idea. More recently, however, Bullinger's dependence on Zwingli's "Reply to Hubmaier" has been decisively proven. "Von dem Touff," then, was written after November 5, 1525.[16] The second problem manuscript is Bullinger's "Answer to Burchard,"[17] in which he also stated the unity of the covenant. This treatise also has been dated as early as early 1525,[18] but new research has demonstrated that it must have been written between late November 1526 and January 1527.[19] Consequently, there is no extant written statement of Bullinger's covenant idea until after Zwingli's "Reply to Hubmair" of November 5, 1525.

Clearly, then, Zwingli preceded Bullinger with his covenant idea. And this matter of precedence is closely related to the problem of dependence. If Bullinger followed Zwingli chronologically in developing his covenant notion, it may follow logically that he was also greatly influenced by,[20] or perhaps totally dependent upon,[21] Zwingli. But was this the case? How dependent was Bullinger on Zwingli for his covenant idea in the 1520s? Was his early covenant theology identical with Zwingli's? An examination of Bullinger's major covenant writings in the 1520s will shed some light on this problem of dependence and at the same time clarify the early development of his covenant idea.

Bullinger's "De Scripturae negotio,"[22] of November 30, 1523, contains important background for his later covenant idea, although it does not treat of the covenant per se. The major point of this short treatise is that the Christian should listen only to Christ (Matt. 17:5), which was equivalent to hearing the Scripture alone.[23] When considering the New Testament understanding of the Scripture, Bullinger maintained that Christ proved everything from the ancient Scripture (John 5:39ff) and the apostles measured all things according to the same Scripture (Acts 15), the Old Testament. Bullinger concluded from this, "In brief, I find the New Testament to be nothing other than the interpretation of the Old. I saw that the latter promises, the former teaches what has been made real; the latter more concealed, the former more open; the latter has to do with veils and figures, the former with clear evidences and the things itself." The marginal note reads, "The New Testament is a commentary."[24] Bullinger proceeded to develop further this astonishingly clear assertion of the importance of the Old Testament. Paul testified that the gospel was promised by the prophets (Rom. 1:1–2), and when he said, "All Scripture is inspired" (2 Tim. 3:16–17), he meant the Old Testament. When Paul spoke of "the sufficiency of the Old Testament, of which Christ is the goal and mediator" (Rom. 10:4ff), Bullinger was forced to decide, "The New Testament is nothing other than the interpretation of the Old." The Old Testament *was* the Scripture.[25]

Bullinger then developed his hermeneutical principle: "I saw from the testimony of the Scripture and the fathers that the one and only Scripture is sufficient." No human addition was necessary; tradition was not useful. The early church had known neither Thomas nor Scotus nor even Augustine. But Augustine himself had stated the key in his dictum, "There is no passage in Scripture so obscure that it is not explained in another passage." Bullinger wrote in the margin: "We interpret Scripture from Scripture."[26] The Holy Spirit would aid in interpreting the Scripture, as promised by Jeremiah (31:33–34). Bullinger would trust neither tradition nor the fathers, but only the Scripture. "Therefore, I add nothing, I subtract nothing. I treat the Scripture alone, interpreting the Scripture with the Scriptures."[27]

The importance of "De Scripturae negotio" for Bullinger's later thought can hardly be overstated. Already Bullinger considered the Old Testament to be of utmost importance for the Christian: the New Testament was the interpretation of, a commentary on, the Old Testament. Bullinger thus saw the unity of the Testaments, if not of the covenant, as early as 1523, an understanding that Zwingli did not reach until 1525.[28] Furthermore, it was both a soteriological and hermeneutical unity. Like Zwingli later, Bullinger saw the Old Testament as promise, the New as fulfillment. Christ was the goal and mediator of the Old Testament as well as the New. Although Bullinger did not refer to testament except in terms of the Testaments (unless one considers his use of Jeremiah 31 as such a reference), the unity of the Testaments in this soteriological sense is nearly the equivalent of asserting the unity of the testament.[29] Only the testamental terminology is missing. Hermeneutical unity was, for Bullinger, in correlation with soteriological unity. Christ was the goal and mediator of the Old Testament; therefore, "the New Testament is nothing other than the interpretation of the Old." To understand the old Testament, one must use the New as a commentary, i.e., one must interpret Scripture with Scripture. These are essential elements of his covenant thought that he first expressed in "Von dem Touff" in late 1525.

"Von dem Touff" was addressed to Heinrich Simler, to warn him about the Anabaptists who, Bullinger had heard, were also active in Bern. His entire discussion of baptism is cast in the matrix of the covenant. Despite the rebellion of man against God (Gen. 3), God, in His free mercy, "made a covenant, testament or will with the fathers Adam, Enoch, Noah and especially clearly and explicitly with Abraham and his seed for eternity." Thus, even though Bullinger may have followed Zwingli chronologically, he immediately introduced a new facet—the covenant had first been made with Adam. The covenant included all of human history, but it became especially clear in its formulation with Abraham. God would be Abraham's God, giving him every blessing, material and spiritual, including a seed in whom all men would be blessed (Gen. 12, 15, 17). In return (*herwyderumb*) Abraham was to walk before God in piety and holiness (Gen. 17:1ff). "And this covenant was made not only with wise old Abraham but also with his children, not for five thousand years but forever."[30] At the outset, then, Bullinger affirmed not only the eternity or unity of the covenant, but also its bilateral nature.

Bullinger underscored this mutual nature of the covenant when he turned to circumcision. Circumcision was the sign of the covenant, i.e., a sign "which obligates to this testament or will." The child, having received the covenant sign, was under the covenant by God's grace until the age of discernment, when he must fulfill the obligation expressed by the sign. Here Bullinger used the analogy of the will (*gmächt*):

> A child is not disinherited as long as it is young and lies in the cradle, but is only disinherited if it, growing up, acts against the wishes of the father as expressed in the written will. It is also known how the will or testament has no validity unless the one who made the testament is dead. Therefore, circumcision was a covenant sign, given not without blood, as a sign that the true Son of God would die and make the covenant firm with His blood. So now you have what the covenant of God with men contains and how circumcision is a sign of the people of God, just as the white cross [is a sign] of a confederate.[31]

Circumcision, then, as the sign of the covenant, obligated both God and man.

This same covenant was then renewed with Isaac, Jacob, Moses, Joshua, Gideon, Samuel, Josiah, Hezekiah, and Maccabee.[32] An era ended, and the covenant was fulfilled in the time of John the Baptist. John preached the same covenant that had been made with Abraham, the fulfillment of which the prophets had promised. John's task was to prepare the Jews for the Messiah, the blessed Seed, the promise of the covenant. John also began baptism, which was "nothing other than an initial sign with which he marked those who . . . would repent and accept Christ as the true Messiah."[33]

Baptism had replaced circumcision because the blood of circumcision, a figure of the future blood of Christ, had been fulfilled. Christ had made the covenant firm with His blood. But the covenantal purpose of baptism was similar to that of circumcision: "First baptism is nothing other than an initial sign of the people of God, which binds us to Christ and to an irreproachable life. Secondly, its effect is to keep us for Christ in the covenant or in a life pleasing to God." Thus Bullinger again emphasized the human obligation. Then he stressed further the unity of the covenant. The apostles baptized with the same baptism as did John and preached the same covenant. Peter clearly stated that the covenant with Abraham continued after Christ (Acts 3:24f) and he baptized the Gentile believers with the same baptism instituted by John (Acts 10:44–11:18). Paul also equated the baptism of John with the baptism of Christ (Acts 19:1).[34]

Bullinger had to answer an obvious question: "If there is only one testament, which up until now we have considered to be two, why then do we call it the old and the new? Answer: there is only one single testament through which all piety originates in him who believes in the Messiah." Therefore, the time before Christ was called the old testament because Christ was promised in the ceremonies; the time after Christ was called the new testament because Christ fulfilled the ceremonies and all things became new. Also the covenant was made with a new people, the heathen. Finally, the covenant sign was changed: beginning with John, baptism replaced circumcision as the sign of the people of God.[35]

This decided the question of infant baptism for Bullinger. If there was but one covenant, and if the children before Christ were included in the covenant by circumcision, the covenant sign, then children after Christ must also belong in the covenant and must be given baptism, the new covenant sign. If the Testator had not disinherited the children (Mark 10:14–16), certainly the apostles could not have done so.[36] After presenting further arguments for infant baptism, Bullinger summarized:

Now then, my dearest Heinrich, you have heard from both Testaments the true basis of baptism: how the human race has a covenant with God in which the high God obligates himself toward us miserable ones as our highest good, as our fullness and sufficiency; and that He therefore wishes to give to us His Son for a firm foundation, who had to seal the testament or covenant with his blood for the young and old; and how this testament has no difference except that Christ fulfilled for us what was promised to them; also that this covenant was made with a new people and all blood was staunched; therefore also that circumcision is changed into baptism; . . . therefore that as circumcision initially bound one to God from the cradle on, so also baptism binds us, by the power of God who has accepted us by grace through His Son.[37]

Bullinger thus had a clear and fairly complete covenant idea by late 1525. Although many of the arguments in "Von dem Touff" can be found in Zwingli's "Reply to Hubmaier," Bullinger's covenant idea was not merely a copy of Zwingli's even at this early date. That Bullinger had already made the general argument and presentation his own is evident in the very manner in which he broached the subject to Simler. Although he did not go into so much detail, he clearly had in mind the same principles as when he wrote "De Scripturae negotio" in 1523. Paul, Christ, and Peter all solved quarrels and arguments with the Scripture, which for them was the Old Testament. Therefore, Bullinger's procedure on the topic of baptism would be to begin with Adam and then to proceed through the prophets into the New Testament.[38] His hermeneutical principle, expressed in "De Scripturae negotio," is thus applied to the covenant in his letter to Simler. Furthermore, even the content of "Von dem Touff" is not identical with Zwingli's 1525 teaching. The arguments for the unity of the testament and for infant baptism are, to be sure, quite similar. But Bullinger already had an idea of covenant with human obligations or stipulations, even though this bilateral aspect was not yet fully developed. There was, however, one item lacking in "Von dem Touff": the application of the covenant concept to the eucharist, a deficiency that Bullinger filled with a treatise sent to Werner Steiner and Bartholomäus Stocker on December 10, 1525, entitled "De institutione et genuino eucharistiae usu epistola."[39]

Bullinger began his argument in this treatise with a few words about Scripture, asserting, "There is no other Scripture except the books of Moses, the interpreters of which are indeed the prophets." To be sure, Christ was the "fulfillment, the light and the end" of the Old Testament, and his apostles were witnesses to the fulfillment of the old promises. Therefore, there would be little profit in reading the New Testament without the Old, for, as Bullinger wrote in the margin, "The New Testament is the explanation of the Old Testament." Immediately following this short statement of his hermeneutical stance, Bullinger introduced the covenant: "Therefore, the Lord appeared to Abraham [and] struck a covenant with him," promising to be all-sufficient to Abraham and to give him a Seed, who would bless all people. He also gave him a covenant sign, circumcision, which, Bullinger added parenthetically, "we understand as a pledge." The sacrament of the covenant was bloody because it was a promise of the blessed Seed, Christ. Furthermore, this covenant was eternal: "This is a single testament, seeing that the Scripture does not know another one besides this one." In fact, the subject of the whole Scripture was how God made the covenant with man and how he kept his agreements and fulfilled his promises.[40] So Bullinger not only stressed covenant unity here but also clearly and closely bound his covenant idea together with his hermeneutical and soteriological principles with respect to the Testaments.

Then he introduced the passover as the second Old Testament sacrament of the covenant. The lamb was both a type of Christ and a renewal of the promises of the covenant. The passover was a remembrance of God's mercy in delivering the people of the covenant from Pharaoh and at the same time a symbol of hope and faith in the lamb who would come.[41] From the passover itself Bullinger moved to a discussion of the Lord's Supper, which was also a symbol of the covenant. Christ was the mediator of the testament, His blood, the seal of the testament. He spoke of a new testament "because our era has the very light of the figures, Jesus Christ, who uncovers all the things covered with age, explains and makes fresh the covenant of God." Since all things became clear and complete in Christ, He spoke of a new testament. But He made no new covenant: "Now therefore when Christ calls this cup a new testament, no one shall imagine that God began a new covenant with the human race." Rather, it meant that Christ renewed and sealed the covenant with His death.[42] Thus, by December 10, 1525, Bullinger had expressed all the elements of his fully developed covenant theology. His view of the eucharist was similar to Zwingli's, but in late 1525 Zwingli had not yet so clearly and thoroughly connected the Lord's Supper with the unity of the testament.

Perhaps it is too early to call Bullinger a covenant theologian, but unquestionably the covenant became the first principle of his theology in the next two years, during which time he used the covenant idea in a variety of circumstances. In 1526, in his first publication, which was directed solely against the Catholics, he asserted his hermeneutical principle: "Scripture must be interpreted from itself and through itself, in faith and love." Then, without developing the idea, he used the unity of the testament against the Gnostics, Cerdo and Marcion. Finally, he mentioned baptism as "an initial covenant sign."[43]

Also during this period, Bullinger utilized the covenant idea in three letters. On February 8, 1526, he wrote to Matthias Schmid, pastor and reformer of Seengen, a recent convert to the Reformed teaching. Bullinger wished to encourage him to continue to preach the gospel to his congregation as a good shepherd. At the very beginning of the letter, Bullinger mentioned the covenant. God, he explained, "in His pure grace and inexpressible mercy made a covenant with us," through which He presented himself as the all-sufficient God. Then Christ, the pledge of God's grace, died and rose again, having been given by the Father for purification, piety, and atonement. Then, in conclusion, Bullinger exhorted Schmid to be a good pastor, to be firm and strong and to preach the Scripture only, using the method of explaining Scripture with Scripture. Thus Bullinger returned to his hermeneutical principle.[44]

The second letter, dated February 27, 1526, was written by Bullinger and Johannes Enzlin, pastor and reformer of the Hausen congregation near Zurich,[45] to Christoph Stiltz, town clerk at Wildberg (Würtemberg), whom they wished to bring to the Reformed teaching. Having spent a large portion of the letter arguing against the Catholic interpretation of the eucharist and for the Zwinglian view, Bullinger then used his idea of the testament to buttress the Zwinglian argument. Citing Paul, "This cup is the new testament in my blood" (1 Cor. 11:25), Bullinger asserted that the wine was not the testament itself, but only a symbol of the testament, just as circumcision had been a symbol despite the fact that God had referred to it as the pact or testament itself (Gen. 17:10ff). Then Bullinger affirmed the unity of the testament: "There is only one testament in the world, which will never be abrogated since it has existed from the beginning." Briefly, Bullinger summarized, "the testament is salvation or the remission of sins, Christ the mediator of the testament, the death and blood of Christ the unveiling and the seal of the testament, the bread and wine the symbol of the confirmed testament, reminding of redemption and union."[46] In this letter, Bullinger spoke more in terms of testament than of covenant, not once referring explicitly to the covenant conditions. He did, however, strongly affirm the unity of the testament.

The third missive, of an entirely different type, was addressed to his fiancee, Anna Adlischwyler. Dated February 24, 1528, the topic was the duties and virtues of a faithful Christian wife. First, he wanted Anna to understand fully the true Christian faith, as expressed in the Scripture. She should read the Bible prayerfully, seeking God's help. In addition, she should understand "that there are a few definite points at which the entire Scripture aims; and the Old Testament begins with the covenant which God struck with Abraham and in him with all His faithful ones, so that He alone would be the single good, the treasure of all goods, on whom alone we should depend and before whom we should walk with integrity [Gen. 17:1ff]. All the histories, all the prophets take aim at that." There were many in the Old Testament who had shown how to depend solely on God and how to walk before Him with integrity. To depend on God meant to have faith like Abraham's. God had not altered the manner in which He dealt with men in the New Testament era: "No new covenant was established in the New Testament; rather, it only demonstrates irrefutably that God wants to be our God, that is, our good and sufficiency."[47] Bullinger did not fully develop his covenant idea here. Nevertheless its basic elements come through amazingly clearly: the covenant was the basic point of the entire Scripture; there was but one covenant in history; and man had the obligation to have faith and to live with integrity.

By 1528, then, Bullinger had repeatedly, in a variety of contexts, used his covenant idea. But his most impressive expression of the covenant concept is found in his "Answer to Burchard."[48] It is his clearest and best sustained development of the covenant of the 1520s, and it was directed toward a Catholic.[49] After a short personal word to Burchard about their quarrel, Bullinger stated that he would address himself to two basic points: whether one should listen to Christ alone and whether the mass was a sacrifice. But as his argument develops, it is the covenant that becomes the framework for his discussion of each of these main topics.

The first point, that one should hear Christ alone, meant that one should pay heed to the Scripture alone. Thus Bullinger's purpose in the first half of the treatise was to demonstrate that the Scripture was sufficient, that tradition, councils, and such were unnecessary. Reiterating his hermeneutical principle, he connected it with his covenant idea in a startlingly clear statement. The apostles, Bullinger argued, preached nothing but the Scripture (Acts 26:22) and they wrote down everything that they commanded the church. The church, then, had both the Scripture that the apostles preached and the apostles' own writings, the New Testament. For the apostles, of course, the Scripture was Moses and the prophets. In fact, Bullinger asserted, the will of God was fully revealed in the books of Moses, "because they are the highest spring, the fountainhead, from which every prophetic and apostolic stream bubbles. For clearly, concisely and plentifully the content of the entire testament, and thus of our salvation, is included in them. But the testament I call a covenant, a peace treaty, an alliance, a disclosure of the will and of the mind or the witnesses of the heart." This was the covenant that God had made with Abraham, in which He bound himself to be the God of Abraham and of his seed, i.e., the salvation of all faithful men, Jew or Gentile, through the promised Seed; in return (*herwÿderumb*) men were obligated to confess God to be their God, obeying Him and walking before Him with integrity. "And this is the sum total of all Scripture, toward which all Scripture always aims, witnessing how only this covenant has been performed continually by both sides."[50]

Following this strong affirmation of the bilateral nature of the covenant, Bullinger emphasized covenant unity. This same covenant was renewed by Moses. Then the prophets, reproving all un-righteousness and urging justice and righteousness, again declared the covenant of Abraham. The prophets also promised the coming of the blessed Seed, Christ, portraying Him "as if they had seen Him, or as if He already had been born." This led Bullinger back to an assertion of the sufficiency of the Old Testament. The ancients before Christ had nothing to complain about. As Paul wrote to Timothy, the Scripture, inspired by God, taught about salvation (2 Tim. 3:14–16). This demonstrated the sufficiency of the Old Testament, for Timothy had been raised "in the law and the prophets," as a Jew.[51]

Burchard might answer: "He says that the law and the prophets are so perfect that no addition is needed; it follows then that the entire New

Testament is superfluous. What would you make of us other than Jews?" Bullinger answered that the New Testament taught the same covenant as the Old, that the covenant was eternal, that there was but one people of God, one church, one testament and faith. Therefore, Bullinger asserted, "if the testament is one and eternal, it must follow that God has made no new covenant, no new testament with us."[52] It was called a "new" testament because Christ was the new light who made the old shadows obsolete and also because a new people was admitted to the testament. Christians after Christ were freed from the shadows; they possessed the reality of the blessing promised to Abraham. These were the only differences between the ancients and those after Christ. Furthermore, the preaching of the New Testament was not written initially. The apostles did not carry the books of the gospel around with them. They preached the inheritance of the testament and established everything by the law and the prophets, the Old Testament. There was, then, no difference in the message before and after Christ. The Old Testament was an announcement to "the Old Christians" that Christ would come; the New Testament, a report that He had come.[53]

Thus Bullinger had first made it clear that the covenant was bilateral, that man was obligated to fulfill the conditions of the covenant. Then, while arguing for the unity and eternity of the covenant, he stressed the element of testament: both before and after Christ men were saved by God's grace, through faith. There was thus a soteriological unity in the Old and New Testaments. But now he asserted that the testament itself should not be confused with the books of the testament. Neither the books of the Old nor of the New Testament were the testament itself; they were instead the contents of the testament, instructing how to keep the testament. "Thus the books are a testament: that is, a description of what concerns the testament. And among the learned such words are called metonyms."[54] Having made the distinction between the records of the covenant and the covenant itself, Bullinger had reached the point where he could affirm hermeneutical unity: "Since the books of the New Testament are an elucidation of the law and of the prophets. . . , we use them in place of a commentary." When the apostles themselves taught, they always referred to the Old Testament, saying, "As it is written," or "As the prophets also say." Bullinger asked: "What is that now except to write a commentary, an elucidation and an exposition?" Therefore, Scripture was its own commentary; Scripture must be interpreted by Scripture. Nothing else was necessary, although Bullinger hastened to add that he did not despise the church fathers as long as they spoke with the Scripture.[55]

Bullinger's argument here is reminiscent of his thesis in "De Scripturae negotio" of November 1523. The case for the importance, indeed almost the precedence, of the Old Testament is identical, and so is the hermeneutical principle.[56] The new element in the "Answer to Burchard" is the careful and thorough manner in which Bullinger connected his view on Scripture with the covenant. Although the connection is apparent in his earlier covenant statements, it was never so clearly and decisively stated. Here Bullinger asserted not only the unity of the covenant but also both the soteriological and hermeneutical unity of the Testaments. The content of the entire Scripture was the eternal covenant. It seems that Bullinger could no longer discuss his hermeneutical principle apart from the covenant idea—even in a polemical treatise addressed to a Catholic—so important had the covenant become for him. In fact, the "Answer to Burchard" demonstrates that by early 1527 the covenant had become the key interpretive motif of Bullinger's theology, the principal formative and organizing factor in his thought.[57]

The covenant idea thus found its Zurich origins in the thought of Zwingli and Bullinger from 1525 through 1527. Zwingli's first statement of covenant unity came in his "Reply to Hubmaier" of November 5, 1525, Bullinger's in his "Von dem Touff," probably later in the same month. Bullinger's definitive declaration on the covenant in the 1520s was his "Answer to Burchard" of late 1526 or early 1527, while Zwingli's is found in his "Elenchus" of July 1527. Even though Zwingli was working in Zurich and Bullinger some miles away in Kappel, it would be surprising if there had been no personal discussion between them about the covenant. There was, in fact, an exchange on the covenant after Zwingli's "Reply to Hubmaier," of which we have some knowledge because of Jud's letter to Bullinger of December 1, 1525, in which he thanked Bullinger for drawing Zwingli's attention to passages in Tertullian and Lactantius that supported covenant unity.[58] Possibly there had been an exchange of ideas even prior to Zwingli's "Reply to Hubmaier," but probably the subsequent discussions included much more than the Jud letter indicates. There was ample opportunity: Bullinger's three visits to Zurich in 1525 for the disputations with the Anabaptists and his five-month period in Zurich, from mid-June through mid-November of 1527.

Whether or not such an exchange of ideas took place, the fact remains that Bullinger's covenant thought was not identical with Zwingli's. First, Bullinger had a firmer and more fully developed hermeneutical basis for his covenant idea. Bullinger originally affirmed the absolute unity of the Testaments in 1523 in "De Scripturae negotio," while Zwingli as late as his "Taufbüchlein" of May 1525 still saw great contrast between the Old and New Testament. Although he expressed the unity of the testament and thus the soteriological unity of the Testaments, even hinting at interpretive unity, in his "Reply to Hubmaier,"[59] he did not develop an analogous hermeneutical apparatus. In the "Elenchus" of 1527, he further elaborated on the importance of the Old Testament, twice using the argument that when Christ and the apostles referred to the Scripture, they meant the Old Testament.[60] Later in the treatise, in connection with the testament, he asserted that there was no difference between the Old and New Testament on the most important matter, the relationship between God and man.[61] Thus the elements were present in the "Elenchus," but Zwingli did not develop these affirmations into a definite hermeneutical principle corresponding to his assertion of the unity of the testament. He never clearly correlated the soteriological unity of the Testaments with a fully developed hermeneutical unity. Bullinger, on the other hand, would not and could not separate his covenant idea from the hermeneutical unity of the Testaments.

Secondly, Bullinger strongly affirmed the bilateral nature of the covenant, the mutual responsibilities of God and man in this contract. Zwingli's lack of clarity is in contrast with Bullinger's explicit assertion of a conditional covenant. In the "Reply to Hubmaier," listing the main points of the covenant with Abraham, he said: "The fourth indicates the obligation, what we are obligated to do toward Him, when He says, 'and walk blamelessly before me.' "[62] In the "Elenchus" he simply restated the obligation from Genesis 17:1.[63] But he did go into more detail in his Genesis commentary, where he first explained that *integer* did not mean perfection but rather always striving for righteousness. The covenant was a pact of friendship between God and Abraham and his seed. Defining the covenant, he said: "This is the pact of God with man: that He himself should be our God; that we should walk with integrity according to His will." Then Zwingli explained more clearly how he interpreted man's obligation in the covenant: "And those who believe with all their heart just as Abraham [did] . . . strive in all ways to walk in God's presence with innocence and integrity, to diminish the weakness of the flesh daily and even hourly. For circumcision signifies this. A milder sign is given to us, which also reminds us of daily cleansing and purging."[64] Thus, for Zwingli the fulfillment of the human obligation was not a condition in the literal sense—it demonstrated the prior faith that was a gift to the elect. And unlike Bullinger, Zwingli did not state that faith itself was a covenant condition.[65]

On the one hand, Zwingli spoke of human obligations in the covenant, and it might be concluded from that that he taught a bilateral covenant.[66] On the other hand, it could be maintained that for Zwingli the covenant remained a unilateral promise to the elect, in reality a theology of testament in which any "conditional" elements were blunted by his doctrine of election.[67] In any case, the contractual element, the mutual nature of the covenant, was simply not a clearly or well-articulated idea in Zwingli's thought. He seems not to have developed his covenant idea sufficiently to consider carefully the implications of the bilateral nature of the covenant. Even in the 1520s, however, Bullinger left little doubt in his reader's mind: the covenant was bilateral, and the human conditions were faith and piety. Then, in 1534, in his definitive work on the covenant, *De testamento*, he clearly differentiated between *foedus* and *testamentum* and heavily emphasized the conditional nature of the covenant.

In fact, Bullinger's initial topic in *De testamento* was the meaning of the words *testamentum* and *foedus*. *Testamentum*, he explained, had three meanings in the Scripture. Often it referred to a last will made by a testator or to the inheritance itself (Matt. 26:28; Gal. 3:15–18; Heb. 9:1–15). *Testamentum* also meant a promise confirmed by an oath. In this sense it was related to the words *testor* (to bear witness) and *testis* (a witness). "Whence many times in the Scriptures *testamentum* is written down in place of *promissio*, and not just any type of promise but one made firm with an oath" (Luke 1:72–74; Acts 3:25). Finally, *testamentum* carried the meaning of pact (*pactum*) or covenant (*foedus*), as in Genesis 15 and 17. "We shall also use it in this way in the exposition at hand."[68] Bullinger thus gave *testamentum* the primary meaning of covenant, although the secondary definitions of inheritance, last testament and promise also were important for him.

The meaning of *foedus*, however, was unequivocal for Bullinger: it meant a treaty or covenant between enemies. The origin of the word, Bullinger opined, was connected with the ancient ritual of killing a sow cruelly in the making of a covenant.[69] Ancient covenants included not only this bloody ceremony but also rules and stipulations or conditions for each side. In ancient times the *fetialis*[70] had been in charge of the entire procedure. The final step in making a treaty or covenant had been to write down a complete record or account of the covenant, especially for the benefit of posterity. Such a written document, Bullinger added, was also the custom in making a last testament: to designate the heirs, to describe the inheritance—everything written and sealed to avoid fraud. A testament, of course, was not in force until the testator died.[71]

The point of all this, Bullinger continued, was that God had followed these human customs in making His covenant with man. The account or record of this covenant had been written by Moses in Genesis 17, although in a broader sense the entire Scripture was the record of the covenant. Moses first stated the parties of the covenant: God and the seed of Abraham. Then he explained the conditions of the covenant: God wished to be the God of Abraham and his seed; in return, Abraham and his seed were bound to walk before God in innocence. Furthermore, Moses made it clear that this was an eternal covenant. Finally, this mutual covenant was sealed with a bloody ceremony. So God had followed every step of the human custom in making covenants.[72]

Later in *De testamento* Bullinger several times reemphasized the conditional nature of the covenant, along with its unity. When God made the covenant with Abraham, He also made clear that man's duty was "to adhere firmly to the one God through faith and to walk in innocence of life for His pleasure."[73] The law, the prophets, Christ, and the apostles all taught the same covenant conditions. Christ himself witnessed that the law "teaches partly the love of God, partly the love of the neighbor. This very thing is also taught by the main points of the covenant. Indeed, the Decalogue itself seems to be just like a paraphrase of the conditions of the covenant."[74] And Bullinger asked,

who did not know that Christ taught "partly faith in God, partly love of
the neighbor? The former explains the first aim of the covenant, the
latter, the second. For faith believes that God is supremely good,
righteous and beneficent towards man. Love truly is the fountainhead
of innocence and purity itself."[75] Zwingli's tentative statements about
the conditional nature of the covenant are hardly comparable to
Bullinger's asseverations of a bilateral covenant in *De testamento*.

One final distinction between Bullinger and Zwingli was the manner
and frequency with which they used covenant unity. Zwingli used it
almost exclusively to argue against the Anabaptists, except for two
treatises in 1526 and 1527.[76] His well-developed discussions of
covenant unity are found in his "Reply to Hubmaier" and his
"Elenchus"; after the latter he did not engage in any lengthy discussion
of the covenant. Bullinger also first utilized covenant unity against the
Anabaptists in his "Von dem Touff," but not polemically, for the
treatise was a warning about them to Simler. Significantly, he did not
again use the covenant against them until his published polemic of
1531.[77] But he did repeatedly write about the covenant in the 1520s:
against the Catholics, particularly in his "Answer to Burchard"; to
encourage those who either were leaning toward the Reformed
teaching or had already accepted it, as in his treatise "De institutione et
genuino Eucharistiae" or his letters to Schmid and Stiltz; and to
enlighten his fiancée, Anna Adlischwyler. Bullinger used the covenant
more consistently, more broadly, and more frequently because it was
the central doctrine for him. It was also an important teaching for
Zwingli, but his point of departure was the sacraments; he nearly
always used covenant unity to defend his sacramental viewpoint.[78]
Since his purpose was basically polemical, he never thoroughly
integrated the covenant idea into his larger system of thought.[79]

The development of covenant thought in Zurich in the 1520s was a
joint effort, with Zwingli apparently taking the lead. The broad
outlines of the covenant ideas of the two men are quite similar. Both
strongly asserted the unity of the covenant, the soteriological unity of
the Testaments. Both thought in corporate terms: God, by means of
the covenant, formed a people, the church. Their teachings on the
sacraments of the covenant were similar. Clearly Bullinger was greatly
influenced by Zwingli. But he added some touches of his own—his
clearer assertion of the bilateral nature of the covenant and his

affirmation of hermeneutical unity, his frequent assertion that the New Testament was nothing but the interpretation of the Old. Even in the 1520s Bullinger had made the covenant idea his own, both in terms of content and in terms of the central position that the concept held in his thought.

Zwingli, then, was within all probability one major influence on the development of Bullinger's covenant theology. A question remains, however, before Bullinger's own thought can be analyzed any further. Was the covenant idea a distinctive mode of thought, unique to the early Reformation in Zurich? Or were there predecessors in Christian thought, from patristic sources or from the late Middle Ages? Bullinger himself never claimed originality for his covenant scheme and in fact cited several church fathers in support of it.

Most frequently Bullinger turned to Augustine for patristic documentation, both in his writings during the 1520s and in *De testamento*. Yet he quoted only two passages at any length. The first, from Augustine's lectures on John, was an affirmation of the unity of the faith: all who were saved, either in Old or New Testament times, believed in Christ. Those before Christ believed that He would come, those after, that He had come. As Augustine wrote: "The times have changed, not faith. . . . At different times, indeed, but we see that both have entered by the one door of faith, that is, by Christ."[80] The second passage quoted by Bullinger, from Augustine's treatise on baptism against the Donatists, involved both the unity of the faith and an assertion that there was but one church in history. According to Augustine:

> That same [church] which bore Abel, Enoch, Noah and Abraham also at a later time bore Moses and the prophets before the coming of the Lord as well as our apostles and martyrs and all good Christians. For it bore all those who appeared, born at different times but joined together in the fellowship of one people; and citizens of the same city have experienced the hardships of this pilgrimage, and some of them are now experiencing them, and others will experience them until the end of the world.[81]

In addition to these two quotations, Bullinger made several other references to Augustine.[82]

Nevertheless, Bullinger's idea of the covenant was not Augustine's. Augustine's was a theology of testament, not a notion of bilateral covenant. Augustine's theology of testament can be found throughout his writings, but especially in the treatises against Manichaeism, Donatism, and Pelagianism; he thus used the unity of the testament to establish the validity and importance of the Old Testament for Christians, to defend Catholic baptism, and to assert the freedom of God's grace. The Old Testament also was Christian Scripture. Although much of it did not apply to New Testament Christians (i.e., the ceremonies that had been fulfilled by Christ), it contained the promise of the New Testament. In a hermeneutical sense, then, the gospel was present in the Old Testament, although hidden in the figures and types; in a soteriological sense, the saints of the old testament belonged to the new, having been justified by faith, not by ceremonies or the law. Those who depended only on the temporal promises belonged to the old testament or covenant. The old testament was letter, the new, spirit. None could be justified by works—from the beginning each saint had been justified by faith. Thus the old testament was carnal, the new, spiritual. Both had existed since Adam, although both had been hidden until Moses revealed the old testament in the law. Then the new testament remained hidden in the old, in the figures, until Christ fulfilled the old and revealed the new.[83] Hermeneutically, then, Augustine perceived the New Testament veiled in the Old; soteriologically he saw the new testament or covenant hidden in the old. Augustine is quite clear on the unity of the Testaments, the testament, and the people of God. There was but one people of God, the church, saved by faith, from Adam to the end of the world.[84] But there is no bilateral covenant in Augustine's thought, despite the fact that Bullinger referred to him so often.

It has been suggested that Irenaeus (d.c. 200) was the primary source for Bullinger's covenant theology; that although Bullinger's single covenant contrasted with Irenaeus' threefold covenant scheme, their presentation of revelation and salvation as an historical drama was quite similar.[85] Irenaeus did indeed have a covenant doctrine, positing not three covenants, but two. His purpose was to demonstrate the unity of faith: Abraham and others in the old dispensation were justified by faith just as Christians after Christ. Abraham knew Christ, and Christ was the fulfillment of the promise made to Abraham. In fact, the Old Testament was filled with promises about the coming of Christ. Christ, however, did not abrogate the natural precepts of the laws as expressed in the Decalogue; rather He restated them. These natural precepts had been written in the heart of man since creation, and in any age their observation was necessary for salvation: they were common to both covenants. Defining the nature of these covenants more carefully, Irenaeus stated that Abraham belonged to both: before his circumcision he belonged to the covenant of uncircumcision by virtue of his faith; afterwards he also belonged to the covenant of circumcision, characterized by the law of works. The covenant of faith, in effect until Abraham, when it was replaced by the covenant of circumcision, was reinstituted by Christ.[86]

There are some ambiguities in Irenaeus' covenant scheme. At first glance it appears to be a theology of testament, but some of its elements hint at a bilateral idea. Although Irenaeus did not specifically refer to conditions as such, his notion that the Decalogue was still in force in the New Testament era finds a clearer expression in Bullinger's conditions of faith and love. Furthermore, although Irenaeus did not develop the idea, his assertion that the covenant of faith both predated and followed the Mosaic era brings to mind Bullinger's conception that the church began with Adam, that the era of circumcision was an interregnum.[87] These similarities suggest that Bullinger may have been influenced by Irenaeus, perhaps more than he admitted, inasmuch as he cited Irenaeus but twice in connection with the covenant in his early writings.[88]

In his early expositions of the covenant, Bullinger depended heavily on Tertullian (d.c. 225) and Lactantius (d.c. 325) for patristic support. By the time he wrote *De testamento*, his enthusiasm had paled: Tertullian merited but one quotation and one passing reference, neither of which was connected with the unity of the covenant;[89] and he did not even mention Lactantius. This is understandable because Tertullian, in the passages cited by Bullinger in "Von dem Touff" and the "Answer to Burchard," had nothing to say about either covenant or testament per se. In "Von dem Touff" Bullinger made reference to Tertullian's "On Repentance." In the passage, Tertullian briefly mentioned God's people in terms of the promised seed of Abraham, who were known "by the sign of repentance," that is, baptism. Then, in a later chapter, he referred to baptism as a "seal of faith."[90] Bullinger had written to Zwingli in late November 1525 to inform him of these passages from Tertullian. Jud replied for Zwingli, and we have a good idea what this meant initially to Bullinger and Zwingli from Jud's paraphrase of Tertullian's judgment "that He [God] sends ahead the baptism of repentance as a seal to those who are about to begin new life, or (that I might use his words) those who are called by grace to the destined seed of Abraham."[91] Thus, by inverting the order of the Tertullian passages and putting them together, Jud created a credible ancient authority. But it was at best a twisted interpretation of Tertullian and not really a support for the covenant idea, let alone covenant unity, but only for interpreting infant baptism within a corporate context. But even this support is only apparent, as Bullinger must have known. For immediately following the reference to baptism as a "seal of faith," Tertullian explained that "We are not washed so that we might cease to sin, but because we have ceased, seeing that we already have been bathed in the heart."[92] Bullinger did not again use Tertullian's "On Repentance," and for good reason. The Anabaptists, after all, could also read Tertullian.[93]

Lactantius actually offered more support than Tertullian, but for some reason Bullinger had also dropped him as a source by the time he wrote *De testamento.* In "Von dem Touff" he made two references to Lactantius, both from "The Divine Institutes." The first, in support of infant baptism, was a passage where Lactantius mentioned briefly that the Gentiles were given baptism as the Jews had been given circumcision.[94] The second passage directly upheld the unity of the testament. Moses and the prophets called their law a testament because a testament could not be confirmed, nor could its contents be known, until the testator died. Christ, therefore, had to die to reveal the testament. Thus the Scriptures were divided into the Old and New Testament; "but they are nevertheless not opposed because the New is the fulfillment of the Old and in both Christ is the same Testator, who, having accepted death for us, made us heirs of the eternal kingdom, the people of the Jews having been renounced and disinherited" (Jere. 31:31–32).[95] Although Lactantius affirmed both the unity of the testament and the Testaments, his argument was not well developed. It was not a carefully thought-out case for the necessity of faith in Old Testament times, as is found later in Augustine. Perhaps Bullinger ceased to use Lactantius because Augustine's argument was so much more effective.

If Bullinger had, for whatever reason, dropped a couple of ancient authorities, he discovered another who served his purpose much more clearly than either Tertullian or Lactantius did. This was the church historian Eusebius (d.c. 339), whom Bullinger quoted at length toward the end of *De testamento* to the effect that all those of true faith since Adam were Christians in fact if not in name. His argument is reminiscent of Irenaeus, but he did not use the terms "covenant" or "testament." Christianity, that is, salvation by faith, began with Adam; the era of circumcision and the law was an interregnum; and the pure religion of the patriarchs reappeared with Christ. Thus Christianity was not new; rather, it was the first and true religion.[96] Along with Augustine, Eusebius was Bullinger's strongest support from the early church. Both, Augustine more clearly than Eusebius, accepted the basic unity of the testament in soteriological terms, Eusebius arguing as an historian, Augustine as a theologian. But neither of them—in fact, none of the church fathers, save perhaps Irenaeus—developed any sort of a bilateral, conditional covenant notion. It was a theology of testament that Bullinger discovered in the fathers, not a theology of covenant.

Another possible source for the Reformed idea of covenant is late medieval nominalism with its pervasive bilateral, conditional emphasis, particularly in the thought of Gabriel Biel (d. 1495). This pact rested on two elements: the nature of man and the self-imposed obligation of God. After the fall the soul of man retained a *synteresis*, a power or natural inclination toward good, which made it possible for man to make the first hesitant step toward God. God had obligated himself to give grace to the individual who made that step, who did his very best (*facere quod in se est*). God had thus made a pact with His church, obligating himself to infuse His grace into each person who did his very best.[97] Biel himself stated it rather succinctly in his sermon "The Circumcision of the Lord": "Thus God has established the rule [covenant] that whoever turns to Him and does what he can will receive forgiveness of sins from God. God infuses assisting grace into such a man, who is thus taken back into friendship."[98] Another, related element of nominalism was the relationship of the Old Testament to the New with respect to the sacraments and the pact. Biel argued:

Let it not seem bad-sounding and fictitious to anyone that God in the New Law has celebrated this sort of *pacta* with the faithful, since you can read that *he did the same thing in the Old Law*. For He says: "This is my *pactum* which you shall observe: every male of yours shall be circumcised." And further on: "Any man the flesh of whose foreskin has not been circumcised, his soul shall be wiped out from the people." Where, in the converse sense, it can be argued: If he *has* been circumcised, *he shall be* saved. And on the basis of the establishment of the *pactum* God assists this circumcision by remitting original sin, and he causes grace, which is the means of leading man to salvation.[99]

The nominalist idea of "pact" seems to have had little if any direct influence on the development of the Reformed covenant idea. It should be noted that Biel did not postulate a single pact but seems to have seen two distinct covenants that were similar. Thus there was neither covenant unity nor testamental unity in nominalist thought. The constant was that God dealt with man by means of a pact in both Testaments. Secondly, the nominalist idea of pact rested on a semi-Pelagian base. Bullinger himself did not operate from such a semi-Pelagian base. Despite the apparent tension in his predestinarian idea, Bullinger carefully protected God's freedom and the Reformation principle of justification by faith alone, never approaching the do-your-very-best element of nominalist theology.[100] Furthermore, there is no evidence that Bullinger was directly influenced by nominalism.[101] His own education at the University of Cologne was based on the *via antiqua*. On the other hand, it seems unlikely that he could have been totally isolated from nominalist ideas; i.e., inasmuch as the nominalist idea of "pact" was current, its bilateral element may have had an indirect effect on the development of Bullinger's own covenant concept. But in its formulation and intent Bullinger's notion of covenant had nothing to do with the nominalist idea of pact. For Bullinger the goal of the covenant was the creation and continuation throughout history of a true community of which all were members by virtue of baptism, just as all were members of Israel by virtue of circumcision. Nevertheless, until the Reformation, the bilateral emphasis is found only in the nominalist "pact," except perhaps for Irenaeus.

Even during the early Reformation, until the 1530s, the concept of conditional covenant was a rarity in Protestant thought. The norm was an Augustinian understanding of unilateral testament, as developed by

Luther after he broke completely from the semi-Pelagian nominalist "pact." Melanchthon's early thought was marked by Luther's theology of testament, although later, in the 1550s, he did construct a covenant idea. In Reformed thought, the idea of testament was pervasive. Among the early Reformed thinkers, Bucer was alone in accepting, in 1527, the Zurich concept of bilateral covenant. Oecolampadius, in mid–1526, did affirm the unity of the people of God in the Old and New Testament, but this was an understanding based on an Augustinian notion of unilateral testament. Many later Reformed thinkers, including Calvin, followed the lead of Luther and Oecolampadius in accepting a testamental rather than a covenantal theology.[102]

There was nothing particularly unique in the Reformation idea of testament, since it had been stated in Christian theology at least as early as Lactantius in the early fourth century. It was, however, a timely restatement, because the theology of testament highlighted the distinctive Reformation emphasis on divine grace and the sole efficacy of faith in opposition to the late medieval tendencies toward works-righteousness and semi-Pelagianism. Bullinger's notion of a conditional covenant, a bilateral agreement between God and man, was a more unusual idea, if not totally unprecedented in Christian thought. The question is, was Bullinger, with his covenant approach, equally able to protect *sola fide* and *sola gratia*?

CHAPTER TWO

Predestination and Covenant in Bullinger's Thought

THE VITAL Reformation doctrines of *sola fide* and *sola gratia* found two different modes of expression within early Reformed circles. The most prevalent was the Augustinian idea of testament, linked with an affirmation of double predestination, which found its classic statement in the writings of Calvin.[1] The other Reformed tradition, existing alongside the more heavily predestinarian Calvinist tradition, was Bullinger's notion of conditional covenant.

Predestination, inasmuch as it was incipient in *sola gratia*, was a generally accepted doctrine from the very beginning of the Reformation, although it was not a source of contention in the earlier years. The importance of the teaching grew, however, until, after midcentury, absolute double predestination increasingly became the test of orthodoxy in Reformed circles. But this did not happen without a struggle. Calvin himself was the author of the controversy, particularly in his argument with Bolsec in the early 1550s. Other battles over predestination followed, such as the quarrel between Bibliander and Vermigli in Zurich, and Zanchi's problem in Strassburg. In the fray, it became more and more difficult to remain neutral, to cling as Bullinger did to his practical approach and to his carefully stated, moderate doctrine of predestination. During the last years of his life, Bullinger seemed increasingly like a man who had outlived his age, a nondogmatic figure in a period that was yearly growing more dogmatic.

During the struggle, the theology of testament became the logical corrollary of an absolute predestinarian stance, while those who held to a covenant notion were more likely to affirm a more moderate single or even a conditional predestinarian teaching. Moreover, Bullinger's own influence on later sixteenth-century covenant thought seems to have been limited to men of questionable orthodoxy in the matter of predestination.[2] Does this mean, then, that Bullinger's own predestinarian doctrine was open to suspicion? Given his notion of conditional covenant, was his a semi-Pelagian or a proto-Arminian position?

"Predestination is the eternal decree of God by which He determined either to save or to destroy men, a most certain end of life and death already having been provided."[3] This statement, written by Bullinger in his *Decades* (1550), appears to be a fairly strong definition of predestination. But elsewhere he asserted that Christ's offering "purifies all the world from its sins" and that it gave "righteousness to all the world."[4] Moreover, in *De testamento* he referred to "that eternal covenant of God made with the human race."[5] Such affirmations, plus the fact that Bullinger seldom chose to discuss the covenant within the context of election, have led some to conclude that Bullinger's covenant idea pushed him to a universalist position, i.e., what was later called Arminianism.[6] Others, however, have offered a second, perhaps prevalent, interpretation, that Bullinger's predestinarian thought developed from a practical teaching of single predestination to a Calvinistic double predestination by the 1560s.[7] Although there are variations on these two themes, they demonstrate that modern interpreters have found Bullinger difficult to categorize.[8]

This same divergence is evident in the Netherlands during the late sixteenth and early seventeenth centuries. Both the Arminians and the high Calvinists saw Bullinger as one of their own. As early as 1590, preachers who did not accept the high Calvinist scheme of double predestination were appealing to the authority of Bullinger. Then the later Remonstrants again and again cited Bullinger and Melanchthon to support their position. In 1612, Samuel Lansberg published a book in defense of the Remonstrant point of view, claiming that the

Arminians agreed with Bullinger on every point. They were, in fact, nothing but his disciples. But the Counter-Remonstrants also claimed Bullinger, insisting that his doctrine of predestination was identical with Calvin's. In 1613 an anonymous book, published in answer to Lansberg, asserted that Bullinger agreed with Calvin, pointing particularly to Bullinger's signing of the Zurich *Gutachten* in support of Zanchi in 1561. Lansberg had misinterpreted Bullinger and twisted his teaching by quoting him out of context. During the next five years preceding Dort, both sides continued to use Bullinger in support of their respective points of view.[9]

Bullinger was still a pivotal and controversial authority at the Synod of Dort. Johann Jacob Breitinger, Antistes of the Zurich church and the leader of the Swiss delegation at Dort,[10] was understandably upset by the Remonstrants' "misuse" of Bullinger's honorable name. Breitinger, in a speech before the Synod, defended Bullinger, his major argument centering on Bullinger's support of Zanchi against Marbach in late 1561. Breitinger had recently discovered in the Zurich archives a letter from Bullinger to Vermigli; according to that letter, Breitinger stated, Bullinger had not only signed the *Gutachten* but had actually asked Vermigli, a high predestinarian, to write the *Gutachten*.[11] Thus, by convincing the Synod that Bullinger agreed with Calvin on predestination, Breitinger vindicated Bullinger and protected the honor of the Zurich church.[12] The question remains, however, whether Breitinger represented Bullinger's viewpoint accurately, since he obviously wanted Bullinger to be within the circle of orthodoxy rather than on the fringes with the "false teaching" of the Arminians.

Bullinger developed the themes of his lifelong teaching on predestination in the 1520s. His was a moderate single predestination, with a twofold emphasis: God's election of those who believe was in, through, and for Christ; therefore salvation was totally of God's free grace. Thus Bullinger wrote, "God therefore included everyone under sin so that He might show mercy to all and the entire world might glorify and praise Him." But "here also all free will, all reason, work and all merit is rejected. . . . And therefore this salvation is not in our will, running, work or merit."[13] Here already the tension is evident— the universal calling of God and the election of God. Bullinger emphasized that those who had faith had been chosen by God in His eternal counsel. Thus election could be known only by one's response to the calling of God through the preaching of His word; i.e., as many as believed were chosen by God. In terms of calling, then, election included all men.[14] But Bullinger also specifically rejected synergism during the 1520s, making several distinct denials of free will, such as his reaction to Erasmus' *De libero arbitrio*: "If there is providence, there is no free will; for otherwise providence is not providence."[15] So in the 1520s Bullinger affirmed election and denied free will, but he also affirmed a universal calling within which man must understand election in history.

Bullinger did not alter his point of view in the next two decades. He was not willing to move toward a doctrine of double predestination that, he felt, made God the author of evil. In 1536, in an oration on predestination and related matters,[16] he asserted that God gave right reason and the means to salvation to those "who struggle to life through Christ; He damns the others, who, having despised Christ and the truth, follow the darkness of the flesh." He then specifically rejected both extremes: those who ascribed salvation to merit rather than the grace of God; and those who, concerning the gift of faith, "cast all things back into absolute necessity so that they make God the author of all evil and of every sin."[17] Thus Bullinger wished both to protect God's integrity and man's responsibility, without denying God's freedom. His affirmation that faith and justification were free gifts of God was balanced by his equally clear denial that God had caused human sin. Man's condemnation was his own fault; man sinned freely, not from compulsion. He had been created good, completely removed from corruption, and "wholly divine."[18]

Man thus sinned by his own free choice. Even though God's election in Christ took place before the foundation of the world (Eph. 1:4), "it does not follow that God's foreknowledge chains us to impious things or that the blame for sin can be cast back on God." Men did not refuse salvation because God foreknew their refusal; rather God foreknew their refusal because they would refuse. Thus there was foreknowledge without predestination, in the case of those who would refuse salvation; but those whom God predestined would have faith because of His election. Predestination to life did not rest on foreknowledge of works, but on pure grace. As for those who were not elect, "God gave them up to a reprobate mind. Sin, then, is not of God, but judgment is."[19] Toward the end of the speech, Bullinger restated this point in terms of the human will: "There is always free will in us, but it is not always good. For either it is free from righteousness when it serves sin, and then it is evil; or it is free from sin when it serves righteousness."[20] In the latter case Bullinger referred to the divinely restored power of the will of the elect; God allowed those who were not of the elect to follow their own impulses toward evil. Thus Bullinger affirmed a single predestination in 1536. He would not and did not speak of reprobation in terms of predestination because, he felt, to do so would make God the author of sin.

Bullinger's doctrine in midcentury, expressed in his *Decades*, had not changed. His overriding concern still was to preserve God's goodness. God created Adam in His own image, perfect, holy, and pure, with an absolutely holy and free will. God also gave Adam a law, forbidding him to eat the fruit of the tree of the knowledge of good and evil, thus requiring obedience and faith. Tempted by Satan, Adam and Eve willingly and freely, with full understanding of the consequences, sinned against God's law. God knew that Adam would sin, but "no necessity follows from the foreknowledge of God so that Adam sinned from necessity because God foreknew that he would sin." God did not decree Adam's sin; in fact, He did not will anyone to sin or to resist Him. All of the passages that referred to God's hardening of the heart, blinding men and giving men over to a reprobate mind referred to God's just judgment, the cause of which was in man, not in God. Even Paul's dictum that God was merciful to whom He wished and hardened whom He wished could not be twisted to mean "that God compels anyone to sin from necessity and thus is made the cause of sin. For the will of God is good and just."[21] This is exactly the same position as presented in the speech of 1536: God did not will anyone to sin and He was not in any way the author of sin.

These distinctions must also be used to interpret his sermon on providence and predestination. Bullinger included foreknowledge and predestination under providence. Foreknowledge, he wrote, is

that knowledge in God by which He knows all things before ʒey happen and holds present before His eyes all things which are, ᴡere and shall be. For to the knowledge of God all things are present; nothing is past, nothing future. Predestination, on the other hand, is the eternal decree of God by which He determined either to save or

to destroy men, a most certain end of life and death already having
been provided. Whence also the same is elsewhere referred to as a
preordination.

Although this bare definition might be construed as an acceptance of
double predestination,[22] it was not. For one thing, he had already
implicitly rejected a decree of reprobation in the sermon on sin; God
was not the author of sin, either in Adam or in the nonelect.
Furthermore, in this sermon, immediately following the definition of
predestination, Bullinger warned against those who curiously and
contentiously disputed about predestination, going beyond the
pronouncements of Scripture, to the point that souls were endangered
along with the glory of God among the simple people. Then he
asserted: "God by His eternal, immutable plan has preordained those
who must be saved or condemned." Again, double predestination
appears to be at hand, but Bullinger continued and further defined his
terms: "The end of predestination or preordination is Christ, the Son
of God the Father. For God decreed to save all, however many, who
have fellowship with Christ, His only begotten Son, but to destroy all,
however many, who are estranged from the fellowship of Christ, His
only Son. For truly the faithful have fellowship with Christ; the
unfaithful are estranged from Christ." Here Bullinger introduced the
unavoidable biblical reference to election before the foundation of the
world (Eph. 1:4), in the context of the purpose of election being Christ
and its proof being faithfulness. Paul meant that "those who are in
Christ are elect." So faith was the proof of election.

> Therefore, if you ask me whether you have been elected to life or
> predestined to death, that is, whether you are of the number of those
> to be damned or to be saved, I respond simply from the evangelical
> and apostolic Scripture: if you have fellowship with Christ, you have
> been predestined to life and you are of the number of the elect; but if
> you are estranged from Christ, however strong you might appear to
> be in virtues, you have been predestined to death and foreknown, as
> they say, to condemnation. Higher and deeper into God's plan I do
> not wish to creep. . . . Therefore, faith is the most certain sign that
> you have been elected, and while you are called to the fellowship of
> Christ and taught faith, the generous God reveals His election and
> benevolence toward you.[23]

Election, then was revealed by faith, and even when commenting on Paul's words about the pretemporal decree of God, Bullinger emphasized experiential faith in this world, in historical time. Furthermore, his reference to those "predestined to death" must not be read out of context. Although it does introduce some ambiguity, it cannot be construed to mean double predestination but must be interpreted in the light of his sermon on sin, where he said that although God foreknew it, men freely condemned themselves to God's just punishment. Therefore God's judgment of those who rejected Christ was predetermined, but the rejection itself was only foreknown.[24] Further support for this judgment is found in the sermon on the gospel, where Bullinger flatly stated:

> Christ and the grace of Christ announced or declared by the gospel belongs to everyone. For no one should imagine that two books are put aside in heaven, in the first of which those are inscribed who are ordained to be saved, and even must be saved by necessity, without question, however they might resist the word of Christ and commit horrible crimes; and in the second those recorded to be condemned are kept, who cannot escape condemnation, no matter how piously they might live. Let us rather hold that the holy gospel of Christ proclaims the grace of God, the remission of sins and eternal life in general to the entire world.

Then Bullinger cited numerous biblical passages with universalist overtones. Why then, he asked, were not all men saved if God was willing for all to be saved? Because, as Christ said, "Many are indeed called but few truly chosen" (Matt. 20:16). God required faith for salvation, but many men rejected the gospel. Only the faithful were saved.[25]

At midcentury, then, several points, theological and practical, instructed Bullinger's teaching on predestination. First he took care to protect God's goodness. God did not decree anyone's rejection of the gospel. He was not the author of sin, neither in the case of Adam's original sin nor subsequently. Men did not sin by necessity, but freely. The gospel of Christ and the grace of God were offered to all men. Those who rejected the gospel did so freely, not because of divine compulsion. Secondly, he wished to affirm God's freedom and the doctrine of salvation by faith alone. Since salvation resulted from

God's free grace, none could have faith unless drawn by God through the preaching of the gospel. Therefore, those who experienced faith were the elect. Although at times the logic of the matter seemed to bring Bullinger to the brink of double predestination, he always drew back, stating his case with the same tensions that he found in Scripture. God's freedom and power were important to him, but so were God's goodness and man's responsibility. Election promised inclusion in the people of God, but it did not threaten exclusion. This was clearly a doctrine of single predestination. Did Bullinger hold to it during the next twelve years of controversy, or did he alter his teaching and accept Calvin's point of view?

In 1551, Calvin became embroiled in a controversy with Jerome Bolsec, a former Carmelite monk. Bolsec publicly charged that Calvin with his doctrine of double predestination made God the author of sin, and Bolsec appealed to Melanchthon's and Bullinger's teaching to support his accusation.[26] Calvin and the Genevan ministers requested the support of the pastors of Basel, Bern, and Zurich against Bolsec. According to their letter, Bolsec espoused universalism: men were elected because of their faith; men were condemned because they deprived themselves of the election common to all men.[27] Four letters were sent in response from Zurich: two official letters from all the pastors and doctors of Zurich, the first to the pastors of Geneva (27 Nov. 1551) and the second to the city council of Geneva (1 Dec. 1551); and two personal letters from Bullinger to Calvin. Calvin found little satisfaction in any of the four. The official responses, similar in content, counseled moderation and reconciliation. They affirmed the election of believers before the foundation of the world, and salvation wholly by God's grace. Although God justly condemned unbelievers, the fault for their unbelief was their own, not God's. God was not the cause of sin. He was absolutely holy.[28]

In his first personal response, Bullinger expressed astonishment at Calvin's expectation of support, since Calvin fully understood Bullinger's point of view from the _Consensus Tigurinus_ and his _Decades_. And indeed his answer to Calvin is nearly identical with his position in the _Decades_. As Paul said, God wished all men to be saved. To be sure, justification was by pure grace, and faith was a gratuitous gift. On the other hand, He wished to condemn all those who did not believe in Christ. Their unbelief was their own fault. Reiterating, seemingly to avoid any misunderstanding, Bullinger wrote, "Therefore, however many men are saved, they are saved by the pure grace of God the Savior; those who perish do not perish by fated, compelled necessity, but because they willingly rejected the grace of God. For there is not any sin in God; that and the fault of our damnation inheres in us." In the "Aphorisms concerning Predestination," which accompanied the letter to Calvin, Bullinger made the same point, that God "condemns unbelievers because of their own sin and guilt, because they did not accept the offered Savior."[29] Thus Bullinger's continued concern was to protect God's goodness and to maintain human responsibility. Although he did not state it as such in this letter, the implication was that Calvin's doctrine of double predestination tended to make God the author of sin. In that respect at least, Bullinger agreed with Bolsec.

This very issue was Bullinger's concern in his second letter: a defense of Zwingli against Bolsec's charge that he had made God the author of sin in his *Providence of God* of 1530. Such a charge was obviously erroneous, Bullinger argued, if only one would read what Zwingli actually wrote on predestination. Then he came close to accusing Calvin of making God the author of sin: "Believe me that many are offended by your statements about predestination in the *Institutes* and infer the same thing that Jerome concludes from Zwingli's book *De providentia*." Then again Bullinger affirmed salvation solely by God's grace and condemnation because of man's own sin and guilt.[30]

Calvin expressed his bitterness in a letter to Farel. He complained about Zurich's "rudeness" in the official missives and said that Bullinger's personal letter was no better, that Bullinger "haughtily despises our necessities."[31] More than a month later, in January 1552, he wrote more tactfully to Bullinger. Why should Bullinger have been astonished at being asked to approve a doctrine so clearly taught in God's word? How could the Zurichers defend such a man as Bolsec? He was stung by Bullinger's criticism of his teaching on predestination in the *Institutes*. If he was in error, perhaps Bullinger would correct him.[32]

In his reply, Bullinger did just that, pointing specifically to items in Calvin's doctrine that particularly bothered him. Calvin's teaching that "God not only foreknew, but also predestined and arranged the fall of Adam" seemed to make God the source of evil and the cause of sin.

Furthermore, Bullinger could not accept the idea that God actually blinded men to the truth and therefore that "the universal promises of God and the words of Christ" were meant only for the few. "And it is certain that not a few men zealous for the truth are offended by these things."[33] It is also clear that Bullinger's position had not changed because of the Bolsec affair.

Bullinger's correspondence with Bartholomew Traheron throws a bit more light on Bullinger's differences with Calvin. Traheron wrote his former teacher requesting his point of view on predestination. The rumor in London was that Bullinger leaned toward Melanchthon, while Traheron and his friends accepted Calvin's viewpoint as expressed in his *De aeterna Dei praedestinatione.*[34] Bullinger's answer, in early 1553, was itself a short treatise on providence and predestination.[35] At the very beginning he indicated his attitude toward Calvin: "It appears to certain people that we cling too much to Melanchthon's teachings because Calvin has written so unconditionally concerning the matter." Bullinger insisted that his own teaching, the orthodox teaching of the apostles, had not changed during his entire ministry, while Melanchthon in the first edition of his *Loci communes* had urged a rigid, fatalistic doctrine. Melanchthon had altered his opinion, worked and reworked it, so that one could not know where he stood.[36] Thus Bullinger denied his affinity to Melanchthon, but he did not bother to go into any detail.

In the first portion of the letter Bullinger dealt with providence and in particular with the crucial question of whether providence made God the author of evil and the cause of sin. This was, of course, an old concern of Bullinger's, from the 1520s and 1530s, but now the issue was much more urgent, since Calvin's fully developed doctrine was beginning to receive such widespread acceptance. His answer is familiar, but now he took care to be extremely clear. God's providence was absolute, but he worked through men, using them as secondary instruments. He permitted sin but He did not cause it, He did not will it or compel it. This permission was, in fact, part of divine providence. Then Bullinger made his point succinctly: "Certainly God is not the author of evil (that which is like a sacred anchor in this disputation), He does not will evil or compel into sin or destine the wills of men to sin, but rather every cause and origin of evil was derived from the wickedness of the devil and free will of man." The free will of man, he continued, had existed historically in three stages or conditions. Before the fall Adam was absolutely perfect, good, and free. As a result of the fall, human understanding and will were obscured but not destroyed. In one sense man had no free will because he could know nothing of the divine. But in another sense man's will was free. He chose freely to sin and to follow corruption. "And thus all deceptions and every sin come from man, so that it is not at all necessary to bring these things back to God as the instigator." Finally, the regenerate man had free will by virtue of divine grace. He could, with the aid of the Spirit, understand and choose good.[37]

Having made his position clear on these crucial points, Bullinger then turned to predestination.

> Predestination, preordination or predetermination is that arrangement of God by which He appointed all things to a definite goal, but especially man as the lord of all things, and this by His holy and just plan, judgment or decree. Now also the election of God is from eternity, by which He indeed elected some to life and others to death. There is no other reason for election and predestination except the good and just will of God saving the elect without cause but damning and rejecting the reprobate with cause.

Although this bare definition might be seen as an affirmation of double predestination, Bullinger clearly did not mean it as such. For, he continued, salvation was completely by grace: men were not elect because God knew they would believe, but they were elect so they would believe. Faith was a gift of God; therefore, all who had faith were elect. Those who did not believe were reprobate. "But," Bullinger explained, "because some do not believe and perish, we do not cast the blame back on God and His predestination, but on the man himself who spurns the grace of God and rejects the heavenly gifts." After referring Traheron to the parables of the talents (Matt. 25:14ff) and of the great supper (Luke 14:16ff) and other such passages emphasizing human responsibility, Bullinger again asserted, "Therefore, the blame is not to be cast back on God and His predestination or compulsion or retention in faithlessness, but on the depraved will of those who refuse."[38]

Clearly Bullinger still had not accepted a double decree of

predestination. Indeed, he specifically rejected reprobation in this sense, denying that "God so rejected certain ones in such a way that even now He hardens them so they might not believe in the truth, to grant the gift of faith to the few. Rather we stress more those universal promises and bid everyone to hope for good." In fact, he continued, predestination had been revealed to show that "God is the lover of men, that He wishes well to men, that He chose all believers for life in Christ and even that He wishes all men to be saved. Whence He instructed that the gospel be preached to every creature." Then, after citing many biblical passages emphasizing God's universal grace, Bullinger warned of the inherent dangers in disputing about God's secrets, such as election and predestination, beyond the words of Scripture. It endangered God's promise and the truth. Therefore, he strove for moderation and an orthodox teaching concerning predestination.[39]

In the Traheron letter, then, Bullinger taught neither Calvin's double predestination, as one might suspect from his initial definition, nor the apparent universalism with which he concluded his argument. Rather, he felt, both God's election and the universal call were taught in Scripture. Election of believers protected free grace and God's freedom; the universal call demonstrated God's integrity and made unbelievers responsible for their own destiny. His position had not changed but was in every way consistent with his earlier teaching, even under the pressure of Calvin and those who agreed with Calvin, such as Traheron.

Bullinger explicitly although tactfully separated himself from Calvin's teaching at the end of his letter to Traheron. Who could censure Calvin's teaching when his motive was to protect the purity of God's grace? It was for this very reason that Calvin taught that God not only foresaw but also arranged and caused the fall of Adam and the ruin of his posterity, and asserted that God created some men for destruction and actually blinded them to the truth to make them instruments of His wrath. Bullinger could never accept such a position; the sincerity of God's grace could be defended without going to such an extreme. The clear implication here is that Calvin's doctrine went beyond Scripture. Nevertheless, Bullinger admitted that God had given great gifts to Calvin and compared him to Augustine, who also went to extremes in some of his writing against the Pelagians.[40]

Undoubtedly Bullinger was feeling the pressure to move to Calvin's position, and one interpretation has been that he did begin to do so in the 1550s, based on three short treatises on the freedom of the will, on providence and predestination, and on whether God is the cause of sin. Bullinger, however, did not write these treatises; the author was Vermigli.[41] Indeed, there is no evidence at all that Bullinger altered his teaching on predestination during the 1550s,[42] although he did find it more difficult to maintain his moderate position, even in Zurich, when Bibliander and Vermigli clashed on the subject.

Theodore Bibliander (d. 1564) became professor of Old Testament in Zurich after Zwingli's death, a position that he held until forced into retirement in 1560. He has been called an Erasmian, an evangelical humanist, a proto-Arminian, and a universalist. Although he apparently never treated predestination systematically, he presented his position clearly enough in 1535 in a letter to Myconius of Basel, his friend and once his colleague in Zurich.[43] He felt that it was "a terrible doctrine . . . that God compelled and forced men by absolute necessity to shameful deeds." God was absolutely holy; He did not will sin or wish the death of sinners. In this respect, one must distinguish between God's predestination and His foreknowledge. God knew some things that He had not predestined. So Bibliander's concern was to protect God's goodness. Rejecting the idea of the election of individuals, he affirmed the predestination of two classes of men: believers and unbelievers. Predestination was not personal; thus Bibliander allowed some latitude for the exercise of the human will. No one was irrevocably lost. Simply stated, "They belong to eternal life by God's grace, by the merit of Jesus Christ, however many fear God and have faith. They belong to eternal death, however many despise God."[44]

Some years later, during the Bolsec affair, Myconius again wrote to Bibliander about predestination, explaining that Bolsec asserted that his teaching was similar to that of Zurich.[45] Apparently referring to his 1535 letter, Bibliander replied: "I am neither a Pelagian nor a Manichean. For the one faction destroyed the grace of God by which alone we are saved by faith. The other settled upon God as the author of perdition and of all evil." Bibliander recognized that man could do nothing at all to gain salvation by himself. "I said that faith is a gift of God so that none might boast." But then he referred to a prevenient grace: "I put anticipatory grace prior to faith, which is the basis of the comforting election by which we have been chosen in Christ, before the foundation of the world." For God wished to be called Father by all men. In fact, He wished men to know that "we all are in the position of sons, provided that we do not force God the Father to renounce us by distrust, sins and impiety itself."[46] Although Bibliander began the letter protesting his orthodoxy, he was obviously out of step in 1552. He had not abandoned his predestination of classes; he introduced the idea of prevenient grace; and he asserted that all were adopted as sons unless they forced God to reject them as such. Therefore, none was irrevocably lost, and the individual will was left some latitude in the matter of salvation. His position resembled Bullinger's in that Bullinger also held the reprobate responsible for his own fate. Both men carefully protected God's goodness, but Bibliander did not protect God's freedom as carefully as Bullinger did. Bullinger posited the personal election of believers, thus avoiding the charges of Erasmianism and synergism.

Bibliander worked and lived in Zurich in harmony with his colleagues for nearly twenty-five years. The occasional criticism of his predestinarian teaching came from Myconius in his personal correspondence with Bibliander, and from Calvin, who complained to Bullinger in April of 1553 about Bibliander's hostility toward him. In fact, Calvin had heard that Bibliander would soon publish a book against his position on predestination.[47] Bullinger replied that Bibliander, "our teacher, without doubt a pious and learned man," was not Calvin's enemy and had no plans to publish a book hostile to Calvin. He suggested that Calvin should write a friendly letter to "my Bibliander."[48] Thus, even during the height of the Bolsec affair, Bullinger avowed his friendship and admiration for Bibliander. One can hardly imagine that Bullinger was not quite aware of Bibliander's viewpoint on predestination. Soon, however, such support and protection would become too costly. Konrad Pellikan, an Erasmian like his friend and colleague Bibliander, died in 1556 after thirty years as professor of Old Testament in Zurich.[49] Bibliander's new associate was Peter Martyr Vermigli, Pellikan's successor as professor of Old Testament.

Vermigli had fled from Lucca in 1542; after spending two months in Zurich, he taught at Strassburg until 1547, when he went to England. Returning to Strassburg in 1553, he met strong opposition from the

Lutheran Johann Marbach, especially on predestination. He happily accepted the Zurich position, leaving his friend Jerome Zanchi, also Italian, in Strassburg to struggle against Marbach. Vermigli's high Calvinist double predestinarianism[50] was well known in Zurich. One might wonder why the Zurichers almost assured a clash by appointing Vermigli. If they had counted on Bibliander's peaceable nature, they were to be disappointed. Vermigli was bent on bringing Zurich over to Calvin's teaching,[51] and in his very first set of lectures, he emphasized absolute double predestination. Meanwhile, Bibliander did not remain silent; rather, he also found occasion to lecture on the subject, apparently explicitly attacking Vermigli's point of view.[52] By late 1559 it had become apparent that Zurich had to choose between the two men. The pastors and theologians chose Vermigli. On February 8, 1560, Bibliander was relieved of his duties and was put on a pension. What did this decision mean? Can one conclude that "On this day Zurich made a decision for Calvin"?[53]

Zurich may well have decided for Calvin, but it does not follow that Bullinger himself did so. Bibliander's point of view was tolerated in Zurich for twenty-five years, until predestination became a crucial issue, in the middle 1550s. When the choice had to be made, Bullinger and his colleagues chose Vermigli precisely because absolute predestination was becoming the orthodox position. The Zurichers simply could not support Bibliander in such an either-or situation, especially since the conflict was known outside of Zurich. But Zurich's decision in favor of Vermigli did not mean that Bullinger fully agreed with him any more than Bullinger's previous protection of Bibliander had signified complete agreement with him. The verdict was dictated by the growing pressure exerted by the high predestinarians, by ecclesiastical politics, at least for Bullinger. Even after Bibliander's retirement, Bullinger could still refer to him privately as "that most excellent man" and, at his death in 1564, as "a most distinguished man."[54] Furthermore, despite the increasing difficulty of holding a moderate position in the face of the new orthodoxy, Bullinger did not accept Calvinist double predestination.[55] He maintained the teaching of the *Decades*, although he did so with a low profile, as in the *Gutachten* for Jerome Zanchi.

Zanchi was converted to Protestantism in Italy under the influence of Vermigli. In 1553 Zanchi replaced the late Caspar Hedio as professor of Old Testament in Strassburg. A few months later, Vermigli returned to Strassburg from England. Marbach's opposition on the eucharist and predestination caused extreme difficulties for both men, and when Vermigli left for Zurich in 1556, Zanchi was the sole remaining Reformed theologian on the faculty. Although Zanchi's view on the eucharist was initially the most important question for Marbach, his position on predestination soon also became a point of issue. Zanchi held to a high double predestination couched in an Aristotelian philosophical theology.[56] When Marbach brought a formal charge of heterodoxy against Zanchi early in 1561, Zanchi drew up fourteen theses summarizing his teaching, precisely stating his predestinarian doctrine in theses 4 through 14.

Zanchi found general support among the German and Swiss Reformed churches, including the church in Zurich. The *Gutachten* from Zurich was written by Vermigli, at Bullinger's request. Bullinger's admiration for Zanchi's learning and abilities is evident from his letter to Vermigli. But it was not his admiration for the man's learning that spurred Bullinger to ask Vermigli to write the *Gutachten*; rather, ecclesiastical politics was uppermost in Bullinger's mind. Strassburg and Zurich had enjoyed close ties since the 1520s that were now seriously threatened by the inroads of Lutheranism. It was imperative to defend Zanchi's eucharistic teaching, to try to save the Reformed tradition in Strassburg.[57] Furthermore, lack of support for Zanchi on predestination almost certainly would have put Zurich and Bullinger in the position of opposing the basic tenet of the new orthodoxy, thus adding to the suspicions that Zurich was weak on this issue. Bullinger found himself in an impossible situation: although he did not agree with Zanchi's viewpoint on predestination, he felt the absolute necessity of defending Zanchi's teaching on the Lord's Supper. So he asked Vermigli, who not only agreed with Zanchi but also knew him well, to write the *Gutachten*. His letter to Vermigli (27 Dec. 1561) reflects both Bullinger's concern about the Reformed eucharistic doctrine and the conflicts in his mind over the predestinarian issue. He requested that Vermigli write "in the name of us all a brief opinion" that Zanchi could present to the judges.

> For I judge that this learned man and faithful minister of Christ who is in danger because of the truth and particularly because of the matter of the Lord's Supper ought not to be forsaken. Further,

about which there is considerable hope, he can help the church very
much if he does not yield in this matter and is not ejected by his
rivals. For if he is ejected, they will destroy and ruin the school and
the church, which have in other respects been weakened enough. I
do not deny that these propositions could have been in some cases
put forth more properly; . . . but since they have been proposed, it
is certain, in order that an evil interpretation might not be added,
that they cannot be rejected.[58]

Vermigli responded swiftly—the *Gutachten* was ready two days later.

Five of Zanchi's theses were particularly crucial with respect to
predestination. In thesis 4 Zanchi asserted: "With God there is a
definite number of those elected to life as well as of the reprobates
predestined to destruction." The Zurichers responded, "That there is
with God a definite number of those predestined to eternal life, as well
as of the reprobates is indisputable."[59] Zanchi's thesis, however, was
misquoted by Vermigli; the *Gutachten* referred to predestination only
for the elect, whereas Zanchi used the term specifically with reference
to the reprobates. The Zurichers did not refer to reprobation in terms
of predestination; rather, those who were not saved were "forsaken"
(*deserentur*). The number of each "class" (*ordo*) was fixed because
God's will was eternal. Despite this general support of thesis 4, there
was no word about predestination to judgment in the *Gutachten*. The
fifth thesis, certainly objectionable to Bullinger, stated: "Just as those
elected to life cannot be lost and thus are necessarily saved, so also
those who are not predestined to eternal life cannot be saved and thus
are necessarily condemned."[60] In his letter to Vermigli, Bullinger
wrote: "The proposition about those to be damned and those to be
saved by necessity seems hard, and, if it were proposed so nakedly to
the people, it would be proposed to more of them with offense than
with edification." Then, after referring to several passages of Scripture
that appeared to agree with Zanchi, Bullinger said that the proposition
could be accepted, "correctly understood."[61] The *Gutachten* itself
agreed with Zanchi that the elect were necessarily saved, that they
could not be lost. Moreover, the reprobate could not be saved because
God would not give faith to them. The Zurichers, however, took care
to reject necessity in terms of constraint, suggesting that Zanchi meant
necessary consequence in the scholastic sense. In thesis 6, Zanchi

stated: "He who is once elected does not become and cannot become a reprobate."[62] The *Gutachten* stated complete agreement with Zanchi on this point.

The thirteenth thesis asserted that the promises of eternal salvation were to be preached to all men but that they pertained to the elect only. The Zurichers agreed that faith was not given to all but the gospel must be preached to all. Zanchi's fourteenth thesis concerned the seemingly universalist statements of Scripture, such as "God wishes all men to be saved" (1 Tim. 2:4); "all" meant "all the elect." The *Gutachten* stated that this interpretation distorted the Scripture the least, that it could not be rejected in good conscience, and that it had been the opinion of Augustine. The *Gutachten* concluded with the statement that the theses contained nothing "either heretical or absurd. Indeed we embrace them partly as necessary, partly as probable." Not only the ancient fathers but also Luther, Capito, Bucer, Brenz, and other illustrious evangelical leaders taught a similar doctrine.[63]

Bullinger's was the first signature on the *Gutachten*. Was Breitinger correct at Dort, then, that Bullinger accepted Calvinistic double predestination in 1561? The *Gutachten* can hardly be seen as proof of such a change. Bullinger's letter requesting Vermigli to draft the document reveals some of his misgivings. Undoubtedly the finished document went beyond anything Bullinger himself had written on predestination.[64] And it affirmed some theses that were stated in a manner repugnant to Bullinger, such as thesis 14. Nevertheless, the *Gutachten* itself was a fairly moderate statement, not once referring to the predestination of the reprobate. Within the general context of the growing pressures to conform to the new orthodoxy and considering the specific possibility of losing Strassburg to Lutheranism, Bullinger, as the Antistes of the Zurich church, felt compelled to support Zanchi. These considerations of ecclesiastical politics are evident both in Bullinger's letter to Vermigli and in the *Gutachten* itself, with its references to Luther, Brenz, Capito, and Bucer, two Lutherans and two Strassburg reformers. There was no mention of either Calvin or Zwingli. The *Gutachten* was a public statement, a political document in support of a Reformed ally and the Reformed church in Strassburg.[65] Bullinger's signature may well indicate his willingness to bend to ecclesiastical necessities and realities. But that this did not signify an alteration of his own doctrine of predestination is evident in the Second Helvetic Confession.

Bullinger began to work on the Confession in 1561, perhaps as a private confession, and completed it in 1564.[66] Then, in 1565 and 1566, he revised and corrected it in consultation with other Reformed churches.[67] First published in 1566, it was a common confession of faith for the Swiss Reformed churches, including Geneva. If Bullinger had been convinced by Vermigli of the Calvinist double predestination doctrine, the Confession would have been a perfect manifesto of that change of mind. Such was not the case, however. Bullinger did make two alterations for the published version in the section on predestination because Beza had objected to a pointed anti-Calvin bias.[68] There were already sufficient strains between Zurich and Geneva without adding to them with specifically anti-Calvin statements in the Confession. These alterations, however, did not affect Bullinger's own doctrine. In fact, his doctrine of predestination in the Confession was a summary of the teaching of the *Decades* and his letter to Traheron.

The chapter on the fall of man contains familiar themes. Man, created righteous and good, fell at the instigation of Satan. He sinned willingly, not from any compulsion. God did not decree the fall. Although God permitted man to sin, God himself was in no way the author or cause of sin. Bullinger condemned "all who make God the author of sin." When the Scriptures spoke of God hardening or blinding men and delivering them to a reprobate sense, "it is to be understood that God does it by just judgment, as a judge and just avenger." Reprobation, then, was a result of sin, not the cause of it.[69] In chapter 9, on the human will, Bullinger posited the same three conditions of the human will that he had in the letter to Traheron: before the fall, after the fall, and the regenerate man. The will of man after the fall was free to sin and did sin without compulsion. Man was not, however, free to do good or to have faith. The will of the regenerate man was freed by the Holy Spirit so that it "of its own accord (*sponte*) wills and is able to do good."[70]

Bullinger moved to predestination and election in chapter 10: "From eternity, by His free and pure grace, with no respect of men, God predestined or elected the saints, those whom He wishes to save in Christ." Thus the elect were chosen not because of any merit of their own but "in Christ and because of Christ." The elect, then, were those who had faith in Christ; those without such faith were the reprobate. But despite the occasional scriptural references to the small numbers of the elect, no man should be rashly judged to be reprobate. Rather than curiously inquiring about one's election, a person should "strive" to enter heaven by the narrow way (Luke 13:24). Speculation could only lead to a fatalistic attitude. For in a practical sense "the preaching of the gospel must be heard and it must be believed. And there is no doubt that if you believe and are in Christ, you are elect." Predestination, then, was to be seen as a comfort because "the promises of God are universal to the faithful, since He says, 'Ask and you will receive. Everyone who asks receives'" (Luke 11:9, 10). Bullinger concluded the chapter with reference to the sacraments and thus indirectly to the covenant: "We have been grafted into the body of Christ by baptism and frequently we are nourished in the church by His flesh and blood unto eternal life. Having been strengthened by these things, we are commanded, according to the precept of Paul, 'to work out our salvation with fear and trembling'" (Phil. 2:12).[71]

These same themes are evident in Bullinger's writings throughout the 1560s. While still working on the Confession, Bullinger published his *Fundamentum firmum* (1563), where he briefly discussed the current dissension over election, which he feared would confuse and dismay the average Christian. Even Christ, who knew the exact number of the elect, admonished everyone to strive "to enter into eternal life." He called everyone and excluded no one. Therefore, all should pray for faith and hope for the salvation so generously promised. Curious questions about predestination only added to the confusion; they cleared up nothing.[72] In his Isaiah commentary of 1567, Bullinger strongly affirmed election but also reiterated that God gave faith to those who desired it and caused the condemnation of no one. Christ died for every man and everyone was called to salvation. God did not wish the condemnation of any man; men sinned and rejected the gospel freely. Faith was the sign of election; the faithful were God's elect. The whole matter of predestination must be connected only with Christ, who died for all men. At one point in the commentary, Bullinger asserted, "A moderate debate concerning election and predestination and rejection will not be healthy unless it is limited to Christ." Elsewhere, discussing the decrees of God, he wrote, "The mandates and decrees of God, pronounced by God without condition, are that He promised the blessed Seed and in this one Seed He elected all who shall be saved; that He established the eternal kingdom in the blessed Seed; that by His death the blessed Seed redeemed the elect of God; that our bodies will be resurrected and that the blessed Seed will judge the entire world. These are the immutable decrees of God." On the other hand, God's decrees of judgment, such as His promise to destroy Nineveh, were mutable, conditioned on repentance. Thus Bullinger still refused to talk about an immutable decree of reprobation.[73] Finally, in his *Bekerung* of 1569, Bullinger repeated his now familiar position. Affirming God's free election, he abhorred a fatalistic attitude. Christ said to preach the gospel to everyone. The promise was given to all, and all were called to salvation. Those who refused were lost by their own fault, not because of any compulsion from God.[74]

Thus Bullinger clung to his moderate position on predestination. His acquiescence to the resolution of the Bibliander affair and his signing of the *Gutachten* for Zanchi did not signify his conversion to Calvinism. Both were ecclesiastical-political actions necessitated by the increasing importance of this new dogma of the new Reformed orthodoxy. His doctrine of predestination throughout the 1560s was essentially a restatement of his teaching in the *Decades*. Throughout his life Bullinger taught a carefully stated single predestination with overtones of universalism.[75]

On the one hand, those who have seen Bullinger as a universalist, both in his own day and since, have clearly been wrong. He never taught that anyone could will to have faith. Faith was God's gift to His elect. On the other hand, there is no evidence that he ever accepted Calvin's teaching of double predestination. If Bullinger himself had been at Dort, he would have disagreed with both parties. Certainly he would have rejected the high Calvinist assertions of necessity or compulsion and of limited atonement, as expressed in the Canons of Dort. Most likely he would have felt uncomfortable among these uncompromising scholastics. Perhaps he would have been more compatible temperamentally with the Remonstrants. And he might well have agreed in general with heir point in the Remonstrance affirming a universal atonement. He would, however, have rejected their teachings on conditional election and the possibility of falling from grace. Bullinger's approach to predestination made it possible for both the Remonstrants and the high Calvinists to find support in his works. His approach was practical and biblical, not speculative and philosophical. He belonged with the first generation of the Reformation and clearly felt uncomfortable with the incipient Reformed orthodoxy of his own day. In short, Bullinger was no scholastic. At Dort he would have been completely out of place. Bullinger would have disagreed with Breitinger on Bullinger.

Bullinger's doctrine of predestination must be understood within the context of his covenant idea, for his system, such as it was, centered around the covenant. And his covenant notion was based on his biblical exegesis and his understanding of how God worked in history, not on logical categories and dogmatic formulations. That is to say, the covenant was not a dogmatic principle in the later Reformed scholastic sense; it was, however, the cornerstone and organizing principle of his thought. Although Bullinger seldom discussed predestination directly in connection with the covenant, he did so briefly in 1560, in his second book against the Anabaptists. He posited a possible Anabaptist objection to infant baptism: since none were saved except the elect, one should wait until a person gave evidence of his election before baptizing him. Bullinger answered that although God's election was secret, the Scriptures included infants among God's people. Salvation was only for the elect, but the Scriptures also taught that God would be merciful unto all who called on Him (Rom. 10:12; John 3:16; Luke 11:9–13; Matt. 7:7–11). Commenting further, he wrote:

> On account of these examples of the teaching of the holy Apostles and above all of Christ, who also said clearly, "Come to me all who labor and are burdened and I will give you rest" [Matt. 11:28], the ministers preach salvation generally to all men and they admit all who come for baptism and desire it for themselves and their own. And they do not dispute at all about God's election, which nevertheless they firmly believe, and they are well aware that the Lord knows only His own. But they also prove their judgment from the word of the Lord, who said, "He who believes and is baptized will be saved" [Mark 16:16]; also, "Whoever is from God hears the word of God" [John 8:47]; also, "All who have been baptized have put on Christ" [Gal. 3:27]; also, "The one who does the truth comes into the light" [John 3:21]. So they are not ashamed to say, "They are the children of God who gladly hear the word of God, believe, allow themselves to be baptized and do good works."

That some were hypocrites was irrelevant because "the church judges from the present, the known and the manifest." In general, the lost could not be known and no judgment at all could be made of children: "Since God has included them in His covenant, we should expect good and not evil from them." Since only God knew His elect, "We should judge according to the word and general promise of God: 'I will be your God and the God of your children.' "[76] Here is the same practical approach as found in his writings specifically on predestination. No one knew the elect except God; therefore, one could not speculate. Those who had faith were the elect, and those who professed faith must be assumed to be the elect. But more importantly, Bullinger stressed the corporate aspect of the covenant, closely connecting baptism with predestination.

A similar corporate emphasis is found in the Confession in the chapter on baptism. There was but one baptism in the church, which "once received continues for the whole life and is a perpetual seal of our adoption. For to be baptized in the name of Christ is to be enrolled, initiated and received into the covenant and family, and so into the inheritance of the sons of God; yes indeed, right now to receive the name of God, that is, to be called a son of God; also to be cleansed from the filth of sins and to be presented with the manifold grace of God for a new and innocent life." The water of baptism was a visible sign of God's working in the soul, invisibly and spiritually. Furthermore, baptism created a community in that it separated God's people from other religions and people, and God thus "consecrates us to himself as a special property."[77] So Bullinger saw baptism as a meaningful sign that initiated the infant into the people of God. One should assume that all who were baptized were also elect. Only if the individual later explicitly rejected the covenant by not keeping its conditions, only then could he perhaps be seen as reprobate. God's covenant community was formed by means of baptism, which obligated a person to faith and a new and innocent life. Election was a matter of inclusion within the covenant, not of exclusion.

In fact, when Bullinger approached salvation historically, from the covenant, his emphasis often tended to verge on universalism, although he always carefully guarded God's free grace. His *Summa* was a summary of what Bullinger saw as the main points of the Christian religion, what every Christian ought to know, to believe, and to do. He did not explicitly discuss predestination, but the topic was often just under the surface. The *Summa* was first published in 1556, just after the Bolsec affair and during Castellio's quarrel with the

Genevans. Bullinger clearly had these disputes in mind when, in the preface, he specifically abhorred such quarrels among Protestants. He promised to avoid these quarrels, and to deliver a simple explanation of the evangelical faith.[78] The *Summa*, essentially an explication of faith, justification, and the Christian life and ethic, was organized around the covenant.

Bullinger introduced the covenant notion at the very beginning, in the article on Scripture. The books of the Bible were separated into the Old and New Testament, just as there were two people, the old and the new, with whom God had made His covenant, testament, or will. The entire Scripture was the book of the covenant. Turning to God and His works, Bullinger stated how God had covenanted and bound himself to men and what He demanded from men, all explained in the Scripture, to the end that all men might be saved. God had created man good, righteous, and holy, and totally free. In no way compelled by God, Adam fell by exercising his own free will. Sin came from man, not from God. But God in His great mercy immediately promised salvation to all the faithful, making "a covenant with the human race," first with Adam, extending it to Noah, clarifying it with Abraham, renewing it by Moses, and concluding it through Christ. God's part of the agreement was to be all-sufficient, especially through salvation in Christ. In return God wanted men to hold Him in trust and faith as the only God "and to walk in His commandments for our entire life."[79]

In the article on sin, Bullinger, again emphasizing that sin came from man, warned that men should not speculate and dispute about why God allowed man to sin. But despite the passages about God's blinding of men and giving them over to a perverse mind, God never compelled any man to sin. It was enough to know that God was just and holy. Rather than following this section with a discussion of predestination, Bullinger turned to original sin, where he reintroduced the covenant. God, because of His covenant, out of His grace,

> wishes to cleanse us and not to reckon our sins toward damnation. In this regard our children are baptized and washed as the children of the ancient [people] were circumcised, so that we might come to confess original sin and our impurity, which, however, along with our other sins, God does not wish to reckon to us, for Christ's sake. The judgment of St. Augustine assists in this matter: "In baptism the

sin is forgiven, not that it no longer is in man or does not remain in the flesh, but that it is not reckoned for our damnation."[80]

Bullinger clearly did not mean that every baptized person was automatically justified; but neither did he qualify this statement. And aside from condemning Pelagianism in rather general terms, he ignored predestination.

Discussing the law, Bullinger asserted that the moral law, the Decalogue, was not abolished but was restated by Christ. Therefore all Christians must fulfill the moral law through Christ and faith, as stated in the covenant conditions.[81] But as Bullinger emphasized in the article on grace, one could be justified only by faith, not through the law. Here again he almost approached predestination: "As God saw the fall and ruin of man from eternity, thus He also prepared the medicine from eternity, with which He wishes to deliver the lost world again, and He proposed that He would allow His Son to become man, to come into the world and to restore the ruin. The holy apostle Paul speaks about that to the Ephesians" (Eph. 1:4–8). There is no word about particular election in this forceful affirmation of universal atonement. Even the quotation from Paul, a favorite passage of the high Calvinists, was placed in this context of a universal atonement. Similar universalist statements occur in the article on faith. Because of the fall, man found himself in need of a savior, "which God decreed in His eternal counsel and ordained Jesus Christ as the Savior of the entire world." Those who did not believe in Christ would be damned eternally for their unbelief.[82]

The actual means by which God brought men to faith, the preaching of God's word and the inward work of the Spirit, was very important to Bullinger. Here election is the topic, although he did not specify it as such. Faith was God's free gift; no one could believe by himself. But even though all men did not receive faith, individuals should not worry and doubt. Rather, "each of us should much more take comfort in the consoling promises of God," for God did not will that any man should be lost (2 Pet. 3:9). One should pray for faith. Furthermore, "in the planting or increasing and maintaining of faith, the holy sacraments are not fruitless or useless." The Lord established them for a purpose. But, Bullinger cautioned, "the word and the sacraments in themselves alone neither give the grace of God to us nor justify us." Moreover, care must be taken not to decrease God's honor by adding "other outward things such as instruments or tools or human works." On the other hand, one "should not spurn the instruments which God does use, nor should he think that the obedience and the works which God requires from us are useless or regard them as unnecessary."[83] This was as much as to say that the covenant conditions could be met by asking for God's help and by using the aids prescribed by God.

The article on the sacraments rounds out Bullinger's argument. The sacraments were "holy actions," signs and seals of God's covenant. They reminded the Christian of his salvation and of his duty to God and man in the covenant. They were outward signs of salvation and justification, "that God has accepted us into the covenant and as children." They firmed up faith and gathered a community, the church. Those who had been baptized had received "the sign of the covenant and of the children of God, yes the seal of regeneration and cleansing." In their physical birth, all were tainted with Adam's impurity, to death and damnation. "But God regenerates us with His grace and cleanses us through His Spirit with the blood of Christ; He renews us inwardly, which baptism, as a true sign, signifies and testifies outwardly. For baptism is an evidence of our covenant with God which cleanses us. That is why it is given with water." Baptism also reminded the Christian of his covenant obligation to live a holy life, which Bullinger treated more fully in the article on good works. The Christian did not despise good works, but rather "he walks in the commandments of God, he serves the neighbor in love, and all his life he delights in the duties and obligations which God has prescribed for him, and he knows that he is obligated to God." In short, he keeps the conditions of the covenant.[84]

Bullinger's doctrine of election was thus closely connected with the covenant, the historical context within which God dealt with His people. Baptism initiated the individual into the covenant community, the church. Baptism was the sign of belonging to God's people and a seal of justification. Having accepted this covenant sign, the individual was obligated to love and trust God through faith in Christ and to love and serve his neighbor. These were the human conditions of the covenant, and if the individual met them he was one of the elect. Election was a positive matter of inclusion and assurance. Thus, when explaining his doctrine of predestination, Bullinger took great care, often not stating it at all, as in the *Summa*, preferring to remain on the practical, historical plane.[85] He did not develop an abstract, theoretical, or speculative dogma, because to do so would go beyond the biblical teaching and the realm of history. It would undercut human responsibility as outlined in the covenant conditions. Bullinger was content to present his understanding of the biblical teaching of single predestination within the context of a universal atonement. When pressed he always cited the universalist passages of the Bible. He never attempted to reconcile everything in a closely reasoned and logical theory of double predestination. Instead he cast his doctrine of salvation within the framework of the covenant, which meant that predestination only made sense within the historical calling of man by God.

Bullinger's position on predestination, then, undoubtedly had its ambiguities and, at least from the vantage point of hindsight, its inconsistencies. It must be viewed, however, within the context of the historical development of Reformed thought and theology. On the one hand, the Reformed tradition of Calvinist orthodoxy subordinated the matter of salvation and the covenant to double predestination. The covenant was in actuality God's testament, a unilateral promise of salvation to the elect. It applied only to the elect because Christ's atonement was limited to the elect. For the Calvinists, God's double decree of predestination was absolute and static. On the other hand, Bullinger stressed the covenant as the vehicle through which God dealt with man; God's election only became binding in history as individuals kept the conditions of the covenant. The covenant, then, was the framework within which *sola fide* and *sola gratia* were understood. The covenant tradition was the other Reformed tradition, which must be distinguished from the incipient Reformed orthodoxy of the second half of the sixteenth century.[86]

Bullinger's approach was biblical and historical rather than systematic and static. For this reason, in order to understand the full importance of the covenant in his thought, his conception of the covenant in history, from Adam to his own day, must be clarified. For Bullinger discovered the prototype for the Reformed community of his own day in the history of God's people within the covenant, especially during the Old Testament period. Although the rule of faith became clearer when Christ fulfilled the covenant, the divine norms for the

Christian community continued to be applicable during the New Testament era, from apostolic times through the Middle Ages into the Reformation.

CHAPTER THREE

"Looke from Adam": The People of God in Old Testament Times

BULLINGER'S APPROACH to the covenant was invariably from a distinctive historical perspective. The history of God's people, the history of salvation, was the history of the covenant. The primary source for this history was the Bible, the "book of the covenant" or "the records of the covenant,"[1] the source for the content of the covenant and the account of God's dealings with His people from Adam through apostolic times. It was within this historical frame that Bullinger viewed his own day. His interpretation of the Reformation, his defense of Reformed society in Zurich, and his judgment of the radicals were reflections of his conception of the history of the faith. For this reason, an understanding of Bullinger's perception of the history of God's people in covenant terms is crucial in appreciating his application of the covenant to his own society.

The Old Testament had special significance for Bullinger, and several important themes stand out in his treatment of Old Testament history and in his commentaries. According to his calculations, the covenant was made with Adam 2,449 years before the first written Scripture, the giving of the law to Moses (1520 B.C.).[2] This time before Moses, the age of the patriarchs, was a period of pure religion. Bullinger thus heavily emphasized the antiquity of the Christian faith and the existence of an oral tradition during the patriarchal era. In this connection, Bullinger saw the period of the Law, from Moses to John the Baptist, as an interregnum between the two ages of the patriarchs and of Christ, when the covenant was uncluttered by legal accretions. Nevertheless, it was during the interregnum of the Law that he discovered the norms for the Christian commonwealth and church, all of which were connected with the covenant. Furthermore, this interregnum was marked by times of extreme apostasy and periodic restorations of the covenant; these restorations set the norm for reformation by the Christian magistrate. Finally, the Jews were rejected as God's special people because of their continuous violations of the covenant, violations capped by their total rejection of Christ, the promised Seed who confirmed the covenant with His death.

Bullinger found all the basic elements of the Christian faith at the very beginning of the patriarchal age, when God first made the covenant with Adam and Eve. There was thus one covenant, one faith, and one church from Adam until Bullinger's own time. His most cogent argument for this unity, *Der alt gloub* (1539),[3] was also his most succinct history of the faith. Bullinger did not posit a covenant of creation, before the fall, but he did state that God gave a law to Adam and Eve in Paradise. This law, expressed in the simple commandment not to eat the fruit of the tree of the knowledge of good and evil, was simply that they must love and obey God.[4] God had created Adam and Eve perfect, with absolute free will, in His own image. Theirs was a willing disobedience and their fall from this perfection entirely their own fault. God could righteously have destroyed them. Instead, in His mercy and grace, He offered restoration and eternal life to all the faithful, promising redemption in the Seed to come (Gen. 3:15). This was the first preaching of the gospel and the genesis of the Christian faith, when God transferred the curse from man to Christ in "the first promise and the authentic gospel."[5]

Such, however, was not the full extent of Bullinger's claims for the protoevangelion. More than simply the first gospel, the promise also was "the basis and entire sum of our holy Christian faith." Through man's own fault, the entire human race fell into death and damnation; in this first promise, God offered salvation to all who believed and held fast to Him. The promise included the basics of Christianity—faith, love and innocence. It lacked nothing about faith and the Christian life. Therefore, because of their faith, Adam and Eve were "true Christians." Having lost eternal life because of their willful disobedience, they received it back through faith in Christ. There was nothing vague or imprecise about Adam's faith as far as Bullinger was concerned. In fact, Adam's knowledge about Christ, the content of his faith, was astounding: he knew about the twofold nature of Christ; he saw the cross "from a distance in faith"; he understood that Christ's suffering brought life once again to the faithful. All this God had written in the hearts of Adam and Eve. Although they had no written Scripture, they lacked nothing. God even gave them a sacrament, the sacrifice, the offering, as a figure of Christ and a sign of thanksgiving.[6] This promise of the blessed Seed, then, was the beginning of the church, which would include all the faithful, all those in the covenant of God.

Bullinger did not explicitly introduce the covenant in his treatment of Adam in *Der alt gloub*.[7] He did, however, clearly do so in several other writings, in which he emphasized that God's covenant was made first with Adam, for the restitution of the human race. From the very beginning, the conditions of the covenant had been that God would be all-sufficient, especially in offering Christ for the redemption of mankind, and that man in return must trust completely in God and keep His commandments. Ever since Adam, true worship and piety had been to keep the covenant.[8]

The true worship, however, was perverted almost immediately. Although Adam undoubtedly taught the faith, the promise of the coming Seed, to both of his sons, only Abel had true faith. His offering, given in faith, was a figure "of the single, perpetual offering of our Savior Christ," a sacrament of coming things. As such it pleased God. But Cain was unfaithful and disobedient, despising God's word (Gen. 4:1–7; Heb. 11:4). While Abel was "an example of the seed of God and of a regenerate, true, orthodox Christian man," Cain was "a seed of the serpent, a child of the devil." The two brothers were thus the progenitors of the two types of people, the faithful and the unfaithful, the founders of the city of God and the city of the Devil. Furthermore, when Cain murdered his brother, "then Abel became the first martyr and witness of God and Christ in the holy church." Bullinger saw Cain as the first apostate and his murder of Abel as the first attempt to destroy the faith. But with the birth of Seth (Gen. 4:25) in 130 (3839

B.C.), the true faith was reestablished, as was "the lineage of the pious to Noah and thence to Abraham, then to David, and from there to Christ."[9] Seth's was the first restoration of the covenant, in effect the first reformation of the church.[10]

The lineage of the faithful continued from Seth (d. 1042) through Enos (d. 1140) and the other holy patriarchs up to Noah, born in 1056 (2913 B.C.). During the same millennium the godless flourished, until God resolved to destroy the unfaithful as an example of His great displeasure with godlessness. Only the faithful Noah and his family were saved from the ensuing flood, which took place in 1656 (2313 B.C.). "Here," Bullinger explained, "our holy true Christian faith was victorious and triumphant. For Noah was of our faith, of the seed of God, and trusted in the blessed Seed, our Lord Jesus. Indeed, the ark or ship of Noah was a symbol of Christ" (1 Pet. 3:20).[11] Through Noah God thus maintained the line of the faithful, despite the general apostasy of mankind.

After the flood, Noah made a sacrifice of thanksgiving to God, and God renewed with him the ancient covenant originally made with Adam (Gen. 8:20–9:17). In connection with the covenant, Noah received some commandments from God, "but none other except those He had given to his forefathers and written in their hearts." The first concerned marriage and bringing up children "in the fear of God, piety, obedience and knowledge." The second forbade violence and deception, "that no one support himself from murders, suppressions of the poor, by usury, force, treachery and deceit." In summary, "whatever concerns the love of God and the neighbor is renewed here with Noah and his children and required from them." This was the oral tradition that had come down from Adam. From the time of Adam the old patriarchal religion had been based on the covenant and its conditions of faith and love, and even though God began anew with Noah, He did not alter the covenant or its conditions. Noah's son, Shem, continued the lineage of the faithful and of the blessed Seed.[12]

Abraham, the descendant of Shem, was born in the year 1948 (2021 B.C.) in Chaldea, where "the pure faith had been darkened somewhat" by idolatry. After Abraham had obeyed God's command to leave Chaldea and to move his entire family to Canaan, God renewed His covenant with him. Here Bullinger took care to emphasize the unity of the faith and the covenant: "For first He [Christ] was promised to

Adam, then the promise was renewed with Noah, and now with Abraham. And all that is but one promise, one Savior and one faith." Abraham's obedience and faith were of utmost importance, for his justification by faith preceded his circumcision by many years (Gen. 15:6; 17:1ff). This was a crucial interpretive point for Bullinger, that "our Christian faith is 2048 years older than circumcision and 2449 years older than the law, the priesthood and the ceremonies of the Jews." It was Abraham's faith that counted. As Christ said, " 'Abraham saw my day and he rejoiced' [John 8:56]. What is the day of Christ except the light of the gospel? He did not see this light physically but with the eyes of faith, and that comforted him and saved him." Because of his faith, Abraham became the father of all believers; his spiritual seed included all the faithful.[13]

The covenant conditions were the same for Abraham as they had been for Noah and Adam. They were simply, faith and love. To keep the covenant was to place one's faith solely in God through Christ and to keep God's commandments, or, as it was given to Abraham, to walk in God's presence and be pure (Gen. 17:1).[14] The faithful person kept these conditions throughout his life.

God also gave Abraham a new sacrament, circumcision, the purpose of which was to include all Abraham's physical progeny within the covenant. God confirmed His covenant with blood, as human covenants were confirmed. Circumcision not only brought God's people into one body and reminded them of their obligations in the covenant; it also was a renewed promise of the coming Seed of Abraham, Christ, who would ratify the covenant with His own blood. Circumcision, then, was both the sign and the seal of the covenant. The faithful in the covenant, those who kept the covenant conditions, became Abraham's spiritual seed as well as his physical offspring.[15]

Both Isaac and Jacob were faithful in the covenant: "They . . . trusted in God alone through Jesus Christ and also lived properly and piously." Joseph also followed the faith of his father and grandfathers, suffering in patience, then ruling with justice and fairness when he received power in Egypt. When Joseph died in 2309 (1660 B.C.), his entire family, the descendants of Abraham, were settled in Egypt (Gen. 50:20–26). One hundred and forty years later Moses led them out of the slavery into which they had fallen.[16]

Moses, born in 2368 (1601 B.C.), was the last of the patriarchs and

God's instrument in creating an organized church and commonwealth among the Jews.[17] Moses, who had "a knowledge of Christ and a faith in Christ," led the Jews out of Egypt in the year 2449 (1520 B.C.). At Mt. Sinai, God commanded the people to purify themselves, "for He wished to bind them to himself, to take them as a people and to give them His commandment and Law."[18] First God gave them the moral law, the Decalogue, then the ceremonial law and finally the judicial laws. When Moses wrote the law, the epoch of the patriarchs ended and the period of the Law, an interregnum between the patriarchs and Christ, began.

Along with this distinct division between the times before and after Moses, Bullinger also placed a much greater value on the patriarchal period. Although occasionally he pointed to the progressive nature of revelation,[19] more often he hinted that the knowledge of the gospel was clearer during the patriarchal age than under Judaism. Bullinger did place great emphasis on written Scripture as God's sole word to man, the only authority for faith and life. But the idea of the oral tradition of the patriarchs also fascinated him. God's direct revelation to Adam about Christ, the blessed Seed, included a law, i.e., a rule for living, God's will for mankind. Thus the covenant was revealed directly to Adam, along with its conditions. Not only was Adam to have faith in Christ, the Savior of the world, but God also taught him that he must serve God as his only God "in purity and righteousness, for all the days of his life. Therefore, He also instructed the confederates to worship with purity and to obey superiors and the other things which later were written in the two tables of the covenant, etc. This, I say, is that living, sure and divine tradition received by the patriarchs from God, through Adam." The ancient oral tradition was the conditions of the covenant or the moral law, which taught faith and piety.[20]

Bullinger's references to this ancient oral tradition were always made in connection with pure worship, the patriarchal faith in Christ, and the law or will of God. In his treatise on the authority of Scripture, Bullinger introduced the subject in the first chapter. The word of God, which had existed in the world since the promise to Adam "concerning the restitution of the human race" (Gen. 3:15), was handed down intact from Adam to Moses. All the patriarchs accepted this word, instituting their whole life and faith according to it.[21] After making a similar argument in connection with the covenant and Scripture in the first article of his *Summa*, Bullinger returned to the topic of this pristine tradition in the article on the law of God. God's first revelation of His law was to the patriarchs, from the beginning of the world, writing in their hearts everything later given in the Decalogue. This law was the will of God, how God wished the faithful to live in all ages, "that we should love Him above all things, serve and depend on Him alone, and give perfect obedience with all our strength, in spirit, soul and body. Then He adds promises and threats."[22] The law, then, was the conditions of the covenant, faith and piety. It was written in the hearts of men before Moses wrote it as Scripture. Bullinger did not set the moral law against the gospel; rather, the law, as the will of God for man, was the gospel, as explained in the covenant conditions. To be sure, salvation always had been by faith alone. But those who had faith were faithful, doing their best to fulfill the covenant condition of piety, to live according to God's will in the covenant.

This connection between the moral law and the gospel becomes quite clear in Bullinger's treatment of the Decalogue. The Decalogue was the moral law, the will of God for man in all times, places, and conditions. Given to Moses on two stone tablets, it was a summary of true religion. The first table, the first four commandments, taught the true love and worship of God. The remaining six commandments, the second table, prescribed man's behavior toward other men. Or, put more clearly in covenant terms, the Decalogue "teaches partly the love of God, partly the love of the neighbor. This very thing is also taught by the main points of the covenant. Indeed, the Decalogue itself appears to be a paraphrase, so to speak, of the conditions of the covenant."[23] Bullinger, then, saw the Love Commandment of Christ as a summary of the Decalogue, of the moral law, and thus a concise statement of the covenant conditions of faith and piety. These two tables of the law were called "the tables of the covenant because they embrace the original main points of that ancient covenant begun with the patriarchs."[24] As for the other laws and commandments that were later added to the two tables of the Decalogue, "they were not added as primary commandments but as bylaws, for the elucidation and better understanding of the ten chapters or commandments. For the entire perfect sum of all laws, the proper form of godliness, of worship, of righteousness and of the good and evil life is already included in the two tables."[25] Therefore, God did not initiate anything new with the Decalogue, but

simply renewed the ancient covenant by means of a written summary
of His will, which previously had been written in human hearts.

Bullinger saw a threefold use of the moral law. First, it gave
knowledge of sin, that no one could be justified by his own powers, but
only through faith in Christ, by the grace of God. Here the purpose of
the law was to convince a person of his own sin and unworthiness and
thus lead him by faith to Christ. Thus it taught justification by faith
alone: "In this regard it is most openly mingled with the gospel and
takes upon itself the office of the gospel." The law also taught the
proper worship of God and how to live in this world to those who were
already justified by faith. Here, then, the law was the explication of the
covenant conditions for the faithful. Finally, the law was the basis for
public order by means of the discipline and punishment of the
Christian magistrate.[26] This third use of the law concretely tied the
covenant conditions to social-political life in the Christian commonwealth.

Bullinger was quite aware that his connection of the moral law with
the gospel left him open to the charge that works were necessary for
salvation. His defense was based on the covenant. The promise of the
blessed Seed was reiterated by Moses in the first commandment, with
the reference to the exodus from Egypt. Then the covenant itself,
renewed with the giving of the law, was fundamentally concerned with
this salvation through faith in Christ. Therefore, since the covenant
was unchangeable, Moses also preached salvation through faith alone
in Christ (Gal. 3:16–18). Bullinger did, however, feel the necessity of
asserting specifically that he maintained the proper distinction between
law and gospel, not mixing them together.[27] Nevertheless, Bullinger
did not distinguish as clearly as many of his contemporaries; this was
certainly no Lutheran distinction between law and gospel.[28]

Aside from this law-gospel issue, the important point made so
clearly by Bullinger was that God's people, before and after Christ,
must live according to the moral law, the will of God, the conditions of
the covenant. God demanded both faith and a life of obedience or good
works from His faithful in every age.[29]

The judicial law, on the other hand, was simply the application of the
moral law to social and political life. It was the civil law of the Jewish
commonwealth and as such applied only to that time and place. It is
important to note, however, that Bullinger found the basis for civil law,
in this case the judicial law of the Old Testament, in the second table of

the Decalogue, in the commandment to love one's neighbor as oneself, and thus in the covenant condition of piety. In any age, civil law among God's people must be based in the moral law, in the covenant.[30]

Bullinger's preference for the patriarchal age becomes even more apparent in his treatment of the ceremonial law. The patriarchs had a pristine religious practice, acting as their own priests, making sacrifices from the heart in faith. Theirs was an exercise in true piety. The simplicity and sincerity of their worship contrasted sharply with the complexity and the externals of the ceremonial law. These more formal, outward ceremonies had been given under Moses because the Jews had become enamored of such external props in Egypt. Bullinger's ambivalent feelings about the ceremonial law are evident. "If the people had not been corrupted in Egypt by dwelling with idolaters but had remained firm and unmoved like their fathers Abraham, Isaac and Jacob, then they might well have continued with the old, short simple form [of worship] as it was with the holy patriarchs. But now, in Egypt, they had seen the outward, expensive worship, with temples, altars, sacrifices, a priesthood, holy days, ornaments, etc." God introduced the ceremonial law because His people had become too corrupt to do without external ceremonies and a priesthood.[31]

Bullinger made essentially the same point in *De testamento* about the ceremonial law, but specifically in covenant terms. The Jews had lived in Egypt so long that "not only were they nearly ignorant of the ancestral religion and the covenant itself, but daily went over more and more to Egyptian idolatry." God first gave the Decalogue as a support "for the collapsing covenant," then the ceremonial law, also as an aid in keeping the covenant. Therefore, just as God gave the judicial law to help the Jews keep the second table of the Decalogue or the covenant condition of piety, so He meant the ceremonial law as a support in keeping the condition of faith or the first table of the Decalogue. The ceremonial law, then, not only had the specific purpose of creating a formal, external worship to satisfy the Jews, but also of supporting the true worship of God in the covenant. Bullinger made it clear that God did not prefer such a detailed, external religious observance. He allowed the ceremonial law only because His people had become superstitious and corrupt. In this sense, the ceremonies were "foreign things" to the covenant.[32]

The sacrifices, however, were much more than mere outward

ceremony. "In another way, what the patriarchs possessed in abbreviated form in the Tradition, that is, in the promise of the blessed Seed, in the righteous rule of life and in the sacrament of the sacrifice, that same thing the Jews now receive more copiously set forth in the law, in the manifold sacrifices and in the sacred rites." All the sacrifices, the ark of the covenant, the candelabrum, the passover, the altar, all these external things were types of Christ and thus had to be used in faith.[33] As Bullinger expressed it in *Der alt gloub*, "Therefore, those who used or performed such worship without faith and the raising up of the soul neither served nor please God. But those who had faith in God, depending on Him alone, raising their hearts higher and not remaining standing on the visible thing, they pleased God." All the blood of the sacrifices signified the future sacrifice of Christ, in whom the worshipper had to place his faith. Thus, along with circumcision and the passover, the other sacrifices and rites were sacraments, visible things denoting the spiritual blessing, redemption by the coming Messiah. When the faithful participated in the ceremonies and sacrifices, "they looked at Christ with the eyes of faith" and considered the promised Seed, "who shall die on the cross for us, cleanse us with His blood and make us alive with His death." This was the true spiritual purpose of the sacrifices and the ceremonial law. "For the outward show and pomp of the offerings outside of and without faith in God and the blessed Seed is worth nothing at all, and is, in addition, an abomination to God."[34] The ceremonies, then, had worth only as an aid in keeping the covenant condition of faith. Even during the interregnum of the Law, salvation was by faith alone through God's grace, not by works or external ceremony.

The problem, from Bullinger's perspective, had been that many Jews took these appendages to the covenant as the essence of the covenant, thus missing the true meaning and message of the law: the gospel, the promised Seed. The Jews therefore misused the law and ignored the true conditions of the covenant. When Christ came, the law would again be written in the hearts of men as it had been during the era of the patriarchs. The ceremonies would then cease and the interregnum of the law would end.[35] As Bullinger stated it in *De testamento*, Christ fulfilled the figures and types in the ceremonial law and thus abolished it. Consequently, "that ancient religion, which was thriving in that golden age of the patriarchs before the law was brought forth, [now] flourishes throughout the entire world, renewed and restored more fully and more clearly by Christ, and made perfect with a new people, namely the Gentiles, as though a new light had been introduced into the world."[36] The period of Judaism was thus an interregnum between two periods of pure religion. Christ renewed the ancient Christianity, the old covenant, but more clearly and with a new people.

Nevertheless, Bullinger's ambivalence about the ceremonial law did not impede him from finding the norms for both the church and the Christian commonwealth during the period. Along with the liberation of His people from bondage in Egypt, God wished to constitute an organized church and commonwealth among them. All the holy patriarchs before the law had been both priests and prophets, but in the organized church after the exodus God established an official priesthood along with the ceremonial law. The Levitical priests led the church, taught the moral law, administered the sacraments and performed the sacrifices. The priests were exclusive servants of the church. Prophets, on the other hand, were shown the future by God. They also explained the meaning of the moral law, attacked error and iniquity, and generally taught and guarded piety and righteousness, the conditions of the covenant. Often the same person was both priest and prophet, such as Jeremiah, but also laymen such as Isaiah were prophets. The priests, then, had to do solely with ecclesiastical affairs. The prophets were concerned with both matters of the church and the commonwealth, exhorting the Jews to keep the covenant not only in worship but in everyday life.[37]

The office of magistrate also was much more ancient than Moses. But soon after the Exodus, God established the Christian magistracy over His people, church, and commonwealth. Like other reformers, Bullinger argued that the magistracy was a divine ordinance, made necessary by human sin to avoid anarchy in society. Government, then, had existed from the beginning of the world. Bullinger's basic support for his teaching came from two biblical passages. The first, the thirteenth chapter of Romans, taught that the magistrate, as the servant of God, received his authority directly from God. The magisterial office was thus holy, and those magistrates who ruled justly were the friends of God. This passage from Romans was the common foundation for all the magisterial reformers' teachings on government. Bullinger's second text, the eighteenth chapter of Exodus, verse 21, was more uniquely his own. There, God, through Jethro, directed Moses to choose governors from the people to aid him in ruling Israel. Although Romans 13 gave divine sanction to government and was thus an indispensable text for Bullinger along with the other reformers, Exodus 18 was an actual example of God directing the choice of Christian magistrates to rule over His people.[38]

The Exodus passage held special importance for Bullinger in defining the character of the magistrate who ruled over God's people. He should be a man of God, a Christian: "Let him fear God, be religious and not superstitious. No idolater preserves the commonwealth; rather he destroys it. Impious men do not increase truth and religion, but punish and banish them. Therefore, let that man of ours be orthodox, of sound faith, one who trusts in God's word." Several other passages further prescribed that the magistrate must be a man of God, pious, and a friend of true religion (Deut. 1:13, 17:14-20; Num. 27:16-17). The commonwealth and true religion would flourish under such a magistrate. Bullinger justified his heavy use of the Old Testament with his insistence that the faithful Old Testament rulers were true Christians who believed in Christ.[39]

The Christian magistrate's divinely ordained task was to ensure that the covenant conditions were observed among God's people. The magistrate's laws must be based on the Decalogue. Laws concerning religion and the church helped in keeping the first table or the condition of faith. Laws relating to man in society were aids in observing the second table, the covenant condition of piety.[40] The direct application of the covenant conditions to civil life and the laws of the magistrate is unambiguously stated by Bullinger in his *De testamento*.

> The judicial and civil [laws], which admonish about maintaining public peace, about punishing the guilty, about waging war and repelling enemies, about the defense of liberty, the oppressed, widows, orphans and the fatherland, about laws of justice and equity, about the purchase, the loan, possessions, inheritance, and about other legal subjects of this sort—are not these things also included in that part of the covenant that prescribes integrity and commands that we walk in the presence of God? Now if anyone thinks this opinion of ours is not valid or clear enough, let him consider the very deeds of Abraham, . . . [who] so far as judicial,

civil or external things are concerned, is seen to have conformed to certain principles. . . ; and [these principles are] nothing else but what the purity of the soul, the sincerity of faith, and the love of truth and the neighbor dictated; indeed, much later, God speaking through Moses taught the Jewish people to observe the same things.[41]

This was the task of the magistrate—to enforce the covenant conditions in society, among God's people. The covenant was the standard for life in the commonwealth, both for those who willingly attempted to keep its conditions and for those whom the magistrate had to force to observe the condition of piety. The Christian magistrate made the covenant conditions clear to all God's people with his just law, based on God's law.

Moses himself was the first magistrate and lawgiver of the Jewish commonwealth. His was, Bullinger reported, the most ancient law extant as well as the first history, the oldest poetry and the first philosophy, for Moses antedated the Trojan War by 350 years.[42] It was Moses who appointed the first governors and judges in Israel and the first high priest, Aaron. However, by establishing a priesthood and appointing a high priest, Moses did not divest himself of authority over matters of religion and the church, or even of doctrine. Such things were properly the concern of the magistrate, for the ruler was a minister of God and of the church. On the other hand, it was the duty of both prophet and priest to instruct the ruler in God's law, as Eleazer instructed Joshua (Num. 27:15–23). Nevertheless, Bullinger asserted, the magistrate had complete authority in both ecclesiastical and civil matters. Even though the ruler might not heed the prophet and the priest, they must obey all lawful commands of the magistrate.[43]

Joshua, who became the ruler of the Jewish commonwealth at Moses' death in 2488 (1481 B.C.), finally led the Jews into the land of Canaan. God promised to bless the undertaking if Joshua would observe the law scrupulously (Josh. 1:2–9). This commission to Joshua, Bullinger observed, demonstrated "that it is the duty of the magistrate to learn it [the law] and govern according to its standard." And Joshua heeded God's demands by circumcising the uncircumcised and explaining God's law to the people (Josh. 5:2ff; 8:30ff). Joshua, pious leader of the commonwealth, died in the year 2520 (1449 B.C.), having ruled for thirty-two years. He had not only led the conquest of the promised land but had also preserved true religion and worship within the covenant.[44]

From Bullinger's perspective, the period of the Judges was both the high point in Israel's history and the most instructive for his own society. For God had initially established not a monarchy "but a republic, a democracy, I say, tempered by aristocracy." Each tribe chose its own magistrates, with the judges presiding as chief magistrates over all Israel, not as lord and king but as judge and consul. Counting Moses as the first judge, this republican form of government lasted for 427 years, until Saul, the first king. Seeing Zurich's reflection in the republic of Israel, Bullinger saw Israel as much happier and better off under the judges than under the later kings. Since Israel's republic endured for 355 years after Joshua's death, and considering that God permitted a monarchy only at the insistence of the people, it even appeared that republicanism was the divinely preferred form of government.[45]

Despite this happy state of the Jewish commonwealth, the period of the judges was marred by "defection from God and His law and desecration or violation of the covenant of God." The pattern was clear: violation of the covenant by falling into idolatry, punishment and oppression, repentance and the raising of another judge to liberate the church and commonwealth. Toward the end of the period, when Eli was judge (1 Sam. 4:18), there was anarchy in Israel (Judg. 21:25). Neither true religion nor public justice and honesty was preserved, because Eli, who was priest as well as judge, did not do his duty as magistrate. As a result, there were religious corruption, war and civil disorder, crime and impiety among God's people.[46]

Samuel, the last of the judges, succeeded Eli, who died in 2845 (1124 B.C.). With a powerful oration (1 Sam. 7) Samuel convinced the people that repentance was the only means "of recovering liberty and salvation." When they returned to God and rejected the idols, He mercifully forgave their sins and gave them victory over the Philistines. In his old age, Samuel attempted to make his office hereditary by appointing his sons as judges. But, Bullinger mused, when the pious man gave his sons as judges without consulting the Lord, it did not turn out well. For the sons were degenerate and avaricious, and their judgments, unjust. This, then, was the occasion that prompted the demand for a king (1 Sam. 8:1ff). Saul became the first king of Israel in 2876 (1093 B.C.).[47]

The institution of the monarchy again brought forth Bullinger's admiration for the republican constitution under the judges.

> God had established through Moses in His law the most excellent, the most admirable and convenient form of republic, depending on the wisest, most powerful and most merciful king of all, God, on the best and fairest senators and not at all on extravagant and arrogant ones, and finally on the people; to which He added the judge, whenever it was necessary. They would have maintained it at any cost had they been wise; but rarely is the multitude wise. In general it is changeable and always fickle, ungrateful and eager for new things.

Samuel, opposed to the monarchy, explained the inconveniences of a monarchial form of government to the people, exhorting them "to renew the pristine condition of liberty or the arrangement of the republic." When Samuel consulted God, He said, "They have not rejected you but me" (1 Sam. 8:7). Bullinger, although obviously preferring the republican form, quickly cautioned that this episode did not indicate that monarchies in themselves displeased God (1 Pet. 2:13) but that God's people had spurned God's more direct rule over them for a human king.[48]

Bullinger pointed out that Samuel's objection to the new monarchy was well taken. Few of the kings of Israel and Judah were true to the covenant. The first king, Saul, lost his kingdom because of disobedience and faithlessness (1 Sam. 13:13–14).[49] The high point of the period of the kings came under David, who was faithful in the covenant.

Bullinger praised David for his piety, which greatly surpassed that of Vergil's Aeneas. The model Christian ruler, he conquered the entire promised land with God's help. "But," Bullinger asserted, "David excelled not so much with arms in war as with law and justice in peace. The civil administration was most excellent and virtuous under his rule. He conducted horrible wars so that pleasant peace could be enjoyed after the enemies and disturbers of the peace had been crushed. But peace is not stable unless the kingdom or commonwealth is governed with just laws, and good judgment is used and justice flourishes."[50]

In matters of religion there was no other king in Israel or Judah who measured up to David. He built up Jerusalem and made it the capital of the kingdom (2 Sam. 5:6ff). Although the prophet Nathan restrained David when he wished to build a temple to the Lord, he did give David a promise from God that his kingdom would endure, that his house would have a perpetual succession in the kingdom. This was, Bullinger explained, a renewal of the promise of the blessed Seed, who would be born from the house of David. It also was a renewal of the covenant. Furthermore, David himself taught clearly about Christ, especially in the Psalms, and had faith in Christ. "Here again," Bullinger asserted, "one can perceive the continuous, perpetual and uninterrupted teaching about true religion, the Messiah and true faith, extending and coming down from God through Adam and all the holy patriarchs to Moses and from there now to David." David's great faith was manifested in keeping the covenant condition of piety, through love of the neighbor. His faith and piety were especially evident in his last will, where he advised his son Solomon, "Keep the obligation of the Lord your God, to walk in His ways and keep His statutes and commandments as it is written in the law of Moses" (1 Kings 2:3).[51] When David died in 2925 (1044 B.C.), Solomon became king.

Solomon was faithful and pious from the beginning of his reign, fostering and promoting the faith in his kingdom. His writings demonstrated his great sagacity and piety, and his wisdom and justice in ruling were well known (1 Kings 4). In short, Solomon's reign was marked by justice, equity, and true piety. It was a time when Israel was true to God and His covenant. But even wise Solomon turned away from God in his old age. His downfall was his many wives (1 Kings 11), for in order to please them he worshipped their gods. As Bullinger explained it: "Thus the young Solomon conducted himself very well in the matter of religion, to such an extent that he could not have done better; but the old Solomon did not act with moderate and conjugal love of women but deluded in immoderation he acted like a madman." Such conduct, especially among old men, "the most foolish lovers," was unbecoming and ridiculous. So despite his many years of piety, in the end Solomon preferred his women to God. His sin had great consequences for Israel. God divided the kingdom—after Solomon's death in 2965 (1004 B.C.), God gave all but one tribe to Jeroboam to rule.[52]

The northern kingdom, its capital at Samaria, was called Israel; Judah was the southern kingdom, with its capital at Jerusalem. This division of the kingdom, Bullinger emphasized, had resulted from idolatry, from false religion. All Israel suffered because Solomon had not been faithful in the covenant. God allowed Solomon's son Rehoboam to retain the rule of Judah because of the promise that David's kingdom and house would endure. The kingdom of Judah, then, was now the vehicle for the coming blessed Seed.[53]

Jeroboam, rather than keeping the pure faith, as he had been commanded when he was given the rule over Israel (1 Kings 11:38), fabricated a false religion in competition with the religion of Judah (1 Kings 12:25ff). Bullinger characterized this new religion as "a defection from the true religion and an ecclesiastical schism," referring to its adherents as "sectarians." It was an example of the severing of the church. Not a single king of Israel returned to the true worship under the covenant. God, in His great mercy, continued sending prophets such as Elijah, Elisha, and Amos, who exhorted the kings to restore the covenant and true religion. But there was no reformation; the Jeroboamite religion, which Bullinger likened to the later papal heresy, continued to flourish. The Jeroboamite heresy sealed Israel's fate: finally, after 265 years, "God led Assyria, that barbarous reformer," to punish Israel with captivity (3231; 738 B.C.) and eventual extinction.[54]

Throughout his treatment of Israel, Bullinger heavily stressed the importance of the character of the kings, an emphasis that he maintained in his discussion of Judah. The faithfulness of the ruler was crucial. For Bullinger the fate of the commonwealth depended on the faith, religion, and character of its magistrates. Judah, in fact, endured longer as a kingdom because of its several pious kings, four of whom were of prime importance to Bullinger, as examples of magistrates who promoted true religion and restored the covenant. These four kings—Jehoshaphat, Joash, Hezekiah, and Josiah—thus established the norm for God's people in effecting reformation in the church and commonwealth.

Jehoshaphat, acceding to the throne in 3026 (943 B.C.), eradicated all idolatry and superstition in Judah. He himself lived in true piety and encouraged the same in the hearts of his people. The result was a return to the covenant, a thorough reformation, and great tranquillity in the kingdom (2 Chron. 17ff). After Jehoshaphat's death, however, Judah returned to idolatry.

Joash, who as an infant had been saved by the priest Jehoiada from an attempted purge of the entire posterity of David, became king of Judah at the age of seven. At the same time, Jehoiada effected a reformation, "and renewed the covenant between God, the king and the people." The idols were destroyed and the true religion restored. Joash himself ordered the temple repaired and reformed the priesthood. After Jehoiada's death, however, Joash allowed idolatry to return. God's punishment was military defeat, Joash's own assassination (3101; 868 B.C.), and the further deterioration of religion.[55]

The third king, Hezekiah (d. 3254; 715 B.C.), was the best king of Judah, in Bullinger's estimation. Hezekiah completely reformed the church in the first year of his reign, by restoring the temple, exhorting the priests and decreeing a mass celebration of the neglected passover. Idolatry was totally extinguished, and true religion flourished. To Bullinger Hezekiah's reformation was "a perfect example of reforming and restoring the church." Hezekiah also was victorious over Sennacherib, king of Assyria, shortly after the Assyrian conquest of Israel. But this great victory was marred by Hezekiah's alliance with Egypt (Isa. 30–31). As Bullinger pointed out, God's people must not put their trust in human covenants, but only in God's covenant.[56]

Finally, there was Josiah, the last pious king of Judah, who took the throne in 3311 (658 B.C.) and effected the final reformation prior to the Babylonian Captivity (2 Kings 22–23; 2 Chron. 34–35). He began by cleansing Judah from idolatry and restoring the temple, where the book of the law was discovered. After Josiah and the people had heard the law, Bullinger explained, "then he bound both himself and the entire people together with God as firmly as possible in the holy covenant." From Josiah's death in 3342 (625 B.C.) until the Babylonian Captivity began in the second year (3355; 614 B.C.) of Zedekiah's reign, there were no godly kings in Judah. First Judah came under the sway of Egypt, then the kingdom was occupied by the Babylonians (2 Kings 24–25; 2 Chron. 36). Idolatry was reestablished, righteousness forgotten, and the covenant abandoned. Because of such faithlessness, Nebuchadnezzar's army burned the temple and deported the people to Babylon.[57]

If these four kings were, for Bullinger, the classic models for the magistrates of his own day in reforming church and commonwealth; the prophets, especially Isaiah and Jeremiah, with their exhortations to restore the covenant and return to the true religion, set the norm for the pastor.

The covenant, in Bullinger's opinion, was a major theme in Isaiah's prophecy, especially within the context of Hezekiah's reign. Commenting on the thirty-third chapter, Bullinger devoted an excursus to the covenant. God demonstrated His mercy and goodness to those "who persevered in His friendship or society, covenant or association." Admittedly there were sinners and hypocrites in Zion, in the church, sinners who did as they wished and hypocrites who simulated piety. But, Isaiah promised the faithful, "those who are joined with God in the covenant so that in this life He dwells with them and they dwell with Him or keep intimate fellowship with Him, then after this life they are never separated from Him, but live with this God in eternity." Bullinger assured his reader that Isaiah spoke of the same covenant that had been made with Abraham. The covenant conditions given to Abraham in the few words, "Walk before me and be perfect or pure," Isaiah reiterated here (v. 15) with many words. In this text, then, Bullinger discovered the covenant conditions of faith and piety. The righteous were those who were faithful in the covenant. Bullinger also made it quite clear here that the condition of piety applied not only to private life but also to civil society and justice. "There is also the political justice of the holy magistrate which restores to each his own, gives what is due, defends and punishes. Those who are the faithful of Christ the Savior are the most just of all in this."[58] Therefore, the faithful, those who keep the covenant conditions, were also the best citizens.

The covenant and the unity of faith in the Old and New Testament were major themes to which Bullinger returned repeatedly in his commentary on Isaiah. There was one church and one Savior from the beginning of the world until the end. Christ was the message of the law and the prophets—all the faithful in every age were saved through faith in Christ.[59] Christianity was the oldest religion and the only true religion. And it was cast in the covenant mold. As Bullinger explained it, the very word "religion" referred to the covenant itself, *religio* finding its root in *religare*, to bind. "For by religion we are bound firmly to God. The bond is the communion of the spirit and true faith. . . . Our religion is also called the covenant in the Scriptures. . . . These are the welcome fetters for the pious, the very covenant of God and the Christian religion."[60] Commenting on chapter 56, Bullinger again connected the condition of piety with human justice. The faithful must not only hear God's word but also follow it, doing justice, which included judicial, social, and political justice. These were the good works of repentance, resulting from the righteousness of faith that could only be found in Christ. To walk before God according to His law, in innocence, purity, and love, was to apprehend the covenant and to keep its conditions as stated in the two tables of the Decalogue. God required these duties of piety from all His faithful.[61]

Bullinger broached the topic of the covenant in the very first section of his Jeremiah commentary. Jeremiah's first sermon was intended to bring Judah to repentance, back into its covenant relationship with God. Rather than keeping the covenant, the Jews had continuously turned to false gods, to idolatry, until every order in the church and kingdom had been totally corrupted—the priests, the teachers of the law, the pastors and the prophets. So Jeremiah accused the entire people of apostasy and violation of the covenant. They ignored God's mercy and faithfulness in the covenant and thus failed to keep the condition of faith. They were not faithful but corrupt. This was a call for repentance and reformation, a return to the covenant. Commenting on the first verse of Chapter 3, Bullinger asserted, "Now indeed it is certain from other passages of Scripture that a marriage or a covenant has been agreed upon and contracted between God and man. The purity of this marriage is violated by idolatry, by the worship and invocation of strange gods." Judah, polluted by idolatry, had broken the covenant and had violated the contract as foully as adulterers repudiated their marriage vows. Although God had every right to reject them in return, instead, because of His mercy, He called for repentance. This time Judah did repent under the leadership of Josiah, temporarily returning to the covenant and thus delaying God's punishment. Jeremiah's call was for a total reformation, a circumcision of the heart, which would result in piety and innocence, the fulfillment of the condition of piety. His demand was that the Jews return to the ancient faith of Adam and the other patriarchs, who knew that sacrifices could please God only if they were offered in true faith, innocence, and love.[62]

Josiah's reformation had resulted from Jeremiah's exhortations, but

Judah ignored Jeremiah after Josiah's death. Commenting on chapter 11, Bullinger explained that this message was not given "under pious king Josiah but under his impious sons." They "withdrew from God, from His law and covenant; but we know about Josiah, that he restored the law and united the entire people by a covenant with God." From the time of Manasseh the princes and the people "cruelly shed the blood of the innocent and the poor." Jeremiah "accuses them of rebellion and of having violated the covenant. However, he also exhorts them to repentance." The sum of Jeremiah's message was "that God required that they hear and do every word of the covenant," which God had renewed with their fathers at the time of the exodus. "For the law of God is called the covenant, the pact and the word of God and of the covenant." It was insufficient simply to hear this word of the covenant; God also demanded action from the faithful, the keeping of the covenant conditions. "If, He says, you walk in my ways, if you both hear and do my word before all things, you will be my people and beloved sons and heirs" (Exod. 19: 5–6). God thus promised to be all-sufficient, just as He had promised to Abraham (Gen. 17). Jeremiah's message, then, was that Judah must renew the covenant rather than continuing to violate it. They must return to the ways of Josiah or they would be punished, just as God had punished Israel.[63]

The Babylonian Captivity lasted from 3355 (614 B.C.) until 3425 (544 B.C.), from Nebuchadnezzar to Cyrus of Persia. Daniel, the chief prophet during the period, not only ministered to the Jews but also bore witness of the true faith and made God's power clear to Nebuchadnezzar, Evilmerodach, Darius, and Cyrus. Cyrus allowed the Jews to return to Jerusalem in 3425 (544 B.C.). After several delays they were allowed to rebuild the temple, because they had learned that true internal worship pleased God more than the external. During this post-exilic period, Haggai, Zechariah, and Malachi prophesied the coming Messiah. Under the leadership of Ezra the priest and the governorship of Nehemiah, a reformation occurred, and the covenant was renewed between God and the people.[64]

Bullinger's biblical sources were exhausted at this point, and he informed the reader that he would now rely on profane historians such as Josephus and Eusebius. He did, however, have a chronological device to tie together the post-exilic years up until the time of Christ: Daniel's prophecy of the seventy weeks of years (Dan. 9:20–27).

According to Bullinger's calculations, the year 3512 (457 B.C.) was the first year of Daniel's seventy weeks of years. This was the year of Artaxerxes Longimanus' decree allowing any Jew in the Persian Empire to return to Jerusalem to help rebuild the city (Ezra 7). The 490 years ended, then, in 4001 (A.D. 32), the year immediately preceding Christ's death. Christ began His ministry in the middle of the last week, thus causing the sacrifices to cease and confirming the covenant in fulfillment of Daniel's prophecy. In Bullinger's opinion, Daniel's prophecy of the weeks of years was one of the clearest prophecies of Christ in the entire Old Testament.[65]

The passage in the ninth chapter, especially verse 27, also elicited Bullinger's major treatment of the covenant in his Daniel commentary. The themes are now familiar. Discussing the Hebrew word *berith*, he heavily emphasized the conditional nature of covenants. Each side in a covenant promised something to the other: "Two or more place themselves under obligations or bind themselves to conditions." Therefore, Christianity was called *religio*, from *religare*, to bind. God made His covenant with the human race from the very beginning, binding himself to man and agreeing to "certain conditions with us which He explained to the blessed patriarchs, such as Adam, Noah, Abraham, and Moses, revealing himself from time to time more and more, and clarifying and renewing this covenant or testament." The covenant conditions for man were repeated often and were finally written by Moses, especially in the Decalogue. Daniel's message was that the Messiah would confirm the covenant with His blood, thus ending the sacrifices and calling all the people of the world into the covenant.[66]

After Malachi there were no prophets who wrote Scripture. The period following the times of Ezra and Nehemiah was one of great difficulty for the church. "Nevertheless," Bullinger assured his reader, "the true faith and religion remained safe and sound with the elect of God through all these tumults." God watched over His people even under pagan rulers. And there was one great reformation, under the Maccabees. However, beginning about 3839 (130 B.C.), sectarian groups came into existence that corrupted the true teaching and obscured the message of the prophets. The Pharisees, mixing human philosophy, especially that of Pythagoras, together with the law of God, did not know Christ, "nor did they retain the old pure teaching about faith and the gratuitous justification of faith and about the promises of God." The Sadducees, in their denial of the resurrection of the body and of angels and spirits, demonstrated their corruption by the Greek philosopher Epicurus. The Essenes lived a life of withdrawal from the world, like monks. These three sects perverted the true teaching of the law. Nevertheless, the uncorrupted true religion still lived among the faithful few, even in the midst of such corruption and schism. Right up to the birth of Christ in the forty-first year of the reign of Augustus Caesar (3969), there were always some who were faithful to the covenant, such as Simeon and Zacharias, the father of John the Baptist.[67]

The old faith, then, the faith of the patriarchs, had also been the faith of the prophets. "They are diligent to explain the law and to clear up the misunderstanding which had arisen among the people. Thus everywhere they point away from the letter to the spirit, from the outward offerings to Christ Jesus, from all idolatry to the one God who saves us through His mercy alone, and not by our own merit but in the blessed Seed." Bullinger insisted that there was nothing about Christ in the New Testament that had not already been taught or prophesied in the Old Testament. Both Jesus and the apostles always appealed to the law and the prophets to confirm their own teachings.[68] Bullinger thus reiterated the unity of the Testaments as well as the testament. The message of the Testaments was the same and so was the substance of the covenant, despite the occasional use of the terms "old" and "new."

The key Old Testament passage referring to a new covenant was the thirty-first chapter of Jeremiah, verses 31 through 34. Bullinger's comment on this prophecy of the new covenant further illuminates his ambivalence about the period of the Mosaic Law. This prophecy of Christ was a comparison of the law and the gospel and a forecast of the abrogation of the ceremonial law. Following the custom of men, God made a conditional covenant with the holy patriarchs. When He renewed the covenant with Israel (Exod. 20, 24), the conditions were read aloud and written on stone tablets, and the covenant was confirmed with the blood of animal sacrifices. This covenant made with Israel on Mt. Sinai was the same covenant that had been made with Adam and Abraham, but one must distinguish between "certain intrinsic things . . . and certain supplemental matters or unnecessary things." The Decalogue was intrinsic to the covenant; the tabernacle, the priests, the sacrifices, and all the other ceremonies were nonessentials. Therefore, Bullinger explained unequivocally, "when we speak of the old covenant, we understand the ceremonies." This also was Jeremiah's meaning. When he referred to "the fathers," he meant the people of the exodus from Egypt, not Abraham. "Therefore, the old testament is the law itself with the entire Levitical worship." God would abrogate this old covenant because the Jews had continually violated it. That is, God would abolish the ceremonies along with the priesthood and sacrifices while maintaining the essence of the covenant. The new covenant would be made with spiritual Israel, with the spiritual seed of Abraham (Gal. 3; Rom. 4), with a new people, the Gentiles. Then God would write His law in men's hearts, as He had done with the patriarchs before Moses, rather than on stone tablets. This meant that God would give His Spirit in the hearts of the faithful, inspiring love and "spontaneous zeal for the law of God." Although this same Spirit had been given "to the ancient fathers in the old covenant, . . . all things are clearer, more abundant and more widely shared in the new covenant" (Joel 2:28). Whereas the old covenant had been made only with Israel, the new covenant would extend the knowledge of God throughout the entire world. Although the faithful in the old covenant also had received remission of sins through the Messiah, in the new covenant all things would be perfected and fulfilled. Christ would consecrate and confirm the new covenant by His blood, thus abolishing the old sacrifices.[69]

The old covenant, then, referred only to the ceremonial law, to the appendages given as aids to the Jews in keeping the condition of faith during the interregnum of the law. Bullinger's "old covenant" was in effect only during this interregnum from Moses to Christ, and the abrogation of the law meant the ceremonial law. The "new covenant" referred to the essential covenant, without any such supplemental aids. Although this new covenant became much clearer with Christ, it had been made first with Adam. This distinction is further clarified by Bullinger in his *De testamento*, where he asserted that the terms "old" and "new," whether referring to the people or the testament, "cannot separate the testament itself and the church of the ancients from our own church." The covenant was not new in its essence. It could be called new only "because that ancient religion, which thrived in those golden times of the patriarchs before the law was given," was renewed and made fuller and clearer by Christ. So the faithful after Christ were more fortunate than those under the law, because they had appropriated "the ancient and primary precept, clearly from the ancient fathers, which, without ceremonies, depended upon faith and innocence, that is, on the chief points of the covenant." The problem with the Jews had been that even when they were not involved with idolatry, they tended to confuse the appendages with the essence of the covenant, depending on the outward sacrifices rather than on these essential spiritual points of the covenant.[70]

The interregnum of the Mosaic Law did not end with the birth of Christ, but only with the commencement of the public ministry of John the Baptist in 3999 (A.D. 30). This, Bullinger calculated, was the middle of Daniel's seventieth week, when the Messiah was to end the sacrifices and confirm the covenant (Dan. 9:27). John, the last prophet, announced the presence of the Messiah, the fulfillment of the law and the prophets, and thus ushered in the new age.[71]

CHAPTER FOUR

The Covenant Confirmed:
Triumph, Apostasy, and Reformation

JESUS CHRIST was the message and meaning of the Old Testament, from the first gospel as given to Adam and Eve up through the law and the prophets. God had chosen to deal with men within the context of the covenant, which had first been made with Adam and then renewed throughout the Old Testament. Christ was the substance of this covenant, and all the faithful throughout the ages had kept the covenant through faith in the blessed Seed and piety of life. Since the spirit and essence of the covenant was the same in both the Old and New Testament, New Testament Christians could not reject the Old Testament. Bullinger was adamant on this point. The New Testament could not be understood properly without the Old Testament, "as little as the exposition without the text. The text is the law and the prophets, the exposition the evangelists and the apostles."[1]

It followed from this unity of the Testaments that the divine norms for church and commonwealth that Bullinger found in the Old Testament were not annulled or significantly altered in the New Testament. There was no essential difference between the Testaments, but since the covenant had been fulfilled by Christ, there were some appropriate changes, most notably the abolition of the ceremonial law and the new sacraments. The pure religion of the patriarchs was restored. Also, everything was clarified and the rule of faith was firmly established by Christ and His apostles. But the essence of the eternal covenant, its promise and conditions, was unaltered.

Bullinger's interpretation of the New Testament, then, consisted largely of a reaffirmation of his already established Old Testament themes within a later historical context. His method of explaining the New Testament in these terms is particularly clear in his treatment of the law in the new era. Both Christ and Paul taught, according to Bullinger, that the ceremonial law was abolished, but that the moral law, the conditions of the covenant, was reaffirmed by Christ and still applied to New Testament Christians.

Bullinger saw Christ's Sermon on the Mount, especially His teaching about the moral law (Matt. 5:17ff), as conclusive evidence that the covenant conditions had not been altered. Here Christ presented the true meaning of the moral law, thus correcting the false interpretation of the Pharisees. "The moral law is the standard for conduct and for our entire life; it was embraced by the Decalogue and by its abbreviation or chief points, faith and love, the love of God, I say, and the neighbor." Although Christians were justified and claimed the perfection of the law through faith in Christ, that did not mean that they were free from the moral law. Rather, the faithful subjected themselves to the moral law, not from compulsion, but willingly and freely. If the abbreviation of the moral law was the love of God and the neighbor, then to subject oneself to the moral law was to keep the covenant conditions. Such love of God and one's neighbor, the fruit of faith, summarized the true spirit of the Old Testament. "That is, all things taught in the law and the prophets go back to that genuine love as a true target for piety and nothing is taught in any of them except love. Therefore, love is the great commandment." The love of God corresponded to the first table of the Decalogue, summarizing the condition of faith; the love of the neighbor summarized the condition of piety as stated in the second table. This true Christian righteousness was in contrast to the false external righteousness of the Pharisees (Matt. 5:20). Their false outward righteousness was the righteousness of the law described by Paul, by which no man could be justified (Gal. 3). Christ was the righteousness of the faithful and He transmitted His righteousness to them through faith. "Those regenerate ones work the works of the sons of God, walking in love, which is the perfection of the law."[2]

In Bullinger's mind, Paul's teaching on the moral law was identical to Christ's. When Paul said that Christians were not under the law but under grace (Rom. 6:14), he meant, "You are servants of him to whom you give obedience" (Rom. 6:16), that the faithful obeyed God and loved righteousness, innocence, and purity. The intention of the law, Bullinger explained, was "piety, faith, innocence and love." As Paul said, to be under the law was to know sin, but the law itself was nevertheless holy (Rom. 7:7, 12). Therefore, to be without the law was "to be without condemnation" (Rom. 8:1). The moral law demonstrated that no one could be without sin; it also pointed to the remedy, faith in Christ, which freed the faithful from the terror of condemnation (Rom. 8:2) but not from the duties of faith and innocence that the faithful, as sons of God, kept willingly. Therefore, Christ did not abrogate the moral law; rather, it continued to be God's will for the faithful in the covenant. The Pharisees had corrupted the true meaning of the law; in the Sermon on the Mount, Christ simply restored the pristine meaning of the moral law, the pure religion of the patriarchs.[3]

Paul, then, according to Bullinger, never taught that the moral law had been abolished for New Testament Christians. Commenting on Galatians (2:15–3:5), Bullinger heavily emphasized that justification was a result of faith alone and not of any works of the law, moral or ceremonial. Then he turned to Paul's use of Abraham as an example of such faith (Gal. 3:6–9). Abraham had believed the same gospel that had first been given to Adam and Eve (Gen. 3:15), which Paul was explaining to the Galatians. All the faithful, even those under the Mosaic Law, had been saved by faith alone. All this, Bullinger commented, had to do with the eternal testament or covenant (Gal. 3:15–25). Just as human testaments could not be altered contrary to the wishes of the testator, no one could add anything to or subtract anything from God's testament. Paul taught, then, that there was but one covenant in which God "wishes to confer the blessing and justification through Christ alone, not through the law." This covenant was made with Abraham 430 years before the law; then the law was added to the eternal covenant so that the covenant would not be destroyed. Paul did not mean, however, that the testament and the moral law were mutually opposed. Rather, the moral law, through its prohibitions, demonstrated human sin, thus leading to justification through faith alone in Christ. The faithful were free from the law, free from the bondage of sin, that is, they willingly lived holy lives. "What is the spirit of the [moral] law," Bullinger asked, "except Christ himself and Christian faith itself? What, I beg, does the [moral] law teach other than faith?"[4]

The ceremonial law was quite another matter. Because the death of Christ was the confirmation of the covenant, it ended the old sacrifices and the entire ceremonial law. As Bullinger put it in his Matthew commentary, Christ fulfilled the ceremonial law and replaced "the figures and the shadows with the actual thing, His own body." The abolition of the passover and the institution of the Lord's Supper in its place were proof, for Bullinger, that Christ himself saw His own mission in exactly this way (Matt. 26:17–29). In His crucifixion Christ was the immaculate paschal Lamb, offering His blood for the redemption of the whole world, for the restoration of the human race. Since a testament could be confirmed only in death, His death was necessary, so that through His blood the faithful could become heirs of God. Like the passover, then, the eucharist was a sign of the covenant (Matt. 26:28) as prophesied by Jeremiah (31:31–34). As the passover had looked forward to the blessed Seed, the Supper was a remembrance of His death. With the symbols of the bread and the wine, Christ "represented what He would impute to us and what the fruit would be of handing over His body and shedding His blood; thus He indicates what He demands from us in turn: faith, piety, love and mutual charity among himself and His members, and that we acknowledge the blessing and give perpetual thanks." Thus Christ's blood, having once and for all purchased eternal redemption, was called the blood of the new testament, in contrast to the frequent animal sacrifices of the old testament, which could not cleanse sin.[5]

Paul's epistle to the Hebrews was, to Bullinger, the classic New Testament explanation of the covenant as well as the clearest exposition of the purpose and abrogation of the ceremonial law. Commenting on the annulment of the law (Heb. 7:12–8:5), Bullinger insisted that Paul had used a synecdoche when he said that the law had ended. Since he could not have meant the moral law, the unchangeable will of God, he spoke only of the external and figurative things, the part of the law that had been given with reference to a particular time and people. One could not say that "the mandates concerning piety and innocence have been effaced," but rather that "the enmity of the law has been washed from our hearts." Under the spirit of the liberty of Christ, the faithful willingly and joyfully did what previously had been a hated burden. Therefore, Christ abolished only the carnal Levitical law along with its ceremonies when He fulfilled its promises. He himself became the one and only priest, the eternal priest with no successor, the mediator for all who had faith. Perfect and sinless, He offered himself as the single perpetual sacrifice and thus ended the daily sacrifices of the Levitical priesthood and the ceremonial law.[6] Within this context, Paul's reference to two covenants (Heb. 8:6ff) was the same as Jeremiah's (31:31–34). The "first covenant" (Heb. 8:7) was an equivalent term for the ceremonial law; the second was the eternal covenant. Here Bullinger launched a lengthy discussion of the covenant by admitting that theologians differed on the subject. Sometimes, he began, "testament" was used in Scripture to denote a last will. In other passages it was a metaphor for the promise of Christ and the remission of sins. "But in respect to this passage," he insisted, "this testament is the covenant and that pact of God by which God declared His will toward us and directly agreed on certain conditions with us." These conditions, first given to Adam and then to all the patriarchs, but especially to Abraham, were that God would be all-sufficient and that man would walk before God in purity. As if to underscore the conditional nature of the covenant, Bullinger wrote, "And these are the conditions of the covenant or pact." This was the essence of the eternal covenant or testament. There was but one church, one God, and one true religion or faith from Adam until the end of the world. The ceremonial law, with its shadows and figures, was called the old testament or covenant; Christ's fulfillment of those figures and of all the law and the prophets was labeled the new testament or covenant. However, Bullinger cautioned, it was "not new as though the ancients did not possess Christ, grace and the remission of sins, but new in comparison with the old and because His own body destroyed the shadows with its approach." For this reason the Scripture was divided into the Old and New Testament: they were the books of the testament, describing God's dealings with His people within the one covenant before and after Christ.[7] Bullinger clearly felt that his own teaching on the covenant and on the moral and ceremonial laws was in total accord with both Christ's and Paul's.

Christ's confirmation of the covenant was thus called the new testament because He abolished the old testament, i.e., the ceremonial law, and restored pure religion. His last words, "It is completed" (John 19:30), referred to this very thing, Bullinger thought, that the law and the prophets had been fulfilled. At the same time, the veil of the temple was torn (Matt. 27:51), which also indicated that Christ's sacrifice had ended the entire old system of sacrifices and temple worship, thus finishing Daniel's final week of years.[8]

The interregnum of the Law was thus terminated. As a result, the sacraments of the covenant were changed. Inasmuch as Christ's death had ended the blood of the sacrifices, the bloodless sacrament of the eucharist replaced the passover. Similarly, baptism was the new bloodless sign that took the place of circumcision.

John the Baptist, Elijah come again as prophesied by Malachi (Mal. 4:5–6), was the historically transitional figure whom God used to proclaim the fulfillment of the promise of the covenant and to introduce the new bloodless sign. His message was that the blessed Seed, the Messiah, had come, in fulfillment of the sacrifices and prophecies of the Old Testament. He exhorted the Jews to repent, to turn to God and amend their lives, to acknowledge their sins, for the kingdom of heaven was about to begin. By divine command, John also instituted the new covenant sign, baptism, which then replaced circumcision as the sign of the people of God and the seal of justification. Baptism gathered the people of God into one church and reminded them of their responsibilities in the covenant. It was the new initiatory rite by which the children of the faithful were brought into the covenant. Furthermore, John made clear that the goal of water baptism was internal, spiritual baptism: repentance or regeneration through faith in Christ.[9]

Christ himself sought baptism from John (Matt. 3:13–17), not because He needed it (He was the Son of God and without sin), but to give His approval to the institution of the new sacrament and to set an example for all the faithful. His baptism also served as a confirmation that Jesus was the Son of God. For immediately after His baptism, the Spirit of God appeared in the form of a dove and God the Father spoke the words: "This is my beloved Son in whom I am appeased." This, Bullinger explained, testified both to Christ's divinity and to His work of reconciliation.[10]

Jesus, of course, had also been circumcised as an infant (Luke 2:21), which Bullinger fully discussed in the sermon, "Concerning the Circumcision of Our Lord Jesus Christ." Circumcision, he began, became the sacrament or symbol of the divine covenant when the covenant was renewed with Abraham. Bullinger stressed that the covenant was eternal, that its essence had never changed since it had first been made with Adam, although certain things were added in accordance with the times for purposes of correction. The divine promise to Abraham was the same as the promise given earlier to Adam and later to Moses—the blessed seed. The human conditions given to Abraham, "what the good Lord requires in return from us, His confederates," were faith and love. "Therefore, soundness of faith is especially required from God's confederates, along with sincere love, holy innocence of life and simple obedience, in the most steadfast hope." Circumcision, then, had been given to Abraham as a sign and a seal of the covenant, signifying the obligations of both God and His human confederates. In the New Testament, baptism became the new sign of the covenant.

Why, Bullinger asked, did Christ wish both to be circumcised with the ancient people and then baptized with the new people? Because He was the Savior of both people. Having become a true human, although born of a virgin and without sin, "He did not think it unworthy to become a confederate with God along with us and openly to receive the symbol of the covenant in His flesh." Then, for the same reason, He also received baptism from John and thus assured the unity of the covenant.[11]

When Bullinger treated baptism, it was nearly always in covenant terms. Baptism was the sign of the covenant whereby God placed His seal of regeneration and purification on His people. It was the seal of repentance, reminding the faithful of their covenant obligations of faith and innocence. Just as circumcision had inscribed the individual "in the register of the confederates and children of God," in the same way one was baptized into the protection and salvation of God. Children of the faithful were to be baptized just as previously they had been circumcised. They were considered to be among the faithful in the covenant until they proved otherwise. The individual did, of course, have to keep the covenant conditions, to persevere in the covenant. Putting it succinctly, Bullinger wrote, "Those baptized are also received and inscribed into the book of the sons of God and are bound to promise a truthful life and to live in a holy and innocent manner."[12]

Bullinger felt that this interpretation was fully supported by Paul. Commenting on the tenth chapter of First Corinthians, he emphasized the unity of the church before and after Christ. The signs of the single covenant, however, the sacraments, had changed with the times. Another favorite passage on this topic was Colossians, Chapter 2, verses 11 and 12, where Paul spoke of the circumcision without hands. This spiritual circumcision, Bullinger explained, was the circumcision by which the faithful in Old Testament times were cleansed through faith in Christ. It also referred to obedience to the divine commandments. The circumcision of Christ mentioned by Paul was baptism, the New Testament equivalent to circumcision. Both signified justification, circumcision anticipating the blood of the promised Seed, baptism looking back to the death of Christ. Both also gathered the people of God into one church.[13]

Christ's confirmation of the covenant had one final consequence for Bullinger—God's rejection of the Jews as His special people. The Jews had repeatedly fallen into apostasy, beginning with the times of the judges and continuing through the post-exilic period. Neither the destruction of Israel nor the captivity of Judah had kept them from violating the covenant with idolatry, although there had always been a faithful few who understood the true spiritual meaning of the law, who had faith in the promised Seed. But when the Messiah actually came, the Jewish people on the whole spurned Him, and God finally rejected Israel as His chosen people. This impending rejection was reflected in the message of John the Baptist (Matt. 3:9–12), that the seed of Abraham was a spiritual seed that imitated Abraham's obedience of faith and innocence of life, both Jew and Gentile. True repentance along with the fruits of repentance, faith, and innocence, was necessary to be the seed of Abraham. Simply being a Jew was insufficient. Christ himself, after His resurrection, having ended the ceremonial law, made it clear in the Great Commission (Matt. 28:18–20) that the gospel was now to be preached to all men, to Gentiles as well as to Jews.[14] This offering of the covenant, the preaching of the gospel, to the Gentiles had been predicted in the Old Testament, especially by the prophet Isaiah. Bullinger even interpreted the Old Testament prophecies about the restitution of Israel as having been fulfilled by

Christ, the apostles, and the universal church of the New Testament. After Christ, then, the faithful Gentiles were included in the same covenant that had begun with Adam. They were joined together with the spiritual Israel before Christ, with the Jews and patriarchs who preceded them in keeping the covenant conditions, in the church.[15]

The early New Testament church, in Bullinger's mind, had some difficulties in adapting to these changes resulting from Christ's confirmation of the covenant. Initially the apostles and the church at Jerusalem did not understand that the Gentiles could become part of the church. But when Paul was converted (A.D. 34), he also was called to be the apostle to the Gentiles (Acts 9). Then, Peter's vision, the subsequent conversion of the Roman centurian Cornelius, and Peter's sermon at Jerusalem (Acts 10–11) convinced the church that the gospel was also to be preached to the Gentiles. Still, it was several years before the relationship between Christianity and Judaism was fully clarified. In A.D. 48, the question of whether Christians had to be circumcised and had to keep the law became a burning issue. Paul and Barnabas encountered a group at Antioch that had accepted Jesus as the Messiah but insisted that none could be justified without circumcision. Returning to Jerusalem to receive confirmation of his teaching of justification by faith alone, Paul discovered there a group of Pharisees making the same demands. The result was, as Bullinger saw it, the first council of the Christian church, the Council of Jerusalem (Acts 15). Peter spoke first, supporting and approving Paul's teaching, recalling his experience with Cornelius and asserting that all the Old Testament saints also had been justified by faith alone, through God's grace and not by the law. The apostle James then added his agreement, citing the prophet Amos (9:11–12) to the effect that "the Jews were about to be uprooted because of sin and the Gentiles put in their place as a substitute." The decision was a consensus of the entire church in Paul's favor. The early church, then, finally understood that the ceremonial law, along with circumcision, had been abolished and that there was but one church gathered from both Jews and Gentiles.[16]

More important, for Bullinger, was the lack of understanding in his own day on the relationship between the Testaments. The divine norms for church and community established in the Old Testament had not been altered in the New. Thus the leaders of church and commonwealth must find their respective roles and responsibilities in the

Old Testament prototype. In these matters, then, little had changed with the coming of Christ.

The most significant difference was that the priesthood had been abolished along with the ceremonial law. According to Bullinger, there was but one ecclesiastical office in the New Testament church—the pastor, the successor of the Old Testament prophet. Prophet, pastor, bishop, presbyter, and doctor were simply different names in the New Testament for the same office. Not only was the office the same; no matter the name, so too was the function: to teach, preach, and administer the sacraments.[17] Christ had prescribed this task of the New Testament pastor when He gave the power of the keys to the church (Matt. 16:17–20). A key signified the power to administer something, like the keys of a steward of a household. The power of the keys, then, was simply "the management of the churches and the function of teaching, rebuking, exhorting and reproaching, and generally keeping the church in proper order, and especially leading it into the kingdom of heaven by the path of truth." When the pastor preached the gospel and threatened damnation, he exercised the power of closing heaven. This ministry of the gospel, the power of the keys, had nothing to do with discipline, which was supposed to be exercised by the Christian magistracy as in the Old Testament.[18]

This meant that the pastor and the church did not even have the power of excommunication. The power of the keys had nothing to do with excommunication from the Lord's Supper, which, according to Bullinger, had not even been practiced in the church until A.D. 250.[19] Bullinger, in fact, opposed the entire concept of exclusion, either from the church assembly or from the Supper. With regard to the Supper, he asserted: "There is no command or example extant which commands the faithful to hinder those from the sacraments as long as they maintain the same faith with us and embrace the same teaching, even if they are lacking in life and morals." The Lord had commanded all the Jews to keep the passover; none were excluded for moral impurity. Only a person legally impure—for instance, one who had touched a corpse—was temporarily excluded. Furthermore, God had forbidden no one to offer sacrifices. The sacrifices, in fact, had been instituted for sinners. Bullinger concluded that there was no support for excommunication in the Old Testament. Therefore, since the eucharist had taken the place of the passover, all Christians should celebrate the

Supper, just as all Jews had kept the passover. Even though no one could have excluded with more certainty than Jesus, He did not even bar Judas from the Supper. Nor did Paul ban sinners from the church at Corinth, commanding them rather to amend their lives. Despite the many notorious sinners there, Paul simply instructed that each should judge himself before partaking of the Supper (1 Cor. 11). Therefore, Bullinger asserted, "Excommunication which excludes sinners because of a dishonorable life is not a divine command, nor does it have an example, but it is a human remedy."[20]

Bullinger felt, then, that excommunication eroded the very purpose of the Supper. It had been given for unity: "The Lord introduced the Supper for the union or the general assembling together of the faithful, not for the scattering, separation and withdrawal from the church." So the Supper was not a means for purifying the church, for separating the tares from the wheat. It was meant instead as an opportunity for the sinner to give thanks; it was thus absurd to exclude anyone who wished to give thanks, "which is the peculiar purpose of the Lord's Supper."[21]

The function of the New Testament pastor, then, like that of the Old Testament prophet, did not include discipline, not even exclusion from the eucharist. It was the Christian magistrate who, like the Old Testament rulers, possessed the authority to restrain, to punish, and to establish all religion according to God's word. He alone had the power of discipline; the ecclesiastical office had none. At the most, a pastor could admonish an indifferent magistrate, and, like the Old Testament prophet, urge him to perform his duty. Christian discipline, in the hands of the Christian magistrate, was "nothing other than the public and Christian guarding of community virtue and Christian conduct, for only the heart judges the most secret things." Discipline was thus the police power of the Christian magistracy in action—judicial punishment for public crimes.[22]

Those who advocated discipline by the church itself, by the pastors or a presbytery, depended heavily on Christ's command to tell it to the church if an offending brother refused fraternal admonition and then, if he ignored the church, to treat him as a publican and sinner (Matt. 18:15–19). Bullinger's interpretation was that such a matter should be taken before the rulers of the church, i.e., the magistrates, for judgment. As a last resort, the pious Christian should treat the guilty party as a publican and a heathen, which meant having nothing to do with him in the ordinary course of life. It did not, however, include banning him from the Supper. Bullinger connected Matthew 18 with Paul's admonition to the Corinthians to hand the incestuous person over to Satan (1 Cor. 5:5), which referred to punishment by some type of disease or other physical distress. Both Christ and Paul thus advocated physical punishment. To treat a person as a publican or a sinner and to hand him over to Satan meant that he should be prosecuted as a criminal and punished publicly by the Christian magistrate.[23]

For Bullinger, then, the Old Testament norm of a pious faithful ruler, who should maintain order, punish the evil and protect the good, and promote true religion, was applicable to God's people in any age. In short, Bullinger saw the task of the Christian magistrate in covenant terms, as the enforcer of the condition of piety, which was social in nature and thus included the Christian's total life in society. The magistrate, basing his laws on God's moral law, aided God's people in keeping the condition of love within the external church or the Christian commonwealth. This covenant condition clearly had to do with "judicial or civil things" such as public peace, property, business transactions, justice, and equity. "For these things also are the duties of piety or things necessary for the holiest churches, so much so that they cannot exist comfortably without them and have never been without them short of danger." The magistrate's function was to enforce these "duties of piety." Not only was this police power of the magistracy necessary to keep in line the tares who had become a clear menace to the peace of the church, but even the faithful, so long as they lived on this earth, needed civil laws that dealt "with people and the social intercourse of life."[24] Bullinger thus saw the Old Testament judges and kings as models for New Testament Christian government.

Apostolic times were not typical, however. The rulers were not Christians, and the early church could not follow this normal practice, which made true Christian discipline quite difficult. Out of necessity, the church had to improvise, controlling its own discipline without the holy work of the magistrate. Nevertheless, even under such difficult and unusual circumstances, the apostolic church never involved expulsion from the Lord's Supper with discipline. Rather than commanding such exclusion, Paul counseled both the Corinthians (1 Cor. 5:9–13) and the Thessalonians (2 Thess. 3:16, 14–15) to avoid intimacy with such sinners. This did not mean to shun the faithless completely, but only that the faithful should not treat them as friends. Nor did Paul envision a pure church—he commanded the Corinthians to remove the evil one, not the evil. Since even the faithful were still sinners, a pure church was not possible. Paul also admonished the Corinthians to choose judges from among the faithful to settle suits and restrain sinners as much as possible by means of rational argument (1 Cor. 6:1–8). Thus the early church, as an incomplete Christian community, managed its own discipline. But, Bullinger insisted, it did not practice excommunication from the eucharist. It did the best it could under the circumstances, until Christian rulers could fulfill their proper function in the church.[25]

Not only were there no Christian rulers, but the church was subjected to persecution by many of the emperors until 312, when Constantine, according to the prophecy of Isaiah (49:23; 60:3), converted to Christianity. According to Bullinger, the conversion of Constantine signaled both the triumph of the church and the end of the abnormal period when there had been no magistrate over the church. Since Old Testament rulers such as Moses and David had possessed authority not only over civil affairs but also over the church and all ecclesiastical matters, excluding only the administration of the sacraments, Christian rulers rightfully possessed the same power. So when Constantine, as the Christian magistrate, asserted his rule over the church, he reestablished the divine order in the Christian commonwealth, effecting a reformation much like that of Hezekiah and Josiah. Exercising his authority over the church, he called the Council of Nicea to judge the false teaching of Arius and thus restored the law of God and brought peace and harmony to the church. The later great Christian emperors, especially Theodosius, Justinian, and Charlemagne, firmly established their authority over the church, the ministers and all ecclesiastical matters.[26]

Thus, from Bullinger's point of view, Constantine had reinstituted normal conditions among God's people, and the church had consequently prospered under imperial authority at least through the reign of Justinian (d. 565). The Middle Ages, however, was the story of growing apostasy, of the progressive subversion of these divine norms: the cooption of magisterial power and the rise of papal supremacy over the church; idolatry; heresy; in short, a massive violation of the covenant. In fact, as early as the fourth century there were signs of the later attempt on the part of the papacy to thwart the lawful power of the magistracy by means of excommunication. When the Emperor Theodosius viciously suppressed a rebellion in Thessalonica (390) during which the imperial governor had been murdered, Ambrose, bishop of Milan, excommunicated the emperor until he publicly repented. Bullinger severely criticized Ambrose, who had no precedent for such an action, "neither the command of God nor an example. Long ago, Nathan the prophet dealt differently with King David" (2 Sam. 12). If the emperor had sinned against the Thessalonians, Ambrose also sinned with his excommunication of Theodosius. Even if the power of excommunication were granted to the church and were a proper means of discipline, neither of which Bullinger would concede, the magistrate could never be excommunicated. Although the ancient church had never used excommunication, it had become so common by the late fourth century that "the foul practice was easily deemed ancient . . . and Ambrose dared to excommunicate the holy Emperor Theodosius." In fact, according to Bullinger, the development of papal tyranny was a direct result of the increased use of excommunication during the Middle Ages.[27]

The proper use of magisterial authority was thus, for Bullinger, crucially important for the well-being of the church. Corrupt clergy, false worship, and schism were a consequence either of unfaithful magistrates, as in the Old Testament period, or of the subversion of magisterial authority, as during the Middle Ages. One of Bullinger's favorite examples of false teaching in the Old Testament was Jeroboam's heresy. It not only broke the fellowship and unity of the old church but also brought civil disaster and the eventual destruction of Israel. In a similar manner, the papacy devised a new worship, denied pure doctrine, and promoted superstition. The papists were the new sectarians of the Middle Ages, false prophets and heretics in the mold of Jeroboam.[28] Bullinger's interpretation of the Reformation rested on this idea that the papacy had developed a new religion and fomented schism from the true church.

Indeed, this rise of papal tyranny and the papal-imperial conflict had been prophesied by Daniel (ch. 7), according to Bullinger, in the vision of the beasts. The fourth beast, representing the Roman Empire, had ten horns that signified the nations that would destroy Rome, such as the Goths and Vandals. Then, in Daniel's vision, a little horn grew up among the other horns, a horn with the eyes of a man and a mouth that spoke great things (v. 8). Bullinger, linking Daniel's prophecy with Paul's warnings about the son of perdition (2 Thess. 2:3ff), judged the little horn to be the papacy—the Antichrist and his kingdom. The eyes like those of a man represented the papal claims to universal power and supremacy, and the mouth that spoke great things, the pretensions of the papacy as arbiter of doctrine. This little horn would change the laws, especially God's law against images and invocation of the saints. He would be more magnificent than his fellow horns, living in splendor like a king and demanding honor and worship from kings (v. 20). He would also make war against the saints (v. 21), a reference to papal action against kings and emperors as well as papal tyranny over the souls of Christians.[29] This, in outline, was Bullinger's indictment of the medieval papacy.

In tracing the evolution of papal supremacy, Bullinger of course rejected the presumed scriptural basis for the power of the papacy, the Roman interpretation of the power of the keys (Matt. 16) and of excommunication (Matt. 18). No such claims to supremacy had been made by the bishops or pastors of Rome to the time of Gregory the Great (590–604). Even Gregory did not claim temporal sovereignty in the manner of later popes, although he did vie with the Patriarch of Constantinople over ecclesiastical supremacy. Then Boniface III (607) received imperial recognition of Rome's spiritual supremacy from Emperor Phocas. Bullinger considered it but a short step from the assertion of such spiritual supremacy to the usurpation of temporal sovereignty. "But after the see at Rome had been elevated in this manner, the popes then more and more meddled in and concerned themselves with temporal matters. Not only did they aspire to empire and sovereignty but also sought to withdraw themselves from obedience to the emperors and place themselves over them, as well as to appropriate their land, people and majesty for themselves." This usurpation of magisterial sovereignty was evident as early as the eighth century, when Pope Gregory III, resisting imperial opposition to images, excommunicated Emperor Leo III in 739 (731). Later, Pope Zacharius was instrumental in the deposition of Childeric III, the last of the Merovingians, thus easing the rise of Pippin, the first Carolingian ruler, to power in France. Pippin repaid the papacy by defeating Aistulf, king of the Lombards, and forcing him to hand over Ravenna and other territories to Pope Stephen II. This was the inception of actual papal temporal supremacy and led to the crowning of Charlemagne as Emperor of the Romans by Pope Leo III in 800.[30] Thus Bullinger linked the earlier, unwarranted papal claims to ecclesiastical supremacy with the later, even more audacious, usurpation of magisterial supremacy.

The development of papal supremacy was also closely connected, in Bullinger's mind, with two other errors of the papacy—the invocation of saints and the use of images—that appeared during the same period, prior to 800. This false worship fulfilled Daniel's prophecy that the papacy would alter God's law. Bullinger compared the papal worship with Jewish idolatry in the Old Testament. Judah also changed the worship, preferring its own ways to God's covenant. Similarly, papal veneration of the saints was a foul violation of the covenant that required the faithful to worship God alone, in innocence. Images were even more clearly idolatrous. Although Bullinger traced the introduction of images back to the fourth century, Gregory the Great was again the key figure. Even though Gregory cautioned against worshipping them, claiming only their utility as a teaching aid, he did permit images and pictures in the churches, and soon they were receiving worship. In the eighth century, the eastern and western churches split, partially, Bullinger indicated, because of the use of images. Emperor Leo III (717–740), "a judicious, pious, kind and courageous man," forbade any further use of images in 726. The resistance of Pope Gregory III (731–741) to the imperial edict and his excommunication of the emperor resulted in the schism of the church (787). Bullinger went into some detail on the continuing controversy between the emperors in the east and the popes in Rome over images, but his central point was that partially because of the image controversy, Pope Leo III transferred the imperium to the west with his crowning of Charlemagne in 800.[31]

Charlemagne himself was a great Christian ruler, comparable to Gideon, David, and Solomon, but after his death corruption abounded, papal tyranny and superstition flourished, and idolatry went rampant. Christian images were, in Bullinger's opinion, no different from pagan idols. Papal idolatry, along with the excommunication for those who defied it, was similar to Nebuchadnezzar's commandment to worship the golden image, with death for those who refused (Dan. 3:1–7). No matter Gregory the Great's dictum that pictures were the Scripture for the laity, they were still sacrilegious idols. To worship such idols was to break the first table of the Decalogue and thus to violate the covenant condition of faith. Christian idolatry flatly contradicted the moral law, God's will for His people in every age.[32]

The papal doctrine on the eucharist was in Bullinger's mind as equally insidious. In the early church the Lord's Supper had been celebrated very simply. The mass itself was the creation of Gregory the Great, but the idea of the physical presence was an invention of later centuries. Bullinger claimed that the church unanimously taught, until the late ninth century, that Christ was only spiritually present in the elements. He verified this consensus with reference to the teachings of Bertram (Ratramn) and John Scotus (Erigena) in the mid-ninth century, both of whom held to the spiritual presence. Paschasius (Radbert) first disputed the orthodox view in 900 in a treatise in which he made the argument that the bread and wine were changed into the body and blood of Christ.[33] This new teaching raised a great debate that still raged in the mid-eleventh century when Berengar (d. 1088) defended the orthodox view of Scotus and Bertram against those who followed Paschasius. Berengar was twice condemned, first by a papal synod in 1051 that damned his teaching and then by the Third Lateran Council of 1179, where he was labeled a heretic. During the twelfth century, Peter Lombard, Gratian, and others defended the new doctrine, which became part of papal dogma under the rubric of transubstantiation at the Fourth Lateran Council, held under Innocent III in 1215.[34]

Bullinger heavily emphasized the novelty of the papal teaching. For 1,200 years transubstantiation had not existed, but after 1215 the faithful were branded as heretics if they did not accept the new papal dogma. For 1,200 years Christians had believed that the presence of Christ in the elements was "sacramental and spiritual, not real or physical."[35] To Bullinger, the elements could only be symbols of Christ's single perpetual sacrifice, which ended the shedding of sacrificial blood, fulfilled the shadows and promises of the Old Testament, and fully satisfied God the Father. The old bloody sacraments had been replaced with bloodless signs because Christ had thus fulfilled the covenant promise first made to Adam. Therefore, the

Supper was a commemoration, a type, and a perpetual symbol of the shedding of blood, of the universal redemption of Christ.[36] With the papal mass, however, "we see a new priesthood and a new sacrifice to the degradation of the single sacrifice and the eternal Priest, Jesus Christ."[37] No doubt the entire Roman mass was repugnant to Bullinger, a denial of the covenant, a refusal to accept the finality of Christ's redemptive work.

This development of false worship went hand in hand with greater papal tyranny within the church and further cooption of magisterial power. These three phenomena were mutually related for Bullinger. The papal claims to ecclesiastical supremacy had become outrageous by the early thirteenth century. Church councils had become papal tools in maintaining consensus in the church, suppressing any who resisted the pope's power. The Lateran Council of 1215 accepted Innocent's decretal on transubstantiation because he was in total control of the church. This papal monarchy fulfilled Daniel's prophecy of the ram and the goat, with the little horn being the papacy (8:9–12, 23–25). And the papal persecution of the church, of the faithful, was similar to the first imperial persecution because it was directed against Christianity itself, against the true faith.[38]

The increased papal usurpation of temporal power was correlative with this growth of ecclesiastical supremacy because, in Bullinger's mind, the papal monarchy in the church itself was an assumption of a power rightfully belonging to the magistracy. After Leo III had created a western emperor with his unlawful crowning of Charlemagne, succeeding popes did their best to keep the emperors under their control. Hildebrand, Pope Gregory VII (1073–1085), made the boldest move to bring the emperor under papal subjection when he excommunicated Henry IV over lay investiture in 1076. "Not only did he excommunicate him and dishonor him," Bullinger wrote, "but also, after he [Hildebrand] freed them from their sworn oaths, his own [Henry's] subjects, even princes and lords, rebelled against him and brought about unspeakable bloodshed." Then Pascal II (1099–1118) fomented the rebellion of Henry V against his father, causing more death and misery. In Bullinger's opinion, the papacy won the investiture struggle when Henry V surrendered the right of investiture to ecclesiastical benefices and prelacies.[39]

The popes, however, were still not satisfied. They continued to persecute the emperors until finally Germany was reduced to chaos during the Interregnum (1254–1273), when there was no emperor. This sorry state of affairs, Bullinger asserted, was fully the fault of the papacy. Throughout the centuries the popes had enlarged their arsenal to include not only excommunication, with its attendant invitation to civil war and sedition, and councils totally under papal control, but also the crusades. Bullinger explained that Pope Urban II (1088–1099) invented the idea of a crusade at the Council of Clermont (1096), by offering an indulgence and eternal life to all who marched east against the Moslems. Later popes, however, did not preach the cross only against the Moslems, "but also against Christian people, against the emperors themselves, against those whom the pope pronounced heretics, in sum against all who would neither worship the pope nor obey all he commanded. In this manner, then, the popes could assemble large and strong armies without great expense, and thus advance their interests." Boniface VIII (1294–1303) openly claimed imperial power in 1300, when by appearing before the Romans in imperial dress, he proclaimed that "the imperial and papal dignity, indeed all spiritual and temporal power, should be and was in the hands of the popes." Boniface also, in his decretals, especially *Unam sanctam*, made the most extreme claims for the papal tyranny.[40]

The papacy, from Bullinger's vantage point, had no warrant or substantiation for its claims to either ecclesiastical supremacy or temporal sovereignty. The papal interpretation of Matthew 16 was totally erroneous: the "keys" had nothing at all to do with ecclesiastical supremacy. The papacy's claim to temporal authority was weaker yet, since it was based on fictitious documents such as the Donation of Constantine.[41] Furthermore, papal decretals such as *Unam sanctam* had no scriptural basis whatsoever. On this point Bullinger used extensive citations from Marsilius of Padua (d. 1342?) to the effect that decretals were not laws but oligarchic ordinances; that the clergy had no power over other men but were themselves subject to the civil ruler; that the so-called plenitude of power was simply a device to usurp temporal power; and that Christ forbade the clergy to possess such power.[42] In addition to Marsilius, others such as John Wyclif, Jan Hus, and Jerome of Prague had also bravely opposed papal power in the late Middle Ages, but to no avail, "for they were suppressed, condemned and slain by the ferocity of tyrants."[43]

Bullinger clearly saw himself as one in spirit with these late medieval forerunners of the Reformation who had opposed the papal assertion of the plenitude of power and had supported magisterial supremacy. But, despite the similarity of goals, Bullinger's opposition had a unique twist—his interpretation of the history of the church within the framework of the covenant. To Bullinger, the papal tyranny, along with its false worship and erroneous view of justification, was a total violation of the covenant, comparable to the total falling away of Israel under the Jeroboamite religion, and similar to the worst periods of apostasy experienced in Judah. This becomes clear in his massive treatment of the source of the papal errors on the invocation of the saints, the worship of images and the mass. Discussing first the names and power of the one God (fol. 3–18), he moved from there to the benevolence of God and the covenant (fol. 18–32). Following this summary of the true religion in covenant terms from Adam to Augustine, he turned to the origin of superstition and idolatry, first among the ancient Gentiles (fol. 32–46), then among the Jews (fol. 46b–54). This was the historical and theological background for papal error, the subject of the remainder of the book: the invocation of saints (fol. 54ff); Christian idolatry as seen in the use of images and the visual arts in the churches (fol. 113bff); and the mass (fol. 180ff). In the conclusion Bullinger returned to the covenant conditions of faith and love and the joining together of the Christian with Christ as symbolized by the Lord's Supper.[44]

The Middle Ages had thus been an era of increasing apostasy, marked by the total subversion of the Old Testament norms for church and commonwealth, a massive violation of the covenant, under the papal aegis. Bullinger also interpreted the Reformation within this larger context of the history of the covenant, as a restoration of the covenant, similar to such restorations in the Old Testament under Hezekiah, Jehoshaphat, and Josiah. The Reformed faith, then, was the old faith and the papal doctrine, the new teaching, the heresy, the deviation from the true ancient religion. The Roman superstition, confirmed in the medieval church by the popes, was contrary to the teaching of the patriarchs, the law, the prophets, Christ, and the apostles. "And thus as often as schisms are thrown at us by the Romanists we always answer with Elijah: 'We do not disturb Israel, but you, oh pontiff, and the house of your father, since you have abandoned the commandments of the Lord and walk after Baal' " (1 Kings 18:18).[45]

Nevertheless, Bullinger clearly felt that the Reformation had not been fully achieved. As in Josiah's day (Jere. 2:29ff), many hypocrites expected the return of papal idolatry. Corruption still abounded, both in faith and morals, both in the church and in the republic. There must be a double reformation, a restitution of both church and commonwealth, or God would judge and reform by fire. Violation of the covenant, whether by abusing the sacrifices in Isaiah's time (Isa. 24:1–2) or by false teaching on the eucharist in Bullinger's day, always resulted in God's punishment. "Whence now also boil up the multiple evils of our time, which are not removed except by proper repentance and a diligent keeping of the eternal covenant."[46] Thus, not only did the papal church still flourish, but some Protestant churches had not been fully reformed.

Bullinger had no such reservations about the Zurich reformation and the Reformed church. The Reformed faith was not new: it was the same as the apostolic faith. The papacy had split the Christian church in much the same way that Israel had been divided into two kingdoms. Also, just as had Israel (1 Kings 19:10–14), the papists had forsaken the covenant. But as God had had a remnant of 7,000 faithful in that day (1 Kings 19:18), so He had a remnant in Bullinger's time, the evangelicals, who were faithful in the covenant.[47] Bullinger made a similar point against the Lutherans. The Zwinglians were not heretics. Their understanding of the eucharist was the sense of Scripture and the primitive New Testament church as well as such distinguished fathers as Tertullian, Ambrose, and Augustine. The bread and the wine were sacramental signs: "Those err most foully who receive the signs for the real things which are signified by them."[48] The Lutherans had not completely broken from the papal error on the eucharist. Their reform was shallow and incomplete. Their teaching on the Supper differed very little from the Roman mass. They had not gone back to the teaching of the early church as the Zwinglians had done.[49]

Bullinger's appeal to the teaching of the apostolic church did not nearly plumb the depths of his primitivism. His defense of the Reformed church against the charges of heresy and schism led him back to much more ancient origins. The evangelical faith was the most ancient religion, beginning in Paradise with the covenant between God and Adam (Gen. 3:15), "the first fundamentals of our faith and salvation."[50] He was careful not to equate this faith with Judaism, which relied on circumcision and the customs and ceremonies of the law. "Truly the Christian [religion] is much older than such things." Not only was Abraham justified by faith before circumcision, but Adam, Abel, Seth, Enoch, and Noah also pleased God through faith without circumcision.[51] This same covenant was renewed with Moses and confirmed by Christ. The papal religion was new, compared to this old faith. Therefore, the Reformed church had not defected from the true church of Christ, but only from the new Roman error and idolatry. Since the Reformed church had all the marks of the true, orthodox Catholic church and since the evangelical faith was based on the ancient, sacrosanct covenant of God, "we are the true seed of Abraham." The faith of Adam, Abraham, Christ, and the Reformed church was one and the same.[52] To Bullinger, then, true reform meant the restitution of the covenant and the restoration of the ancient religion of the patriarchs and Christ. The pattern was found in the Old Testament.

Reformation, as a restitution of the covenant between a people and God, encompassed all matters in the commonwealth, both ecclesiastical and civil, and must be effected according to the law of God. It should include schools, worship, the sacraments, morals, laws, courts, economic matters, and any other matters that "pertain to the welfare of the church and the commonwealth." The pastors must explain the meaning of God's law and urge the magistrate toward reform. The magistrate ought to obey the laws of God and carry through a complete reformation, both ecclesiastical and civil.[53] Bullinger's favorite examples of such reform came from the kings of Judah such as Josiah, Jehoshaphat, and Hezekiah. All magistrates ought to follow the lead of these holy kings in reforming their commonwealths.[54]

As these Old Testament kings were models for sixteenth-century magistrates, so the prophets provided the pattern for pastors. In 1528, perhaps in a mood of youthful idealism and optimism, the twenty-four-year-old Bullinger acted the role of prophet in his *Anklag und ernstliches ermanung Gottes*, an anonymously published exhortation to the Swiss Confederacy to repent. Written in the first person, as though God himself were speaking through author, the *Anklag* neatly sums up how Bullinger viewed the Reformation in terms of the covenant and how he perceived the relationship between his own day and Old Testament times. "I have loved you and faithfully protected you," Bullinger wrote. "I have made you wealthy and praiseworthy as my Israelites, Greeks and Romans were." Now God had sent pious, true and learned prophets to preach repentance. He would no longer suffer the wickedness of the Confederates, for He had done no less for them than for Israel.[55]

Bullinger then summarized the history of the Swiss Confederacy, from Morgarten (1315) to the late fifteenth century. "In all those wars and battles I was your God, I fought for you, I protected you." Who else had God blessed so greatly? "Since I have demonstrated my love for you with great signs, it is thus now up to you to show your love for me with clear signs. Then, as I have been up until now, I will be your God and you shall be my people."[56]

Reformation was the only way to demonstrate such love for God. The pensions and mercenaries that oppressed the poor and corrupted young men must be abolished. The old confederates, simple, noble, hard-working, God-fearing people, had protected the poor. So must the Confederation do now. "You in the government," Bullinger exhorted, "should not take all authority to yourselves as sovereign princes. Your land is not an oligarchy but a democracy, a republic. Therefore, you should be fathers to your poor people; you should consider your people as fellow citizens." The magistrates should rule according to the laws. "You should be gods, my representatives in justice and righteousness." Such a reformation of the government must be accompanied by a total reformation. The Catholic states must abolish the false papal worship and turn to the true faith, which taught the love and support of the neighbor, the help of the poor, the orphans, and the widows. They must reform the worship and the celebration of the eucharist. The mass was a recent creation of the papacy. The early church had not offered daily sacrifices but had celebrated the eucharist in thanksgiving for the single, perfect offering of Christ for the sins of mankind. Idols and pictures also came from the papacy, for "I have forbidden idols over a hundred times. . . . You have the pictures from the popes and not from me." Nor could the saints be mediators. One must depend on God alone and serve Him with love and innocence.[57]

The crux of it all, however, was the covenant. "Dear Confederates, remember now that in baptism you have bound yourselves to me with an oath stronger than the one with which you have bound one state to another among yourselves." In this baptismal oath the Confederates had promised to hold God as their only God. God had sent many prophets to point out their error, but the papacy had always called them heretics and killed them. If the Confederates persisted in their apostasy, God would forsake them. "Therefore, abandon your ways and serve me with faith, love and innocence." They must follow God's word in both the Old and New Testaments, for the teaching was the same in both. It was called the New Testament because it described "how I, the almighty God, have now sealed, perfected and renewed the covenant which I made with Abraham through my Son Jesus, who shed his blood for forgiveness of sins, which is the testament, and not only for the sins of the Jews but also of the Gentiles who are now a new people in this covenant." So the Confederates must choose pious pastors to preach God's word.[58]

Bullinger returned then to God's temporal blessings to the Confederation. God had given them a beautiful and plentiful land, with wealth, rich harvests, lakes and rivers. Now they must obey God. His desire was that "you be obedient to my word, keep me for your God with faith, love and innocence." Keeping these covenant conditions would again bring unity to the Confederacy. God had blessed Jehoshaphat when he allowed God's word to be preached, when he established the good and uprooted the evil along with all idols. God demanded the same from the Confederation: a complete reformation. They must abolish false worship, renew the democracy, and concern themselves with the general welfare. If not, God would punish them as He had Israel. Judah, on the other hand, "clung only to me, walked before me innocently and in my commandments, and put away the idols along with all human inventions." For a long time God had blessed the Confederation similarly, but He would punish them severely if they did not reform their worship and abolish pensions and mercenaries, tyranny and oligarchy. "If you are inconstant, not protecting the right and punishing the evil, if you do not abandon your wars and sins and begin a Christian government, then I will do to you as [I did to] Judah and Israel."[59] Thus Bullinger played the prophet, measuring the Swiss Confederation in covenant terms against Israel and Judah.

In a later writing, he even more clearly identified Zurich itself with the old people of the covenant. Zwingli was cut from the same cloth as the great prophets of the past, such as Moses, Isaiah, and Paul. He possessed every desirable virtue: an exemplary life, a simple clear presentation of the truth, learning and persuasiveness in the face of adversity. "For through this man," Bullinger enthused, "God restored for us the glory of His church. This one restored the chief points of the testament and eternal covenant, and renewed the decayed things." Like Hezekiah and Josiah, Zwingli caused the images and idolatry of the papacy to be removed and again cleansed the defiled sacrament for the people of God; he destroyed innumerable superstitions, including the false papal interpretation of the keys. Not only did he defeat the papal kingdom of Antichrist but also the hypocritical Anabaptists. Zwingli, then, was the great prophet who restored the covenant among God's people. But Bullinger also extolled him as the restorer of liberty and compared him to the likes of Brutus and Solon. Because of his "burning love for justice, flaming zeal for equity and insatiable passionate longing for the happiness of the fatherland," he subdued the idle extravagance, the blood money from mercenaries and the cruel oligarchy. He restored "the ancestral frugality, uprightness and the holy sovereignty." He was comparable to Jehoiada, the Old Testament priest who restored the kingdom to King Josiah, thus effecting a reformation and a restoration of the covenant (2 Chronicles 23). Because of all this Zwingli was killed while defending the Christian commonwealth and armed by "the holy decree of the magistrate." Like Jeremiah, John the Baptist, and Stephen, he died for the true faith.[60]

The intent of this panegyric of Zwingli was to demonstrate that the defeat at Kappel and Zwingli's death there could not have been God's judgment against Zurich.[61] Still, the comparison of Zurich with the old people of God, that of Zwingli with the Old Testament reformers, and the identification of reformation with a restoration of the covenant come through clearly. Zurich was a covenanted community that had been reformed according to the word of God. All the norms for such a Christian commonwealth had been established in the Old Testament before Israel became a kingdom under Saul. Bullinger went back to these Old Testament norms in judging Reformation society. Although the rule of faith was most clearly expressed in the New Testament, the apostolic church was atypical in terms of the Christian commonwealth. Israel during the republican period of the judges supplied the pattern for the Christian community, and the several restorations of the covenant under the kings of Judah set the standards for reformation.

CHAPTER FIVE

Covenant and Community: Zurich

BULLINGER SAW the Reformation as a restoration of the covenant. The covenant norms for Christian society established by God in the Old Testament were thus fully applicable to the Christian commonwealth of Zurich. Everyone was under the covenant by virtue of baptism, the initiatory rite that enrolled the individual in the people of God, just as circumcision had done before Christ. Inasmuch as baptism placed everyone under the great promise of the covenant, every member of Christian society was responsible to fulfill the conditions of the covenant. The Christian community, the visible church, the kingdom of God on earth included both the faithful and hypocrites, as Christ had explained in the parable of the tares (Matt. 13). So the visible church was inclusive, just like the old church of Israel, which had contained a spiritual and a carnal Israel. Also as in Israel, the conditions of the covenant applied to society as a whole, since the inclusive visible church was coterminous with civil society. The same people of God formed both the church and the commonwealth. Therefore, the pastors of the church, like the Old Testament prophets, exhorted both magistrates and people to keep the covenant conditions; the magistrates, servants of God like the judges and kings of Israel, enforced the covenant condition of piety in the Christian commonwealth. One might say, then, that the church and the magistracy were the institutions of the covenant. The corresponding offices were those of pastor and magistrate, whose cooperation was absolutely necessary.[1]

In his *De prophetae officio* of 1532, Bullinger presented the public function of the pastor largely in prophetic terms: the correct exposition of the Scripture; opposition to error and evil deeds in the commonwealth; and the guardianship of the wealth of the church against its misuse or misappropriation by the magistracy.[2] Like the prophets of Israel, the duty of the modern prophet was "to explain the sacred Scripture, to oppose errors and impious actions, to defend piety and truth, and finally not only to instill but also to impress righteousness, faith and mutual love upon the minds of men in every possible way."[3] The task of the pastor, then, was intimately related to the covenant conditions of faith and piety.

In fact, when discussing the exposition of the Scripture, Bullinger explicitly underscored the chief importance of the covenant: "Thus I admonish you, oh prophet of God, that more frequently, when you are about to expound the Scripture, you should reflect on what the essential point of the holy Scripture is and to which matter all things return. Many [the Lutherans, presumably] say it is the law and the gospel—but incorrectly. For the testament, which is the title of the whole Scripture, is also the essential point of the entire Scripture." Such a statement was not astonishing, Bullinger continued, for he referred to the pact, covenant or compact by which God agreed with the entire human race to be an all-sufficient God. There were also, however, conditions that man had to meet: "Man is morally bound to strive after purity so that he might have a perfect and upright heart towards this God, that he might walk in His ways. . . . These chief points of the covenant, what do they dictate other than faith and innocence? From faith arises the knowledge of God . . . [and] innocence draws behind itself truth, perseverance, fairness, purity of life and love." Since these conditions of the covenant were the essential message of the entire Scripture, Old and New Testament, the modern prophet must use them to gauge his exposition. Just as the carpenter used his rule and plumb line, the pastor could test his interpretation against the Love Commandment. If it did not contradict faith or violate love, the exposition was sound. So the fundamental task of the prophet was to teach the Christian commonwealth about the covenant conditions—faith and innocence of life.[4]

Bullinger's discussion of the second role of the prophet—to condemn error and evil deeds, to guard faith and piety—further reveals the importance of the covenant conditions in the commonwealth. As the guardian of the faith, the prophet should not hesitate in opposing both the papal and Anabaptist errors. To protect the true religion, he must bring such error to light. He must preach God's word to the people so that "they might not only hear it but also portray it with faith and innocence of life." For "faith, both private and public, ought to be protected with great care since it is the sinew of the entire commonwealth." Either lack of individual faith or error in public faith would lead to increased impiety, against which the prophet must be equally vigilant. Prodigality and idleness were the greatest of curses for a Christian commonwealth. Bullinger warned that immoderation resulted in "usuries, thefts, the venal law court, bribery, wars, tumults, insurrections and whatever slaughters and crimes you wish." The prophet must vigorously censure excess and inculcate moderation, and thus destroy avarice. Bullinger's goal was that "the ancestral frugality and liberality, the most holy customs of our fathers may return." But for such to happen, the prophet had to be fearless in combating evil in the commonwealth.

> Therefore, if you love the fatherland, or rather the church of God, set yourself to meet evil at the opportune time. Act like the earlier prophets of God, who spared absolutely no one, not even princes and kings themselves, striving in every way to blockade the road into the kingdom against evil things and, if they had already gotten in, to provide an exit, at one time warning and imploring princes and people in a friendly way, but at another time threatening all the worst things.

Bullinger recognized the inherent difficulties in prophesying judgment against the magistracy; nevertheless, it was the prophet's duty to remind the ruler of God's law, to preach against bad civil laws, and to demand obedience to the word of God from the magistrate.[5]

For all that, however, Bullinger instructed the prophet to employ his independence with restraint. As Christ never withdrew from sinners, not even from Judas, so the pastor's goal should be repentance, not punishment. Thus he should first exhort the offender privately, as Nathan did with David (2 Sam. 12). Then, if necessary, he could condemn the offense in a public sermon, so long as it was a public crime. The pastor, then, should treat such matters with patience, gentleness and moderation lest he might drive the sinner even farther from God. On the other hand, in the case of a hardened unrepentant individual, he must be steadfast and firm, not indulgent, thus preventing the seduction and destruction of the faithful by such impious ones.[6]

The most important tasks of the prophet, then, were interpreting the covenant conditions in his sermons and guarding against subversion of faith and piety in the Christian community. In order to be effective, Bullinger added, the prophet must himself lead a pure and innocent life, his sermons should be simple and clear, and he needed perseverance and courage. Moses, the greatest prophet of God, had possessed just such virtues. He led the commonwealth of Israel not only with teaching, laws, warnings, and a holy life, but also with perseverance. Again and again he brought God's people back to the chief points of the covenant. The modern prophet must likewise persevere in God's work.[7]

The magistrate was also a minister of God. In fact, the cooperation of pastor and magistrate in God's work was the very marrow of the Christian commonwealth. For, in Bullinger's mind, church and commonwealth were distinguishable, if at all, only in a very limited sense, as can be seen in his exhortation to the prophet: "If you love the fatherland, or rather the church of God. . . ." Bullinger did not view the commonwealth in terms of church and state but rather as the people of God gathered together in a Christian society based on the covenant. The church did not exist within society; it was society. Both magistrate and pastor played their roles within the same sphere, whether it was called church or commonwealth. It was the Christian community. However, even though the spheres of church and civil society were not distinguishable for Bullinger, the offices of pastor and magistrate had a clear line of demarcation, just as in the Old Testament church. The pastor's duty was spiritual in nature; the power of the keys (Matt. 16) was simply the preaching of the gospel, the exposition of God's word, which included prophetic denunciation of error and evil. And in these matters the magistrate was bound to heed the pastor. So the magistrate did not preach or administer the sacraments. But neither did the pastor rule or judge. The magistrate ruled the church, and the pastors were subject to the magistrate, with the exception that the preaching of God's word was free.[8]

Bullinger fully realized the potential conflict in such a bifurcation of duties. One serious area of disagreement between the two offices in Zurich concerned Bullinger's third task for the pastor-prophet— guarding against the misuse or the misappropriation of ecclesiastical wealth by the magistracy. He did not deny the propriety of magisterial control of such wealth. It was true that the deacons controlled and distributed the wealth of the apostolic church (Acts 6) when there had been no magistrate. But when rulers became Christians, they also took their proper place as stewards of ecclesiastical wealth. Then, as papal superstition increased, the clergy gained control of this wealth and used it wrongfully. But with the Reformation and the secularization of ecclesiastical property, church income again came under the power of the magistracy, where it belonged.[9] Bullinger thus saw the magistrate as the proper manager of the resources of the church as a steward of God. He was, however, obligated to manage this wealth properly. This matter of the management of ecclesiastical income became an issue in Zurich in 1532. The council, because of the financial exigencies resulting from the Kappel War, attempted to appropriate all surplus income from the secularized monasteries for its own use. So Bullinger's treatment of the topic in the same year was a timely exercise of his prophetic role in the commonwealth, one that rather neatly illustrates his conception of the proper relationship between the offices of pastor and magistrate.

He reminded his readers how the papal church had misused and squandered the resources of the church so that "the poor were miserably oppressed with cold and hunger and the studies of colleges were neglected and superstition and rudeness fostered in their place." Such abuse, of course, had ended with the Reformation. But Bullinger feared that the magistrate might similarly divert this revenue from its proper use; in that case, the prophet must protest.

> Therefore, most esteemed brothers, considering that our church does possess wealth, let us not be negligent, but let us repeatedly exhort that it be distributed scrupulously, either to studies or to the poor. Now if you should see that such [wealth] is divided as spoil and stolen because of the depravity of the few, for heaven's sake let us not be silent even if by speaking we put our lives in great jeopardy.

Bullinger's insistence that the ecclesiastical revenues were dedicated to the public ministries of the church carried a certain urgency, especially with regard to the support of schools. "For," he warned, "if the studies of good and sacred literature should perish, the concern for piety also will quickly die." He was sure that the divisions, errors, and disturbances of his own day were a result of former ignorance, of the papal contempt for good learning.

> Therefore, however many want a decision for the glory of Christ, for the rebirth of truth, for the church of God and for themselves, let them apply themselves with all their strength to this: that the ecclesiastical wealth might be distributed conscientiously and honestly, particularly so that studies might be advanced, lest posterity be brought back into that captivity from which only recently we have at last extricated ourselves.[10]

The Reformation itself was at stake in the resolution of this issue of the use of church revenues.

In other writings, Bullinger put equal emphasis on the importance of education. Along with the church, schools also had to be reformed, for they provided leadership for both the church and commonwealth. The example of Israel was most instructive. The Israelites established schools in forty-eight towns to educate their prophets. Christ himself had founded a school of sorts with His apostles and disciples, and the early church also had schools for educating its pastors. So one essential purpose of schools was the education of pastors and teachers. The curriculum should include not only biblical studies but also the liberal arts—mathematics, physics, economics, politics, and jurisprudence. Nevertheless, the basic aim of all education was piety. The scholastics were good examples of men who neglected good learning and forgot this aim of piety. In order to inculcate piety, discipline, even if it was harsh at times, was essential in the schools. Without proper discipline the students would grow up to become corrupt rather than pious leaders of the church and commonwealth. Therefore, the health and welfare of the Christian community depended somewhat on the quality of education.[11]

Besides the support of education, Bullinger noted other proper uses of ecclesiastical wealth in his *Decades*. Such income should be used for pastors' salaries, sufficient to provide the necessities of life and the maintenance of their households. Furthermore, part of this wealth should support the poor, the aged, the sick and those otherwise impoverished through no fault of their own. Bullinger cautioned that God would judge the commonwealth that neglected such social services. Christ himself (Matt. 25:31–46) as well as the apostle Paul (1 Cor. 16) had shown a special concern and sympathy for the poor. Great care should be taken, then, in the reformation of the church, lest the poor be defrauded. If ecclesiastical revenues were inadequate, then the wealthy ought to contribute to the support of the poor. If, on the other hand, there was a surplus, it should be saved for future needs rather than diverted to an improper use. Finally, church income could be used to maintain buildings necessary for worship and the service of God.[12]

Bullinger acted the role of the prophet with some consistency in this matter of ecclesiastical wealth. The creation of the *Obmannamt* in July 1533 was a compromise solution, with the *Obmann*, as the overseer of all monastic property, administering the surplus income, sometimes for ecclesiastical purposes and at other times for civil needs. Bullinger continued his prophetic stance, however, at least into the 1550s when he published his *Decades*. Consistent with the office of pastor in the Christian commonwealth, his weapons were the pulpit and the pen. He stated God's law as he understood it and thus reminded the magistrates of their duty and God's judgment.

According to Bullinger, then, the visible church was an inclusive body with membership based on the initiatory covenant rite of baptism. Everyone was subject to the covenant conditions—faith and piety. It was the duty of the pastor-prophet to explain these conditions in his sermons and writings, both to the people and the magistrates, and to safeguard faith and innocence of life by condemning error and vice, including fiscal mismanagement, in the commonwealth. Bullinger's treatment of the functions of the magistracy further reinforced this virtual identification of the visible church with the political assembly.

Like Luther, Bullinger argued that government was absolutely necessary because of the sinful nature of men. Because of this human self-love, without a magistracy there would be anarchy as there had been in Israel after the death of Samson (Judges 17:6). God had thus ordained government to protect the good and punish the evil. A Christian society also needed the magistrate because a proclivity to sin still remained in the faithful and because there were always hypocrites in the church, a point that Bullinger illustrated with reference to the period of the Judges and Moses' many problems with Israel. Paul also taught that men could not survive without government and that the magistrate, as God's servant and regent, received his authority directly from God (Rom. 13). So all men needed the magistrate, and all government was ordained by God.

God's people, however, must have a Christian magistrate, a man of God. When God first gathered His people into a visible church and commonwealth, Bullinger expalined, He also, through Moses, ordained the Christian magistracy (Exod. 18:21). Ever since Moses the Christian magistracy had been the divine norm for God's people, throughout the period of the judges and kings of the Old Testament, and then, after a three-century period when there had been no rulers in the church, beginning again with Constantine in fulfillment of Isaiah's prophecy (Isa. 49). Although the papacy had subverted the norm during the Middle Ages, the divine institution of the Christian magistracy had been restored by the Reformation.[13] Through such a ruler God himself ruled His people. Kingdoms based on human wisdom, such as Athens and Rome, always perished. But not so with God's kingdom: "The Jewish and Christian kingdom alone has always stood high when it held steady to God and His word." This was God's charge to the Christian magistrate—to rule well by following the word and law of God. Then God would bless the commonwealth with prosperity and good fortune.[14]

The Christian magistrate, by Bullinger's definition, ruled the visible church. Just as in Israel, his authority included the care of religion as well as temporal judgment. To think otherwise was absurd in Bullinger's opinion. The magistrate should thus follow the examples of Moses, Joshua, David, Solomon, and the pious kings of Judah in reforming the church, in propagating true religion and abolishing false worship, and in making sure that the pastors preached the simple gospel of Christ. The magistrate did not, of course, preach or administer the sacraments. These functions were the province of the pastors alone. But since the Christian magistrate was the head of the visible church, the pastors must obey him and be subject to him. If the magistrate was diligent in his care for the faith and religious matters, the commonwealth would be preserved in health and happiness.[15]

In a broad sense the task of the Christian magistrate was to keep the commonwealth as a covenanted community, to encourage and enforce the fulfillment of the covenant conditions, the love of God and the neighbor. In Bullinger's mind, civil righteousness and justice were the matters involved under the condition of piety. So the civil laws of the magistrate, just like the judicial law of Israel, were simply aids in keeping the condition of piety, and his laws concerning religion were aimed at helping in the keeping of the condition of faith. All relationships in the Christian commonwealth, civil or ecclesiastical, should be regulated according to these covenant conditions.[16] Generally speaking, then, the Christian magistrate should rule so his subjects would fulfill their responsibilities both to God and the neighbor. More specifically, Bullinger stated that the office of magistrate included three functions: "For he orders, he judges and he punishes."[17] The magistrate, then, was legislator, judge, and police power.

As legislator the Christian magistrate could not base his laws on natural law, for according to Bullinger, the natural law was but a pale reflection of God's law. The basic purpose of natural law was to make the Gentiles aware of sin. Since they had not possessed the written law of God, natural law taught them God's will (Rom. 2:14–16). Natural law contained two principal points: "First, acknowledge and worship God; secondly, keep fellowship and friendship among men." To an extent, then, natural law coincided with the Love Commandment; it was the faint human memory of the conditions of the covenant as God first gave them to Adam. But, since grace did not accompany it, natural law was insufficient for salvation. It only gave knowledge of God and sin.[18]

The Christian magistrate could depend only on divine law, which had been written on the hearts of men at the beginning of the world. The knowledge of this divine law had been somewhat obscured by sin—it was, in fact, this diminished understanding of the divine law that men called natural law. God continued to write His law on the hearts of the faithful patriarchs, however, so it was not totally obscured in the period before Moses. Finally, the divine law was given to Moses, written on two stone tablets. Although Christ had abrogated the ceremonial and judicial laws, the moral law of God was eternal. The Decalogue, the summary of divine law, applied to all God's people in every age. "For," Bullinger asserted, "the Decalogue is the true, absolute and eternal rule for true righteousness and all virtues, prescribed for all places, men and times. For the summary of the Decalogue is that we love God and each other. God requires this always from all men everywhere." The first table of the Decalogue taught faith and worship of God. The second table "teaches what we owe to the neighbor." The Decalogue as a whole contained "all the duties of life" and lacked nothing "concerning piety and humanity."[19]

The law of nature and the law of God, then, both taught the will of God for man—man's duty toward God and man's responsibility toward men. In fact, the very first sentence of Bullinger's second decade, which is devoted to the law, reads: "The summary of all laws is the love of God and the neighbor."[20] The Love Commandment was thus the summary of both the covenant conditions and all law. Conversely, all law was the explication of the conditions of the covenant. Bullinger, therefore, saw the covenant conditions or the Love Commandment not simply as a personal ethic but also as the basic law for the social, political, and ecclesiastical organization of Christian society. The foundation for all law was God's law, the conditions of the covenant, written in the Scripture, the records of the covenant. God's law was the basis for the laws of the Christian magistrate.

This standard was to be applied to laws concerning worship and the maintenance of religion, or in some cases the restoration of true religion, under the guidance of the pastor-prophet. Bullinger thought that civil law must also find its basis in God's laws. Heathen peoples' laws were answerable to the law of nature. God's people had a higher standard—the divine law, the eternal will of God. The best civil laws were those that "according to the condition of any place, people, circumstances and time most closely approach the precepts of the Decalogue and the rule of love."[21] More specifically, Bullinger explained, law must promote justice, equity, peace and honesty in the commonwealth. Honesty could be best promoted by morals legislation, the goal of which should be "that discipline and honesty shall be planted and maintained in the commonwealth, namely that nothing of an unbecoming, willful and shameful nature is done." Justice and equity could be promoted both by good laws and just courts. Finally, such laws, based on God's law, would promote peace and harmony in the Christian community.[22]

Therefore, just as the judicial law of the Jews had been based on the moral law and enforced by the magistracy to help the Jews keep the second table of the Decalogue, so the civil laws of the Christian magistrate were meant to aid his subjects in keeping the covenant condition of piety or love of the neighbor. And just as the ceremonial law had been intended to aid the Jews in keeping the first table of the Decalogue, so the ecclesiastical laws of the Christian magistracy helped in fulfilling the condition of faith or the love of God. This is not to say that Bullinger equated the laws of the Christian magistrate with the Jewish judicial and ceremonial laws that had been abrogated by Christ. He did, however, see the laws of the Christian commonwealth in the same light as the Jewish laws: they were intended to help in keeping the covenant conditions, in walking in obedience to God's commandments in piety and innocence, in doing good to all men. If the magistrate was a man of God with a knowledge of God's word, his laws would promote justice and piety among his people in accordance with his divine calling.[23]

The Christian community needed honest courts as well as good laws. Good laws alone were not sufficient to assure justice and equity in the commonwealth. Courageous, just, honest judges were equally important. The judge must hate covetousness, for even the wisest judge could be blinded by gifts and bribes. The judge also must ignore the status and wealth of the accused. For, Bullinger admonished, "the basis of justice and laws is the truth, the faith, and honesty, that we remain firmly in the right and not allow ourselves to drift off. Here the ruler must be an Egyptian judge, that is, an irreproachable, courageous, resolute [person] . . . who swerves from the path of justice neither because of partiality, fear nor bribes." He advised the magistrate to read Deuteronomy and then to follow the example of the pious rulers of the Old Testament, and thus learn to fear God and not to wander from God's law. In other words, justice was to be found in the person of the Christian magistrate who in turn had discovered it in the source—God's word.[24]

As legislator, then, the Christian magistrate's responsibility was to make good and just laws, based on God's law. As judge he was obliged to give fair, honest, and impartial judgment, with God's help, which was available in the Scripture. But in order to fulfill these roles as legislator and judge, the magistrate needed the authority to enforce justice, the function of police power. Bullinger saw this task implied in the very institution of the magisterial office. He had been given the sword by God along with the command to protect the good and punish the evil. "For the sword is the divine vengeance or the instrument by which God punishes His enemies for the wrongs done unto Him" (Jere. 25:29; Ezek. 21:9; 30:24). It was as though God himself wielded the magistrate's sword. Thus he was the servant of God in the truest sense when he exercised his police power. Admittedly, Christ had admonished, "Resist not the evil" (Matt. 5:39), and the Lord had said, "Vengeance is mine" (Rom. 12:19). But, Bullinger insisted, these referred only to private vengeance and did not apply to the magisterial office. Public vengeance by the lawful magistrate was "by no means prohibited by God in the church of Christ."[25]

Christian discipline, in Bullinger's system, fell within the scope of this magisterial police power. Excommunication, a papal invention and a tool of tyranny, had no place in the Christian commonwealth. All discipline, all police power, was in the hands of the magistrate and must direct itself toward repentance and betterment. The goal was not a pure church but the protection of the greater good, as Christ taught in the parable of the tares (Matt. 13:28–30). The tares, or the hypocrites, could never be eliminated from the external church; but if the tares were obvious, if punishment would promote wholesomeness and uphold good government, such use of magisterial police power was not forbidden by Christ in the parable. Bullinger's was a theory of magisterial sovereignty: the pastors had no police power; the magistracy ruled the visible church. In Bullinger's mind, both religious and civil offenses were public crimes, punishable by the Christian magistrate for the improvement and welfare of the Christian commonwealth.[26]

The extent of this magisterial authority is evident in the offenses Bullinger saw as punishable by the magistrate. The magistrate must exercise his police power against all who disturbed or destroyed "honesty, justice, public and private peace of citizens. Let filthiness, indecency, lust, rape, fornication, adultery, incest, sodomy, extravagance, drunkenness, avarice, deceptions, ruinous usury, treason, murder, parricide, sedition and whatever else there is of this type be punished." A more complete catalogue of offenses could be found in Leviticus, chapters 18 and 20. The Christian magistrate also had penal power over specifically religious offenders such as "apostates, idolaters, blasphemers, heretics, false teachers and mockers of religion." That such religious offenses must be punished severely, even with death, was clear from God's commandments in the Old Testament (Deut. 17:2–7; Exod. 22:20; Num. 15:32–36).[27]

The magistrate must use moderation, however, in exercising his police power, Bullinger cautioned, taking care to match the penalty to the people and the seriousness of the crime. Generally there were two types of people involved in the violation of religious laws: the malicious leaders who seduced others into following them and those who were seduced. The Christian magistrate must keep the former in check like a contagious disease. He should exercise forbearance toward the latter, however, while attempting to bring them to the truth. Also, some offenses were less tolerable than others. "There are those which directly and openly aim at the subversion of the commonwealth unless they are put to sleep in time." Once the seriousness of such a religious offense had been demonstrated by the Scripture, then "one may most severely punish the blasphemers and destroyers of the church and commonwealth." On the other hand, less serious errors that did not subvert the church or endanger the commonwealth ought to be punished more lightly, in keeping with the offense. In every case the magisterial police authority should be wielded in love, with the goal being an amendment of life on the part of the offender.[28]

This affirmation of magisterial power in religious matters raised for Bullinger the question of coercion of faith. Faith was, of course, a gift of God; nevertheless, "men are judged by words and deeds." Although the magistrate could not make men righteous, he could and should punish the evil to protect the good. In fact, Bullinger asserted, one must distinguish "between faith as it is the gift of God existing in the heart of man and as it is the external profession declared and testified before men." So long as false faith was hidden it could not be punished. But as soon as a person propagated his false faith and infected his neighbors, he must be silenced.[29] The magistrate could indeed force people to do right. There were two types of men, Bullinger explained, those who did right freely and those who did right because of coercion. This was the basic task of the magistrate—to protect the good and punish the evil. Therefore, the Christian magistrate, with the support of the pastors, must concern himself not only with property and things of this life but also with discipline, the worship of God and repentance among his people.[30]

The magistrate was sovereign in the Christian commonwealth. God would bless the commonwealth if the magistrates were pure and the people obedient and pious, as in the time of Hezekiah in Judah. However, God would punish the commonwealth if it ignored His commandments, if it neglected His covenant, just as He had punished Israel and Judah. The works of the pious Christian magistrate were indispensable if the commonwealth was to live under the covenant, obedient to God and His laws. Such was and always had been God's way for His people.[31]

The double connection in Bullinger's mind between the magistracy and the covenant and between the Reformed church and the Old Testament church is quite explicit in some notes from 1534.

1. There is one God, one testament and one spirit of both the old and the new people.
2. Consequently the religion, the faith and the church of the ancients and ours is also the same, a few certain figures having been subtracted which had been introduced in consideration of the people and the times.
3. Moreover, since there was a magistracy in the ancient [church], it follows logically that it has not been annulled in ours.
4. Furthermore, it is his duty to restrain blasphemy, to forbid heresies from the church and to take care of discipline.
5. It is also his duty to guard the evangelical truth and its worshippers with arms, if it is truly necessary, against the wrongs of the godless ones.
6. If the magistrate neglects this, dealing in the meantime [only] with civil justice and the like, he is impious and less than perfect [since he neglects religious matters].

Bullinger entitled this short sketch: "What the duty of the magistrate is in the church of Christ, who lawfully defends it against the seditions of heretics and the attacks of tyrants."[32] The Reformed church, then, because of the covenant, was the same church as the Old Testament church. Therefore, the Christian magistrate was sovereign: he possessed the same power over both religious and civil life as the Old Testament rulers had possessed.

The church or the Christian commonwealth had always existed within the framework of the covenant. Baptism enrolled the individual among the people of God and obligated him to keep the conditions of the covenant. Even if he did not appropriate the spiritual blessing of the covenant through faith, he still remained under the covenant as part of the Christian community, subject to the covenant conditions that not only prescribed man's relationship with God but also set the standard for all social relationships within the Christian commonwealth. The pastor-prophet made God's will known in the church by urging everyone to fulfill the condition of faith and by impelling all to live according to the condition of the love of the neighbor. The Christian magistrate assured that everyone had the opportunity to fulfill the condition of faith and enforced the condition of piety by means of just laws, honest courts, and the exercise of police power. Everyone, including the pastor, was subject to the magistrate. On the other hand, the magistrate, in order to know and understand God's will, must listen to the pastor. Therefore, although Bullinger's position on magisterial sovereignty was unequivocal, pastor and magistrate cooperated in keeping God's people true to the covenant.

The covenant was much more for Bullinger than simply a theological device or an organizing principle of his theology. The covenant condition of love was the basis for both personal and social ethics as well as for law, justice, and social policy. Laws relating to man in society, concerning such matters as crime, social welfare, and economic affairs, were aids to the Christian citizen in keeping the covenant condition of love or piety.[33] Bullinger's treatment of two topics of social and legal significance—marriage and usury—nicely illustrates his consistency in applying the covenant to daily life, as well as the strength of his conviction about the respective roles of pastor and magistrate and his solicitude for public morality in the Christian commonwealth.

During the Middle Ages the sacrament of marriage was entirely under the jurisdiction of the church. There was no legal divorce in the modern sense, although nullification was possible if the "consent" had been defective. In such a case, a true marriage had never existed. A flaw in "consent" was an impediment on the part of one party unknown to the other party before the consummation of the marriage. Nullification could be based on a number of such impediments, but the most important were impediments having to do with degrees of kindred and affinity: consanguinity to the fourth degree, affinity by marriage, and spiritual affinity. Nullification based on defective "consent" was thus in practice, if not in theory, equivalent to absolute divorce. On the other hand, a consummated marriage based on "consent" with no flaw was a true indissoluble marriage. It could not be nullified. Even for adultery, only "judicial separation" could be granted. Legally, then, there was no divorce in the Middle Ages, although nullification may in effect have been the equivalent of divorce.[34]

The creation of the *Ehegericht* on May 10, 1525, by the Zurich council, was Zurich's declaration that marriage was under the jurisdiction of the civil magistrate. The preface of the ordinance, directed to the ministers and people of Zurich and its territories, justified the creation of the court by referring to the chicanery, hypocrisy, and the high costs involved in going to Constance or some other "foreign" court. Everyone could now receive true justice at a fair cost from the new court. There were six judges: two from the ministers of the city, two from the small council, and two from the great council. The court of appeal was the council. Under the rules concerning marriage, the ordinance specified only those impediments of consanguinity that were stated in the eighteenth chapter of Leviticus. The council also requested that each marriage be ratified in the church in the presence of the congregation. The church ceremony did not legalize the marriage but was simply a custom to which the council made concession.[35]

Section 4 of the ordinance dealt with divorce. Divorce, which was permissible under certain circumstances, meant complete dissolution of the marriage with the right to remarry. There was no "judicial separation" as in Catholic canon law. Adultery, proven before the court, was the basic ground for divorce. The second stated ground was impotence: since God had instituted marriage to avoid unchastity, a divorce could be granted if one partner was incapable of sexual relations. Rather than specifying further grounds, the ordinance simply stated that every problem could not be anticipated and that the judges could decide cases "as they are taught by God and circumstances."[36]

Initially, then, the *Ehegericht* judged only marital cases. Furthermore, it was controlled by the council: four of the six judges were from the council; the council was the final court of appeal; and the power of punishment was retained by the council except for the authority to ban an offender from the sacrament, which the church continued temporarily to exercise.

The council expanded the role of the *Ehegericht* in 1526, and thus created a true morals court. A statute of March 21 gave the *Ehegericht* jurisdiction over fornication.[37] Then, on December 15, another ordinance completed the transition to a morals court, with the council setting penalties for adultery and fornication, including exclusion from the sacrament, as a trustee of the church.[38] An ordinance in 1538 further expanded the role of the *Ehegericht* by placing additional offenses under its jurisdiction—blasphemy, denial of God's word, gambling, gluttony, drunkenness, and failure to attend church services—and by giving the court the right to impose statutory punishment.[39]

The *Ehegericht* thus played an extremely important role within the Christian commonwealth of Zurich. It was the link between the church and the magistracy. The Christian magistracy completely controlled discipline in Zurich. The magistracy had created the *Ehegericht*, and it was part of the machinery of government. The court was the voice of the magistracy in church affairs. Zurich was governed by a Christian magistracy that had complete authority in both civil and ecclesiastical matters, which included marriage and divorce.

The simple transfer of authority from the bishop's court at Constance to the *Ehegericht* at Zurich was not, however, a sufficient foundation for the Reformed concept of marriage. The rejection of marriage as a sacrament also demanded a reexamination of the institution by theologians. Bullinger's *Der christlich Eestand* (1540) was his contribution to the Protestant redefinition of the institution of wedlock.

At the outset, Bullinger asserted that marriage was an ordinance of the church that had been instituted by God before the fall, in Paradise, between Adam and Eve. God had ordained this holy ordinance of marriage for three specific reasons: to bear children, to avoid sexual unchastity, and for the comfort and companionship of mankind.[40] Bullinger further discussed the nature of marriage in terms of contract and connected marriage directly with the covenant. "The little word *Ee* is an ancient German word. Sometimes it is used for law (*gsatzte*) and justice (*recht*), at other times, for union (*vereinigung*) and agreement (*verkumnuss*). Therefore, the Old Testament has been called the old *Ee*, the New Testament, the new *Ee*, inasmuch as they contain the law which God gave to the old and new people, as well as the covenant which God began with both people." The Latin term (*coniungium*) carried a similar meaning. Like the covenant, then, marriage was an agreement or contract, and in Bullinger's mind, marriage was closely connected with the moral law and the covenant.[41]

In the course of his discussion, Bullinger was careful to point out that marriage was contracted under the laws of the magistrate, who had authority over all outward matters.[42] Then he proceeded to treat four topics that had legal and moral significance: consanguinity, the church ceremony, fornication and adultery, and divorce. Each was a matter of potential conflict between the spheres of church and magistracy, and Bullinger's treatment of them shows how he practiced his role as prophet and how he applied the covenant to everyday life in the commonwealth.

His discussion of consanguinity itself, overly long and complex, made the basic point that Leviticus 18 forbade marriage or sexual relations in the second degree of consanguinity. He added four tables to make God's law absolutely clear to his readers. These prohibitions applied to all people of all ages, not only to the Jews, for God had planted His will in the hearts of other people both before and after the written law. Thus all people knew that it was wrong to marry in the second degree of consanguinity, as could clearly be seen even in the pagan law codes. In keeping with his covenant idea, Bullinger argued that Christ had not abrogated the moral law for Christians.

> Therefore, the objection that some make, that the law of Moses was abrogated and abolished for Christians, does not help at all. Chastity, modesty and honor have never been abolished by God. The judicial things in the law are not thus abolished so that they no longer ought to exist among Christian people. We are indeed free insofar as we are not bound to the conditions which were given particularly to the Jewish people because of the circumstances of the time and the nature of the land and the people. But God has not freed us from equity, propriety, honor, and piety, and He never abolished the same law.

None could claim to be free from honorable laws under the guise of Christian liberty.[43] The covenant condition of piety, the moral law, applied to God's people in all ages.

Bullinger acknowledged that many rulers had prohibited marriage to the third degree. It would be better not to go beyond God's law, but magistrates did have the authority to do so. Inasmuch as consanguinity was an outward matter, the law of the magistrate must be obeyed even if it exceeded the moral law.[44]

The second topic of legal significance was the church ceremony, the *Kirchgang*, which Bullinger considered to be very important. He believed that the *Kirchgang* should take place shortly after the legal betrothal or contracting of the marriage. The 1525 ordinance had only urged the couple to have a church ceremony. Perhaps Bullinger had been instrumental in the passage of the 1534 ordinance that ordered the *Kirchgang* to come before the consummation of the marriage. Although he did not appeal to the 1534 ordinance, he did adamantly insist that the *Kirchgang* had to precede consummation. He appealed to what he called the ordinance of God to seek first the kingdom of God. The *Kirchgang* would give God's blessing to the marriage. It also publicized the fact that the couple was married in God's sight and gave the pastor opportunity to educate the people concerning the true nature of marriage. It would give the marriage a good beginning.[45]

Bullinger was particularly concerned about customs at betrothals and weddings that perverted the divine ordinance of marriage and destroyed the spiritual significance of the *Kirchgang*. He complained: "In some places there is a terrible custom, that at the betrothal a great meal and huge banquet is served, and even the same night the betrothed couple lie together, and only several weeks later go to the church." Furthermore, even the *Kirchgang* itself had been corrupted, with the partying beginning early the morning of the wedding and continuing after the ceremony, so that "so much is wasted in one day that it would have been sufficient for the newly married couple to live for a half year." There was also shameful, lustful dancing at such wedding parties, improper behavior for Christian people. Bullinger urged: "Here each Christian man should consider what sort of a lewdness and perverse custom this is and how such an iniquitous foul thing is practiced among Christian people, who should be holy." God had not forbidden proper parties and modest dances, but such excess and abuse made a mockery of the holy wedding. Such behavior could only lead to a deterioration of morals in the Christian commonwealth, especially among the youth.[46]

Fornication and adultery were two other problems of public morality and legal import that Bullinger treated in the *Eestand*. Both, he felt, violated the institution of marriage. Fornication was a violation of God's will that men should marry. Furthermore, it was a violation of the covenant, as Bullinger made clear in an argument based on Paul's exhortations to the Corinthians (1 Cor. 6:15ff). Just as marriage made one body of two people, so also the spiritual marriage between Christ and believers made one body. Therefore, in the same way that the husband sinned against the one body created by marriage in committing adultery, the believer also sinned against the spiritual body of Christ in fornicating. "For he dishonors the grace of Christ and defiles the holy covenant made between him and Christ. . . . The fornicator sins against the covenant and the spiritual marriage with which we ought to be drawn together with Christ." Fornication, then, was a serious violation of the covenant condition of piety. "Fornication separates us from God [and] breaks the covenant which we have with God." Bullinger then spent several pages denouncing the arguments made against marriage by fornicators and extolling the virtues of married life. Particularly odious to him was the old argument that houses of prostitution would prevent a greater evil. Such an argument among God's people was in itself a public shame, for fornication drew the mind away from God and made men "faithless" (*pundtbrüchig*). The magistrate should abolish prostitution.[47]

Bullinger regarded adultery as a much more serious offense, however, and apparently felt it was common in Zurich. Adultery was such an evil act that God himself had set the penalty at death (Lev. 20:10; Deut. 22:22). Even the pagans had considered it a heinous crime, punishable by death. Bullinger insisted that the death penalty was not too severe:

> I know well that this statement about the punishment of adultery will be regarded as harsh and unbearable by many pious people. But if they would weigh the matter rightly . . . and consider what adultery is and what results from it, they would not be so astonished

by the punishment. Adultery is a destruction of and the greatest dishonor of the ordinance of God, an evil proceeding from the devil and the idle flesh, an open and brazen falseness, a shameful faithlessness, and a willful covenant breaking and oath breaking.

Marriage was a perpetual alliance made before the entire congregation, sealed by vows of fidelity and faith. To break these vows was, then, to break both the marriage between man and wife and the spiritual marriage with Christ. If such faithlessness was a "small misdeed," Bullinger wrote, "then I must confess that the punishment of adultery by the old ones was too harsh. But if it is just to punish harshly faithless oath breaking and contempt and disdain of God and all honor, then also the punishment of adultery is just and not too harsh." God's law prescribed death for the adulterer, and God's law had not changed.[48]

Bullinger sharply differed from the Zurich magistracy on this point. The *Ehegericht* did not give the death penalty for adultery. In fact the penalties were not unduly harsh: the first offense brought three days in jail on bread and water; the second and third offenses doubled and tripled this penalty; a fourth offense brought exile from the canton.[49]

Bullinger approached the topic of divorce in the last chapter of the *Eestand*. The ordinance of 1525 had cited adultery and impotency as legal grounds for divorce, and the *Ehegericht* had granted divorces for extreme incompatibility, desertion, physical and mental illness, and fraud.[50] Although Bullinger was not willing to be quite so liberal, he did state at the outset that divorce came under the jurisdiction of the magistracy. He explained that divorce had been permitted by God for the good of man, as a medicine, but like all medicines, it was dangerous. Although it could cure, it also could kill. So Christian married people should take care that they would not need the medicine. Moreover, divorce was not to be granted for frivolous reasons. Christ himself gave adultery as the ground for divorce (Matt. 5:32), but this did not exclude similar or greater grounds. The Christian emperors had allowed divorce for crimes greater than or equal to adultery, such as murder. Striking out at the Catholic opposition to divorce, Bullinger asserted that God had instituted marriage for the good of man, not for his destruction: "Those who in no case will help the distressed married person, and accordingly will not allow divorce in any manner or way, act just like the Pharisees who, according to the letter of the law of the Sabbath, allowed men to be ruined and disgraced." Furthermore, he argued, the innocent party could remarry when the divorce was legal. The Catholic prohibition of remarriage was nothing but a snare to draw people into sin. Indeed, Bullinger continued, there would be no reason to argue about the remarriage of the innocent party if the guilty party was put to death. "To allow the adulterer to live is against the law of God which has condemned him to death. In such a case the faithful one considers the guilty one as dead, even though he lives through the negligence and permission of the world. Such negligence should not take away the freedom and privilege of the innocent party."[51]

Bullinger had given three reasons for the institution of marriage: to bear children, to avoid unchastity, and to find comfort and companionship. Although he argued that there was a legal basis for divorce if the second or third were unfulfilled, the key to his argument was his interpretation of Matthew 5:32. Adultery, the least offense for which divorce could be granted, violated the second reason for marriage. Any offense that violated the third reason for marriage, if it was judged to be as bad or worse than adultery, was also a ground for divorce. Essentially Bullinger argued that any capital offence was a basis for divorce. If such crimes were properly punished, the marriage would be dissolved by death. Thus, if the guilty party was not executed, the innocent party could consider him as dead and remarry after a legal divorce. His argument precluded divorce when the first reason for marriage, the bearing of children, had not been fulfilled, even though the *Ehegericht* had granted divorces because of barren marriages and illness. Illness and barrenness were not crimes but acts of God. Bullinger's argument was thus based on his interpretation of Matthew 5. Unlike Luther and Bucer, his position on divorce was not primarily based on the violation of the nature of marriage.[52]

Bullinger's treatment of marital matters clearly illustrates his view of how the covenant condition of piety ought to be applied to everyday life and how it should be enforced in practice. On the one hand, he completely accepted the authority of the magistracy in matters of marriage and divorce. On the other hand, he carefully explained God's law as expressed in the record of the covenant. In consonance with his covenant notion, he repeatedly asserted that God's law had not changed for Christians. In the *Eestand* his aim was to clarify God's law concerning marital matters so that both the magistrates and the citizens would understand it. Generally he agreed with the Zurich authorities, but he carefully exercised his role as prophet when he saw a conflict between God's law and the position of the magistrates. His indictment contained two charges of significance: the *Ehegericht* did not impose the death penalty for adultery, and it granted divorces on insufficient grounds. His desire was that the magistrates would understand the divine law on marital matters and would uphold public morality by enforcing God's law in the Christian commonwealth.

Bullinger's redefinition of usury further underscores the social dimension of his covenant condition of piety. The obstacles to such a reformulation were formidable. The canon law definition of usury as anything added to the principal had dominated European thought for five hundred years; the practice of usury had been forbidden by the church since the fifth century. The medieval prohibition was based on interpretations of natural and Roman law, Aristotle, and scriptural prohibitions. The theories of the medieval canonists and theologians were intricate and sophisticated, hardly susceptible of easy generalizations. There were, however, two impediments to the exaction of usury that seemed to be of particular importance to the Protestant reformers of the sixteenth century. One was the theory, first stated by Aristotle, then formulated in Roman law and reformulated by Aquinas, that money was sterile or barren; it was a medium of exchange, but not productive.[53] The other obstacle came from the biblical prohibitions, particularly Deuteronomy 23:19–20: "Thou shalt not lend upon usury to thy brother; usury of money, usury of victuals, usury of anything that is lent upon usury: unto a stranger thou mayest lend upon usury: but unto thy brother thou shalt not lend upon usury" (A.V.).[54] When the Protestant reformers considered the topic of usury, they dealt mainly with the biblical prohibitions and the sterility of money, ignoring the detailed analysis of the scholastics.

The reformers faced a more difficult problem than that of the medieval scholastics. Although the absolute prohibition of usury made little economic sense in the sixteenth century, the medieval prohibitions still weighed heavily. They were no longer bound by canon law, but tradition, the biblical prohibitions, and the Scholastic-Aristotelian theory of money continued to impede the development of a new theory of usury. The reformers were additionally confronted by the challenge of the radical sectarian groups. The radicals, generally opposed to any type of usury, appealed both to the Old Testament prohibitions and to Luke 6:35. For the most part, the magisterial reformers took a middle position: on the one hand, they opposed the radical demands that they felt were socially and economically subversive; on the other hand, they were unwilling to move toward a more liberal attitude on usury.[55] Calvin has been presented by scholars as the first to repudiate the medieval prohibitions and to formulate an economic ethic more compatible with the economic realities of the sixteenth century.[56]

It is not true, however, that Calvin was the first to do so. Bullinger developed a new theory of usury in 1530, anticipating much of Calvin's later argument. His argument on usury is found in an appendix to his *Fraefel*, entitled "Fründtlicher bericht vonn dem handel der Zinsen, wider die verwornen uffruerischen Sect der Widertoeuffern."[57] This, then, was Bullinger's reply to the radicals' teaching on usury. When the radicals fell back on the scriptural prohibitions of usury to support a communalistic ethic, Bullinger felt compelled to come to grips with the problem. The resulting ethic was a new approach, based on the Love Commandment and thus on the covenant condition of piety. Furthermore, it was a viable theory within the context of the economy of the sixteenth century. Bullinger discarded the medieval ethic, reinterpreted the Deuteronomic prohibition, and laid to rest the Scholastic-Aristotelian theory of money.

Bullinger began the "Bericht" with the admission that writing about temporal property and wealth was dangerous, admonishing his readers to accept the writing in the spirit that it was given. None should seize it as a pretext to indulge in greediness; its purpose was to judge economic life in the light of God's word, especially the Love Commandment. Then, in the first part of the treatise, he considered the Anabaptist teaching on usury or *Zins* and set up the context for his own position by defining the law, sin, *Zins* and *Wucher*.[58]

The crucial Anabaptist text was Luke 6:34–35, which Bullinger rendered, "You should lend and expect nothing from it. For if you lend only to one who can return, what thanks is there? Sinners also do that." According to Bullinger, the Anabaptists argued from Luke that whoever loaned with a contract of *Zins* was not a Christian. Bullinger replied that the passage must be interpreted within its context, the

Sermon on the Mount, which was Christ's exposition of the law of God. The law, or "the eternal will of God," was stated in three degrees, which Bullinger illustrated with the commandment against covetousness. The commandment itself was the first degree of the law: it introduced man to the fact that he was indeed covetous, that he "lacks the honor of God." The second degree of the law, the commandment against theft, checked the covetousness in man. It protected the neighbor and was thus an expression of the Love Commandment. But if covetousness resulted in theft, in violation of the second degree, then the third degree of the law prescribed the punishment. Therefore, the first degree of the law described the holiness of God and the weakness of man; in the second degree "the law is a rule and a correction of our life, it is good, holy and righteous;" in the third degree it was a punishment.[59] The second degree was the equivalent of the covenant condition of piety; the third degree concerned magisterial enforcement of that condition in Christian society.

Bullinger then applied this scheme to Luke 6, which was an expression of the first degree of the law; thus it concerned the gift and not the loan. Then, since man was of a "selfish and greedy nature," the second degree was given: "You shall not defraud your brother; you shall lend to him and not overcharge him with *wucher*." This degree would not be necessary if men would give freely of their goods. "But since this is not the case, this command follows and thus restrains our selfishness and protects the neighbor." Here Bullinger clearly identified the Love Commandment with the second degree of the law—God's will for the Christian in human society. But if this should be violated, the third degree prescribed the punishment, for God "has ordained the magistrates to punish the fraud and to dispose of the usurer."[60]

Bullinger then proceeded to reject the scholastic definition of usury and to reinterpret the entire concept. "In the Scripture and even in speech *wucher* is not always used for a wickedness (*laster*) and an evil act, although it is usually taken for the fraudulent, usurious profit." Thus there were two types of *Wucher*: honorable (*eerlicher*) and dishonorable (*schantlicher*). The two could be distinguished by the application of the Love Commandment to the situation.

We accept the honorable [*Wucher*] as a reasonable, proper and fair profit, when the neighbor is neither destroyed nor cheated. It is dishonorable, however, when the neighbor is rendered helpless, is cheated or at all taken advantage of. Therefore, when the *wucher* arises from oppression, greed and fraud, and strives against the word of Christ: "Do not unto others what you would not want to happen to you," it is then encumbered with evil and injustice; it is wrong, dishonorable and an unchristian offense, forbidden and condemned in the Scripture.[61]

So Bullinger clearly distinguished between a reasonable, fair interest and extortion.

Applying this distinction to the traditional Old Testament prohibitions, Bullinger asserted that they condemned only dishonorable *Wucher*. First he treated the Deuteronomic prohibition, contending that this "permission of *wucher* was not an eternal mandate, but only a privilege like the bill of divorce. . . . For as Christ said, they were stiff necked. With this they cheated their own people the less; something was permitted to them to prevent greater evil. Here *wucher* is to be understood as the dishonorable profit."[62] He interpreted the other Old Testament prohibitions, including Exodus 22:25, Leviticus 25:35–37, Psalm 15:5, and Ezekiel 18:8, in the same manner: although God permitted dishonorable usury in the case of a stranger, among the Jews themselves only honorable usury was permitted. The yardstick was the Love Commandment. The Anabaptists did not make this proper distinction in the usage of the word, and thus they took all *Zins* and contracts to be an unchristian *Wucher*. But God's law had never prohibited the taking of reasonable profit that benefited both parties, under the regulatory powers of the magistrates.[63]

Bullinger contended, then, that the Old Testament prohibited only dishonorable usury, not the honorable *Zins* or *Wucher*. At this point, he turned to a defense of the honorable *Wucher* in connection with the productive loan. Although he was concerned mostly with investments in land, he also included significant references to commerce and business.[64] First, he carefully excluded illegal loans and small personal loans: "I exclude the blind contracts which are made without the knowledge of the magistracy to defraud the simple ones, and speak of capital and proper substantial affairs and not at all about the small running debts." He asked: "Is it right, when there are large investments in businesses, manors, and commodities, that he who loaned it must have a noticeable loss, and that, on the other hand, he who used it should have a considerable profit over his expenses and labor? Would it not be more godly and more just to work out a compromise? For why should he not be permitted to receive a profit from his possessions if this is not detrimental to his neighbor?" If such profits were wrong, then all occupations (*aempter*) would be usurious, "for no one works to lose, but to earn a reasonable profit (*ein billichen gwün*). . . . If the neighbor can benefit from the *Zins*, and not be overcharged, it is not only a blessing from God, but also a good deed in that the neighbor is enriched and prospered by the use of your property." Therefore the productive loan was an example of the honorable *Zins*, if fair interest rates were set according to the regulations of the magistracy.[65]

The defense of the productive loan implied that money was not sterile, and in fact Bullinger explicitly rejected the Scholastic theory of money. Referring to the *Institutes* of Justinian, he explained that some thought that "since money or the *pfennig* is not able to bear fruit and profit as does the soil, one should not be able to place any *Zins* on money." The argument seemed sound enough until one considered the fact that money was "the nerve, energy, diversification and execution of all business."[66] Thus did Bullinger recognize the relationship between a money economy and capitalistic enterprise. Money was productive in such a loan. There were many large businesses, he continued, which must be based on capital, as "commerce . . . and the majority of guilds are." Furthermore, Bullinger inquired, "Is it not reasonable that he who has supplied every expense should be able also to accept a part of the profit which he has earned for the other with his work, if it is not to the detriment of his neighbor? If only love and justice should be the judge of it, and not a mad, envious head, then no one who engages in such activity is to be excluded from the Christian name."[67] Therefore, both experience and reason argued that money was productive.

Returning to Luke 6, Bullinger contended that this had nothing to do with the productive loan: Christ was not concerned there about "commerce, business or temporal profit," but only with helping one's brother in need. The matter of *Zins* must instead be gauged by the Love Commandment, which summarized "all the law and the prophets." Therefore, if the *Zins* did not defraud the neighbor, it was not contrary to Christ's words. To have wealth and to take profit was not in itself evil: "only greed, duplicity and deceit makes it evil." Indeed, God's law never had prohibited reasonable and equitable *Zins*.[68]

Bullinger then considered more directly the problem of *Zins* on land
or the traditional rents paid by the poor farmer. On this subject, he
reverted to one of his favorite logical devices: the argument from the
greater to the lesser. Since serfdom was not contrary to the Scripture
(the greater), a fortiori neither was the exacting of rent (the lesser). He
began with the familiar argument for the institution of slavery: "The
serfdom, bondage, or slavery originated with Ham, the son of Noah; it
fell on him because of his shame and unchastity, through the occasion
of his drunkenness." Some sort of bondage had existed ever since.
Even the Apostles did not abolish bondage (Eph. 6:8; 1 Tim. 6:1–2);
these passages concerned not only "house servants (*Hussknecht und
Dienst*), but also, indeed especially, bondage (*Leibeigenschaft*)."
Fearing that his argument would be used as an encouragement of
serfdom, he emphasized that his purpose was not to justify the
practice—he used the argument simply as a logical device. He warned
the lords against mistreatment of their serfs. Nevertheless, "the poor
and the bondsman never have the right to revolt" but must suffer
patiently, awaiting relief from God. Although a Christian was
permitted to have bondsmen, in Bullinger's opinion the lord would
perform "a better work if he would free his own." He concluded that
since the greater (owning bondsmen) was permissible for Christians, so
was the lesser (exacting the equitable rent).[69] Although Bullinger was
concerned here with the plight of the small, poor farmer, he did not see
restitution of the *Zins* or abolition of the *Zins* as a remedy. There could
be no restitution if the *Zins* contract had been prepared legally before
the magistrate. Moreover, restitution was impractical: it could only
result in the further concentration of wealth in the hands of a few.[70]

Concluding the treatise, Bullinger exhorted the poor, the rich, and
the magistrates. Although the pleas of the poor for help were just, he
felt that their plight was not solely from lack of aid but more from their
laziness and lack of thrift. He warned them:

> If you do not accept your calling and do not direct your affairs
> according to the course of circumstances and the times, if your
> expenses are generally more than your income, . . . then you must
> live in extreme poverty all your life. . . . [Therefore] fear God,
> work faithfully, be truthful, accept your calling, be thrif-
> ty. . . . Then in a short time your affairs will stand well. Appreciate
> help from others and pay what you owe. If not, then expect the
> chastisement of God.

The rich, on the other hand, must remember that "all wealth belongs to the Lord and you are only the administrator for a while. For this reason you are to be charitable to the poor, not defrauding them nor oppressing them with *Zins*." And if they should be hit by misfortune and be unable to pay, "remember that it is less trouble to supply the land and the expenses than to do the work." His final bit of advice was directed to the magistrates:

> You rulers are the fathers of the people of God. Therefore, act like Solomon and Nehemiah: protect your people and do not allow them to be fleeced by every usurer. You are the guardians of justice and equity; therefore, remove and abolish all usury and all injustice. Smash the unjust sales; order them to be discontinued. Warn that no one will any longer go unpunished. Be sincerely concerned, and do not allow the land to be burdened nor the hard work of the poor to be robbed and defrauded. Indeed, let no one take advantage of the others. God will be with that.[71]

Thus, if the magistrates did their duty as the guardians of justice and equity, as enforcers of the covenant condition of piety, dishonorable usury and economic injustice would disappear in the Christian commonwealth.

Bullinger's economic ethic contained both familiar and new elements. His partial intent in writing the "Bericht" had been to counter the radical argument against *Zins*, to reaffirm the right of accepting the traditional rents and to establish clearly the duty to pay *Zins* that were owed. In these respects his opinions were hardly unique.[72] But along with these traditional elements, Bullinger also affirmed the Christian right to accept *Zins*. He sanctified the practice of taking the honorable *Zins* or *Wucher*. Bullinger redefined usury with respect to the biblical prohibitions, defended the productive loan, and rejected the medieval theory of money. And this reinterpretation appears to have been the first among the Protestant reformers. He quite clearly anticipated Calvin in his theory on usury. Despite the fact that Bullinger's interpretation of Deuteronomy differed from Calvin's, it solved the problem just as neatly. And if anything, his defense of the productive loan and repudiation of the Scholastic theory of money was more precise and forceful than Calvin's more famous solution fifteen years later.[73]

Bullinger's teaching on usury was fully consistent with his covenant idea. Indeed, the covenant condition of piety or love for the neighbor was the basis for his entire social ethic, including the realm of economics. In *De testamento* he listed the loan and other economic matters among the items that were included under "that part of the covenant that prescribes integrity and commands that we walk in the presence of God."[74] To Bullinger, the second degree of the law was the equivalent of the Love Commandment, and it explained how sinful man could keep the conditions of the covenant. So when Bullinger referred to the Love Commandment, he meant more than Calvin's general appeal to Christian love and equity, although that was certainly involved. For Bullinger, the Love Commandment was the summary of the conditions of the covenant, God's eternal will for His people.

The importance of the covenant is quite evident in Bullinger's interpretation of the Deuteronomy text. Since God's law did not change, Bullinger could not simply apply the prohibition to those historical circumstances as Calvin did. Bullinger agreed with Calvin that the permission of usurious interest was nothing but a temporary privilege. Unlike Calvin, however, he thought that the prohibition among brothers applied only to the dishonorable *Wucher*, which violated the covenant condition of love. If Calvin appealed to a brotherhood where interest was authorized, which was quite different from a brotherhood where it was abominated,[75] Bullinger simply suggested that the medieval concept of brotherhood was false. Honorable usury had never been prohibited among brothers—Jews or Christians. For the Jews the standard of economic behavior had been the Decalogue. This standard had not been altered for Christians but was simply restated in the Love Commandment.

Thus, when Bullinger was confronted with the radicals' strict and logical application of the communitarian ethic to the contemporary situation, he did not simply equivocate or revise the medieval theory as did Luther and Zwingli. Like Calvin later, he abandoned the old theory and formulated a new economic ethic that corresponded more closely to the actual economic conditions of his day. Yet, in forming his new economic ethic, Bullinger drew from the record of the covenant. The guide for daily economic activity in Christian society was the Love Commandment, the conditions of the eternal covenant of God.

For Bullinger, then, the covenant served as the foundation for social policy and law among Christian people and thus as the framework for his social-political theory. The covenant was in fact the cement that unified God's people in the Christian community. Because of its great importance, Bullinger used the covenant concept not only in his commentaries and more formal historical and theological works but also in printed sermons,[76] in his *Summa*, a theological compendium for laymen, and in his catechism of 1559. No doubt Bullinger intended that the Zurich church should understand its covenant relationship with God and the concomitant obligations.

The 1559 catechism underscores the significance Bullinger gave to the covenant for the commonwealth, that he was quite serious about God's people in his own day living according to the conditions of faith and piety under the aegis of the Christian magistrate. Written for use by older students in the Zurich schools, the catechism heavily emphasizes the covenant. The first section, on the Scripture, referred to the "primitive church of the prophets and apostles," the men who wrote the books of the Old and New Testament in which the complete and authoritative teaching about salvation and piety was to be found. The student then moved into the doctrine of God and from there to a separate section on the covenant. God's promise to man was twofold: the spiritual promise of eternal salvation, first given in Paradise (Gen. 3:15), and the promise of a good temporal life. God had explained this to man by using the human custom of making a pact or covenant: "For just as men unite themselves most closely with some covenant or other, so God united with men by the eternal covenant." Made first with Adam, God renewed the covenant with Noah and especially with Abraham and all his seed, "that is, with all faithful men of all times and nations. Whence it is most clearly evident that we are all the confederates of God."[77]

The student then affirmed his covenant responsibilities. God's part was that He wished to be man's only and all-sufficient God, "in whom we have all things, those of the soul as well as the body, both of the present and the future [life]." The next question made a point of the bilateral nature of the covenant: "What does God require in turn from us and what is that duty of ours? Answer: That we willingly acknowledge these things, receive them with true faith and adhere to this God, our Confederate, with a sincere and pure heart." This meant to worship God alone, to have complete trust in Him, which would result in a zeal for righteousness, innocence and moderation. Those who stood firm in the covenant were called "religious ones and confederates, friends and allies of God." Unlike the monks, they were true confederates of God "because they are obligated by the bond of piety as they are united and tied to God." This point is driven home with a play on words: religion (*religio*) was derived from *religare*, to tie, thus referring to that bond with which "God tied man to himself and bound him with piety," which made it necessary that "we serve Him as Lord and obey Him as Father."[78]

The law was simply a fuller explanation of the covenant conditions. The moral law, God's will for man, was summarized in the Decalogue, the first table pertaining to man's duty toward God, the second table describing man's debt to his neighbor. The student then covered each of the Ten Commandments, emphasizing that they applied to all Christians, not only to the Jews. The ceremonial law concerned only the external worship of the Jews and, having been abolished by Christ, did not apply to Christians after Christ. The judicial law, based on the Decalogue, was the civil law of the Jewish commonwealth. Christian rulers were free to adapt it as the times, people, places and circumstances demanded, so long as true religion, public honesty, peace, and tranquillity were protected.[79]

The question on the purpose of the law had a twofold answer. First, it convinced a person of sin and thus led him to faith in Christ, the goal of the law, eternal salvation. Then it also was a rule for living. Although no man could perfectly keep the law and even though true satisfaction of the law could be found only in the imputation of Christ's perfection through faith, the Christian must nevertheless be zealous in his attempt, with God's help, to follow God's will as summed up in the Love Commandment. The next section of the catechism covered such matters as faith, sin, justification, sanctification, the church and its ministers, and good works. Responding to the question on good works, the student answered that although works did not justify, faith produced good works "according to the rule of the word of God, for the glory of God and the advantage of the neighbor."[80]

The covenant conditions again were emphasized in the section on the sacraments, where the student recited: "A sacrament is a sacred symbol or holy rite or sacred action established by God with words, signs and things, whereby in the church He keeps in remembrance His greatest blessings and repeatedly renews them; also by those sacraments He seals and represents what He performs for us and what He requires in turn (*vicissim*) from us." The sacraments, then, were both seals or visible signs of God's invisible grace and reminders to God's people of their covenant responsibilities. Although the signs were seals of God's promises, they did not in themselves confer grace. Reminding the individual of adoption and salvation, the sacraments acted as a seal of God's spiritual blessings as the Holy Spirit kindled faith in the heart under the influence of the word of God. Thus the water of baptism reminded the baptized "that it is their duty to repent throughout their entire life and wash away the filth with which they are daily sprinkled." By baptism the infant was adopted into the family of God, just as the ancient infants were circumcised, for "the children of the faithful are included in the eternal covenant of God." The obligations of baptism continued throughout life. This meant continuous repentance or turning back to God, acknowledgment of sins and faith, perpetual service, and a faithful life. "And this is the duty of the baptized, that is, of all of us. Of which we ought to be reminded frequently."[81]

The Lord's Supper was just such a reminder. Eaten in remembrance of Christ's death, it called to mind the duty of piety and love of the neighbor. The bread and the wine, symbols of Christ's body and blood, "enliven and invigorate our souls to life eternal." This was spiritual eating, to eat through faith sacramentally, in memory of the single sacrifice of Christ. The eucharist was thus a solemn thanksgiving, to be accompanied by prayer, a pious life and love toward the neighbor. "God requires and approves of these things."[82] Undoubtedly the catechism, highlighting the covenant throughout, gave the students a clear picture of their covenant responsibilities.

The covenant thus determined the tone and quality of daily life in the Christian commonwealth. True religion was to worship God with piety, keeping the conditions of God's covenant. Piety was "the fear of God, faith, hope and love," or love of God and the neighbor. Therefore, to be pious or godly was to have faith and to love one's neighbor as oneself, to keep the covenant conditions.[83] God's will for His people here on earth was a Christian commonwealth, like Zurich, where the magistrate enforced the covenant conditions and where the people obeyed the laws of the magistracy. The possible weakness in Bullinger's theory was his affirmation of magisterial sovereignty, his great faith in the Christian magistrate. The pastors had no recourse should the magistrate refuse to accept their interpretation of God's law. Their only court of appeal was the Scripture. In case of a turn toward tyranny or false religion, they could only threaten God's judgment, as the Old Testament prophets had done. The whole system depended on the Christian magistrate. Bullinger, however, obviously had great confidence in the power of God's word. There was nothing to fear as long as the pastors were free to preach the word of God. Then God could work out His will among His people.

Bullinger was sure that God's will for His people had not changed— the people of the covenant were still bound by the conditions of the covenant. This had been true for the church of Israel and it still held true for God's church, including the church of Zurich. "Our covenant which God made with us is everlasting and confirmed by the blood of Christ. Therefore it pertains to us and we who believe are in the covenant of God to the end of time, and we are the church of God, Israel, and the people of God."[84] The Reformation had been a restoration of the covenant from the papal darkness of the Middle Ages. The Christian commonwealth of Zurich, then, was a covenanted community, the new Israel.

CHAPTER SIX

The Covenant and Controversy:
The Radical Challenge

THE ANABAPTISTS were a direct threat to Bullinger's covenanted commonwealth. The covenant must be the frame of reference in assessing Bullinger's antagonism toward them. Insofar as the covenant shaped his view of Christian society, to that extent it also defined his critique of the radicals. Thus far this study has avoided any reliance on Bullinger's polemics against the radicals in order to demonstrate that his covenant concept and the consequent view of the Christian community stood on their own merits, apart from the Anabaptists. This is not to argue that the Anabaptist threat had no influence on the development of his covenant notion. Nor is it true that Bullinger avoided striking out at the Anabaptists in many writings other than his polemics against them. Rather, the contention is that the covenant was a pervasive idea in his thought, that he built his entire concept of Christian society and ethics on the covenant idea, that he employed the notion in a wide variety of situations, that he interpreted the entire experience of God's people within the context of the covenant theme. That the covenant was not a special doctrine devised against the Anabaptists is apparent in Bullinger's critique of papal claims: the idolatry and apostasy of the papal church was a massive violation of the covenant conditions of faith and piety, comparable with the

Jeroboamite apostasy.[1] Furthermore, the Lutherans were culpable inasmuch as they partially retained the Roman mass and did not fully restore God's covenant.[2] Then Bullinger's defense of magisterial discipline against those who argued for ecclesiastical discipline, the Calvinists, was also based in his covenant idea.[3] Bullinger's covenant idea, then, cannot be seen as a strategem against the Anabaptists. Rather than interpreting his covenant concept within the context of his opposition to the radicals, his implacable opposition to them must instead be put within the covenant perspective.

Because Bullinger saw the Anabaptists as the prime threat to the existence of the Christian commonwealth as a covenanted community, his polemics against them contain much of what he wrote elsewhere on such topics as the covenant, the sacraments, the church, and the magistracy. Consequently, his point of view can never be divorced from his feelings about the radicals. On the other hand, Bullinger's aversion to them cannot easily be explained apart from his theory of the Christian commonwealth. His opposition to them cannot be understood simply to have been based on his desire to protect the Zurich church from their sectarian spirit or to defend Zurich from the Lutheran charge of sectarianism,[4] although these elements were certainly important. The underlying reason for his animosity toward the Anabaptists was their total rejection of the very idea of a covenanted Christian commonwealth, in Bullinger's mind, God's will for His people on earth. Accordingly, his opposition to them must be understood within the total framework of his theory of covenant and Christian commonwealth.

Even though the Anabaptist position on the church may have constituted their most direct threat,[5] Bullinger felt that their teaching on the church sprang from a much more basic error, their misunderstanding of the covenant, which itself was a consequence of their inadequate understanding of the Scripture. More specifically, Bullinger traced the entire network of Anabaptist errors back to one fundamental source—their renunciation of the authority of the Old Testament, where Bullinger found all the norms for the Christian community as well as the origins of the covenant.[6]

Bullinger expressed his perception of the Anabaptist position on the Old Testament in a letter to Berchtold Haller in the summer of 1532. Haller, having heard that the Anabaptists rejected the Old Testament, had requested Bullinger's advice on dealing with them at the impending Zofingen disputation.[7] Bullinger advised Haller to begin with the proposition: "When disagreements and crises occur among Christians with regard to the faith, they should be resolved and clarified with the holy Scripture of the Old and New Testament." This would elicit a negation of the Old Testament at the very outset, and Haller could then demonstrate how they were misinterpreting their New Testament proof texts. Haller should be especially careful about their use of the word "law." They would miss the double meaning of the term, arguing, "The law has been annulled (Heb. 3:13). Therefore, the authority of the old record is nil for purposes of debate." Paul, however, used a synecdoche, using the larger term *law* to refer only to the ceremonial law. The moral law, the eternal will of God, had not been annulled. In this sense, the law meant the entire Scripture, both the Old and the New Testament.[8]

Once Haller had established the authority of the Old Testament, he should turn to hermeneutical principles, for if differences were to be resolved, the exact meaning of Scripture was necessary. Therefore, Haller should propose the thesis: "The Scripture should not be interpreted according to the opinion and spirit of men but by and through itself, also by the rule of faith and love." Since proof texts could often be found to support either interpretation of a passage, such an approach to the exposition of the Scripture was inadequate, especially when dealing with a text which could not be given a literal interpretation. Consequently, the Scripture must be viewed as a whole, the clearer texts explaining the more obscure. Furthermore, "a given text must be explained according to the context, faith and love." If the Anabaptists tried to pile up proof texts in place of interpretation, Haller should follow these hermeneutical principles. "Those texts which we wish to use to explain another passage must either be clearer than the one concerning which there is contention, or opposite to it, so that anyone can see by the incompatibility that another sense exists than the one produced by the words themselves. In that case the context must be scrutinized, faith preceding and following love."[9]

Bullinger was not suggesting that Haller should trick the Anabaptists by proposing these hermeneutical principles. His point was that any interpretation not in harmony with the Love Commandment had to be suspect, since Christ himself said that the entire law and the prophets hung on these two commandments (Matt. 22:37–40).[10] Furthermore, the rule of faith and love was an essential interpretive principle for Bullinger, which he applied consistently, whether or not he had the Anabaptists in mind.[11] The Love Commandment not only summed up the conditions of the covenant, faith and love, but supplied these same two elements as guidelines for the expositor. Since the entire Scripture was the record of the covenant, all preaching and interpretation of Scripture must aid in fulfilling the covenant conditions. Therefore, the conditions themselves, faith and love, became a basic hermeneutical guideline for Bullinger, the goal being to place any text within the larger context of the Scripture—the covenant.[12] Nor was Bullinger's position on the importance of the Old Testament for Christians formulated specifically with the Anabaptists in mind, but rather in late 1523,[13] before the radical movement had even come into existence. He was, of course, frequently critical of the Anabaptist position on the Old Testament. He also, however, often vigorously defended the great authority of the Old Testament within a more neutral context, because his entire covenant idea depended on it.[14]

This, the preservation of the unity of the covenant, was exactly Bullinger's point when he defended the authority of the Old Testament against the Anabaptists. Christ had not abolished the moral law but only the ceremonies, which He had fulfilled. Although He had thus freed the Christian from the condemnation of the law, the moral law remained as the holy and correct guide for living and for civil society. The Old Testament still had great authority in the church because New Testament Christians were one with the old people of God. "These are truly one people of God, in one church and communion, in one covenant or testament; and they have one and the same redemption and salvation, one and the same teaching, one faith, one spirit, one hope, one inheritance, one calling and equivalent sacraments."[15] The Anabaptists, however, rejected that whole concept of covenant unity, arguing that Christ made a new covenant of faith. Their rejection of infant baptism rested on their insistence on this new covenant and thus stemmed from their rejection of the Old Testament.

When Bullinger treated infant baptism he again dealt with the covenant. Baptism was a sign of the people of God, a covenant sign equivalent to the circumcision of the Old Testament. The covenant made with Abraham was an eternal covenant, and the Anabaptist contention that Christ had established a new covenant, abolishing the old, was erroneous. God's promise that He would be the God of Abraham and his children remained firm after Christ. Since children had been included in the sign of the covenant in the Old Testament, they also were included in baptism, for God would not be less merciful in the New Testament period than He had been in the Old. The covenant was sometimes called "new" because it had been renewed and confirmed by Christ and because the heathen were now included. Bullinger made several arguments from the New Testament to demonstrate that children were still included in the covenant. Christ said that little children were in the kingdom of God (Mark 10:14), and He referred to children having faith (Matt. 18:6). With regard to the latter, Bullinger explained that the Scripture spoke of faith and the faithful in two ways. First, there were those who heard the word of God and believed; this did not refer to children. But the Scripture also referred to the faithful, which did include children, because "they are counted and reckoned among the faithful out of the free grace of God, who has included the children in the covenant." Therefore, Christ could not have excluded children from the Great Commission (Matt. 28:19–20). Furthermore, Paul clearly taught that baptism was the new sacrament of the covenant, replacing circumcision (Col. 2:11–12), and he himself baptized entire households (1 Cor. 1:16; Acts 16:33), which must have included children.[16] Baptism was thus "a sign of the people of God and the seal of the covenant."[17]

The Anabaptists' error on baptism, then, resulted from their rejection of the unity of the covenant. Furthermore, Bullinger felt, their misunderstanding of the covenant led to their false teaching on the church and their perversion of the covenant signs into marks of holiness. "The holy baptism, which the Lord gave for an initiatory covenant sign to all who are in His covenant, they make into a sign of their separated faction and their own contrived holiness. The Lord's Supper, which is a universal remembrance of the death of Christ and a general thanksgiving, they restrict and will allow it to no one except their fellow holy sectarian brothers." The radicals, Bullinger asserted, thus misunderstood the nature of the external church. Ignoring the marks of the true external church, they claimed that the true church must be separated from the world, composed only of true believers.

Otherwise it was a false church and believers must separate from it. Bullinger thought that the history of the church proved them wrong. The church had always included the unfaithful, the hypocrites. Judas had been in the church of the apostles, and Christ himself had taught that the tares must grow among the wheat until the end of the world (Matt. 13). The Corinthian church had even included fornicators, for which Paul had rebuked it severely (1 Cor. 5); but it still had remained a true church of Christ. Furthermore, the Old Testament prophets had continually condemned ungodliness but had never started a new church. There always had been and always would be unfaithful people in the church.[18]

In connection with his criticism of Anabaptist sectarianism, Bullinger also defended the Reformed church as a true church of Christ. It had all the marks of a true church—apostolic teaching, prayer, true use of the sacraments, and fellowship or Christian love. He admitted that there were defects in the evangelical church, as there had been in the apostolic church, but there were also many faithful people. The radicals should consider how bad conditions had been under the papacy and be thankful for the vast improvement. They were the new Donatists. When they separated from the evangelical church, they severed themselves from the vine itself, from the true church of Christ. Their separation was quite different, Bullinger insisted, from the secession of the evangelical church from Rome, which had occurred because of defective teaching, not so much because of the defects of the people. The Roman church lacked all the marks of the true church. Since just the opposite was true of the evangelical church, the Anabaptists had no reason for separating from it.[19] This argument was simply a restatement of Bullinger's contention that the Reformation was the restoration of the covenant after centuries of papal neglect and error.

On at least one issue Bullinger saw the Anabaptists and the Roman church in much the same light—their use of excommunication. The papacy had employed excommunication as an instrument of tyranny and a weapon against magisterial sovereignty. The Anabaptists also undermined magisterial authority with their use of excommunication in connection with their doctrine of a pure, separated church. Bullinger's argument against the radicals on this point was very similar to the position he took against the Heidelberg "presbyterians" in

1568.[20] The Lord's Supper was not for the pure few, but for sinners, for the entire church. Therefore, there should be no exclusion or excommunication from the Supper. If the ban was used at all, it must be aimed toward repentance, not punishment.[21] There is no question that Bullinger opposed the use of excommunication and that he felt all discipline should be in the hands of the magistrate. On the other hand, he did admit the right of other Reformed churches, such as Basel and Geneva, to accept a presbyterian sort of discipline including exclusion from the Supper. If this was inconsistent, it was not because excommunication was an adiaphorus issue for Bullinger.[22] Nor did such a concession imply a tolerance for the practice.[23] Rather it was based on the realities of ecclesiastical politics. It was an attempt to avoid an open rift between Zurich and Geneva and an admission that neither Bullinger nor Zurich could control the practice of foreign churches. Bullinger was firmly committed to an open communion and magisterial discipline throughout his career.[24]

In Bullinger's opinion, then, the Anabaptist teaching on Scripture and the covenant determined their concept of an exclusive church, which in turn colored their approach to baptism and church discipline. But the issue of excommunication and discipline reveals that the crucial point in question was not so much the radical definition of the church as it was their corresponding position on the magistracy. In the end the dispute was over who controlled the police power, who ruled God's people in the external church. The crux of the problem for Bullinger, then, was that the Anabaptists' doctrine of the church implied a profound threat toward the role and competency of the Christian magistrate and a subversive attitude toward the Christian commonwealth. The social-political implications of their sectarianism threatened the very existence of the covenanted community.

Bullinger's entire historical perspective came into play when he treated the radical position on the magistracy. First, he defended the existing relationship between the magistracy and the church in Zurich. According to Bullinger, the Anabaptists charged that the evangelical church was a false church because it placed its trust in the protection of the magistracy. Bullinger replied that the relationship was proper and scriptural. "The magistrate was instituted by God for the good of the entire human race and still today God appoints the rulers to plant, further and maintain peace, justice and every honesty among men.

God, through pious rulers, helps His own on earth and does well toward them; on the other hand, He restrains the evil ones and punishes them. Faithful, upright people understand that; they are thankful to God for His goodness [and] are obedient to the magistrate." Following this general statement, he developed his now familiar argument. There had been a magistrate over God's people ever since He had first gathered them into a visible church and commonwealth (Exod. 18). The single time Israel had been without a ruler, there had been chaos and anarchy (Judg. 17–21). Godless rulers had brought great unrest, war, and bloodshed, but with God-fearing pious kings such as Jehoshaphat, Hezekiah, and Josiah, God's people had found peace, prosperity, and happiness. Sometimes God had punished His people with tyrants such as Nebuchadnezzar, but good pious magistrates had always been a blessing from God. To the contention that such Old Testament arguments did not apply to Christians, Bullinger replied, "The old church and our church is one church [and] we in the New Testament can rightly quote the old Scripture and confirm or condemn every teaching we choose to confirm or condemn with the actions or examples of the old, faithful people." In any case, Paul taught the same doctrine about the magistracy (Rom. 13; Titus 3:1–2), as did Peter (1 Pet. 2:13–14) and Christ (Matt. 17:24–27).[25]

The argument that the Christian could then be forced to idolatry by a pagan magistrate was both invalid and irrelevant. Bullinger, defending the magistrates of the Reformed church, scathingly retorted, "You Baptists should not be so ignorant and unthankful to speak in such a way against magistrates who do not force you to any idolatry but lead you to the true faith." Should any magistrate force to idolatry, everyone knew Peter's teaching to be obedient to God rather than to men in such a situation (Acts 5:29). To the objection that true Christians needed no magistrate, Bullinger replied that even though there was always a righteousness and perfection in God's elect, there also "remains the weakness of the flesh until the end." The Anabaptists were imagining a Christian community and Christian men "who never did exist, nor do exist, nor ever will exist." God's people were still prone to sin, as could be seen in Moses' many problems with the Israelites as well as in Paul's difficulties with the Corinthians (1 Cor. 6:1–8). Therefore, the magistracy was a necessary office in the church.[26]

Bullinger admitted that some Anabaptists did accept the necessity of the magistracy. But then they attacked the Christian magistracy, claiming that no Christian could be a ruler. This direct attack on the Christian magistracy and thus on Bullinger's entire theory of Christian society elicited a sharp response. If the magistracy was good and the ruler a servant of God, he wondered, why could the Christian not be a magistrate? The Anabaptist argument astonished him. "For if no Christians can be rulers, then they (namely those who are Christians) must resign from the government, if indeed they wish to be Christians. Who then will sit in their place? No Christians, since they cannot be rulers; therefore, the unfaithful ones must sit in their place. It is well to bear in mind what they will do and how they will rule. . . . [But] God has ordered in His law . . . that no unbeliever shall rule over the people of God" (Prov. 16). The Anabaptists thus desired to take authority from those who ruled best and give it to those who would rule worst. What honest man could wish to destroy good government? If the Anabaptists understood the consequences of their teaching, Bullinger was sure that this proved that they were "conscious subversives and troublers of a good Christian government."[27]

Here Bullinger's ideal of the Christian magistrate clashed directly with the Anabaptist idea of the fall of the church at the conversion of Constantine and the subsequent development of a state church. The Anabaptists appealed to the time of the primitive church, when there had been no magistrates in the church. Bullinger countered with the argument that there had indeed been magistrates who were Christians, even though they did not control the government. More significantly, this situation had only been temporary until the prophecies about kings coming into the church (Ps. 2:10–12; Isa. 49:22–23) had been fulfilled by the conversion of Constantine.[28] Bullinger thus appealed to a more ancient primitivism than did the Anabaptists, to the establishment of the divine norm for God's people under Moses.

The basic misunderstanding of the radicals on the proper relationship between the civil and ecclesiastical spheres was evident, Bullinger felt, in their treatment of two teachings of Christ. The first was the occasion when Christ forbade his disciples to rule (Luke 22:24–26). This was no general prohibition of Christian rule but simply a differentiation between the offices of pastor and magistrate, Bullinger explained. "Here the Lord separates the callings. He does not want the preachers under the guise of religion to draw dominion unto themselves and make themselves like princes." So, far from abolishing the Christian magistracy, the Luke passage strengthened it. In Bullinger's opinion the Anabaptist interpretation of Christ's assertion that His kingdom was not of this world (John 18:36) even more clearly demonstrated their confusion. They insisted that this meant that the church should be separated from secular society and that the magistracy should have nothing to do with the church. The kingdom of the world and the church could not be mixed at all. Bullinger's reply was a summary of his concept of the Christian commonwealth.

> As long as the rulers of the temporal kingdom remain under the prince of the world and of darkness, not believing in Christ, . . . then certainly the kingdom of the world and the kingdom of Christ should not at all be drawn together. But if the rulers of the temporal kingdom abandon the prince of darkness and cling to the Prince of light, Christ Jesus, in whom they have faith, whom they worship and honor, and also if they further and protect the Christian faith, then they are no longer in the kingdom of this world but in the kingdom of Christ and therefore no longer temporal but Christian princes.

The Christian magistracy, then, was simply the fulfillment of the prophecies about rulers coming into the church.[29]

If such was a mongrelization, Bullinger continued, it had been created by God when He called princes into His church. "But it is not a mongrelization (*mischlung*), since the princes are no longer temporal but in a spiritual capacity. Therefore it indeed is no mongrelization but a fine, good Christian ordinance which the Lord himself brought into existence." When rulers accepted the faith, they came into the church not only as ordinary men but as rulers, ruling according to God's word, abolishing false worship and idolatry and establishing evangelical teaching, prayer, worship, discipline and piety. It was not possible to say "that some mixture of paganism and Christianity has occurred here, or that the church has thus become a temporal kingdom or that temporal rulers have come into it." For they had not come into the church "as temporal rulers to rule the church according to the world but as Christian rulers to govern everything in the church of Christ according to the will and word of Christ, so that Christ himself might live and rule in the midst of His church." The Christian magistrate thus served God through his office as ruler of the church. Who could possibly be a better ruler over God's people than the Christian magistrate, the faithful friend of God?[30]

None of this argument differs significantly in content from Bullinger's general position on the Christian magistracy and commonwealth as expressed for nearly one-half a century in all sorts of writings.[31] It was not so much the Anabaptists' sectarianism per se that disturbed him as it was their correlative rejection of the Christian commonwealth as a covenanted community under the Christian magistrate. Bullinger saw the Anabaptists not only as heretics because of their teaching on the Old Testament and the covenant, and as schismatics because of their position on the church, but also as subversives because of their posture toward the Christian commonwealth. Their subversive attitude was evident in their rejection of magisterial sovereignty, their repudiation of the oath, and their refusal to bear arms.

The Anabaptist rejection of magisterial sovereignty, Bullinger charged, was similar to the papal teaching that the ruler must be excluded from matters of faith and the church, which had resulted in so many centuries of harm both to the faith and the Christian church. "But in this day," Bullinger lamented, "when from God's grace the light of the truth shines so brightly and is preached by us, so that everyone sees that the Christian rulers have not been excluded from things of faith, the prelates no less than the Baptists scream against us." Bullinger then dropped the comparison in order to deal specifically with the Anabaptists, referring the reader to his other writings for his answer to the Roman church. Still, his treatment is in some ways reminiscent of his critique of the medieval papacy, particularly in his charge that the Anabaptists had confused the offices of pastor and magistrate, which caused utter confusion in the church. The two callings were different, that of the pastor to administer the sacraments, preach, and teach, and that of the magistrate to rule, forbid, and punish. But both pastor and magistrate were subject to the same spiritual sword, the Scripture. And both were God's servants and thus subject to Him, which Bullinger illustrated by the examples of Jehoshaphat (2 Chron. 17) and Josiah (2 Chron. 34). "Therefore, we do not confuse the offices, so that the pastor should assume the task of the magistrate, by sitting in court and council, ruling, commanding and punishing. Such belongs to the magistrate and not to the pastors."[32]

Not only should the magistrate take in hand matters of faith and religion, Bullinger continued, but he must do so for the common welfare and well-being of his people. Historically the best governments had been those in which the rulers had met their God-given responsibility in matters of faith, who had abolished false worship and protected true religion. The pious Old Testament rulers from Joshua to Josiah had ruled the church: they had called synods of priests, issued mandates about religious matters, commanded priests, and assured the preaching of God's word. Christian rulers had no less authority. Beginning with Constantine, in fulfillment of Isaiah's prophecy, the Christian emperors took their rightful place in the church. The magistrates of the evangelical church thus had solid historical and biblical precedent, despite the erroneous claims of the Anabaptists and papal prelates.[33]

The subversive nature of the Anabaptist position against magisterial sovereignty was clearer yet, Bullinger felt, in their rejection of the judicial power of the magistracy. They claimed that Christ taught to resist no evil but to turn the other cheek (Matt. 5:39). Therefore, the Christian needed no law and could not use the courts. Bullinger scornfully asked, "What is more shameful than to destroy a well ordered government with the overthrow and evasion of the court and the law?" Since hypocrites as well as the faithful, tares along with the wheat, would always be in the church (Matt. 13:24–30), courts and laws were necessary to protect the good and restrain the evil. The correct understanding of Christ's words, then, was that the Christian should not resist evil with unnecessary force or take private vengeance but should allow the law and the court of the magistrate to take vengeance as directed by God. Invariably Bullinger appealed to Paul's exhortation to the Corinthians (1 Cor. 6:1–8) when discussing Christian courts. Paul told them to choose "faithful, wise and prudent men" to judge disputes. Even though this measure had been temporary, certainly not meant to deprive the proper magistrate at Corinth of his justice, it did demonstrate that Christian judges were not contrary to God's law. Honest, just courts and God-fearing judges were pleasing to God and served Him (2 Chron. 19:5–7). "Indeed to support court and law is not the least among the most distinguished good works" (Isa. 1:16–17; Zech, 7:9–10). Who could imagine that God would be less pleased with such a good work in the New Testament? "In short, the Lord has taught us nothing more truly through His gospel than to do good, to help, aid, love and protect our fellow men, which all men can do through the grace of God, for which reason, however, those are in the magistracy. Therefore, it is demonstrated with fundamental truth that court and law do not strive against the gospel but can and should be in the church." It also clearly proved that the evangelical teaching about magisterial power was based on Scripture.[34] At one stroke, then, Bullinger both defended magisterial sovereignty and connected the judicial power of the magistrate with the covenant condition of love of the neighbor.

He saw a further threat to magisterial sovereignty in the Anabaptist rejection of the police power of the magistrate, which they based on the Sixth Commandment (Exod. 20:13) and several New Testament passages including Christ's words about not withstanding the evil (Matt. 5:39). Since killing was contrary to Christian love and the church was spiritual, only the ban could be used, not the sword. Bullinger responded that not only was the magistrate exempt from the commandment not to kill (Exod. 22:18–20), but he did so on the command of God, "for the sake of public justice, for the deliverance of the pious and for the preservation of public peace and the well being of the entire people." It would, of course, be tyranny if the magistrate executed people arbitrarily, according to his own whims. He must use his sword according to God's law, against such offenses as witchcraft (Lev. 20:27), false teaching (Deut. 13; 18:20–22), blasphemy (Lev. 24:16), disobedience to parents (Deut. 21:18–21), murder, adultery, and other such crimes listed in Leviticus, chapter 20. To the Anabaptist objection that all this belonged under the Mosaic sword from which the Christian had been freed, Bullinger replied, "The sword and the death penalty by the magistrate was not first instituted by Moses as a ceremonial law to be abolished at the time of Christ, but was established by God from the beginning, as a natural, always necessary law." All governments before Moses used the death penalty, then God gave it to Israel and later to the New Testament church (Rom. 13). "Therefore, the sword of punishment remains in the church."[35]

Nor was such punishment contrary to Christian love. Rather it was a positive exercise of true love. For, Bullinger asserted, the magistrate had the obligation to love "not only the few guilty, evil acting or dangerous people, but also, and even much more so, the great community of the innocent." Unwarranted leniency would strengthen evil in the commonwealth rather than restraining it. The magistrate could not allow the evil contingent to prey on the innocent under the pretence of love, against true love. "It must likewise be admitted that just as the discipline of the father is for the good of the son and not contrary to love, so also the legal killing by the magistrate is for the greater welfare not only of one man but of the entire community, and therefore not against love."[36]

The refusal of the Anabaptists to accept magisterial police power in the church, coupled with their insistence on using only the ban, was self-serving and seditious, Bullinger thought. Who did not understand what would happen if the magisterial police authority was suspended? Certainly the ban would be a totally inadequate deterrent. Confusion and disorder would reign. "What else then do you plant with your teaching besides a horrible destruction of a well regulated church?" Historically the church had found that only the magistrate could bring improvement. The Anbaptists, however, devised their "pure angelic church" for the few, at the same time taking away "the protection of the church which we have (assembled from the good and the evil according to the teaching of Christ)."[37] Bullinger thus directly connected their sectarianism with what he saw as subversive tendencies. Their doctrine of a pure church must be opposed in order to preserve the inclusive Reformed church, the Christian commonwealth, the covenanted community.

If the Anabaptist rejection of magisterial sovereignty showed their subversive attitude, Bullinger was sure that their pacifism was explicitly treasonous. The basis for their opposition to war was the same: Christians could not go to war because of the Sixth Commandment and Christ's teaching on not resisting evil. They also referred to Isaiah's prophecy about beating swords into plowshares and the wolf dwelling with the lamb (Isa. 2:4; 11:6–9), linking this with New Testament teachings about peace, love, and unity. But, Bullinger answered, all this is fulfilled daily in the church by the faithful. Since, however, many were not of the faithful and were thus not so well disposed and friendly to others, mistreating and killing pious, innocent people, God instituted the magistracy for the protection and defense of the good ones, including going to war if necessary. Bullinger explained that he did not intend to discuss "the unnecessary mercenary wars," or the justifications for war, or how dangerous war could be even when it was justified. His sole purpose was to prove "that a Christian magistrate (in the greatest emergency, where there is no other alternative, and neither concession nor compromise, neither right nor forbearance can help anything, but that evil men would destroy a people with force and insolence) is duty bound to protect his innocent people to the best of his ability with war or self-defense."[38]

Bullinger's actual argument was based partially on analogy and partially on Scripture and history. If the magistrate had the authority to execute for murder, he must also have the right to repel an enemy attack. Furthermore, Bullinger argued, since the magistrate had the duty to protect such possessions as inheritance and property, he must be "much more obligated to protect and preserve the greater and more important possessions such as religion, freedom, life, honor, city and country." Moreover, godly princes in all ages had fought against tyranny and had protected pious, innocent people with the sword. The judges and kings of Israel fought for the homeland, for true religion and in behalf of honest, oppressed people. God himself had given Israel laws concerning war (Deut. 20), and in the New Testament Paul called these wars a work of faith (Heb. 11:32–24). Therefore, the necessary, defensive war was just and lawful.[39]

It was, then, also lawful for the Christian citizen to fight in such a war. But, Bullinger complained, in an emergency, when it was necessary to defend people, honor, freedom, and homeland, "then the pernicious, intolerable, destructive sect of the Anabaptists corrupt a good part of the people and the troops," and their position on nonresistance gave "the enemy no little advantage but great aid." Their attitude would render ineffective any magisterial defense of God's people. It was, although Bullinger did not use the term, treason: "Such Anabaptist teaching about disobedience during the dangers of war is not only against the government, against honor and oath, but also unnatural, contrary to all love, loyalty, reason, and humanity." Should they, Bullinger asked, allow the old and sick to be mistreated, the church, the schools and youth to be destroyed, young daughters and wives to be violated? Should they stand idly while "all discipline, honor, peace, and all well being, as well as the divine worship, the honorable household and Christian government are torn to pieces and totally destroyed?" The Old Testament people obeyed their rulers in time of war and so should the Anabaptists. Of course, Christians should hope for and pray for peace. Peace was always far preferable to war. But if the citizens refused to aid the ruler in defense, war would surely bring much evil and destruction.[40]

Surely one cannot simply assume that this attack was merely malevolent rhetoric on Bullinger's part. He did not really misrepresent the Anabaptist position,[41] and he seems to have been truly disturbed by their pacifism. In a society where every able-bodied man was expected to be a soldier in times of war, it was to renege on one's duty to refuse military service. It was unthinkable.[42] Thus, to Bullinger, their refusal to bear arms was proof positive that the Anabaptists were treasonous people, disloyal, and a real danger to the continued existence of the Christian commonwealth.

Finally, Bullinger saw the Anabaptist denial of the oath as a threat to the internal structure of the commonwealth. The oath was an integral part of sixteenth-century civic life. In a largely illiterate society, it was the equivalent of the modern signature.[43] The Anabaptists argued that Christ had forbidden all swearing (Matt. 5:33–37), as had James the apostle (James 5:12). Therefore, the Christian could not take an oath. Bullinger denied this interpretation on the basis that Christ, also in the fifth chapter of Matthew, taught that He had not come to destroy but to fulfill the law (v. 17). Since none of Christ's teachings could annul the moral law, His teaching on the oath was identical with that of the Decalogue, which forbade the false or frivolous use of God's name. So Christ also forbade swearing or cursing in everyday, ordinary speech; but He did not forbid either the legal swearing of the oath or the oath given freely out of love for the neighbor. Only cursing was forbidden, for it was contrary to love and the law. James simply repeated the teaching of Christ, so the same interpretation had to be given to that passage. "The oath is useful and necessary for the political order."[44] It is notable that again the differences between Bullinger and the Anabaptists hinged on the interpretation of the Sermon on the Mount and thus on the relationship between the Old and New Testament, that is, on the unity of the covenant.

The purpose of the oath, Bullinger continued, was to ensure that a man actually would do what he promised to do. The prescribed form and outward ceremony of the oath were divinely ordained, firmly based in God's word (Jere. 4, 5; Exod. 23; Josh. 23). First, one should swear an oath only by the living God. Also, one should swear in truth, with no mental reservations, intending to honor the oath fully. Further, the oath should not be given lightly. Finally, nothing contrary to God's word should be sworn. Keeping these rules in mind, the oath was crucially important to the Christian commonwealth. Since it served to preserve all virtue in this world, "the oath is not only useful for all men and governments but also necessary." As with the Old Testament people of God, the oath was to be used to promise faith and subjection to God in the covenant and to bring the people under the true religion through reformation, as had happened under Josiah and other pious kings. Thus "the oath preserves and maintains us in one religion." Furthermore, it forced all who took office to do their sworn duty. In fact, it made firm all agreements. Also, the oath assured fairer and more just courts, settled all sorts of quarrels, and created peace among the citizenry.[45] In short, the oath was crucially important for church and commonwealth.

As Bullinger put it in a sermon in 1558, "By the oath we are bound in one body, both ecclesiastical and political, and preserved in tranquillity and peace. . . . Briefly, it is the bond of ecclesiastical and political government, the binding of covenants and contracts."[46] The oath was an instrument to ensure unity, the preservation of the truth and fairness. It was the glue that held together the Christian community and helped the people of God in keeping the covenant conditions. "The neighbor is protected, the truth is made manifest and innocence brought to the light. Therefore, to swear the oath cannot be wrong. For it has its basis in the two commandments in which all the law and the prophets are comprised."[47] Bullinger thus saw the Anabaptist denial of the oath, like all their errors, as springing from their misunderstanding of the Scripture and their consequent rejection of the eternal covenant. More specifically, their rejection of the oath impeded the magistrate in his enforcement of the covenant conditions among God's people. Therefore, at least implicitly, the Anabaptists encouraged disobedience to God and civil disorder, for even the faithful needed the oath to resist temptation. "Reasonable people, then, see what an intolerable, evil sect the Anabaptist sect is. For take away the oath from the government, and then see whether you will have not loosed the bond which holds together the entire body of the public welfare and of the legal government."[48] The commonwealth could not exist as a covenanted community, under God's laws, keeping the covenant condition of love, without the oath.

Bullinger was convinced that the entire complex of Anabaptist ideas, on the church, baptism, the magistracy, war, and the oath, was subversive and, if not in intent, at least in their practical social and political impact, revolutionary. Since the radicals proposed these ideas as the alternative to the existing religious, social, and political system, the threat was not imaginary,[49] although Bullinger probably inflated its gravity. However, because he did see the Anabaptists as an immediate danger, Bullinger, as a guardian of his society, turned every weapon in his arsenal, including the magisterial sovereignty in which he so fervently believed, against them.

In the end it all came down to the question of whether the Christian magistrate could coerce faith. Given Bullinger's theory of the commonwealth as a covenanted community and considering the age in which he lived, his answer almost had to be affirmative. However, lest it be thought that Bullinger argued for such compulsion only for the Anabaptists,[50] it should be noted that he made the same argument in terms of the Catholics in his defense of Queen Elizabeth against the papal bull *Regnans in excelsis* (1570). Like the Old Testament rulers, Elizabeth had the right and duty to curb false religion and superstition and to compel her own subjects to worship rightly. To argue conversely was to think like an Anabaptist: "Indeed, in the matter of compulsion to good or to faith and true religion, in times past the Donatist heretics, just as today the Anabaptists, taught such [as the Catholics], that no one ought to be compelled to faith or to good but that each must be allowed [to follow] his own conscience." It was, of course, best to bring men to the faith gently, but however it was done, the magistrate must bring the people into the ways of God. Thus magisterial punishment, even death, for violating God's laws and denying the true, evangelical faith was lawful and good.[51]

Bullinger's argument with regard to the Anabaptists themselves was similar, although somewhat more detailed. His affirmations of the legal use of magisterial police power in matters of faith spanned his entire career at Zurich. His most detailed treatment is in his *Ursprung*, his most acerbic in a letter to Tobias Egli (13 October 1570),[52] and his most effective in an opinion written for the Zurich council in 1535.[53] Bullinger's basic concern was for the unity of the faith in the commonwealth. He feared that toleration would lead to such diversity of error that the true faith might be obliterated. Since the evangelical pastors preached the true faith, based on the prophetic, gospel, and apostolic writings, they exhorted the magistracy to allow no other teaching. Those who taught another doctrine must be punished to avoid the infection of the entire community by the false religion.[54] There were two issues at stake: whether faith could be coerced and whether the magisterial police power extended to matters of faith.

The Anabaptists contended that since faith was a gift of God, no one could be forced to believe. Bullinger admitted that none could be forced to have faith in the heart, that such was a gift of God to His elect. On the other hand, no one should blame God for lack of faith, for the promise was universal. A person should pray for true faith and the increase of faith, hoping that he has been chosen by God. Thus, the reason for compelling attendance at worship was that all might hear the gospel, according to the Fourth Commandment. "Such a commandment of God, so far as it relates to faith and love, is not abolished." Everyone was part of the larger covenanted community and thus subject to the conditions of faith and love. What if the schoolmaster said to his students that since learning was of God's grace, he would use neither rod nor commandment? How would they learn? The fact that faith was a gift of God could not rule out the punishment of disobedient people. Piety, and the many commandments against an evil life, were also a gift of God. If someone should be brought before the magistrate for a crime and say, "I have not received the grace from God so you should not punish me, which magistrate would accept such an excuse? Therefore, even though faith is a free gift of God, men should nevertheless be restrained with commandments and compelled to the word of God, and the disobedient should be punished."[55]

Bullinger's point, then, was not that a person could be forced to believe, but that he could at least be compelled to hear God's word and that the magistrate could punish the disobedience resulting from a lack of faith. Even if such compulsion resulted in hypocrisy, as the Anabaptists claimed, it was still better to suppress the evil and disobedient ones, not allowing them to spread their evil throughout the community, than to let them destroy good laws and honest people. "We admit that God wants to have a willing servant and that coerced love is not of precious value. But one must, on the other hand, also confess . . . that heartfelt and voluntary [love] grows out of forced, unwilling [love]." In such a manner, then, the magistrate, using his police power, could elicit willing obedience to God's will as expressed in the covenant condition of love. Like the Old Testament kings, the pious magistrate must make sure that God's people heard the gospel and obeyed God's commandments. Therefore, if anyone introduced false teaching into the community, if anyone was disobedient, the magistrate's punishment was right and lawful. "That, then, strictly speaking is not called forcing to faith, but making unruly, disobedient, quarrelsome people peaceful and obedient. Thus unity, peace and quiet are maintained."[56] Although actual faith could not be coerced, civil obedience could be.

The second, closely connected issue was whether the magisterial police power ought to extend to capital punishment for religious offences. The Anabaptists, of course, thought not. Bullinger, however, answered affirmatively: "No one should be punished or killed because of the correct, true faith, but false and wrong faith should be restrained and, if possible, not allowed to appear. Blasphemers and shameful seducers in matters of the faith should be punished and can be killed." He then replied more specifically to the Anabaptist arguments. To their assertion that such punishment was contrary to love, Bullinger answered that it would make as much sense to say "that to punish and to kill the murderer and the blasphemer, the rebel and the evil doer would also be contrary to love and therefore no one can be punished any longer." Münster was a good example of misguided love, when the true faith had not been compelled and false teaching left unpunished. Since faith was a secret matter of the heart, the Anabaptists countered, how could it be controlled by the magisterial police power? Bullinger agreed that only God could be aware of secret false faith or heresy. "But if it bursts open and spreads like a cancer so that not only are many pious people poisoned and destroyed by it but also that God and His word are blasphemed and publicly mutilated, then a magistrate should and may well punish such an outward evil act. . . . Therefore, the magistrate must judge the unrepentant Anabaptists not merely for their unbelief in the heart but for public actions and blasphemous goings on." First they sinned with false faith, but then they compounded this sin with their proselytizing. Not only did they cause discord in the church by their separation, but they disobeyed the magistracy, even refusing to take the oath of obedience.[57] In Bullinger's mind, then, the magistrate should punish the Anabaptists for the outward, ecclesiastical and social-political manifestations of their false faith.

The Anabaptist argument based on the parable of the tares (Matt. 13) was no more convincing to Bullinger. If, as they contended, the tares signified false teaching and Christ had forbidden uprooting them, then every evil could grow unabated. But, Bullinger countered, that was not the meaning of the parable. Christ taught here that since the evil ones could never be completely eradicated in the church until the end of the world, no one should separate from the church because of them. He did not forbid punishment; rather He was concerned lest the good seed also be uprooted in the process. "Therefore, if there is no danger of a worse evil resulting from the punishment but a greater good can follow, why should the punishment not be allowed?" Although the church could not be pure until the last judgment, until that time the pastors with teaching and the rulers with punishment should build up the church, always taking care "that the good seed is not uprooted along with the tares."[58] Bullinger thus turned the parable of the tares against the Anabaptists, as he did with several other minor arguments.

There was no doubt in Bullinger's mind that punishment, even execution, of the Anabaptists was just. He could not view "faith" apart from the community. To him "coercion of faith" was not an attempt to force anyone to believe but a matter of polity and public policy. He accused the Anabaptists of striking out against "good civil administration [*policei*] and laws" in their teachings on the magistracy and the church.[59] For such subversion they must be punished like any other criminal. The judges, however, must take care not to become vengeful, but to act with moderation. They must distinguish among the people involved, some of whom were harmless, innocent people misled by false teaching, who could be won back to the faith. Of the leaders, some also were susceptible to argument and might be convinced of their error. But the obstinate ones, "as certain destroyers of the church, of religion and of all good government, should and must be removed, subdued or compelled in good time and with great severity, so that their corruption might not spread itself like a cancer and entangle, corrupt and destroy many pious people." The magistrates must further differentiate between mildly erroneous teachings and the serious heresies that threatened the Chrstian community. Finally, the punishment must fit the offense. The unrepentant blasphemers, the destroyers of the church and the subverters of government "can be subjected to corporal punishment." But harmless error must be punished differently: "There should and must be a moderation in all things." Harsh punishment was inappropriate for offenses that could be remedied with words or a milder corrective, such as a money fine or imprisonment.[60]

Bullinger was rather sensitive to the charge that such use of magisterial police power was tyrannical. Let it be understood, he retorted, "that we do not demand, like bloodthirsty bloodhounds, the blood of any innocent person with this legitimate teaching about punishment, but we propose that which pleases God, taken from His word, in conformity with all justice and equity, which is also useful and necessary for the church of Christ." It would be a terrible sin if the magistrate should punish the innocent, the good, and the righteous instead of the guilty, the evil, and the unrighteous. To execute good evangelical people under the name of Anabaptism, as if they were Anabaptists, would indeed be tyrannous. Therefore, the magistrate must take care, judging and punishing justly, in the fear of God, for he himself would be judged by Christ for any abuse of his office and power.[61] In Bullinger's mind, Zurich was no tyranny, but a Christian commonwealth ruled by a Christian magistracy according to God's will as expressed in the covenant conditions.

Bullinger had no doubts about the threat posed by the Anbaptists both to the existing social-political-ecclesiastical situation in Zurich and to his theory of the Christian commonwealth as a covenanted community. Their point of view on the magistracy and the church was diametrically opposed to Bullinger's, and he unerringly discovered the origins of their contraposition in their hermeneutic. Just as Bullinger's conception of Christian society was based on the unity of the covenant, so the Anabaptists, rejecting the Old Testament norms, built a competing view of society on the new covenant of Christ. Their entire complex of ideas, their exclusive view of the church, and their rejection of the Christian commonwealth resulted, in Bullinger's opinion, from their insistence that Christ made a new covenant.

In his *Epitome*, Bullinger likened Israel after the death of Samson (Judg. 17–21) to what would happen in his own society if the Anabaptists had their way. With no effective magistracy there had been anarchy, both civil and religious. These misfortunes in Israel proved that "those who wish to diminish the position of the kingdom or commonwealth according to the gospel standard" were wrong. Those who would deny the coercive power of the magistrate should note the sorry condition of Israel during this time, when neither true religion nor public justice was properly protected by the magistracy. It had been a time of infamy and disgrace for the people of God. Bullinger found the norms for Christian society in the Old Testament, not in the New. God's will for His people, that they live according to the covenant conditions in a Christian commonwealth under the sovereign Christian magistrate, had been carefully defined in the Old Testament. The Reformation had restored the covenant in Zurich just as Josiah or Hezekiah had restored God's people in the covenant. The commonwealth of Zurich had the same covenant relationship with God as Israel under Moses or Joshua. And like Israel under the judges, Zurich was a republic, a commonwealth, the form of government preferred by God himself.[62] The Christian commonwealth of Zurich was the new Israel.

The Anabaptist program for reorganizing church and society according to their understanding of the Sermon on the Mount and on the basis of their new covenant in Christ was thus unthinkable to Bullinger. The Anabaptist challenge raised visions of the overthrow and dissolution of the covenanted Christian commonwealth, the epitome of God's will for His people in society. Inasmuch as the Reformation was, for Bullinger, a renewal of the eternal covenant, the success of the Anabaptists would have signaled the failure of the Reformation.

Epilogue

BULLINGER'S WAS the other Reformed tradition. The core of this tradition was the covenant, and the issues on which Bullinger most clearly disagreed with the Calvinist Reformed tradition—predestination and the Christian community—were kindred to his covenant notion. The theological idea of the covenant, as expressed by Bullinger, paled as the sixteenth century wore on, even taking on the hues of heterodoxy late in the century.[1] In the seventeenth century, however, the covenant idea found new life in the face of the dull and cold Reformed scholasticism of the day, with its heavy Calvinistic emphasis on absolute double predestination. Although the covenant ideas of the seventeenth century were hardly identical with Bullinger's, the essential ingredients of these later covenant ideas were nevertheless inherent in Bullinger's earlier notion.

Whether Bullinger directly influenced the seventeenth-century covenant theorists is another problem. John Cameron's covenantal scheme, developed early in the seventeenth century (1608), appears to owe something to Ursinus[2] and thus to Bullinger indirectly. The covenant thought of Moïse Amyraut was dependent on Cameron[3] and thus inferentially on Bullinger. Johannes Cocceius' covenant theology of the midcentury (1648) undoubtedly was directly indebted to

165

Bullinger, although paradoxically to Olevianus as well.[4] In England, the idea of covenant, the "Zwingli-Bullinger-Tyndale tradition," found a revival in the seventeenth century in the thought of such men as John Preston, Richard Baxter, and Bishop Ussher, as the alternative to the Calvinist thinkers such as William Perkins, William Ames, and John Bunyan, who held to a theology of testament, although under the rubric of double covenant.[5] Bullinger's influence is indisputable in this English covenant tradition. Moreover, it was precisely these men, especially Preston, who were the fount of New England covenant thought.[6] And it was the New England Puritans who, like Bullinger, made the covenant the basis for Christian society. The social covenant was based on the religious covenant; political society thus existed within the framework of the covenant. This was as true for New England as it had been with Israel.[7] The "new" covenant ideas of the seventeenth century were thus clearly not a further development of Calvinism. Rather they were part of the other Reformed tradition which must be traced back to Zurich, particularly to the thought of Bullinger.

Bullinger was also the source for the development of the alternative approach toward the Christian community, with his theory of magisterial sovereignty. An idea of Christian community was not in itself unusual. The climate of opinion of the late Middle Ages and the sixteenth century favored such a conception of society. It was the additional elements of covenant and magisterial sovereignty that made Bullinger's theory unusual, different from the thought of any other major reformer.

Bullinger was undoubtedly influenced by Zwingli on the matter of magisterial sovereignty. During the 1520s, Zwingli developed a theory of magisterial sovereignty based on an Augustinian dualism and reflecting the late medieval Zurich tradition of republicanism and corporate unity.[8] Zwingli expressed his theory most clearly in a letter of 4 May 1528 to Ambrosius Blarer.[9] Blarer was inclined to accept Luther's dictum that the kingdom of Christ was internal, which meant that the magistracy could not involve itself in church affairs.[10] Opposing this view, Zwingli argued from the New Testament that "elders," as at the Council of Jerusalem, were the equivalent of councilmen or senators, civil magistrates. Therefore, the councils at Bern, Zurich, or Constance also represented the consensus of the church of those cities. Furthermore, Paul's teaching about the magistrate in Romans 13 meant that even impious magistrates must be obeyed. Surely, Zwingli argued, the Christian magistrate was worthy of greater, fuller obedience than a pagan. Zwingli also appealed to the Old Testament. Even though the entire law, ceremonial, judicial, and moral, had been abolished by Christ and the Love Commandment had been substituted for it, the Old Testament kings David, Josiah, and Hezekiah were nevertheless better examples to follow than pagan kings. Love bound Christians to follow their example, "provided that religion, circumstances and peace require it."[11] Zwingli did, then, identify the church and the civil community, the Christian and the citizen,[12] as well as affirming magisterial sovereignty within that civil-ecclesiastical community.[13]

Even though Zwingli anticipated many of the basic elements of Bullinger's theory, his conception of the Christian state was not identical with Bullinger's. Neither his hermeneutical nor his historical basis was the same. Although Zwingli did affirm the unity of the covenant, he did not connect this theological idea with his view of the Christian community and the Christian magistracy. Bullinger saw a much clearer unity and a direct continuity of the Old and New Testament people and commonwealths, with the covenant and its conditions, the moral law, as the historical link. There can be no doubt that Bullinger owed a heavy debt to Zwingli in formulating his theory, but his definition of the Christian community and his affirmation of magisterial sovereignty was much more deeply rooted in the Old Testament than was Zwingli's. Zwingli originated the concept. Bullinger fleshed out the idea of magisterial sovereignty within the Christian community and constructed a substantial theory on the basis of the unifying historical theme of the covenant. For Zwingli the unity of the covenant remained a purely theological idea; it did not become the basis for his social-political thought.[14]

Luther, of all the "magisterial" reformers, was least inclined to think in terms of the Christian community and magisterial sovereignty. While he found no practical alternative to a princely, territorial church, this was not the ideal relationship between the church and civil government. Luther did not conceive of two separate spheres in the modern sense, but neither were his two regiments identical. The two might cooperate, but they were still distinguishable, each competent only within its respective sphere. The civil government had authority over the body and material things, but not over the spiritual realm. Although the magistrate might become a *Notbischof* in an emergency, ordinarily he had no more authority in the church than other Christians. Nor did Luther identify the citizen with the Christian; the community and the church were not identical. The Christian commonwealth was not Luther's ideal.[15]

Bucer came closer to the viewpoint of Bullinger and Zwingli. He did share the idea of the Christian state but held back from advocating the sovereignty of the magistracy within that community. Bucer conceived of a close cooperation between church and civil power but agreed with Oecolampadius that church discipline should be given over completely to the community, to some sort of a consistory. All these ideas came together in midcentury in his *De regno Christi*, where he advocated a Christian commonwealth in which the ecclesiastical and civil authorities together would make the rule of Christ a social reality.[16]

Calvin not only conceived of a Christian state but also fashioned one in Geneva. Like Bucer, he distinguished between the ecclesiastical and civil spheres. Spiritual matters, including discipline and excommunication, were church matters. The two spheres operated separately yet cooperatively to form the Christian commonwealth.[17] Despite the fact that both Bucer and Calvin identified the citizen with the Christian in society and both had a theory of the Christian community, neither of them advocated magisterial sovereignty within the commonwealth; instead, like Oecolampadius, they gave the church the power of excommunication. They thus steered a middle course between the Zurich theory and practice and the radical insistence on a separated church and congregational discipline.[18]

Territorial churches, of course, sprang up almost wherever Protestantism was successful. In both the Lutheran and the Reformed territories and cities, the community and the church were seen as one entity, practically if not in theory, and with the notable exception of Geneva, magisterial sovereignty was a nearly universal reality up until midcentury.[19] Of the earlier reformers, however, only Bullinger and Zwingli developed theories of magisterial sovereignty that supported this reality. Like Zwingli's, Bullinger's own concept was based in late medieval corporatism and antipapal thought; but unlike Zwingli's, Bullinger's theory had the historical substructure of the covenant.

This distinction between Zwingli and Bullinger has already been suggested by Staedtke, who, referring to their approaches to the covenant, remarks that Zwingli argued systematically, while Bullinger saw the covenant in terms of the history of salvation.[20] To be sure, the covenant was the umbrella under which Bullinger gathered the history of salvation. It gave unity to God's redemptive activity from Adam on, thus tying together the faith from one age to another and giving continuity to the historical church. But his covenant concept had a much broader historical application than this. The covenant also defined the people of God. The history of the covenant was the history of God's people on earth, and the covenant became Bullinger's vehicle not only for the history of salvation and of the faith but also for the history of the covenanted Christian commonwealth, along with the divinely ordained structure for this community. Therefore, since the Reformation was a renewal of the covenant, it was necessary also to renew the proper institutions within the covenanted community, including a sovereign magistracy, and to follow the norm established by God among His people in the Old Testament in doing so. The social and political standards for the sixteenth century were to be found in the source, the record of the covenant in the Old Testament.

As the history of salvation and of the faith, Bullinger's covenant idea was marked by some development. God's people in the New Testament knew Christ more directly, they had been freed from the ceremonies, and the Gentiles were included. But in terms of the history of the covenanted Christian community it was a much more static concept. Bullinger's social-political stance was essentially conservative. He used the past to support and vindicate the institutions of his own society. Reading history backwards, the present formed the past, and put the stamp of divine approval on contemporary society. This was Bullinger's own "Whig interpretation" of the history of God's people.

The covenant gave Bullinger's theory of the Christian commonwealth its distinctive flavor, but it was not the only definitive factor. The element of community also reflected the common late medieval corporate emphasis, a localized version of the idea of *corpus Christianum*, as seen in Moeller's instructive study of the Reformation in the imperial cities. Emphasizing the corporate character of these cities, Moeller sees the blurring of the borders between civil and spiritual life. He refers to such a community as a "sacral society" or as a "*corpus Christianum* on a small scale."[21] All elements of this society, including the clergy, had to submit to the municipal jurisdiction, the government taking over many ecclesiastical and spiritual functions. This communalism went so far as to identify earthly welfare and eternal salvation; that is, the citizen's salvation was closely bound together with his civic life.[22] Within this context the ambiguities created by Bullinger's combination of single predestination with conditional covenant can be clarified. Since the entire community was put under the covenant conditions by baptism, salvation became a community responsibility. Single predestination tied together with a conditional covenant is more understandable within such a corporate society. All were included in the community by baptism. Some, refusing to believe, opted out of the spiritual promise, but they could never renounce the covenant responsibility of love within the community. Even without faith they were still members of the corporate society. Within this context a certain amount of coercion in religious matters made sense. Even though faith in the heart was a gift of God, the individual's spiritual welfare was nevertheless a community responsibility.

No doubt Bullinger was influenced by this late medieval corporatism, especially by its institutionalization in Zurich. The civil government in Zurich had been imposing its will and authority over the church and the clergy for decades prior to the Reformation. By the early 1520s, the only missing ingredient was Zwingli.[23] Zwingli developed his theory of magisterial sovereignty during the same time that the magistrates were exercising such authority in implementing the reform measures. So when Bullinger succeeded Zwingli, he not only had a personal theory of the Christian commonwealth, but he also stepped into an actual situation in which corporatism had long been a reality and where magisterial sovereignty was a recent development. Bullinger was tailor-made for the task of leading the Zurich church, because the actual situation in Zurich rather neatly corresponded with his own conception of the ideal Christian community.

The influence of this late medieval communal ideal, generally obscured by Bullinger's heavy use of Old Testament authority, comes through clearly in his last will and testament. He exhorted the magistrates to pray for the wisdom to rule well, according to God's will; then God would allow "a pious community" to be committed to their care "as fathers of the people." For, Bullinger reminded them, "You, my lords, the councillors and the guildmasters from the Constaffel and from the guilds together with the members of the great council, are a single head of the united body, the community."[24] Bullinger obviously shared the corporate ideal with Zwingli and other contemporaries. The difference in Bullinger's theory of Christian society lay in the ubiquity of the covenant that gave the theory a distinctive theological framework. The covenant both sanctified the Christian community and placed it within the historical context of God's will.

Bullinger was also influenced by late medieval antipapal thought, especially by Marsilius of Padua, whom he knew and cited as early as 1538.[25] Marsilius identified the *universitas fidelius* with the *universitas civium*. The church and the civil community were one and the same, under the authority of the human legislator, the civil government. The priesthood had no secular or coercive authority, and it was subject to the civil government in all temporal affairs and ultimately even in spiritual matters.[26] Marsilius' identification of the church with the civil community and his insistence that only the civil government had public power was quite similar to Bullinger's conception of the Christian community under the sovereign Christian magistrate. Bullinger's thought approximated Marsilius' in another significant manner. Although Marsilius' theory was based on popular sovereignty or republicanism, the effect was absolutist, for Marsilius postulated an undivided sovereignty for the human legislator without stipulating limits on that sovereignty. The people was the source of power for Marsilius, but he placed no limits on the extent of power.[27] Although Bullinger did not discuss popular sovereignty, the source of power being divine, he did praise republicanism as the most felicitous form of government. This approbation of republicanism could not, however, work out its own logic in Bullinger's thought because of his theory of sovereignty; any hint of popular sovereignty was smothered by his conception of magisterial sovereignty.

Bullinger was not a political theorist, but his theological idea of the covenant cloaked a radical theory of magisterial sovereignty; when stripped of its theological terminology, it sounds much like the concept of indivisible sovereignty in the thought of such men as Erastus and Bodin. In the last few pages of his never published "Tractatus de excommunicatione" of 1568, Bullinger made some notes from a manuscript Erastus had sent him; one telling paragraph outlines Erastus' concept of sovereignty.

> There is a single, highest governor which we designate by one name, the magistracy, whether he is one in number who possesses the authority or many govern the commonwealth together. When he alone cannot attend to every function and entrusts some functions to be ruled by others, the many nevertheless do not become the magistracy. For all the highest men manage the entrusted office in his name. As it is monstrous to form a two-headed body, so it is an unnatural commonwealth which is ruled in such a manner that there are separate magistracies in it. . . . In sum, there is one, single magistracy in the Christian commonwealth to whom God has entrusted the external government of all things, whether they pertain to the civil or to the pious and Christian life. The right and authority of ruling and administering justice is not granted to the ministers or to any others.[28]

Although the terminology is more precisely legal and political than that which Bullinger might have used, these words could easily have come from his pen. Erastus' position on indivisible sovereignty was essentially a restatement of Bullinger's own theory of magisterial sovereignty.[29] In one sense Bullinger's viewpoint was medieval, in that it was firmly based in Christianity and advocated a Christian community. But if Erastus anticipated the concept of undivided sovereignty generally ascribed to Bodin,[30] Bullinger must be given his place in this line of development. At the least, his theory tended to sanctify the supremacy of political authority, providing a religious justification for the further growth of lay power, already far advanced by the middle sixteenth century.

Indeed, Bullinger's own theory did not differ significantly from Bodin's early theory, as expressed in his *Methodus ad facilem historiarum cognitionem* of 1566.[31] Bodin did not include the element of absolutism in his early theory, but he did clearly express the idea of the supreme authority of the civil government within a state, whether that state was a monarchy or a republic. In the latter case, the senate would be sovereign. In any case, true sovereignty was indivisible. Finally, sovereignty was limited by law, i.e., the ruler had a legal obligation to rule according to accepted law.[32]

The parallels with Bullinger's theory are striking, except that the limits that Bullinger placed on magisterial sovereignty were less clear and perhaps more difficult to apply. The only real limits in Bullinger's theory were imposed by God. The pastor could play the prophet, he could exhort and threaten God's punishment, but retribution and correction could only come from God. There were no legal limits, except those imposed by God's law. But even on this matter of limits to sovereignty, the difference between Bodin and Bullinger is more apparent than real. Like Bullinger's divine limits to power, Bodin's legal limitation was impotent if the sovereign wished to ignore it. Because both men defined sovereignty as indivisible, there could be no effective limits, whether legal or divine.

The problem was that limited sovereignty was congenial only with divided or popular sovereignty. Bodin discovered this in the 1570s with the development of French resistance theory by the Huguenots. His answer to the problem, *Les six livres de la république* of 1583, was an argument for royal absolutism. For Bodin, sovereignty was now both indivisible and absolute. Resistance could never be legitimate, since the sovereign was not limited in his exercise of power.[33]

This is not to say that Bullinger ever developed an actual theory of absolutism. He did face a problem similar to Bodin's, but his solution was not nearly so neat and lucid. Bullinger did not allow his idea of "limited" sovereignty to express itself clearly in his thought. Although he never completely denied the possibility of resistance,[34] neither did he develop a theory of the right of resistance.[35] There was thus an inconsistency, some might say a contradiction, in his thought. While he praised republicanism and spoke of divine limits to power, his theory of undivided magisterial sovereignty tended to reinforce authoritarianism. His constant use of the pious Old Testament kings as models for the Christian magistracy canceled out his enthusiasm for republicanism under the judges. He did not reconcile these competing models; he never dealt with the inherent inconsistency between an indivisible and limited sovereignty. His emphasis, however, was focused on the idea of indivisible magisterial sovereignty, which when fused with the concept of a covenanted community had a definite authoritarian tone. He placed great confidence in the Christian magistrate, who by means of social controls kept the community in its covenant relationship with God and at the same time assured social order.

For Bullinger, then, there were no practical limits to the sovereignty of the magistracy. Furthermore, his idea of magisterial sovereignty determined that his covenant concept would operate within a context where the magistracy had complete authority in both civil and religious life. The Puritans in Massachusetts used their social covenant in much the same way, as an instrument of social and political control. There was an emphasis here on man's obligations within society. But others drew different political implications, revolutionary and liberal implications, from the covenant idea. Here the ruler's obligations were emphasized. Whether or not Bullinger directly influenced the Puritans, there is some likelihood that his covenant idea had some general effect on the author of the *Vindiciae contra tyrannos* (1579), probably Philippe Duplessis-Mornay.[36]

Mornay's idea of the covenant was very similar to Bullinger's. But because Mornay's political thought was structured around popular sovereignty, the political implications he drew from the covenant were quite different and much more radical than Bullinger's. Mornay explained that at the coronation of kings in the Old Testament there was a twofold covenant: the first was "between God, the king and the people that the people will be God's people; the second, between the king and the people that if he is a proper ruler, he will be obeyed accordingly."[37] The first question, whether subjects must obey rulers whose orders contradicted God's law, was concerned with the first covenant. Mornay used the Old Testament examples of Joash and Jehoiada, as kings who kept the stipulations of God's covenant, whom God blessed, and Saul, who broke the covenant and lost his kingdom. Moving on to Christian kings, Mornay affirmed the unity of this covenant: "Just as the Gospels succeeded to the Law, Christian rulers have replaced the Jewish kings. The covenant remains the same; the stipulations are unaltered; and there are the same penalties if these are not fulfilled. . . ."[38] The conditions, or stipulations, of the covenant were found in the two tables of the Decalogue, the love of God and the neighbor. Mornay's answer to his first question was negative: rulers who flagrantly violated God's law or covenant and ordered their subjects to do the same must not be obeyed. Obedience to God took precedence over Paul's and Peter's exhortations to obey magistrates.[39]

The second question, whether such a ruler who violated God's law could be actively resisted, also involved this first covenant between

God, the king, and the people. This covenant was made with the people as a whole in order to entrust the church to the entire community rather than to one individual. The king and the people as a whole promised and obligated themselves, a corporate body acting as one individual. Thus the king was responsible to see that the people kept the covenant, and the people was obligated to ensure that the king did likewise. Based on this doctrine of popular sovereignty, Mornay affirmed the duty of resistance by lesser magistrates in the case of a ruler who broke the covenant and defied God's law. Such resistance was lawful for the entire kingdom or any part of it. Although private individuals did not have the obligation to resist, they also participated individually in the covenant by virtue of baptism and thus could, if truly led by God, forcibly resist.[40] Concluding his treatment of the second question, Mornay asserted: "We have shown that the people as a whole, or the officers of the kingdom whom the people have established, or the majority of these, or any one of them, very gravely sin against the covenant with God if they do not use force against a king who corrupts God's law or prevents its restoration, in order to confine him to his proper bounds."[41] Resistance for religious reasons thus rested on the first covenant.

Mornay's third question, concerning resistance for secular reasons, involved the second covenant, between the king and the people. Here popular sovereignty was decisive: "For God willed that every bit of authority held by kings should come from the people after Him, so that kings would concentrate all their care, energy and thought upon the people's interests."[42] The people had confirmed Saul, David, and Solomon as kings. The election of kings had been the custom in early France. Therefore the people as a whole, as represented by lesser magistrates, was greater than the king. Kings were established by the people as guardians of justice and law. In short, the king was not above the law.[43] In the second covenant, the political covenant, the king promised to rule according to justice and law. This was an absolute promise. The people promised to obey as long as the king ruled justly. Their promise was thus conditional. The two covenants, however, the religious and political, cannot be seen as distinct and separate. In the case of Josiah, he promised to observe the precepts and commandments in the Book of the Covenant, i.e., "the precepts of religion and justice." Mornay saw the two covenants in tandem: "By the first covenant, or compact, religious piety becomes an obligation; by the second, justice. In the first the king promises to obey God religiously, in the second, to rule the people justly; in the former, to maintain God's glory, in the latter, to preserve the people's welfare."[44] All government rested on such a compact, either explicit or implied. A tyrant, one who ruled contrary to justice and equity, must be resisted. Since the transfer of authority from the people to the ruler was conditional, the lesser magistrates or notables of the kingdom had the obligation to resist the ruler who broke the compact.[45]

Bullinger's covenant idea is found *in toto* in Mornay's covenant scheme. Mornay clearly belongs in the covenantal Reformed tradition, even though his political use of the covenant was so different from Bullinger's. Bullinger's theory of indivisible magisterial sovereignty made the covenant into an instrument of social and political control. Mornay's resistance theory, on the other hand, presupposed a truly limited magistracy. His was a theory of popular sovereignty. Another difference between the two men was that Bullinger did not posit a second, political covenant; his was a single covenant. But he applied the one covenant to both religious and civil life; the conditions of the covenant related both to matters of faith and to public policy and justice within the community. Thus, even though Bullinger did not refer to a purely political covenant, the political implications of the covenant were inherent in what might be called his political theology. The difference between the two men was that Bullinger, consistent with his idea of indivisible sovereignty, used the covenant to assure obedience to the magistracy, while Mornay, building on a concept of popular sovereignty, used the covenant to construct a resistance theory.

One further political influence of the notion of bilateral covenant can be found in seventeenth-century England. The *Vindiciae contra tyrannos* went through several Latin and English editions in England from 1581 to 1689.[46] Locke himself was undoubtedly familiar with the *Vindiciae*,[47] and the idea of the covenant was clearly an important element in the development of social contract theory.[48] Although the specific connections between the theological concept of the covenant and social contract theory are a subject for another study, the general debt of later thinkers such as Locke to the bilateral covenant idea seems indisputable.

The first, the covenantal, Reformed tradition thus had a varied and diverse history after Bullinger's death. It proved to be remarkably vital by influencing not only Reformed theology but also political theories in the late sixteenth and seventeenth centuries. It was the other Reformed tradition, and its genesis must be located in the thought of Heinrich Bullinger.

Appendixes

APPENDIX A

Covenant and Testament
in the Early Reformation

THE ZURICH covenant notion found its earliest configuration in Zwingli's "Reply to Hubmaier" of November 5, 1925 and its full form in Bullinger's "Answer to Burchard" of late 1526 or early 1527. The covenant idea as expressed by Bullinger, the bilateral approach within the confines of *sola fide* and *sola gratia*, was quite unusual in Christian thought; in fact, there were no progenitors of Bullinger's concept of the covenant prior to the Reformation, save perhaps Irenaeus. However, several early Reformation figures—Luther, Melanchthon, Oecolampadius, Cellarius, Capito, and Bucer—have been suggested as possible predecessors. But a closer scrutiny of their thought, using the distinction between bilateral covenant and unilateral testament, will demonstrate that such was not the case. Most of these men had no concept of covenant at all, but rather a theology of testament, and those who did come to a covenant idea did so after the origins of that idea in Zurich.

Oberman, declaring that the Reformation idea of covenant did not appear *ex nihilo*, suggests that the young Luther had a covenant notion that he had developed from the nominalist "pact." Oberman cautions that Luther was not a covenant theologian, because the covenant was not the key to his theology. He differed from Bullinger, Oberman explains, insofar as the covenant for Bullinger was the target of both the Old and New Testament. The more crucial distinction between Luther and Bullinger, however, was the difference between testament and covenant. Discussing Luther's first lectures on the

181

Psalms (1513–1515), Oberman himself points out that Luther, although rejecting the nominalist "pact," began to develop his own concept, clearly differentiating between the old and new covenant, the old and new law. The old covenant was a bilateral covenant of works. The new covenant was unilateral, resting solely on God's mercy. In this new covenant, God bound himself not to the "workers" but to the "believers."[1] The nominalist "pact," then, was relegated to the old covenant of works. Luther's new covenant of faith was the incipience of his theology of testament, which had Augustinian, not nominalist, roots.[2]

Hagen, in his study of Luther's lectures on Hebrews (1517–1518), judges that for the young Luther "only one Word comes forth from God." That one word was called testament, promise, law, or gospel. Thus, Luther saw old and new testament men both before and after Christ, depending on how each received God's Word: to receive the testament of God as letter was to be an old testament person; to receive it as spirit was to be a new testament person. This Augustinian understanding of testament bypassed the hermeneutical problem of the relationship between the Old and New Testaments. It was a soteriological understanding; the new testament was the eternal promise of God.[3] Essentially this was Luther's later distinction between law and gospel, as Bornkamm argues so persuasively.[4] Elsewhere, Hagen summarizes the further development of Luther's theology of testament in the 1520s. He began to see the sacraments in terms of testament: baptism was a "covenant" in which God promised salvation; the eucharist became a testament. Finally, he made it quite clear that the testament was a unilateral gift to God.[5]

Bornkamm demonstrates that Luther also affirmed the unity of the testament—i.e., the "new covenant" had existed with Adam and was eternal. The "old covenant" began with Moses and ended when Christ fulfilled the "new covenant." Thus the church began with Adam, and continued without interruption throughout the Old Testament era. The people of God in the Old Testament period were Christians, that is, they appropriated the promise through faith.[6] Luther's assertion of the unity of the testament troubles Cottrell; for, if Cottrell is correct that Zwingli held to a "covenant of grace" only, a unilateral testament, there is little to choose between Zwingli and Luther. But, he infers, Zwingli still preceded Luther in his understanding of the unity of the testament, because Bornkamm's documentation is nearly all post–1530.[7] Hagen, however, cites Luther's "Lectures on Deuteronomy" of 1525, where Luther stated that the eternal new testament was promised from the beginning of the world.[8]

Luther, then, postulated an eternal testament beginning with Adam, a "Christian" church from the beginning of the world. From Moses until Christ this new testament existed side by side with the old testament of the law. Then Christ fulfilled the new testament and abolished the old. The Old Testament

Scripture contained the promise of the new testament, in the sacramental signs, in the prophecies, and in the figures. The new testament was a testament of faith and grace, the old one, of law and works. So Luther, breaking completely from the semi-pelagian nominalist "pact," transmitted the Augustinian understanding of unilateral testament into the sixteenth century. In Zurich, unilateral testament evolved into bilateral covenant, and as the Reformation progressed, both testament and covenant became more distinctively Reformed than Lutheran.

Melanchthon, however, has been seen by some modern scholars as an influence on the early development of covenant theology.[9] He did appropriate and elaborate upon Luther's theology of testament in the first edition of his *Loci communes* (1521). Like Luther he asserted that both law and gospel were found in both the Old and New Testament. The gospel was first given to Adam (Gen. 3:15)—Adam, in fact, was justified by faith, as were all who had faith in the promise during the Old Testament era.[10] Melanchthon paralleled this soteriological unity with a "hermeneutical divide" between the Old and New Testament.[11] The Old Testament contained material promises conditioned by the law. On the other hand, "In the New Testament good things are promised unconditionally, since nothing is demanded of us in return." The law, including the Decalogue, was totally abrogated in the New Testament. Having quoted Jeremiah 31:31–34, Melanchthon explained, "In this passage the prophet mentions a twofold covenant, the old and the new; the old, justification by the law, he says, has been made void." He thus turned again to soteriology in terms of law and gospel or old and new covenant. He asserted that the demand of the law was removed by the gospel; the freedom of the gospel, or the new covenant, was that those who believed would spontaneously desire what the law demanded. "In this way the fathers who had the Spirit of Christ were also free even before his incarnation." They were justified by faith. Thus the law was abrogated, but "only in the case of those who have believed in the later covenant, namely the gospel." Those who had faith, then, including the Old Testament saints, were free from the law because the Spirit fulfilled the law for them.[12] Melanchthon's argument was thus both soteriological and hermeneutical. Hermeneutically the difference between Old and New Testament depended on the historical and temporal incarnation of Christ. First, the Old Testament was basically law, the New, essentially gospel. Secondly, the Old Testament promised Christ, the New revealed Him. Finally, the Old Testament was not really a testament "because the Testator did not die. In the New Testament the Testator died."[13] Soteriologically, the difference between the old and new testament cut through time; both existed from Adam. Melanchthon, then, affimed the unity of the testament as early as 1521; but there was no hint of a mutual or bilateral covenant.

Melanchthon altered his position on the moral law in the second edition of his *Loci* (1535). The moral law was eternal divine law that pertained to all people. Equivalent to the law of nature, it was summarized in the Decalogue. The moral law was never abrogated because it summarized the wisdom of God. Thus it was reiterated in the gospels; it told men how to live.[14] This accent on the moral law meant a greater emphasis on sanctification, on becoming holy in this life, for the man of faith. As he so succinctly put it in his 1559 German translation of the *Loci*: "We are free from it [the moral law] with respect to justification and condemnation but not with respect to obedience."[15] It also resulted in the breaking down of that hermeneutical divide: there were, to be sure, still differences between the Old and New Testament, but the moral law tended to tie them more closely together. Finally, there was a hint that God imposed conditions on man even in the New Testament, although Melanchthon did not connect this directly to the testament or covenant.[16]

Later in his life, however, Melanchthon did tie the condition of faith together with an idea of covenant. Commenting on Malachai in 1553, he asserted:

> The old testament is the old covenant by which God obligates himself to give a certain abode and commonwealth to the people, among whom, however, He wishes to gather an eternal church; and in turn He obligates this commonwealth to obedience of the law and the preservation of the doctrine and of the promise in its political constitution. The new testament is the promise of the new and eternal justice and life because of the dying Son, in which God obligates himself to give us remission of sins and reconciliation, justice and eternal life, and in turn obligates us to believe in the promise, which is gratuitous, that is, it is given only because of the Son, not because of the law.[17]

The mutual nature of the new testament is stated even more clearly in Melanchthon's "Ordination Examination" of 1559. In the section on infant baptism he explained that baptism was not only a covenant between God and infants but also between God and all adults who had faith. By faith one renewed the covenant of baptism; through faith one possessed the promise of grace and the inheritance of eternal life. The man of faith knew that "a mutual covenant was made between God and the baptized." God, because of Christ, accepted the sinner, forgave his sins, and sanctified him to eternal life. In turn (*vicissim*) man must recognize God as the true God through faith in Christ. "Thus the stipulation of a good conscience and the mutual obligation of God and the baptized man is made" in baptism, which Christ ratified and made efficacious. "The same stipulation and mutual obligation is confirmed for those who turn to God, because they are wholly reinstated in possession of the promise of grace and the inheritance of eternal life."[18] Thus the stipulation connected with baptism was fulfilled through faith that resulted in a good conscience. Or baptism itself was a stipulation in the sense that it asked the question whether one wished to believe in Christ. The affirmative answer fulfilled the obligation of the new covenant.[19]

For Melanchthon, then, faith was the stipulation of the covenant. But was this a true condition, or did God fulfill it for man? Discussing human will, Melanchthon stated that Adam was created with a perfect, free will that was greatly weakened by original sin. After the fall man lacked the power to keep God's law, to become righteous; he could not begin "inward obedience" without God's help. On the other hand, man was not a passive recipient of God's grace. God gave aid to those who were willing, "who feel in their hearts a small spark and longing to be in the grace of God again; they should know that God both made the beginning in them and will further strengthen them, but they should at the same time exercise the faith they have and pray."[20] Thus the stipulation of faith was closely connected with obedience to the moral law, from which believers were not exempt.[21] Man's will was active, then, but he could not keep God's law, that is, have inward obedience, without grace, without God's aid. Still, God's commandments were possible to keep, both external works and inward obedience, with the help of Christ.[22] Melanchthon's locus on predestination further clarifies his position. He did not proceed in terms of divine decrees; rather, he cautioned that only the Scripture must be followed. All were elect, he asserted, who had faith. Those who had eternal salvation by grace through faith were thus "also predestined to eternal blessedness." The promise was offered to all men, thus "we should include ourselves in the *all*, and should reflect that the greatest sin is not willing to believe in the Lord Christ, and not willing to receive His grace." It was a universal promise. On the other hand, only those who were called were "to be numbered among the predestined, that is, among those who listen to and learn God's word."[23]

So Melanchthon presented a balanced, carefully stated doctrine of predestination. The promise of grace was universal. Although aided by God's grace, the human will was not passive but active in the matter of salvation. Man was responsible in a real sense for his faith or lack of faith; salvation was by God's grace, but man had to cooperate, at least in desiring grace. Related to this "synergism" was his insistence on the necessity of good works as an evidence of salvation, the emphasis on the Christian's obligation of inward obedience to the moral law. Melanchthon's stipulation of the covenant was not so different from Bullinger's conditions of faith and piety. But Melanchthon also differed from Bullinger in that he continued to structure his thought around the dichotomy between law and gospel, between old covenant and new covenant, his new testament simply becoming the new covenant with mutual overtones. If Melanchthon's "synergism" allowed him to develop an idea of covenant, the generally stronger predestinarian ideas among Reformed thinkers impeded the development of a bilateral idea and generally resulted in a theology of testament.

Oecolampadius (d. 1531), in Basel, was utilizing a notion of covenant or testament in his commentaries during the 1520s. Trinterud asserts that this was a contractual concept, and he implies that Oecolampadius was the progenitor of Rhineland covenant theology, preceding both Zwingli and Bullinger.[24] Moreover, Oecolampadius was the only contemporary author whom Bullinger cited in *De testamento* in support of the unity of the covenant. He quoted from Oecolampadius' commentary on Jeremiah, which had only been published in 1533, under the editorship of Capito.

> Before God that eternal covenant, which is arranged differently according to the diversity of the times, is one. And also in relation to the inward things of man it always has been and always will remain one, not only as it is in eternal predestination. . . . Notice, however, the great diversity of the covenants. The Lord made a pact with Abraham with words and demanded nothing except obedience from him. But under Moses many strange and dreadful things were added, things known not only to the one leader but evident things to the entire multitude. Then it was fortified with so many adjective legalities, all of which return to those ten words of the tablet of the covenant.[25]

Nevertheless, even though Bullinger quoted Oecolampadius in support of his idea of covenant unity, both the emphasis and implications differed from Bullinger's covenant notion. The passage from Oecolampadius was his interpretation of Jeremiah 31:31–34, Jeremiah's prophecy of a new covenant between God and His people. And Oecolampadius did emphasize the eternity and unity of this new covenant, which concerned only the inner man. As he explained, "We discovered a two-fold covenant, old and new, carnal and spiritual, external and internal, perfect and imperfect." This two-covenant scheme colored his entire approach. The old covenant, given by Moses, was imperfect and carnal; it concerned the outer man, demanding obedience by the compulsion of written laws. The new covenant was a covenant of faith, promising inward spiritual things that were given by the Spirit. The law was carnal in the old covenant, spiritual in the new. Both covenants had existed since Adam; but the new covenant was not fully revealed or perfected until Chrst.[26]

All this precedes the passage quoted by Bullinger. The portion deleted by Bullinger further clarifies the difference between the covenants. The differences lay not only in terminology but also in substance. In fact, the old covenant was invalidated because the people did not keep it. So, Oecolampadius asserted, "the covenant of Abraham, the covenant of Moses, the covenant of Christ are quite different in essence." Furthermore, God promised "an entirely new" covenant through Jeremiah, "and yet the same is ancient and eternal." Then, following the passage quoted by Bullinger, Oecolampadius explained that the new covenant was not new in the sense of time, but because it had been clarified, established and perfected by Christ. All the elect, all people of faith from the beginning of the world participated in the new covenant. It was the new spiritual law written in the heart by God.[27]

According to the Jeremiah commentary, then, Oecolampadius posited an old and a new covenant, carnal and spiritual, respectively, corresponding to law and gospel. The new covenant applied only to believers, to the elect, and thus his covenant idea takes on the characteristics of unilateral testament, an Augustinian idea of testament not unlike Luther's. He did refer to the conditions of the covenant, which were equivalent to the new spiritual law written in the heart,[28] but nowhere did he clearly state the bilateral nature of a covenant. The new covenant contained the promise of its fulfillment by the Spirit.

The Jeremiah commentary, published in 1533, was compiled from Oecolampadius' sermons on Jeremiah from 1527 and edited by Wolfgang Capito. Ernst Staehelin does not consider it an authentic work of Oecolampadius, stating that Capito edited too freely, adding too much of his own.[29] Trinterud's source for his assertion about the contractual nature of Oecolampadius' covenant idea was an earlier work, Oecolampadius' Isaiah commentary, compiled from lectures given at the university in 1523 and 1524 and published in 1525.[30] There is much material on the covenant in the Isaiah commentary, but it does not significantly differ from the point of view in the Jeremiah commentary.

Trinterud asserts that Oecolampadius, in the Isaiah commentary, held to the "view that the eternal covenant of God with man was the law of love. This law was written on man's heart at creation, and was only expounded by the written law of the Bible. To be blessed of God man must keep this covenant by obeying the law. Here the entire law-contract structure is seen." In response to this, Cottrell says, "this interpretation does not seem warranted by the text nor by the commentary as a whole."[31] Indeed, the text cited, but not quoted, by Trinterud contains not a hint of a conditional covenant idea. Commenting on Isaiah 24:5, Oecolampadius wrote, "We speak of the law of nature which was written on the hearts of men, of which all other laws whether by Moses or the prophets are the explanation, which condemns us because we have demolished the law of nature, which had to be restored." The Jews had violated the legal aids that God had given to help them keep the law of nature, such as the sabbath, circumcision, and the ceremonies,

> which were not abolished or destroyed inwardly for Christians but are fulfilled today by the law of the Spirit. For Christ did not come to dissolve the law but to fulfill it. By the eternal covenant I understand the law of love. For this is not a new commandment but has been a commandment from the beginning. Moreover, the law of love is the law of the Spirit. Whoever loves his neighbor has fulfilled the law (Rom. 13:10; Gal. 5:14).[32]

Trinterud ignores the obvious question: what did Oecolampadius mean by the law of love or the law of the Spirit that he equated with the eternal covenant? That he meant the gospel is clear from his comment on Isaiah 51:4, where he explained that the new law would be given not from Mt. Sinai but from Mt. Zion on the day of Pentecost. "Truly that is the law of the Spirit, of which Jeremiah 31 and Hebrews 10 speak, 'And this is the testament. . . ' " (Heb. 10:16).[33] Clearly then the promise of the new law of the Spirit was the promise of the gospel, of the testament. There was no law-contract involved. Elsewhere Oecolampadius said: "And those who have that faith have laid hold of the testament of God, which God has written in the hearts of men, not with ink but with his Spirit (for to lay hold of the testament is to have faith)."[34] So Oecolampadius did not see the testament in terms of commandment, but as promise. He spoke of no conditions in connection with that promise, but only of God writing the law of the Spirit in the hearts of men. Furthermore, he posited two distinct covenants, corresponding to law and gospel. And even though he spoke of Old Testament saints belonging to the church, his emphasis was on the contrast between Israel and the New Testament church, between the people of God in the Old and New Testament. Thus, in the Isaiah commentary, Oecolampadius posited a theology of testament, but he saw neither the unity of the Testaments nor the unity of the testament. The theme was that the new testament was distinguished from the old by justification by faith rather than works-righteousness.[35]

Cottrell discovers the same emphasis on the new covenant as the law of love in Oecolampadius' sermons on 1 John (1524). Moreover, in his Romans commentary (1525), Oecolampadius discussed the covenant in terms of promise and emphasized the distinctions between the old and new covenants. It was not until the early summer of 1526 that he began to equate the people of God in both the Old and New Testament. In his comment on Malachi 3:4, he clearly stated the unity of the testament: "Hence it is even inferred: there is no distinction between the fathers of the new and old testaments, other than that the latter followed, the former preceded Christ. All of them ate the same spiritual bread and possessed the same spirit of faith."[36] Thus only a few months subsequent to the statements of Zwingli and Bullinger, Oecolampadius also accepted the idea of the unity of the testament. But it was an Augustinian notion of unilateral testament, not a bilateral covenant.

Martin Cellarius has also been mentioned as an early covenant theologian,[37] and he did have much to say about covenant in his *De operibus Dei*. God made his eternal covenant with Abraham, the external sign of which was circumcision. But the important part of the covenant was the promise of Christ, not the sign.[38] The possession of the sign in no way guaranteed the possession of the promise. There were in fact, two covenants; that is, the internal covenant was hidden in the external pact of circumcision. There were two peoples: the carnal seed of Abraham and the elect people of God who were given faith by the Spirit. The reprobate were part of the pact of carnal circumcision, but they were like Ishmael, who "neither wanted to be nor could be reconciled by the covenant of peace . . . because of the ineluctable decree of damnation and reprobation."[39] Cellarius thus connected a double covenant and a double people with double predestination. There is nothing at all to suggest a conditional covenant.

Wolfgang Capito of Strassburg was another early covenant theologian, according to Trinterud.[40] Capito's position has been clarified, however, by James M. Kittelson in his recent biography. Capito did not equate baptism with circumcision, which was a *conditio sine qua non* for all covenant theologians and even for most who held to a theology of testament. He did use the term "covenant," but he meant the free testament which God revealed only to the elect.[41] He did affirm the hermeneutical unity of the Old and New Testament nearly as strongly as Bullinger, as well as the soteriological unity of the testament. All the elect in all ages were justified by faith. His was an Augustinian idea of testament, filtered through Luther, not a bilateral covenant.[42]

Martin Bucer is also included in Trinterud's host of early covenant theologians, although he offers no documentation.[43] Bucer is an excellent example of the confusion involved in interpreting sixteenth-century concepts of covenant or testament. Hagen concludes that Bucer had a rather fully developed Augustinian theology of testament in his commentary on the gospels in 1527.[44] Schrenk asserts that the covenant became especially important for Bucer's understanding of the sacraments because of his reaction to Cellarius. He also bases his judgment on the gospel commentary of 1527.[45] Lang discusses Bucer's use of the covenant in connection with the sacraments but then remarks that the covenant idea did not play a decisive role in Bucer's system.[46] Koch adds to the confusion with his assertion that for Bucer the covenant had "the character of a legal agreement [*rechtlicher Vertrag*], which God concludes with his elect."[47] This conclusion seems to be based solely on the fact that Bucer used the term *pactum* in his Romans commentary. The quotation given by Koch does not suggest a contract but rather an unconditional promise: "Therefore, this covenant is nothing other than an agreement (*pactum*) by which God promises and offers eternal life to them [the elect]."[48] This confusion clearly demonstrates the necessity of differentiating between bilateral covenant and unilateral testament, no matter the terminology used by any given thinker. For Bucer the terms *foedus* and *pactum* referred to God's unilateral promise to give eternal life to His elect. His was a theology of testament, at least until 1527, as a glance at a few of his writings will demonstrate.

Bucer's *Grund und Ursach* of late 1524 will focus his position just prior to the development of the covenant notion in Zurich by Zwingli and Bullinger. Bucer referred here to the eucharist as a renewal by Christians of their spiritual, eternal covenant and testament in the Lord. Later he asserted that Christ's blood was the basis on which "the abundantly gracious, new, eternal covenant has been established between God and us."[49] All the Scriptures, and especially Jeremiah 31:31–34, referred to this event, and the eucharist was a sign of this new testament. But Bucer did not further clarify what he meant by the eternal, new testament. Not only did he not affirm the soteriological unity of the testament, but he also posited great contrast between the Old and New Testament, at one point equating the Pope with Moses, at another contrasting the carnal customs of the Old Testament with the spiritual character of the New Testament.[50] The Christian was free from the law of the Old Testament, but he would keep the divine law of faith and love.[51] Although there are many Zwinglian elements in the *Grund und Ursach*, the basic elements of a theology of testament, let alone a covenant idea, are missing. Bucer affirmed neither the unity of the testament nor of the Testaments. He did refer to an eternal testament or covenant between God and the Christian, but the agreement involved, between God the Father and Christ, was that Christ *would establish* the eternal testament. So it was eternal in the sense that it was never ending, not because it also had existed before Christ's death.

Later in 1524, in his polemic against Treger, Bucer had more to say in relation to the unity of the church and of faith in the Old and New Testament. Abraham had been "a true Christian . . . a true disciple of Christ." There had, in fact, been those who had had faith and salvation from the beginning of the world; all the writers of Scripture—from Moses to the apostles—had the same faith. All were members of the invisible church. He also referred to "the church of the Jews."[52] Thus, in his reply to Treger, Bucer clearly affirmed the unity of faith and the existence of a single church from the beginning of the world. These references are scattered, however, and not at all developed. Nor did he connect these ideas with the notion of eternal testament. In 1524 Bucer appears to have been groping for a concept to tie everything together; but he did not discover it.[53]

In his comments on the Psalms in 1526, Bucer again spoke of the "eternal covenant and testament." The offering of Christ for the salvation of men had been the greatest example of God's grace and mercy. Through faith the believer became "an heir of God," a recipient of eternal life, because Christ "has established the new testament and the eternal covenant between us and the Father" (Jere. 31:31–34).[54] Although Bucer still did not specify the unity of the testament, it can perhaps be assumed because of his affimation of the unity of faith in the reply to Treger. So in 1526 Bucer had a theology of testament, no matter how underdeveloped.

But the very next year, in his gospel commentary, Bucer does seem to have come to an idea of covenant. He affirmed the unity of the old and new testament: in both, the believer was united with God through faith. Along with this testamental unity, he also argued for the unity of the covenant, although maintaining the distinction between the old and new covenants. The old covenant was external: it promised the land of Canaan and gave an external law along with the ceremonies. The new covenant, which promised the Spirit and an inward law, was eternal and had been made with the elect from the beginning of the world. In the new covenant one knew God through faith and exercised his faith by living piously and righteously in this life. The ceremonies and external rites of the old covenant were only appendages to the eternal new covenant that related to that time and those circumstances. Only faith and love of the neighbor were necessary in the new covenant. "This is the new and eternal covenant between us and God, that since we are convinced that He himself is the propitiation for us, thus in return we strive to make our entire life acceptable to Him." The elect in the Old Testament also understood the law in this way. In fact, "Moses clearly taught in all things to have faith in God and to love the neighbor."[55] In many ways Bucer sounds like Oecolampadius here except that he specifically stated that man had responsibilities in return for divine grace. Although he did not actually refer to conditions or stipulations, he did affirm the unity of the covenant and declare that faith and love were requisites of the covenant.

The host of early Reformation covenant thinkers is thus reduced to a single partisan. Almost all of them held to a theology of testament. True, Melanchthon finally came to a covenant understanding, but not until the 1550s. Only Bucer can be counted among those who developed some sort of real covenant idea in the 1520s, but even he did so only after the Zurich conception of the covenant had been fully stated.

Covenant and Testament
in Calvin's Thought

SCHOLARS HAVE debated for some time about the nature of Calvin's covenant idea, whether it was a notion of unilateral testament or bilateral covenant. Perry Miller argues that the Puritans went far beyond Calvin's interpretation, that Calvin himself did not develop the covenant idea to any great extent.[1] Along the same line, Trinterud states that for Calvin the covenant was simply God's promise to man, fulfilled by Christ. It was not a conditional promise; the mutuality of the Rhineland and English covenant ideas was missing in Calvin. Thus Calvin's was essentially an idea of testament.[2] James Torrance also strongly implies that Calvin's covenant of grace was a unilateral, unconditional covenant.[3] Finally H. H. Wolf sees Calvin in the light of testament rather than conditional covenant.[4] Schrenk, however, sees a conditional covenant, arguing that Calvin received his covenant notion from Zwingli and Bullinger and that he even followed the wording and structure of Bullinger's concept.[5] Others also argue that Calvin had a fully developed covenant idea, including the conditional element.[6]

No one denies that Calvin had some sort of covenant idea. The issue is whether Calvin appropriated Bullinger's covenant notion or simply amplified the idea of testament. Those who detect no conditional element often stress that Calvin's was a "covenant of grace." But such terminology is confusing inasmuch as it implies that a conditional covenant necessitated a semi-Pelagian approach to grace. Bullinger, along with his conditional covenant, also affirmed the Reformation principle of *sola gratia*. Whether Calvin's was a notion of testament or of covenant does not depend on whether his was a "covenant of grace," then, but rather on the relationship he saw between testament or covenant and predestination.

In the *Institutes*, Calvin's basic definition of covenant is discovered in his concept of adoption. The covenant was equivalent to God's adoption of His chosen through the mediation of Christ. So it was a covenant of grace, a "freely given covenant, whereby God had adopted his elect."[7] Again and again Calvin referred to the covenant of adoption, emphasizing free grace.[8] Thus membership in the "covenant of life," in the "spiritual covenant," depended on God's adoption of those whom He had freely chosen.[9] At times Calvin did seem to include more than the elect in the covenant. Thus all of Israel was in the covenant; through Abraham God had chosen all Israel, His general election of the entire nation. But, Calvin continued, "We must now add a second, more limited degree of election," by which God rejected some but kept others as sons.[10]

Hoekema claims that this section of the *Institutes* demonstrates that Calvin "does not identify membership in the covenant of grace with particular election."[11] But this is to ignore Calvin's distinctions about the covenant, which parallel his distinctions between general and particular election. Speaking of Israel as a nation in respect to the promised land, Calvin said, "Now we must note that where 'land' is mentioned, it is a visible symbol of the *secret separation that includes adoption*."[12] This "secret separation that includes adoption" must be compared with Calvin's references to two different covenants. Speaking of law and gospel, Calvin asserted that the law was equivalent to old testament and the gospel to new testament. Augustine had said the same thing, Calvin added, that the children of promise, the regenerate, from the beginning of the world had belonged "to the new testament." Although the patriarchs lived under the old testament, they aspired to the new.[13] Elsewhere Calvin asserted that the patriarchs possessed the "spiritual covenant," which promised eternal life and contrasted with the "carnal covenant," which had to do only with earthly things.[14] Finally, he made a similar distinction in comparing "the covenant of the law with the covenant of the gospel."[15] Calvin thus carried on Oecolampadius' dichotomy between the old carnal covenant and the eternal new spiritual covenant as an affimation of the unity of the testament. The same church existed among the Jews—although their understanding was weak, they were promised the same inheritance.[16] Their covenant "was supported not by their own merits, but solely by the mercy of God who called them." Theirs was "the covenant of the gospel," the spiritual promises which were fulfilled by Christ.[17] This was an Augustinian idea of testament, not a theology of conditional covenant. There was one testament of grace that applied to all who were of the elect.

Hoekema also refers to the "real," if not "meritorious," conditions of the covenant in Calvin's thought.[18] But Calvin spoke only of the "condition" of piety, not of faith. That is, the condition of faith was fulfilled for the elect, who were then responsible to live a godly life. Calvin, after all, was no antinomian. At times he seems to say that faith also was a human condition: "By their own defect and guilt, I admit, Ishmael, Esau, and the like were cut off from adoption. For the condition had been laid down that they should faithfully keep God's covenant, which they faithlessly violated." But this is only apparent, for Calvin then said that the reprobate, such as Esau (Rom. 9:13) were rejected solely on the basis of God's will, not because of their works.[19] Without attempting to resolve the tension between God's will in election and man's responsibility, suffice it to say that faith was only a hypothetical condition for Calvin. The condition was fulfilled for the elect; the reprobate could never fulfill it. But the believer did have a responsibility to live according to the moral law that was written in his heart by the Holy Spirit.[20] This was Calvin's third use of the moral law, close to Melanchthon's understanding. In another context he stated that God required "uprightness and sanctity of life" from those admitted to the fellowship of the covenant.[21] So the condition concerned the life of the faithful after God had given faith. The elect were adopted in Christ, thus gaining the inheritance of the testament.

Calvin's famous section on the unity of the covenant must, then, be interpreted to be an affirmation of the unity of the testament. His basic point was, in fact, the unity of the faith of the peoples in the Old and New Testament. He asserted: "The covenant made with all the patriarchs is so much like ours in substance and reality that the two are actually one and the same. Yet they differ in the mode of dispensation." He further explained that the covenant with the Jews was spiritual, supported by God's mercy, not by their works. They also were justified by faith alone; the spiritual covenant was common to the patriarchs, Moses, and the prophets. They all sought eternal life in this covenant of mercy, which, although only a feeble spark when given to Adam (Gen. 3:15), became progressively clearer through the centuries until fully revealed in Christ. Christ was the pledge to the Old Testament fathers, in whom they placed all their trust.[22]

The differences that Calvin saw between the Testaments are more instructive. First he cautioned that these differences were matters of dispensation, not of substance. Although the promises were the same in both Testaments, the spiritual promises of the testament or covenant were represented by temporal promises in the Old Testament. Secondly, the Old Testament typified Christ with images and ceremonies. It was here that Calvin made the distinction between the covenant of the law and the covenant of the gospel. God's elect in the Old Testament were under the covenant of the gospel, the promise of which was Christ. Even though the ceremonies were but accessories to this covenant of the gospel, these additions or appendages also bore the name covenant at that time. But the old covenant of the law had no real substance—it consisted of shadows that veiled the new covenant of the gospel. Thus after Christ the covenant of the law was terminated with the confirmation of the covenant of the gospel. Furthermore, the old testament was literal, the new, spiritual. Here it appears that Calvin has moved more directly to a soteriological contrast of testaments, rather than a hermeneutical distinction between Old and New Testaments. His contrast at this point is an Augustinian difference between old and new testament. Citing Jeremiah's prophecy about the new covenant (Jere. 31:31-34), Calvin explained that Paul interpreted this to mean that the new covenant was the gospel and the old covenant, the law (2 Cor. 3:6-11). The new spiritual covenant brought life, the old literal covenant, condemnation. Fourth, still operating on this soteriological level, Calvin said that the Scripture referred to the old testament in terms of bondage, to the new in terms of freedom (Rom. 8:15; Heb. 12:18-22). The patriarchs fled to the refuge of the gospel when oppressed by the law, although they were still compelled by the ceremonies. Citing Augustine, Calvin again affirmed that the gospel, the new testament, had existed since the beginning of the world. Thus the old testament, the law, did not include the spiritual and eternal promises of the old dispensation before the birth of Christ. In fact, Calvin asserted, the patriarchs "so lived under the old testament as not to remain there but ever to aspire to the new, and thus embraced a real share in it." Calvin's final difference was that God confined His covenant of grace only to the Jews in the Old Testament, whereas after Christ He included all nations. These were the different ways, Calvin concluded, in which God had accommodated himself to man in different ages.[23]

These two chapters of the *Institutes* of 1559 were taken almost in their entirety from the 1539 edition. Calvin did not deal with election in them at all.[24] Furthermore, in the 1539 edition he did not mention the covenant in the section on predestination except for his reference in the very first sentence to the "covenant of life" that was not preached equally to all men.[25] However, in the 1559 edition, Calvin closely connected the covenant with election in both major sections on predestination, one of which was entirely new and the other greatly expanded.[26] So in the 1539 edition, Calvin stated both a doctrine of predestination and of covenant, but he did not directly relate them to each other. In the 1559 edition, he presented a more complete doctrine of predestination, which had clearly become more important than the covenant to Calvin. It was the 1550s controversies about predestination, particularly Jerome Bolsec's charge in 1551 that Calvin's doctrine of predestination made God the author of sin, that impelled Calvin, in his own defense, to clarify and enlarge the significance of his teaching on predestination.

Calvin's immediate response to Bolsec was his *De aeterna Dei praedes-tinatione*, a more fully developed and more elaborate defense of double predestination than in the earlier editions of the *Institutes*. Even in this 1552 treatise, Calvin began to subordinate his covenant idea to predestination, asserting, "On no other ground can that covenant of God stand inviolable . . . except the Lord in his free will decrees to whom He will show grace and whom He wills to remain devoted to eternal death."[27] Much of the new material in this reply to Bolsec found its way into the considerably enlarged sections on predestination in the 1559 edition of the *Institutes*, where the covenant was also defined completely within the scope of double predestination.

Calvin's covenant theology, then, was really a theology of testament, similar to that of Augustine. The new testament or covenant, the gospel, was equivalent to the spiritual covenant by which God adopted the elect in all ages. The old testament or covenant, the law, was the same as the carnal covenant by which God condemned the reprobate. Calvin cast his covenant idea within the mold of election; the result was a notion of testament, unlike Bullinger's covenant idea, despite the often similar terminology. He made distinctions between the old "carnal" covenant and the new, eternal spiritual covenant, between law and gospel, and indeed between Old and New Testament, which Bullinger did not make. In this respect he sounds much more like Oecolampadius. Nor did he clearly tie his ethic to the covenant—i.e., the covenant did not become the basis for a community ethic. Calvin did not see covenant in terms of corporation. The reason was that he held to a theology of testament, despite his occasional references to man's responsibility in the covenant. To be sure, there are paradoxes and ambiguities in Calvin's idea; but because he subordinated covenant to predestination, these paradoxes and ambiguities are precisely the same as those inherent in his doctrine of double predestination. In Calvin's thought the covenant was subsequent, logically and theologically, to election. For Bullinger the covenant was antecedent to everything else. In short, Calvin's idea of testament, like Augustine's, simply served to unify God's grace from one dispensation to the other. It was the framework within which God dealt with His elect in all ages.

Trinterud is correct, then, in asserting that the mutual, contractual element was missing from Calvin's covenant idea, that it was simply God's promise of grace.[28] Miller is clearly wrong in saying that "Calvin made hardly any mention of the covenant."[29] Hoekema claims too much for Calvin's covenant idea, failing to take into account the framework of testament for Calvin, at least as stated in 1559.[30] To give quotations from Calvin's "Sermons on Deuteronomy" (1555 and 1556) to prove that Calvin taught a conditional covenant does not solve the paradoxes in his covenant idea any more than quoting him on human responsibility can solve the paradoxes and ambiguities involved in his doctrine of election. Calvin did have a fully developed idea of testament but not of conditional covenant, which would have cut into his doctrine of election. Miller may be weak on Calvin generally, as Marsden claims,[31] but Miller is correct in his suggestion that the later Puritan idea of covenant as contract weakened God's sovereignty and thus eroded election in a way that Calvin never allowed.[32] However, even though Miller recognizes that covenant theology did not come from Calvin, in the end he confuses the origins of covenant thought by tracing it back to Perkins and Ames in England.[33]

Calvin, then, like Oecolampadius before him, reaffirmed the basic Reformation distinction between law and gospel by means of the Augustinian notion of testament encased within double predestination. Within this framework, he defended *sola gratia* against those who, like Bolsec, seemed to be undermining the very foundation of the Reformed faith.

APPENDIX C

Calvinist Orthodoxy and the
Paralysis of the Covenant Idea

MORE THAN a century ago Alexander Schweizer argued that predestination was the central dogma of sixteenth-century Reformed Protestantism, i.e., that the logical consequence of the doctrines of justification by faith, the fallen human will, the free gift of grace and perseverance was the development of the idea of absolute, double predestination.[1] And it is true that the reformers without exception accepted a doctrine of predestination. However, during the earlier Reformation, these principal doctrines, which Schweizer sees necessitating the dogma of absolute predestination, were affirmed as biblical teachings; they were not stated as dogmatic principles. That is to say, there was a scriptural thrust, a willingness to take seriously *sola scriptura*, even if that meant unresolved logical and philosophical problems, an approach that was essentially antithetical to the later scholastic method of Reformed orthodoxy. Only in the second half of the century did the high Calvinist doctrine of double predestination begin to become the test of orthodoxy in Reformed circles.

It has often been stated that the seventeenth-century covenant theology was a reaction to the heavy emphasis on the divine decrees, that it served as a corrective to the supralapsarian, double predestinarianism of the Reformed scholastics. As Lindsay puts it, "There can be little doubt that there was a tendency in the Reformed theology of the latter half of the seventeenth century to allow the metaphysical to override the religious element in their dogmatic systems." Covenant theologians such as Witsius and Cocceius reestablished the historical element and reaffirmed human responsibility by means of the covenant conditions.[2] McCoy, in his study of Cocceius, points out that the Reformed scholastics of the seventeenth century deduced their entire systems from the eternal decree of predestination, thus tending "to render meaningless the interaction between God and man and to destroy the significance of history and salvation. Cocceius' own covenant system restored this lost meaning."[3] Dorner says specifically that Cocceius' covenant theology undermined double predestination and that the original covenant (in Paradise) was "represented as bearing a character of universalism."[4] Heppe also refers to the "essentially universalist basis" for the idea of the covenant of grace in the seventeenth century.[5] Miller's point about the contractual covenant concept, that it undercut predestination and eroded God's sovereignty, is similar.[6]

For all that, however, the seventeenth-century formulations of a bilateral covenant concept were a restatement of the earlier Reformed covenant idea. During the second half of the sixteenth century, conditional covenant and absolute predestination, as alternative ways to approach *sola fide* and *sola gratia*, joined combat. Bullinger's *De testamento* of 1534 was the clearest early articulation of the notion of bilateral covenant, and during the next two decades or so, conditional covenant remained a live option to the more common notion of unilateral testament. But Calvin's statement of testament in connection with double predestination prepared the way for the temporary victory of testament over covenant. During the latter half of the century Calvinist orthodoxy grew in strength, and the crucial doctrine of double predestination increasingly became the test of orthodoxy in Reformed Protestantism, resulting in the paralysis of the idea of bilateral covenant. The latter was initially stated within a framework of single predestination, although it had an underlying quality of universalism to it. But by the late 1550s it began to take on the overtone of universalism, and later of Arminianism, so rigid had the lines become. So Bullinger's influence in covenant or testamental thought in the late sixteenth century was diminished. Although the categories and even the terminology of the testamental theologians after 1560 often reflected an indirect influence from Bullinger, the substance of their thought must be traced back to Calvin and the Augustinian tradition preceding Calvin. Only in the seventeenth century would Bullinger's type of conditional covenant again come into its own.[7]

A survey of these trends, using a few basic thinkers, will serve to clarify the fate of Bullinger's covenant idea in the latter sixteenth century. Three men in particular were quite important in the further development of the Reformed idea of covenant or testament after 1550: Wolfgang Musculus of Bern, and Zacharius Ursinus and Caspar Olevianus of Heidelberg.

Musculus (1497–1563), who became a Protestant in 1527, was clearly influenced by Bullinger, although his covenant idea was not identical with Bullinger's. He discussed two covenants in his *Loci communes* of 1559. The general covenant was God's promise after the flood, made with the entire earth, man, and beast (Gen. 8:21; 9:9–11); it was an earthly, temporal covenant, which represented the general grace of God. The special and eternal covenant, made first with Abraham, was God's covenant with His elect, with those who had faith. The conditions, or "chief points," of this covenant were, on God's part, that He would be the God and Savior of those who participated in it. The conditions for the confederates were faith and obedience, as expressed to Abraham, "Walk before me and be upright." The special covenant, then, was the eternal covenant of God's grace in which were included "all the elect and believing." Musculus stated that even though God did not make the covenant explicit until Abraham, all the faithful and elect from Adam on had participated in it. Furthermore, the essential things (*substantialia*) of the covenant must be distinguished from the appendages (*accessoria*), such as the promise of the land of Canaan and circumcision. The essence of the covenant was the chief points: God's promise and the human conditions. The essence was eternal; the appendages were temporal and temporary. The essence had not been altered since Adam: there was one promise of grace, one covenant, one people of God, one church from the beginning until the end of the world.[8]

Except for his close and quite explicit connection between covenant and election, this sounds much like Bullinger. Musculus' doctrine of predestination, however, was not Calvinistic, but rather one of single predestination. Early in the *Loci* he discussed the fall of man and its effects. Adam had been created a perfect being with free will; thus he sinned freely. Man could not blame God for his fallen nature. Although God had foreknown the fall, He had not caused it. Rather, He had permitted it to happen. After the fall, man's freedom was limited: he could not will to do good, but, Musculus stressed, man freely chose evil. Sin was willful and men were thus justly condemned by God for their sin, disobedience, and lack of faith. In the locus on faith, Musculus stated that men could not will to believe because they were so corrupted by sin. Thus faith was a gift of God to the elect. Moving on to election, Musculus averred that God had chosen some for salvation before the foundation of the world. His election was based neither on foreknowledge nor on any good in the elect, but purely on grace. Although the elect could not be known with certainty, "all the faithful are to be considered as elect ones in whom there are no manifest proofs that they are estranged from the true faith and from the spirit of the children of God." He also treated the reprobate under the locus on election, although he introduced the topic with criticism of those who were contentious on the topic (Calvin presumably). He emphasized that reprobation fell within the sphere of the free grace of election. If some were elect, it followed that "some are reprobate, namely those who are not of the number of the elect." Reprobation was not a matter of decree but of refusal. They were refused because God did not choose them.[9] This definition of reprobation must be correlated with Musculus' earlier statement that man freely disobeyed God and refused to believe. Thus he held back from a Calvinistic double predestinarian formulation, and despite his discussion of reprobation, his was a doctrine of single predestination. Although Musculus' treatment of predestination was more sharply focused and more clearly based in formal logic than Bullinger's, the two men were essentially in agreement on predestination and on the covenant.

Both Ursinus (1534–1583) and Olevianus (1535–1587) were younger men, students of the earlier Reformers. Ursinus,[10] professor of dogmatics at the University of Heidelberg, had studied with Melanchthon for seven years in Wittenberg. After a brief term as teacher in Breslau, he went to Zurich in 1560, where he came to a Reformed point of view under the influence of Bullinger and especially Peter Martyr Vermigli. In the summer of 1561, recommended by Vermigli, he accepted the position at Heidelberg. The covenant was an important aspect of Ursinus' theology.[11] In fact, Ursinus introduced the covenant at the very beginning of his commentary on the catechism. The moral law was equivalent to God's commandment to Abraham to walk in God's presence and to be upright; the gospel was found in the promise to bless all people in Abraham's seed. Furthermore, the subject of the entire Scripture was the covenant between God and those who had faith.[12] Then, in the locus on the covenant, Ursinus emphasized its conditional character:

> The covenant which God made with men through the Mediator is a promise and a mutual pact, by which God obligates himself through and because of the Mediator to forgive sins in those who believe and to give them eternal life; by which in return men obligate themselves to receive this great gift by true faith and to show true obedience to God, that is, to live according to His will. This mutual pact is confirmed by the sacramental signs.[13]

The conditions or obligations were the same both before and after Christ, for the covenant itself was one in substance, although its circumstances and administration differed in the Old and New Testament.[14] This statement of the unity of the covenant and its conditional nature corresponds generally with Bullinger's view, and Ursinus' general covenant scheme was probably influenced somewhat by Bullinger. But the language with which Ursinus stated the mutuality of the covenant agrees very closely with Melanchthon's in his comments on Malachi,[15] and his treatment of the law is also reminiscent of

Melanchthon.[16] Although Bullinger also affirmed the eternity of the moral law, the Melanchthonian law-gospel scheme gave Ursinus' covenant idea a different flavor from Bullinger's. It almost appears that Bullinger's covenant notion was superimposed on a Melanchthonian foundation.

Although Ursinus did not mention election in his discussion of the covenant, he did hold to a strong double-predestinarian doctrine. In the locus on predestination, he posited two parts, election and reprobation, making a point of the fact that both were divine decrees. It was not that God had simply not chosen the reprobate; rather they were reprobate because He had decreed it. Furthermore, neither election nor reprobation was based on works; their cause could only be discovered in the good pleasure of God. The purpose of both decrees was the glory of God.[17] In a letter to Jacobus Monau, a Lutheran critic in Breslau, he similarly placed predestination under the doctrine of God and made essentially the same points. Apparently Monau had accused Ursinus of teaching an unscriptural doctrine, for after a brief presentation of his doctrine, Ursinus defended himself against the following charges: that he went beyond Scripture to speculation about God's secret will; that his doctrine was fatalistic like that of the Stoics, making man totally passive; that he made God the author of sin; that he based his doctrine on reason; that he ignored the universal promises of Scripture; and that the teaching on perseverance made men careless. Ursinus concluded that double predestination afforded great security and assurance. Monau's teaching was not that of Luther, but "truly heathenish," indeed "a gateway to hell."[18]

Ursinus is a bit of an enigma, then. On the one hand, he taught a mutual covenant, close to Bullinger and dependent on Melanchthon; on the other hand, he affirmed a rather rigid doctrine of double predestination. He clearly falls within the sphere of Calvinist orthodoxy and perhaps under the rubric of scholasticism. Although he does not seem to have quoted Aristotle directly, he otherwise fits the mold of Calvinist scholasticism as recently outlined by John Donnelly: the attempt to organize his theology in a logically coherent system, the use of human reason in forming and defending his theology, and a strong interest in speculative questions such as predestination.[19] Furthermore, Ursinus, in his letter to Monau, aligned himself with Beza and Vermigli on predestination,[20] who were among those most responsible for the development and growth of Calvinist scholasticism.[21] Although Ursinus did allow the tension between mutual covenant and double predestination to remain in his thought, one must ask how seriously he took the human conditions in the light of the hard logic of his predestinarianism. It would seem that his conditional covenant was subsumed by his doctrine of double predestination.

There is no such ambiguity in the thought of Olevianus. He was a thorough Calvinist, a disciple of Calvin himself and in close agreement with Beza.

Olevianus is particularly important because he wrote the first systematic treatise on the covenant from a Calvinist point of view, in which he tied election and the covenant into an inextricable knot. He began by quoting Jeremiah's promise of a new covenant (Jer. 31:31–34; Heb. 8:8–10). It was a covenant or testament that promised knowledge of the true God, a gracious remission of sins in Christ and the renovation of the image of God in man. It was a promise to the elect only.[22] Olevianus added a new twist to the covenant idea, moving the emphasis from Abraham to the creation and fall. He introduced the notion of a covenant of creation, which after the fall became the legal covenant or the natural covenant.[23] God created man in His image, but when man broke the covenant of creation by believing Satan's lies, this image was obscured by sin. Thus all men became natural heirs of Adam. The law of creation then became the legal covenant, by which God obligated man to perfect obedience to His law, as known in the law of nature and in the Decalogue. None could fulfil this obligation.[24] God thus established another covenant, a covenant of grace, which was unconditional. This purely gratuitous covenant stood firm only by God's mercy, "not by any stipulation of our strength."[25]

Olevianus made precisely this point when discussing predestination in his comments on Romans 9. Discussing Jacob and Esau as examples of all the elect and reprobate, he explained,

> Certain men, therefore, are elect. Accordingly, that which many suppose, that all without distinction are elect, but on the condition that they believe, is false. . . . For certain ones are predestined to life eternal, so that, because they are predestined, they also are going to receive the gift of faith from God. Against that, certain ones are not elect to life; and because they are not elect, they are not going to receive the gift of faith, but are going to disdain the offered grace with particular obstinancy.

Thus the cause of faith or lack of faith rested in God's decree of predestination. The reprobate were vessels of wrath "whom God prepared for damnation."[26]

The covenant of grace, then, was based on God's free and absolute decree of election, by which He adopted certain men as sons, heirs of God and coheirs of Christ. The elect, heirs of the testament, were given faith by God; the reprobate were excluded from the testament of grace.[27] But for a testament to be valid, for the heirs to receive the inheritance, the testator had to die. Thus Christ, with His death, confirmed the eternal testament of grace, by writing the law of God in the hearts of the elect. As Adam had destroyed the image of God in man, making all men his natural heirs, so Christ restored the image of God in the elect, making them heirs of the testament. The new covenant, then, offered righteousness and obedience to the elect through Christ.[28]

Olevianus' covenant of grace was the Calvinistic notion of unilateral testament; it rested on absolute election. He transferred the idea of conditions to the natural or legal covenant, thus nicely smoothing out the tensions in Calvin's own thought. The logic inherent in Calvin's teaching on predestination and the testament bore fruit in the careful statement of the same themes by Olevianus. Soon Olevianus' scheme would be standardized in the Reformed dichotomy between the covenant of works and the covenant of grace, the Reformed counterpart to Luther's distinction between law and gospel.

A brief glance at the covenant notion of Franciscus Gomarus (1557–1644) will show how this double-covenant idea had become entrenched among the Reformed scholastics by the 1590s. Gomarus' supralapsarian, double-predestinarian position is well known. He was the leader of the high Calvinists in Holland against James Arminius and the Arminians, and his statement on predestination was even more extreme than the infralapsarian position represented by the Canons of Dort.[29] Gomarus stated that the covenant, properly speaking, consisted of mutual obligations: God would give eternal life if man would meet God's stipulations. But, he continued, "this covenant is two-fold, Natural and Supernatural." The natural covenant, known by nature, required perfect obedience from man. First contracted immediately after creation, in Paradise, it demanded natural uprightness and love for God, along with the special prohibition not to eat from the tree (Gen. 2:17). The natural covenant was restated in the Mosaic law. Thus the natural covenant was the old covenant or the law and it "is unable to be called a testament." The supernatural covenant was a purely gratuitous covenant, "by which God not only offers Christ and perfect obedience in Him for reconciliation and eternal life to men, but also gives the condition of faith and repentance by His Spirit." This eternal testament or new covenant was initiated immediately after the fall with the promise of Christ in the protoevangelium (Gen. 3:15), renewed with Abraham and Israel, and confirmed by Christ. Comparing the two covenants, Gomarus again stressed the conditional nature of the old covenant and the unconditional nature of the new covenant: that is, faith was a gift, and God thus fulfilled the condition of the new covenant for the believer. Thus the old covenant was a true covenant; the new covenant was in reality a testament.[30]

Clearly the double covenant, double predestinarian scheme was well established on the continent by the 1590s. In England, William Perkins taught essentially the same high Calvinist combination of testament and predestination. Perkins' *Golden Chaine*, first published in Latin in 1590, was devoted to the teaching and defense of a supralapsarian doctrine of predestination. After a definition of God and a discussion of God's decree, i.e., the work or action of God, he turned, in chapter 7, to God's action toward men: "God's decree, inasmuch as it concerneth man, is called predestination: which is the decree of

God, by which he hath ordeined all men, to a certain and everlasting estate; that is, either to salvation or condemnation, for his own glory." The creation and the fall were God's means of effecting His decree of predestination. Adam and Eve were created "perfect, but mutable: for so it pleased God to prepare a way to the execution of his decree." Having treated the fall and original sin, Perkins then returned to predestination in chapter 15: "Predestination hath two partes; Election and reprobation. . . . Election, is God's decree, whereby on his owne free will, he hath ordeined certaine men to salvation, to the praise of the glory of his grace."[31] The foundation of the decree was Christ, and the means of executing the decree of election was God's covenant (chapter 19): "Gods covenant, is his contract with man, concerning life eternall, upon certain conditions. This covenant consisteth of two partes; Gods promise to man, Mans promise to God. Gods promise to man, is that, wherby he bindeth himself to man to be his God, if he breake not the condition. Mans promise to God, is that, whereby he voweth his allegiance unto his Lord, and to perfourme the condition between them."[32]

Perkins could not have stated more clearly the conditional nature of a covenant. But, like Olevianus and Gomarus, Perkins blunted the conditional aspect. For "there are two kindes of this covenaunt. The covenant of works, and the covenant of grace [Jere. 31:31–33]. . . . The covenant of works, is Gods covenant, made with condition of perfect obedience, and is expressed in the morrall law."[33] Fulfillment of this condition would result in eternal life, failure in eternal death. For Perkins, then, the covenant of works was the law; or the law was an abridgment of the covenant of works. The whole law was summarized in the Decalogue, and the Decalogue in the Love Command-ment. The purpose of the law and thus the goal of the covenant of works was to define sin and to condemn the sinner (chapters 20–30). Thus Perkins attached the covenant conditions to the covenant of works; the conditions were the law, and the law was unfulfillable.

The covenant of grace (chapter 31), concerning only the elect, was the promise of Christ and salvation. In fact, "this covenant, is also named a testament: for it hath partly the nature and properties of a testament or will." For one thing it was confirmed by the death of the Testator (Heb. 9: 16–17). "Secondly, in this covenant, we do not offer much, and promise small to God, but in a manner do only receive: even as the last wil and testament of a man, is not for the testators, but the heires commoditie."[34] Perkins' point was, of course, that faith was a gift, that the covenant of grace was unconditional. The covenant of grace, then, was the gospel; it was one in substance from the beginning of the world to the end. Following a discussion of the sacraments and the degrees of the execution of God's decree of election, with appropriate accompanying charts, Perkins turned to the decree of reprobation toward the end of the book.

In the preface, Perkins had explained that *A Golden Chaine* was a defense of the true doctrine of predestination against the new Pelagians, the Lutherans, and the semi-Pelagian papists.[35] In his treatment of the decree of reprobation (chapters 52–56) he opposed the new Pelagians, the Arminians of Holland, who, according to Perkins, taught that God wanted all men to be saved in Christ; that God did not decree the fall of Adam; that salvation was offered universally to all men; and that God's entire decree was based in foreknowledge. Perkins denied each point: God had not willed that all men be saved; He had decreed Adam's fall; He had decreed reprobation; and He had not offered grace to all men. God's entire decree of predestination had resulted from God's will, not His foreknowledge. God had rejected the reprobate.[36]

Perkins' double-predestinarian, double-covenant scheme was essentially that of Olevianus and Gomarus, although he connected the covenant and predestination more closely than they had. The general scheme was worked out more fully in Perkins' thought. Quite cognizant of the difference between testament and covenant, he shifted the conditions to the covenant of works, or the law, and presented the covenant of grace, or the gospel, as testament, thus preserving absolute double predestination, the mark of the new Reformed orthodoxy. Yet, aside from his adept handling of covenant and testament within the framework of double predestination, Perkins said nothing new. The dichotomy between law and gospel had been carefully developed by Luther, as had the doctrines of human depravity and justification by faith alone. Moreover, Calvin himself had made ambiguous references to the carnal covenant, the covenant of the law, and the covenant of the gospel. And Oecolampadius had distinguished between the old covenant and the new covenant with the elect. Perkins, then, fell into the testamental tradition of the early Reformation. He did smooth out the paradoxes of Calvin's thought, by making logical inferences from the divine decree of predestination in the development of his system of double covenant. Bullinger's notion of covenant was relevant to Perkins only in the sense that he had to deal with the problem of condition, not in how he dealt with it.

The early Reformation Augustinian idea of testament prevailed over covenant in the late sixteenth century because predestination was becoming the test of orthodoxy for the Reformed scholastics. For men like Gomarus and Perkins, the "covenant" was simply a convenient way to express their absolute double predestinarianism, with the idea of conditions necessarily being relegated to the covenant of works or the law. The alternative Reformed tradition, based on Bullinger's notion of conditional covenant, was greatly attenuated by the late sixteenth century, because those who accepted such a covenant idea also tended to hold to a weaker, single predestination or even to universalism. As the century wore on, they met more and more suspicion and hostility from the Reformed scholastics.

Perkins was representative of later Tudor Puritanism with his high Calvinistic double-covenant scheme.[37] The earlier Puritans, however, such as William Tyndale, seem to have been more influenced by Bullinger and Zurich. Although it is difficult in Tyndale's case to establish firmly the sources of his covenant idea, there is no doubt that he taught a contractual covenant. In the preface to his 1534 New Testament, he introduced the covenant as the major topic of the Scriptures. "The generall covenaunt wherin all other are comprehended and included is this. If we meke oure selves to God/ to kepe all his lawes/ after the ensample of Christ: then God hath bounde him selfe unto us to kepe and make good all the mercies promysed in Christ/ throwout all the scripture." The law, he continued, was comprehended in the Decalogue, which in turn was summarized in the Love Commandment. Keeping the law, then, meant loving God and one's neighbor. All the promises of God referred to God's promise in the covenant and thus they were conditional promises: "For all the promyses of the mercie and grace that Christ hath purchased for us/ are made upon the condicion that we kepe the lawe." Then Tyndale began to enlarge upon what he meant by keeping the law.

> Also ye se that two things are requyred to begin a Christen man. The fyrst is a stedfast fayth and trust in Almightie God/ thorow the deservinge merites of Christes bloude onlye/ withoute all respect to oure owne workes. And the other is/ that we forsake evell and turne to God/ to kepe his lawes and to fyght agaynst oure selves and oure corrupte nature perpetuallye/ that we maye do the will of god every day better and better.[38]

So Tyndale's conditions, faith and piety, were the same as Bullinger's.

Tyndale did not mention predestination in his discussion of the covenant. Trinterud makes him into a strong predestinarian,[39] but Tyndale did not specifically limit the covenant to the elect. In the "Prologe to the Romayns," commenting on chapters 9 through 11, he presented a doctrine of single predestination. By means of predestination,

> oure iustifiynge and salvacion are clene taken oute of oure handes/ and put in the handes of God only/ which thinge is most necessary of all. For we are so weke and so uncertayne/ that yf it stode in us/ there wolde of a trueth no man be saved/ the devell no doute wolde deceave us. But now is God sure that his predestinacion cannot deceave him/ nether can eny man withstand or let him and therefore have we hope and trust agaynste synne.

That is a fairly strong statement of single predestination, but then he went on for nearly a page and a half warning against the dangers of getting too caught up in the doctrine. One should not "serche botomlesse secretes of Goddis predestinacion" wondering whether or not he is predestined. Rather, one should educate oneself to Christ in order to understand the meaning of the law and gospel as taught by Paul, then fight against sin and learn tribulation. At that point "the necessite of predestinacion will wave swete and thou shalt well fele how precyouse a thinge it is."[40] Tyndale did not, however, reconcile the conditional nature of his covenant teaching with predestination. In fact, he appears not to have discussed predestination except where a treatment was demanded, such as in a consideration of Romans 9–11, and then only briefly. The covenant idea was implicitly, if not always explicitly, universalist.

The origins of Tyndale's covenant notion are still somewhat obscure. Trinterud sees the influence of Zwingli and Oecolampadius, but Clebsch hesitates to accept continental influences.[41] Møller accepts an influence "by some sort of Zurich theology,"[42] and the chronology of the development of Tyndale's covenant idea seems to warrant such a conclusion. Although the seeds of Tyndale's covenant concept may be seen as early as 1528, his idea was not well developed until 1533 and 1534, too early to have been influenced by Bullinger's *De testamento* of 1534. Bullinger did, however, use the covenant idea in print as early as 1531 in his first polemic against the Anabaptists.[43] Certainly Zwingli's works were available to Tyndale, and the possible influence of the 1529 Zurich Bible has been suggested.[44] There was, then, ample access to Zurich literature on the covenant.

If Zurich influence on Tyndale himself cannot be established with certainty, there is more evidence of such influence on Miles Coverdale, a friend and close associate of Tyndale's. Coverdale's interest in the covenant is evidenced by his 1541 translation of Bullinger's *Der alt gloub*,[45] a clear statement of the covenant. Moreover, Coverdale published the first English translation of the entire Bible (1535), including Tyndale's translations from the Old Testament and his entire New Testament, but not his prefaces and notes. However, in his own preface, Coverdale echoed Tyndale's covenant theology.[46] The first edition of Coverdale's Bible was unauthorized, printed on the continent. Some scholars have argued that it was published at Zurich by Froschauer, which would establish a clear link between early English covenant thought and Zurich, although the Zurich printing has recently been denied.[47] If Zurich is rejected as the place of publication, Coverdale's 1541 translation of *The Olde fayth* still remains, the first incontestable proof of any personal influence by Bullinger on Puritan covenant thought.

At about the same time, in the early 1540s, John Hooper was drawn to the teachings of Zwingli and Bullinger.[48] Apparently under some pressure because of his acceptance of the Zurich teaching, Hooper left England for Strassburg, then went on to Zurich in 1547. During his two-year visit he became Bullinger's close personal friend and disciple. Among other ideas he appropriated Bullinger's covenant theology, which he most explicitly maintained in the preface to his "A Declaration of the ten holy commandments," published in 1548 while he was still in Zurich.

> But foreasmuch as there can be no contract, peace, alliance, or confederacy between two persons or more, except first the persons that will contract agree within themselves upon such things as shall be contracted . . . ; also, seeing these ten commandments are nothing else but the tables or writings that contain the conditions of the peace between God and man . . . ; it is necessary to know how God and man was made at one, that such conditions could be agreed upon and confirmed with such solemn and public evidences, as these tables be, written with the finger of God.

God was bound to aid and preserve man and to give him eternal happiness. Man's condition was to obey God's commandments and to love Him. This, then, was a bilateral covenant. It was first made with Adam (Gen. 3:15), renewed with Abraham (Gen. 17), restated by Moses (Exod. 19) and confirmed by Christ, "the arbiter of this peace."[49]

Hooper's position on predestination was quite moderate. All men were included in the promise of grace, but some "exclude themselves from the promise in Christ." This was true even in the case of Esau: "Howbeit these threatenings of God against Esau [Mal. 1:2–3; Rom. 9:13], if he had not of his wilful malice excluded himself from the promise of grace, should no more have hindered his salvation, than God's threatening against Ninive, Jonah i." Man's own sin was the cause of his rejection by God. Election, on the other hand, resulted from God's mercy in Christ. But, Hooper continued, "he that will be partaker of this election must receive the promise in Christ by faith. . . . So we judge of election by the event or success that happeneth in the life of man those only to be elected that by faith apprehend the mercy promised in Christ. Otherwise we should not judge of election." God did not force any man; it was man's duty to "receive the grace offered, consent unto the promise, and not repugn the God that calleth."[50] Thus men were rejected because of their sin, not because of any action of God. Furthermore, the elect had the responsibility of responding to God. Hooper's language comes close to universalism, the term "election" seeming to be synonymous with "promise." The strongest position that can be ascribed to him is that he taught a very temperate single predestination.[51]

The essential elements of Hooper's covenant teaching were similar to Bullinger's. However, Bullinger's version did not continue to find favor with the later Tudor Puritans. After Hooper, Calvin's theology of testament tended to displace Bullinger's covenant idea. Until the 1580s the major expression of the Calvinist idea of testament was found in the Genevan Bible of 1560. Then Fenner, Cartwright, and especially Perkins restated the Calvinist idea within the framework of absolute double predestination.[52] But just at the time that Bullinger's covenant scheme was losing its appeal in England, it was becoming an important factor in Dutch Reformed theology, in the thought of such men as Veluanus, Snecanus, and Wiggertsz.[53]

Joannes Anastasius Veluanus, one of the earliest Dutch Reformed leaders, was a product of several apparent influences: the old Dutch biblical piety, Erasmus, Melanchthon, Zwingli, and Bullinger. His first publication in 1554, *Der Leken Wechwyser*[54] (*The Layman's Guide*), established him, along with Bullinger, as a major influence on the growth of Reformed Protestantism in the Netherlands, at least until Calvinism became strong in the north.[55] He also published two works on the eucharist.[56] The covenant is present, if not the dominant motif, in all three works, usually in connection with the sacraments. In *Der Leken Wechwyser*, he presented the covenant as having first been made with Adam. It was then renewed with Abraham and successively throughout the Old Testament, and confirmed by Christ. He elaborated this in his treatment of the sacraments:

> Here the following points are to be noticed. First, the sacraments are true signs of the grace of God toward us, so that God's spirit comforts our hearts and strengthens us in the faith with them. Secondly, they are a covenant, in which we obligate ourselves to the service of God. . . . God makes a covenant with the Christian and the Christian makes a covenant with God. Baptism is a true sign of both, just as circumcision was a covenant sign between God and Abraham's children. (Gen. 17:11–14; Rom. 4:11).

God's covenant with man was based on the promise of Christ. The conditions for man were to believe with God's help, to follow the Holy Spirit, and to live a virtuous life.[57] In *Vom Nachtmal Christi*, Veluanus referred to the covenant in the section entitled, "The true interpretation of Zwingli and his followers in this matter."[58] Then, in *Von dem waren leib Christi*, he again brought up the covenant, in connection with the sacraments of the Old and New Testaments.[59] Thus, although the covenant was not the major principle of Veluanus' theology, he did use the concept fairly often, usually with reference to his sacramental teaching. Moreover, his was a conditional covenant. He specifically rejected double predestination and in fact came close to affirming a universalist position.

Denying the Calvinistic distinction between God's secret will and revealed will, Veluanus asserted that the invitation to God's grace was genuinely universal. God decreed in eternity to save those who allowed themselves to be taught as much as possible and who remained obedient. This, he added, had been the teaching in the old church before Augustine, and the earliest Christianity was the purest Christianity. More explicitly, he explained that men should seek God's help, using their sick free will, for "the good God grants salvation to all called men and to all in the same manner and no one is bound to perdition by predestination."[60] This synergism is also evident in his *Von dem waren leib Christi*, where he argued against absolute predestination in the section that also contains his covenant idea. The sacraments were such sure seals of grace that each baptized person and each communicant could say: "I have the hand and seal of God himself that He willingly grants me conversion and eternal salvation and that He will gladly help me with that with His Spirit." It was as though God had said: "I have not predestined you to damnation." God meant inwardly what He expressed outwardly. The call to salvation was truly universal. "And therefore the sacraments are quite comforting testimonies of God against the dangerous temptation of the one-sided predestination of God, which fantasy only leads many people astray." Furthermore, God's grace also encompassed unbaptized infants who died.[61]

Veluanus' position on predestination seems to have been somewhere between Erasmus' and Melanchthon's teachings. His covenant idea, however, was most likely the product of Bullinger's influence. Although Veluanus did not directly support his covenant idea from Bullinger, a casual glance at his writings demonstrates that he knew and respected Bullinger's works.[62]

Gellius Snecanus sounds more like Bullinger on the covenant than any of the later sixteenth-century covenant thinkers.[63] In his major work (1585), he emphasized the unity of the covenant and its conditional nature. The covenant was eternal. It was made first with Adam, renewed with Abraham, and confirmed by Christ the Mediator. Although its substance had never changed, its administration encompassed three periods: before the law, under the law, and after the law. God had clearly expressed the conditions of the covenant, faith and love, to Abraham: "In these few words is included whatever pertains to true faith and love, both towards God and towards man. The sum of the entire Scripture and of piety consists in these two conditions of the divine covenant."[64] The sacraments of the covenant, in both the Old and New Testament, were signs and seals of the covenant. Although the children of believers were included in the covenant by baptism, only those who kept the conditions of faith and love were ultimately participants and members of the covenant. Bullinger would have agreed almost totally with Snecanus on the covenant, with the sole exception that Snecanus seems to have picked up the idea of a covenant before the fall.

On predestination, however, his position was nearly in agreement with that of Arminius. In 1590, he wrote that "the doctrine of conditional predestination is not only conformable to the word of God but cannot be charged with novelty." He claimed that during the early Reformation in Friesland those who opposed conditional predestination had been seen as innovators, but now he was seen as such. Then he asserted, "Let all orthodox professors of theology openly exhort their students not to ascribe to the writings of anyone

[referring explicitly to Calvin] more authority than the rule of faith permits."
Beza attempted to have Snecanus silenced, but in 1596 he published his
Introduction to the Ninth Chapter of Romans. The point of view was similar
to Arminius' argument.[65]

Cornelius Wiggertsz, the third covenant thinker in the Netherlands
indebted to Bullinger,[66] was an outspoken universalist. According to
Wiggertsz, the covenant was made with Abraham and all his descendants just
after the fall. No one was excluded from the covenant except for unbelief.
Children took part in the promise of the covenant by means of the sacrament,
either circumcision or baptism. For adults the conditions for remaining in the
covenant were faith in Christ and a life of obedience and thanksgiving. Since
the confederates already possessed salvation through Christ, original sin
could not condemn them. The covenant was based in Christ, "who was the
second Adam and the life giving Spirit for the salvation of all men . . . just
as earlier Adam's sin was 'efficacious' for the condemnation of all men." Only
those who persevered in Christ could continue under the grace of the covenant. On predestination, he said: "First God decreed from eternity that all
who believe in the name of His only begotten Son shall have eternal life. Secondly, the eternal foreknowledge of God is to be held firmly, since He knew
from eternity who would become His own. Neither His predestination nor His
foreknowledge can be applied to the persons, but only to the qualities."[67] So
acceptance into the covenant did not assure salvation. One had to persevere in
the covenant relationship with an active faith, as Adam had done. Wiggertsz,
who did not die until 1624, was defrocked and excommunicated in 1598.
Among those professors at the University of Leiden who signed his
condemnation was Franciscus Gomarus.

Those who agreed with Bullinger in teaching a conditional covenant had
one thing in common: with the exception of Ursinus, none of them held to
absolute double predestination. Some, like Tyndale and Musculus, taught a
moderate single predestination in keeping with the original Reformation
emphasis on justification by faith alone. Others, such as Veluanus and
perhaps Hooper, were closer to Melanchthon's "synergism." Finally,
Snecanus and Wiggertsz held to a more distinctively Dutch tradition, which
culminated in Arminianism. For many, the problem with Bullinger's
covenant idea was the tension produced by an affirmation of conditional
covenant within the framework of *sola gratia*. Seemingly Luther's assertions
on human nature and justification led to a denial of the freedom of the will and
thus inevitably to an acceptance of predestination. Within such a context, the
notion of conditional covenant was paradoxical. Few were willing to accept
such a paradox, especially during the latter part of the century; they released
the tension either by adjusting their doctrine on man or by means of a

theology of testament rather than covenant. Men like Snecanus and Wiggertsz maintained a conditional covenant by reaffirming some freedom for the human will, thus turning to a position of universal grace. Others, such as Perkins and Gomarus, resolved the paradox with a theology of testament within the context of absolute double predestination.

Calvin had initiated this latter trend with his bitter battles with his opponents on predestination in the 1550s, which is not to say that the later Calvinist position was identical with Calvin's. Calvin's doctrine was carefully formulated from his understanding of Scripture, and it was based in his Christology and soteriology.[68] The Calvinist scholastics, on the other hand, perhaps as early as Jerome Zanchi,[69] placed predestination under the doctrine of God and made it a matter for philosophical speculation. Nevertheless, of all the earlier reformers, it was Calvin who felt the necessity of emphasizing double predestination so heavily,[70] and it was his followers, many of them taught by Calvin himself, who formulated the new Reformed orthodoxy. By the late sixteenth century, these Calvinist scholastics were gaining theological ascendancy, and absolute double predestination was becoming the test of orthodoxy in the Reformed churches. Any other position was viewed with suspicion or treated as heresy. One consequence of this was the paralysis of the idea of conditional covenant, of the alternative Reformed tradition, because of its apparent universalist tendencies; it seemed to correspond logically with conditional election. The pinnacle for the high Calvinists was the Synod of Dort (1618), where even Bullinger himself had to be defended.

Yet the double predestinarian scheme of the new orthodoxy presented its own problems: its cold rationalism, its emphasis on the philosophical rather than the historical aspects of the faith, and especially its implicit antinomianism. The solution of some Reformed theologians of the seventeenth century was to reintroduce an aspect of human responsibility by reasserting history over philosophy within the framework of a conditional covenant. Perry Miller contends that the later Puritans made a conditional covenant out of Perkins' covenant (testament) of grace. The basic condition was faith, which further obligated the believer to live according to the law (the covenant of works). Sanctification thus became the seal and assurance of election. This tight rope walk between Arminianism and antinomianism did not deny the absolute election or the free grace of God. Rather it affirmed both the free grace of God and the responsibility of man, thus enabling the Puritans at the same time to hold firmly to absolute election and to emphasize the necessity of living according to God's law.[71] Brian G. Armstrong argues cogently that the covenant theology of John Cameron and Moïse Amyraut at the Academy of Saumur was essentially a corrective to the rationalism and the unhealthy prominence given to predestination in the thought of the Calvinist scholastics.[72] Finally, the covenant theology of Cocceius, also conditional, aimed at a restatement of historical and biblical theology and a renewed emphasis on the element of human responsibility in opposition to Reformed scholasticism.[73]

This, then, was the solution given by various covenant theologians of the seventeenth century to the rigor mortis of high Calvinist scholasticism—the rebirth of the notion of conditional covenant, the renascence of the earlier Reformed tradition. This is not to say that any of the seventeenth-century covenant formulations was identical with Bullinger's, for the seventeenth-century theologians retained many of the accretions of a century, such as the double-covenant notion. Whether or not Bullinger directly influenced these later covenant concepts, his own theology of the covenant stands as a towering monument in anticipation of these ideas.

Notes

Prologue

1. *HBBibl I*, p. vi. Staedtke, in *HBBibl I*, lists 772 entries, which include all known translations and editions. Bullinger's unpublished writings total about 300.
2. See Joachim Staedtke, "Bullingers Bedeutung für die protestantische Welt," *Zwingliana* 11 (1961), pp. 372–388; and Fritz Büsser, "Die Ueberlieferung von Heinrich Bullingers Briefwechsel," *HBBW I*, pp. 7–21.
3. This biographical information has been gleaned from Fritz Banke, *Der junge Bullinger 1504–1531* (Zurich, 1942); Carl Pestalozzi, *Heinrich Bullinger. Leben und ausgewählten Schriften* (Elberfeld, 1858); Gustav von Schulthess-Rechberg, *Heinrich Bullinger der Nachfolger Zwinglis* (Halle, 1904); and from Bullinger's own *Diarium*.
4. Pestalozzi argues that the Bremgarten school was woefully inadequate to prepare one for the university. *Heinrich Bullinger*, pp. 9–10. Blanke, however, asserts that at least fifty cases can be cited between 1462 and 1526 of boys who matriculated from this school into the universities without additional preparation. *Der junge Bullinger*, p. 12.
5. *Diarium*, pp. 2:24–3:5.
6. See the appendix of Egli's edition of the *Diarium*: "Vita Henrichi Bullingeri usque annum 1560," p. 125. Hereafter cited as "Vita."
7. Pestalozzi argues that Heinrich was sent to Emmerich because the school there was run by the Brethren of the Common Life. *Heinrich Bullinger*, pp. 10–13. Blanke disagrees: "This view is false." Bullinger never mentioned the brethren in his *Diarium*, and they in fact were not his teachers. Although the brethren did

217

have two "houses" in Emmerich, they were student hostels, not schools. Bullinger lived in neither, but in a private home. *Der junge Bullinger*, pp. 30–31. More recently, however, Hans Georg vom Berg has made a convincing argument that Bullinger was indeed influenced by the brethren at Emmerich. "Die 'Brüder vom Gemeinsamen Leben' und die Stiftsschule von St. Martin zu Emmerich. Zur Frage des Einflusses der Devotio Moderna auf den jungen Bullinger," *HBGesA I*, pp. 1–12.

8.   *Diarium*, p. 5:1.

9.   *Diarium*, p. 6:6–7, 13. Concerning Luther's influence on the young Bullinger, see Ulrich Gäbler, "Der junge Bullinger und Luther," *Lutherjahrbuch* 42 (1975), pp. 131–140; Staedtke, *Theologie*; Susi Hausammann, *Römerbriefauslegung zwischen Humanismus und Reformation: Eine Studie zu Heinrich Bullingers Römerbriefvorlesung von 1525* (Zurich, 1970).

10. One of the two sketches of Bullinger's life in English is not only very brief but also at times misleading, implying, for instance, that Bullinger's formal course of study at the Bursa Montis was theology. G. W. Bromiley (ed.), *Zwingli and Bullinger* (Philadelphia, 1953), p. 41. See also David J. Keep, "Henry Bullinger, 1504–1575: A Sketch of His Life and Work with Special Reference to Recent Literature," *London Quarterly and Holborn Review*, 191 (6th ser.): 35 (1966), pp. 135–146, which is exceedingly brief and general.

11. See Blanke, *Der junge Bullinger*, p. 76.

12. "Vita," p. 126; see also *Diarium*, pp. 8:23–26.

13. *Diarium*, p. 9:11–18.

14. "Brief über das Abendmahl an Matthäus Alber." 16 Nov. 1524. *ZW* 3, pp. 335–354. For the evolution of Zwingli's thought on the eucharist, see G. R. Potter, *Zwingli* (Cambridge, 1976), pp. 150–159.

15. *Diarium*, pp. 13–16. For the published works, see *HBBibl I*, nos. 1, 2, 3, 10. For the entire seventy-two titles, see Staedtke, *Theologie*, pp. 266–292.

16. There are three extant letters from Heinrich to Anna. The first is the letter in which he asked her to marry him, dated 30 Sept. 1527 (*HBBW I*, pp. 126–141). The second is a reply to a letter from Anna (late 1527 or early 1528), in which she had apparently expressed some misgivings, perhaps under pressure from her mother, who opposed the marriage (*HBBW I*, pp. 145–149). The third letter, dated 24 Feb. 1528, was written at Anna's request. Among other things, it includes Bullinger's views on the duties of a faithful wife (*HBBW I*, pp. 150–176). Concerning the betrothal and marriage, see *Diarium*, pp. 11:14–23; 18:15–21. See also Blanke, *Der junge Bullinger*, pp. 87–112, and R. Christoffel, *H. Bullinger und seine Gattin* (Zurich, 1875).

17. The book against the Anabaptists was his *Fraefel*, to which he added his position on *Zins* as an appendix. For a fairly detailed account of the background for the *Fraefel* and of the events leading up to the disputation, see Heinold Fast, *Heinrich Bullinger und die Täufer: Ein Beitrag zur Historiographie und Theologie im 16. Jahrhundert* (Weierhof [Pfalz], 1959), pp. 28–30.

18. See Endre Zsindely, "Heinrich Bullingers Berufungen im Jahre 1531," *Zwingliana* 12 (1968), pp. 668–676.

19. Actually the title *Antistes* was not yet in use. It was conferred on Bullinger in 1532. The *Antistes* received any instructions from the magistracy, directed the correspondence, and was superintendent over the other ministers of Zurich. M. Gelzer, "Antistes," in *Die Religion in Geschichte und Gegenwart* 1, p. 459.

20. For a brief discussion of Zurich's intricate foreign policy prior to the Kappel War, see G. R. Potter, "Zurich and the Reformation in Switzerland," *History Today* 15 (1965), pp. 12–19. See also Potter, *Zwingli*, pp. 414ff, for the aftermath of the war.

21. *Actensammlung*, no. 1797.

22. Printed in *Reformationsgeschichte* 3, pp. 284–291. See also Blanke, *Der junge Bullinger*, pp. 148–149.

23. *Reformationsgeschichte* 3, pp. 293–296.

24. *Actensammlung*, no. 1853 (for previous morals legislation see nos. 1077, 1385, 1534, and 1619; cf. "Grossen Sittenmandat" [March 1530], no. 1656). See also Leonhard von Muralt, "Zwingli als Socialpolitiker," *Zwingliana* 5 (1930), pp. 276–296.

25. For the initial exchange of correspondence, in March 1532, see Fast, *Bullinger und die Täufer*, pp. 180ff.

26. *Ibid.*, p. 33. Fast suggests that Jud may have edited the publication. Jud did mention the brethren in his initial letter to Bullinger. *Ibid.*, p. 180. Weisz implies that Jud was simply reverting to the position that he shared with Zwingli prior to the *Ehegerichtsordnung* of 1525. Leo Weisz, *Leo Jud. Ulrich Zwinglis Kampfgenosse 1482–1542* (Zurich, 1942), p. 90.

27. *Katechismen*, pp. 148–181.

28. Hans Hüssy, "Aus der Finanzgeschichte Zürichs in der Reformationszeit," *Zwingliana* 8 (1948), pp. 341–345, 356–357; P. Schweizer, "Die Behandlung der zürcherischen Klostergüter in der Reformationszeit," *Theologische Zeitschrift aus der Schweiz* 2 (1885), pp. 174–179; Carl Pestalozzi, *Das zürcherische Kirchengut in seiner Entwicklung zum Staatsgut* (Zurich, 1903), pp. 13–16. For a more recent assessment, see Hans Ulrich Bächtold, "Bullinger und die Obrigkeit," *B-T 1975*, pp. 77–86.

29. *Actensammlung*, no. 1889 (the Synod had been created in April 1528 [no. 1391]). See Kurt Maeder, "Bullinger und die Synode," *B-T 1975*, pp. 69–76.

30. See Erland Herkenrath, "Bullingers Beziehungen zur politischen Führungsschicht Zürichs," *B-T 1975*, pp. 63–67.

31. See *H B Bibl I*, nos. 422, 425, 568, 587. See also below, chapters 4 and 6.

32. See especially Fast, *Bullinger und die Täufer*. Cf. below, chapter 6.

33. For a discussion of the entire sacramentarian controversy and of the events leading up to the Consensus Tigurinus, see Ernst Bizer, *Studien zur Geschichte des Abendmahlsstreits im 16. Jahrhundert* (Darmstadt, 1972 [1940]).

34. Joachim Staedtke (ed.), *Glauben und Bekennen: Vierhundert Jahre Confessio Helvetica Posterior: Beiträge zu ihrer Geschichte und Theologie* (Zurich, 1966).

35. See Kenneth Hagen's statement of this distinction: "From Testament to Covenant in the Early Sixteenth Century," *SCJ* 3:1 (April 1972), pp. 1–24. For Luther and Calvin on covenant and testament, see below, appendixes A and B.

220   *Heinrich Bullinger and the Covenant*

36. See especially C. B. Hundeshagen, *Die Conflicte des Zwinglianismus, Lutherthums und Calvinismus in der Bernischen Landeskirche von 1532–1558* (Bern, 1842), and J. Wayne Baker, "In Defense of Magisterial Discipline: Bullinger's 'Tractatus de Excommunicatione' of 1568," *HBGesA I*, pp. 141–159.

37. Th.D. dissertation, Princeton Theological Seminary, 1971.

38. Ludwig Diestel, *Geschichte des Alten Testamentes in der christlichen Kirche* (Jena, 1869), pp. 278–306; cf. "Studien zur Föderaltheologie," *Jahrbuch für Deutsche Theologie* 10 (1865), pp. 209–276, where Diestel did not even mention Zwingli.

39. Antonius Johannes van t'Hooft, *De Theologie van Heinrich Bullinger in betrekking tot de Nederlandsche Reformatie* (Amsterdam, 1888), esp. pp. 43–44.

40. Emmanuel Graf von Korff, *Die Anfänge der Foederaltheologie und ihre erste Ausgestaltung in Zürich und Holland* (Bonn, 1908), pp. 15–27, 30–31, 53.

41. Gottlob Schrenk, *Gottesreich und Bund im älteren Protestantismus vornehmlich bei Johannes Coccejus* (Darmstadt, 1967 [1923]), pp. 36–63.

42. *Ibid.*, p. 40. McCoy, in his more recent study of Cocceius, also gives a sketch of the sixteenth-century origins of the covenant idea, including a few paragraphs on Zwingli and Bullinger. Charles Sherwood McCoy, "The Covenant Theology of Johannes Cocceius," Ph.D. dissertation, Yale University, 1956, pp. 63–66. For a brief examination of seventeenth-century covenant thought, see T. M. Lindsay, "The Covenant Theology," *The British and Foreign Evangelical Review* 27 (1879), pp. 521–538.

43. Otto Ritschl, *Dogmengeschichte des Protestantismus* (Göttingen, 1926), pp. 412–414. See also Heinrich Heppe, *Geschichte des Pietismus und der Mystik in der reformirten Kirche, namentlich der Niederlande* (Leiden, 1879), pp. 207–208, where Bullinger is given a prominent place in the development of Reformed covenant theology. Zwingli is presented as the originator and Bullinger as an important secondary figure in both P. Jacob, "Bund. IV. Föderaltheologie, dogmengeschichtlich," in *Die Religion in Geschichte und Gegenwart* 1, 1518–1520; and Jürgen Moltmann, "Föderaltheologie," in *Lexikon für Theologie und Kirche*, 4, 190–192.

44. Leonard J. Trinterud, "The Origins of Puritanism," *CH* 20 (1951), pp. 37–57; John Murray, *The Covenant of Grace: A Biblico-Theological Study* (London, 1954), esp. pp. 3–7; G. D. Henderson, "The Idea of the Covenant in Scotland," *Evangelical Quarterly* 27 (1955), pp. 2–14; Everett H. Emerson, "Calvin and Covenant Theology," *CH* 25 (1956), pp. 136–144; Joseph C. McClelland, "Covenant Theology: A Re-evaluation," *Canadian Journal of Theology* 3 (1957), pp. 182–187; S. A. Burrell, "The Covenant Idea as a Revolutionary Symbol: Scotland, 1596–1637," *CH* 27 (1958), pp. 338–350; Hans Heinrich Wolf, *Die Einheit des Bundes: Das Verhältnis von Altem und Neuem Testament bei Calvin* (Neukirchen, 1958); Jens G. Møller, "The Beginnings of Puritan Covenant Theology," *JEH* 14 (1963), pp. 46–67; Richard L. Greaves, "John Bunyan and Covenant Thought in the Seventeenth Century, *CH* 36 (1967), pp. 151–169; James B. Torrance, "Covenant or Contract? A Study of the

Theological Background of Worship in Seventeenth-Century Scotland," *Scottish Journal of Theology* 23 (1970), pp. 51–76; George M. Marsden, "Perry Miller's Rehabilitation of the Puritans: A Critique," *CH* 41 (1970), pp. 91–105; Kenneth Hagen, "From Testament to Covenant": and Richard L. Greaves, "John Knox and the Covenant Tradition," *JEH* 24 (1973), pp. 23–32.

45. Trinterud, "Origins of Puritanism," pp. 40–41. For Oecolampadius, Capito, and Cellarius, see below, appendix A.

46. Møller, "The Beginnings of Puritan Covenant Theology," *passim.* Møller does not use the terminology "theology of testament" but does distinguish between the conditional covenant of Zwingli and Bullinger and the Calvinistic idea of covenant, which was not conditional.

47. Hagen, "From Testament to Covenant," pp. 15–20, 23. These few pages are the best printed treatment of Zwingli's covenant thought.

48. *Theologie*, esp. pp. 227ff.

Chapter One

1. Schrenk first suggested that Zwingli took the covenant idea from the Anabaptists, who saw baptism as *Bund. Gottesreich und Bund*, pp. 36–37. Cottrell argues convincingly against such claims for Anabaptist precedence. "Covenant and Baptism," pp. 302–314.

2. See Cottrell, "Covenant and Baptism."

3. Staedtke, *Theologie*, pp. 227–228, 274.

4. The radicals rejected each of these points: they did not accept covenant unity; they failed to develop an idea of bilateral covenant, which underscores the necessity of defining terms carefully; and they directly opposed the inclusive corporate emphasis present in both Zwingli and Bullinger.

5. Cottrell, "Covenant and Baptism," p. 374. This analysis of the development of Zwingli's covenant thought is largely based on Cottrell's study.

6. Cottrell, "Covenant and Baptism," pp. 50–58, 96–97, 116–125. Cottrell (pp. 28–29) denies Robert C. Walton's argument that Zwingli thought in terms of the unity of the Old and New Covenants as early as 1522 (*Zwingli's Theocracy* [Toronto, 1967], pp. 79, 105–106).

7. "Von der Taufe, von der Wiedertaufe und von der Kindertaufe," *ZW* 4, pp. 188–337.

8. Although several earlier authors have seen Zwingli's first emphasis on the unity of the covenant in the "Taufbüchlein," Cottrell forcefully and convincingly denies it. "Covenant and Baptism," pp. 159–166, 172.

9. "Antwort über Balthasar Hubmaiers Taufbüchlein," *ZW* 4, pp. 577–647.

10. Cottrell argues that covenant unity emerged in Zwingli's thought during the summer of 1525. He bases his argument on Zwingli's "Erläuterungen zur Genesis" (*ZW* 13, pp. 1–290), not published until March 1527, where there is an obvious emphasis on covenant unity. The commentary resulted from Zwingli's *Prophezei* lectures from June 19 to Nov. 5, 1525. Jud and Megander edited the

commentary, which was a compilation from notes on these *Prophezei* lectures. "Covenant and Baptism," pp. 174–185. There are some severe difficulties in making such use of the commentary, which Cottrell himself notes. First, Zwingli said in his preface that he had included not only his own ideas but also the ideas of others. Cottrell feels that the commentary was mostly Zwingli's (*Ibid.*, pp. 177–178). Secondly, to what extent does the commentary represent Zwingli's thought during the summer of 1525? Cottrell's answer is vague (*Ibid.*, pp. 178–179). Even if the sections on covenant unity were not part of the 1525 *Prophezei* lectures, it seems likely that in 1527 Jud and Megander would have included Zwingli's by then well-developed idea of covenant unity in explaining such crucial passages as Genesis 17. Since there is no independent corroboration, this seems at least as likely as the argument that Zwingli developed the idea of covenant unity as early as the summer of 1525.

Cottrell also discovers covenant unity in Zwingli's "Subsidium sive coronis de eucharistia" (*ZW* 4, pp. 440–504), of August 17, 1525. "Covenant and Baptism," pp. 189–192. Cottrell uses the "Subsidium" to bolster his argument that the *Prophezei* lectures of 1525 made up the entire Genesis commentary of 1527. This argument seems a bit weak, in that Zwingli still did not specifically assert that there was only one people of God. The most important quotation from the "Subsidium" reads, "The covenant which was struck with Abraham is so strong and by no means abrogated that unless you keep it always you will not be faithful." *Ibid.*, pp. 191–192 (*ZW* 4, p. 500: 15–17). Since Zwingli did not follow through with his full teaching on covenant unity, it seems likely that the "Subsidium" contained not a synopsis of a *Prophezei* lecture that later became part of the Genesis commentary but rather the first tentative step toward covenant unity, fully developed only later in 1525.

11. Cottrell, "Covenant and Baptism," pp. 201–208. Zwingli did not substantially enlarge his position in the next twenty months. In Aug. 1526, he reaffirmed covenant unity and for the first time related election to the covenant ("De peccato originali declaratio ad Urbanum Rhegium." *ZW* 5, pp. 359–396. English translation in *ZLW* 2, pp. 1–32). Then, in Feb. 1527, he again affirmed covenant unity ("Amica exegesis, id est: expositio eucharistiae negocii ad Martinum Lutherum." *ZW* 5, pp. 548–758). Cottrell, "Covenant and Baptism," pp. 222–223, 229.

12. "In catabaptistarum strophas elenchus." *ZW* 6: 1, pp. 1–196. English translation in *UZSW*, pp. 123–258.

13. Cottrell, "Covenant and Baptism," pp. 237–245, 248. Although Zwingli continued to use the covenant concept and to stress covenant unity in his later works, Cottrell judges that "they do not reflect any advancement or change in his covenant thought" (p. 250). He does discuss them, however (pp. 250–263); he also presents a systematic rather than chronological analysis (pp. 265–294).

14. Zurich ZB, Ms. A82, fol. 75r–81r. Staedtke, *Theologie*, no. 32, pp. 273–274.

15. Simler, 2, p. 90.

16. See Johann Martin Usteri, "Vertiefung der Zwinglischen Sakraments- und Tauflehre bei Bullinger," *Theologische Studien und Kritiken* 56 (1883), pp. 730–731; and Fast, *Bullinger und die Täufer*, pp. 20–21. See also Fast's "On the

Beginnings of Bernese Anabaptism," *MQR* 31 (1957), pp. 292–293. Joachim Staedtke, in his "Die Anfänge des Täufertums in Bern," *TZ* 11 (1955), pp. 77–78, suggests May 1525 as the earliest possible date, but in his *Theologie*, p. 274, he places the letter in the autumn of 1525.

17. "Antwort an Burchard." Zurich ZB, Ms. A82, fol. 56v–73v. Staedtke, *Theologie* no. 31, pp. 272–273.

18. "Etwa Anfang 1525." Staedtke, *Theologie*, p. 274; see also Staedtke's "Heinrich Bullingers Bemühungen um eine Reformation im Kanton Zug," *Zwingliana* 10 (1954), pp. 36–39.

19. Hans-Georg vom Berg, "Noch einmal: Zur Datierung von Bullingers 'Antwort an Johannes Burchard,' " *Zwingliana* 10 (1978), pp. 581–589. See also Endre Zsindely, "Aus der Arbeit an der Bullinger-Edition: Zum Abendmahlsstreit zwischen Heinrich Bullinger und Johannes Burchard, 1525/1526," *Zwingliana* 13 (1972), pp. 473–480; and J. Wayne Baker, "Das Datum von Bullingers 'Antwort an Johannes Burchard,' " *Zwingliana* 14 (1976), pp. 274–275.

20. Cottrell concludes that Bullinger was dependent on Zwingli on the basis of a quotation from Bullinger from 1527. Jack Warren Cottrell, "Is Bullinger the Source for Zwingli's Doctrine of the Covenant?" *HBGesA I*, pp. 76–77.

21. Fast, *Bullinger und die Täufer*, p. 19.

22. Zurich ZB, Ms. A82, fol. 45r–50r.

23. "De Scripturae negotio," fol. 45v–46v; see Susi Hausammann, "Anfragen zum Schriftverständnis des jungen Bullinger in Zusammenhang einer Interpretation von 'De Scripturae negotio,' " *HBGesA I*, pp. 31–35.

24. "De Scripturae negotio," fol. 46v–47r.

25. "De Scripturae negotio," fol. 47r. Novum Testamentum aliud non esse quam Veteris interpretationem.

26. "De Scripturae negotio," fol. 48r. Scripturam ex Scriptura interpraetamus.

27. "De Scripturae negotio," fol. 48v. This interpretive principle was, of course, in itself not unique to Bullinger, but a common Reformation hermeneutical motif. Staedtke says that the principle was taken over from humanism, citing Faber Stapulensis and Erasmus, the major difference being that the humanists neglected the literal sense in favor of the mystical sense. *Theologie*, p. 78, note 25 (see also pp. 57ff, where Staedtke discusses "De Scripturae negotio" along with other early Bullinger writings). Hausammann disagrees with Staedtke, presenting Gerson as the greatest influence on Bullinger's interpretive method. *Römerbriefauslegung zwischen Humanismus und Reformation*, pp. 123–130. Hausammann discusses Bullinger's hermeneutic with respect to Luther in her "Anfragen zum Schriftverständnis," *HBGesA I*, pp. 35–47.

28. Zwingli continued to think basically in terms of contrast between the Testaments until 1525. See Cottrell, "Covenant and Baptism," p. 122; Hagen, "From Testament to Covenant," pp. 18–19; and Edwin Künzli, "Zwingli als Ausleger des Alten Testamentes," *ZW* 14, pp. 897–899.

29. Hausammann also sees this understanding of the unity of the Testaments as pointing toward his later covenant idea. "Anfragen zum Schriftverständnis," *HBGesA I*, pp. 39–40.

30. "Von dem Touff," fol. 75v.

31. "Von dem Touff," fol. 75v–76r. In his "Reply to Hubmaier," Zwingli only mentioned the human obligations in passing, with reference to the institution of the covenant in Gen. 17, but he did not at all develop the idea of obligation. *ZW* 4, p. 631: 1–4. He also used the term *pflichtszeichen*, but in the general sense of sacrament, as he stated in his *Taufbüchlein* (*ZW* 4, p. 218: 3–4), where he also specifically rejected the idea of any real human conditions—the obligations of the testament were God's alone (*ZW* 4, p. 293: 19–27).

32. "Von dem Touff," fol. 76r. Zwingli also named most of these men in his "Reply to Hubmaier," *ZW* 4, p. 630: 20–23.

33. "Von dem Touff," fol. 76v. Nütz anders xin, dann ein anfencklich zeichen. . . .

34. "Von dem Touff," fol. 77v–78v. Zwingli's treatment of the unity of testament or covenant in his "Reply to Hubmaier" is not nearly so well developed as this (*ZW* 4, pp. 634–637).

   The Acts 19 passage refers to the disciples of John, whom Paul met at Ephesus, who had not received the Holy Spirit. After they fully understood that John preached Christ, Paul baptized them, even though they seem already to have been baptized by John. Zwingli argued that John had only taught them, that they were first baptized by Paul (*ZW* 4, pp. 268–277, esp. p. 277: 7ff). Bullinger took the same position.

35. "Von dem Touff," fol. 78v. Zwingli's argument is similar in his "Reply to Hubmaier," *ZW* 4, pp. 637–638.

36. "Von dem Touff," fol. 78v–79r. Zwingli made the same argument, that the children in the New Testament were no less God's than those in the Old, in his *Taufbüchlein* (*ZW* 4, p. 333: 24ff), and then connected this argument with the unity of the testament in his "Reply to Hubmaier" (*ZW* 4, p. 637: 27ff; 641: 5ff).

37. "Von dem Touff," fol. 80v.

38. "Von dem Touff," fol. 75r.

39. Zurich ZB, Ms. A82, fol. 81r–89v.

40. "De institutione eucharistiae," fol. 81v.

41. "De institutione eucharistiae," fol. 82r.

42. "De institutione eucharistiae," fol. 85r.

43. *Kaetzeryen*, sig. bi–bi(v), ci. Incidentally, Bullinger also made a passing swipe at Burchard in this work (sig. aiv[v]).

44. *HBBW I*, pp. 93: 1–12, 97: 23–98: 1.

45. For Enzlin, see *HBBW I*, p. 85, note 1. The Hausen congregation was the first that Bullinger served as pastor, during 1528 and 1529.

46. *HBBW I*, pp. 110: 1–111: 9. In this letter, Bullinger sounds somewhat like Zwingli in his "Subsidium" (*ZW* 4, pp. 499–501).

47. *HBBW I*, pp. 153: 6–11; 154: 19–20.

48. "Antwort an Burchard." Zurich ZB, Ms. A82, fol. 56v–73v.

49. Even in the 1520s, then, the covenant was not used by Bullinger exclusively to oppose the Anabaptists, as Fast might lead one to believe (*Bullinger und die Täufer*, pp. 132ff).

50. "Antwort an Burchard," fol. 61r. Und disz ist die gantz summ aller geschrifft für und für reicht: anzoeugende wie nun diser pundt zuo beiden siten/ stat gethon

sye. (The Schweizerdeutsch diphthongs $\overset{o}{u}$, $\overset{e}{u}$, $\overset{e}{a}$, and $\overset{e}{o}$, are reproduced in the notes as uo, ue, ae, and oe.)

51. "Antwort an Burchard," fol. 62r–62v.
52. "Antwort an Burchard," fol. 62v. Und so nun das testament einig und ewig ist, muosz ye volgen das Gott gheinen nüwen punt/ ghein nüwes testament mitt uns gemachet habe.
53. "Antwort an Burchard," fol. 63r–63v.
54. "Antwort an Burchard," fol. 63v. Also sind der buecher ein testament: das ist/ ein inhalt wie das testa. gehandlet. Und heissend soelich reden by den gelerten, Metonymiae. . . .
55. "Antwort an Burchard," fol. 64r–64v. Under "the pious fathers and servants of God," Bullinger listed Tertullian, Augustine, Lactantius, Cyprian, Origen, Ambrose, Athanasius, and Jerome.
56. "The New Testament is nothing other than the interpretation of the Old." "We interpret Scripture from Scripture." "De Scripturae negotio," fol. 47r, 48r.
57. For Staedtke's discussion of the "Antwort an Burchard" and of Bullinger's position on the Scripture, see *Theologie*, pp. 57–79.

    Bullinger also used the covenant idea in the second half of the "Antwort an Burchard," in connection with the eucharist: the comparison of the divine testament with a human testament, i.e., the Testator must die (fol. 67r); the covenant condition of piety (fol. 69v); the eucharist as a replacement for the passover because all the figures were fulfilled (fol. 70v); Christ as the fulfillment of the covenant made with Abraham (fol. 71r).
58. *HBBW I*, pp. 81–82.
59. *ZW* 4, p. 639: 12–26.
60. *ZW* 6, pp. 56: 6–9; 110: 19–27. Since it has been clearly established that the "Antwort an Burchard" was written by Jan. 1527 at the latest (see above, note 19), it may well be that Bullinger influenced Zwingli, during late June, prior to the publication of the "Elenchus," on both this hermeneutical point and on the idea that the covenant began with Adam.
61. *ZW* 6, pp. 169–170. See Gottfried W. Locher, *Die Theologie Huldrych Zwinglis im Lichte seiner Christologie* (Zurich, 1952), pp. 96–98, where he demonstrates the soteriological unity in Zwingli's thought.
62. *ZW* 4, p. 631: 1–2.
63. *ZW* 6, p. 157: 6–7.
64. *ZW* 13, pp. 101: 30–102:2; 106: 21–24; 105: 5–6; 107: 13–23.
65. See the "Elenchus," where Zwingli stated that the elect were known by the fruit of election, i.e., faith upon reaching maturity, and that the others proved their rejection by not showing such fruit. *ZW* 6, p. 178: 27–29. It should be noted, however, that Zwingli did not stress condemnation. As Locher says, Zwingli felt that one must be considered of the elect until the reverse was obvious. Gottfried W. Locher, "The Shape of Zwingli's Theology: A Comparison with Luther and Calvin," *Pittsburgh Perspective* 7 (June 1967), p. 22. See also Locher's "Die Prädestinationslehre Huldrych Zwinglis: Zum 70. Geburtstag Karl Barths," *TZ* 5 (1956), pp. 526–548. For Bullinger on predestination, see below, chapter 2.

66. Hagen argues that Zwingli moved from a theology of testament in 1522 to an idea of bilateral covenant by 1525. "From Testament to Covenant," pp. 16–20.
67. See Cottrell's argument along these lines. "Covenant and Baptism," pp. 271–272.
68. *De testamento*, fol. 2–3b.
69. *Foede*, adverb from the adjective *foedus*—foul, horrible. The etymology and the play on words are really more complex than that, however. To make a covenant is *ferire foedus*, one meaning of *ferire* being *to kill*. Thus the metonymy *to make a covenant*, from *to kill a sow cruelly*. See Karl Ernst Georges, *Ausführliches Lateinisch-Deutsches Handwörterbuch*, 12th ed. (Hannover, 1969), vol. 1, col. 2723.
70. Also *pater patratus* (*Von dem Testament*, sig. Aiii), the chief priest of a group of priests, who concluded and sanctified treaties and covenants. Georges, *Handwörterbuch*, vol. 1, col. 2742–2743; vol. 2, col. 1507.
71. *De testamento*, fol. 4–4b.
72. *De testamento*, fol. 4b–6.
73. *De testamento*, fol. 16. Nostrarum partium est uni Deo per fidem constanter adhaerere, & ad placitum eius in innocentia vitae ambulare.
74. *De testamento*, fol. 17b. Partim amorem Dei, partim amorem proximi tradit. Hoc ipsum et foederis capitibus traditur. Quin ipse Decalogus conditionum foederis veluti paraphrasis quaedam esse videtur.
75. *De testamento*, fol. 23b–24. Partim fidem in Deum, partim amorem proximi tradat? Illa priorem foederis rationem exponit, haec posteriorem. Fides enim credit Deum summe bonum iustum & beneficum esse in hominem. Charitas vero ipsius innocentiae integritatisque fons est.
    For other assertions of the conditional nature of the covenant see *De testamento*, fol. 11b–15b, 17, 21b–23b, 28–31b.
76. "De peccato originali declaratio ad Urbanum Rhegium," *ZW* 5, pp. 369–396; "Amica Exegesis, id est expositio eucharistiae negocii ad Martinum Lutherum," *ZW* 5, pp. 562–758.
77. *Fraefel*. See chapter 6, below.
78. This is true with the possible exception of his "De peccato originali declaratio"; but even there his argument concerned the nature of baptism itself. See Cottrell, "Covenant and Baptism," pp. 219–226.
79. Staedtke's conclusion is similar. *Theologie*, p. 228; and "Bullingers Theologie— Eine Fortsetzung der zwinglischen?" *B-T 1975*, p. 91.
80. "In Ioannis evangelium tractatus CXXIV," XLV, 9. *PL* 35, col. 1722–1723. English translation in *PNF* 7, p. 252. Bullinger cited "In Ioannis" in his "Von dem Touff" (fol. 77v) and quoted this passage at some length in *De testamento* (fol. 26b–27b). Regarding the influence of Augustine on the early Bullinger, see Ulrich Gäbler, "Bullingers Vorlesung über das Johannesevangelium aus dem Jahre 1523," *HBGesA I*, pp. 20–21.
81. "De baptismo contra Donatistas," I, xvi, 25, *PL* 43, col. 123; *PNF* 4, p. 422. Quoted by Bullinger in *De testamento* (fol. 27b–28); cited in "Antwort an Burchard" (fol. 62v).

82. In "Von dem Touff" Bullinger cited "Ad Valerium contra Iulianum." (fol. 77v). In his "Antwort an Burchard" (fol. 60, 62v, 64v, 65v), he referred to "Ad Marcellinum," "De utilitate agendae poenitatem," "Ad Petrum diaconum," plus many passing references. In *De testamento*, he cited "Contra Guadentium" (fol. 40b), "De civitate Dei" (fol. 41b), and "Contra Faustum" (fol. 41b). Staedtke says that Augustine had the greatest influence of any church father on Bullinger. *Theologie*, p. 45.

83. This summary of Augustine's position is based on "De peccatorum meritis et remissione, et de baptismo parvulorum," I, 27, 53–54 (*CSEL* 60, pp. 50–53; *PNF* 5, pp. 35–36); "De natura et gratia, contra Pelagium," XLIV, 51 (*CSEL* 60, pp. 270–271; *PNF* 5, pp. 138–139); "De spiritu et littera," XIII, 21–XXV, 42 (*CSEL* 60, pp. 173–196; *PNF* 5, pp. 91–101); "Contra duas epistolas Pelagianorum," III, iv, 6–13 (*CSEL* 60, pp. 492–501; *PNF* 5, pp. 404–408); "De gratia Christi, et de peccato originali, contra Pelagium," II, xxiv, 28–xxx, 35 (*PL* 44, col. 398–403; *PNF* 5, pp. 246–250); "De gestis Pelagii," V, 14–15 (*CSEL* 42, pp. 64–68; *PNF* 5, pp. 188–190); "Contra Faustum," IV; X; XV, 4; XXXII, 6, 14 (*CSEL* 25, pp. 268–271, 310–313, 421–423, 595–596, 600–603; *PNF* 4, pp. 161–162, 176–177, 213–214, 274, 276–277); "De baptismo contra donatistas," I, xv, 23–24, xvi, 25; IV, xxiv, 32 (*PL* 43, col. 121–123, 174–176; *PNF* 4, pp. 421–422, 461–462); "De civitate Dei," IV, 33; V, 18; X, 25; and esp. XVI, 26 (*CSEL* 40, 1, pp. 207–209, 251, 487–490; 40, 2, pp. 171–174; *PNF* 2, pp. 82, 101, 195–196, 325–326).

84. For an excellent, more technical, and more thorough discussion on Augustine, see Kenneth Hagen, *A Theology of Testament in the Young Luther: The Lectures on Hebrews* (Leiden, 1974), pp. 33–43; see also James S. Preus, *From Shadow to Promise: Old Testament Interpretation from Augustine to the Young Luther* (Cambridge, Massachusetts, 1969), pp. 9–21.

85. Staedtke (*Theologie*, p. 43) says that the "covenant theology of Irenaeus made the deepest impression" on Bullinger but offers no documentation.

86. "Against Heresies," IV, v, vii, ix–xvi, xxi, xxii, xxv, xxxii, xxxiv (*ANF* 1, pp. 466ff; *PG* 7, col. 983ff).

87. See below, chapter 3.

88. In *De testamento* (fol. 37b), he made a passing reference to Irenaeus, not in support of the covenant notion, but in connection with the Ebionite heresy. In *De origine erroris II*, he mentioned Irenaeus, along with Tertullian, Lactantius, Eusebius, and Augustine, as fathers who taught in terms of covenant (sig. Bii[v]); then he went on to develop his concept of the covenant (sig. Biii–Bv). For Irenaeus on the covenant, see Adolph Harnack, *History of Dogma*, vol. 2, pp. 305–311. Harnack counts four covenants.

89. He referred to Tertullian along with Irenaeus against the Ebionites, without any citation. *De testamento*, fol. 37b. The quotation (*De testamento*, fol. 30b–31), concerning the reasons for the Old Testament sacrifices, is from "Adversus Marcionem," II, xviii–xix (*CSEL* 62, pp. 359–362; *ANF* 3, pp. 311–312). For Bullinger's study and use of Tertullian, see Staedtke, *Theologie*, pp. 42–43. Cf. Hausammann, *Römerbriefauslegung*, pp. 78ff.

90. "Von dem Touff," Zurich ZB, Ms. A82, fol. 77v; "De paenitentia," 2,4, per paenitentiae subsignationem (*CSEL* 76, p. 142: 19–22; *ANF* 3, p. 658); 6, 16, Lavacrum illud obsignatio est fidei (*CSEL* 76, p. 156: 60–61; *ANF* 3, p. 662).

91. 1 Dec. 1525. *HBBW I*, p. 81. Bullinger's letter to Zwingli is not extant. This exchange of letters suggests that Bullinger used the fathers not so much as sources for his covenant idea, but as "proof texts."

92. "De paenitentia," 6, 17 (*CSEL* 76, p. 156: 62–63; *ANF* 3, p. 662). See also "De baptismo," XVIII, where Tertullian advised against infant baptism (*CSEL* 20, p. 216; *ANF* 3, p. 678). Tertullian not only opposed infant baptism but also held to a doctrine of baptismal regeneration, as did other early fathers. See J. F. Bethune-Baker, *An Introduction to the Early History of Christian Doctrine up to the Time of the Council of Chalcedon* (London, 1920), pp. 378–382. See also Arthur Cushman McGiffert, *A History of Christian Thought, vol. 2: The West from Tertullian to Erasmus* (New York, 1933), pp. 19–21.

93. In the "Antwort an Burchard," Bullinger again referred to Tertullian in support of covenant unity (Zurich ZB, Ms. A82, fol. 62v; "Adversus Marcionem," IV, i–xliii [*CSEL* 47, pp. 422–568; *ANF* 3, pp. 345–423]), although Tertullian himself did not refer either to testament or covenant in the passage.

94. Zurich ZB, Ms. A82, fol. 77v; "Divinae institutiones," IV, 15 (*CSEL* 19, p. 329: 14–18; *ANF* 7, p. 115). For Bullinger's use and study of Lactantius, see Staedtke, *Theologie*, p. 45.

95. "Divinae institutiones," IV, 20 (*CSEL* 19, p. 364: 1–365:5; *ANF* 7, pp. 122–123). Bullinger also cited this passage in his "Antwort an Burchard (Zurich ZB, Ms. A82, fol. 62v). For Lactantius, see Joseph Fischer, "Die Einheit der beiden Testamente bei Laktanz, Viktorin von Pettau und deren Quellen," *Münchener Theologische Zeitschrift* 1 (1950), pp. 96–101.

96. *De testamento*, fol. 50–51b; "Historia ecclesiastica," I, iv (*PG* 20, col. 75–79; *PNF2* 1, pp. 87–88).

97. Heiko A. Oberman, *The Harvest of Medieval Theology* (Grand Rapids, Michigan, 1967), esp. pp. 132, 148, 167–170; Steven E. Ozment, *Homo Spiritualis: A Comparative Study of the Anthropology of Johannes Tauler, Jean Gerson and Martin Luther (1509–16) in the Context of Their Theological Thought* (Leiden, 1969), esp. pp. 25, 45–46, 55–58, 199. See also Oberman, "Wir sind pettler: Hoc est verum: Bund und Gnade in der Theologie des Mittelalters und der Reformation," *Zeitschrift für Kirchengeschichte* 78 (1967), esp. pp. 244–245; Oberman, "Facientibus quod in se est Deus non denegat gratiam: Robert Holcott, O. P. and the Beginnings of Luther's Theology," *Harvard Theological Review* 55 (1962), esp. pp. 317–330; and Martin Greschat, "Der Bundesgedanke in der Theologie des späten Mittelalters," *Zeitschrift für Kirchengeschichte* 81 (1970), pp. 44–63.

98. Heiko A. Oberman, *Forerunners of the Reformation* (New York, 1966), p. 173.

99. As translated by Preus, *From Shadow to Promise*, pp. 131–132. Italics his. Preus concludes that Biel had discovered "the basis of a real continuity between the Old and New Testaments in the *pactum*, the covenant, understood historically" (p. 232).

100. See below, chapter 2, for Bullinger on predestination. In his Matthew

commentary Bullinger specifically rejected the nominalist semi-Pelagianism: "Huic pharisaicae iustitiae similis illa esse videtur, quam nostro saeculo quidam docentes dixerunt, Fac quod in te est. . . ."*Matthaeum*, fol. 55b.

101. Staedtke sees an indirect nominalist influence through Luther in Bullinger's early doctrine of justification. *Theologie*, pp. 190–193.

102. For the discussion of Luther, Melanchthon, Oecolampadius, Cellarius, Capito, and Bucer, see below, appendix A. For Calvin, see appendix B. For the treatment of the development of testamental theology and covenantal theology during the latter sixteenth century, see appendix C.

Chapter Two

1. See appendix B for Calvin on predestination and the covenant.

2. For the fortunes of the covenant idea and for Bullinger's influence in the second half of the sixteenth century, see appendix C.

3. *Decades*, IV:iv, fol. 217 (*PSD* 3, p. 185). The first Roman numeral in the citations from the *Decades* refers to the specific decade, the second, to the sermon within that decade. The translations from the *Decades* are my own, although *PSD* has always been consulted.

4. "Antwort an Burchard," fol. 67r–67v. Dorumb woellend wir ietzund beweren das das einig oppffer Christi also volckommen ist/ das es gheines ersetzens bedarff/ und alle welt von iren sünden reinget. . . . Merckend hie frommen Christen wie Paulus so unverholen dem einigen lyden Christi . . . zuo gipt aller welt grechtigheit.

5. *De testamento*, fol. 21b. Foedus illud Dei aeternum cum hominum genere pactum.

6. M. A. Gooszen, *Heinrich Bullinger en de strijd over de Praedestinatie* (Rotterdam, 1909), pp. 97–98; see also Korff, who refers to the "universalist stress" in Bullinger's thought (*Die Anfänge der Foederaltheologie*, p. 24); and Schrenk, who speaks of the characteristic "universalist formulation of Bullinger's covenant idea" (*Gottesreich und Bund*, p. 41, n. 21); see also Heppe, *Geschichte des Pietismus*, p. 207.

7. See, for instance, Justus Heer [Emil Egli], "H. Bullinger," *RTK* 3, 536ff; Emil Egli, "Zur Erinnerung an Zwinglis Nachfolger Heinrich Bullinger geboren 1504: Akademischer Rathausvortrag am 7. Januar 1904," *Zwingliana* 1 (1904), pp. 424–425, 437; Joachim Staedtke, "Der Zürcher Praedestinationsstreit von 1560," *Zwingliana* 9 (1953), pp. 536–546.

8. For the complete historiography on Bullinger and predestination, see Peter Walser, *Die Prädestination bei Heinrich Bullinger im Zusammenhang mit seiner Gotteslehre* (Zurich, 1957), pp. 9–22.

9. Walter Hollweg, *Heinrich Bullingers Hausbuch: Eine Untersuchung über die Anfänge der reformierten Predigtliteratur* (Neukirchen, 1956), pp. 117–129.

10. For Breitinger at Dort, see J. J. Mörikofer, *J. J. Breitinger und Zürich* (Leipzig, 1873), pp. 24–37.

11. Breitinger's speech is printed in *Historiae*, pp. 959–976.

12. Hollweg, *Hausbuch*, pp. 136–137.

13. From Bullinger's comments on Ephesians from the middle 1520s (title no. 59, Staedtke, *Theologie*), as cited in Staedtke, *Theologie*, pp. 136–137.

14. *Ibid.*, pp. 134–140.

15. *HBBW I*, p. 87. Also quoted in Staedtke, *Theologie*, p. 140.

16. "Oratio de moderatione servanda in negotio providentiae, praedestinationis, gratiae et liberi arbitrii," given 28 Jan. 1536; printed in *Historiae*, pp. 763–827; discussed by Walser, *Prädestination*, pp. 163–167; translated loosely (with large sections deleted) by Alexander Schweizer, *Die protestantischen Centraldogmen in ihrer Entwicklung innerhalb der reformierten Kirche, 1st half: Das 16. Jahrhundert* (Zurich, 1854), pp. 258–264. Cf. *HBBibl I*, no. 721.

17. *Historiae*, p. 777. Bullinger did not make clear to whom he was referring in the latter case.

18. *Historiae*, pp. 780, 784–789, 792–793. Prorsus divinus.

19. *Historiae*, pp. 794–796. Walser, I think, misinterprets this section, saying that Bullinger tied predestination to foreknowledge. *Prädestination*, pp. 165–166.

20. *Historiae*, p. 825.

21. *Decades*, III:x, fol. 163b–164, 165b–167 (*PSD* 2, pp. 368–370, 377, 380–384).

22. Walser sees it as such, but he also admits that he can find no firm doctrine of reprobation in Bullinger. *Prädestination*, pp. 130–132, 135.

23. *Decades*, IV:iv, fol. 217–217b (*PSD* 3, pp. 185–187).

24. See Hollweg, *Hausbuch*, p. 307.

25. *Decades*, IV: i, fol. 184b–185 (*PSD* 3, pp. 32–34).

26. Bolsec's appeal to Bullinger was similar to the later appeal to his authority by the Remonstrants. Indeed, many who were caught in the web of the latter sixteenth-century Calvinist orthodoxy seem to have appealed to him. Samuel Huber in Bern in the 1580s used him against Abraham Musculus, for instance. See Gottfried Adam, *Der Streit um die Prädestination im ausgehenden 16. Jahrhundert* (Neukirchen, 1970), esp. pp. 75, 83–85.

27. 14 Nov. 1551. *CO* 8, col. 206–207. See also Beza's letter to Bullinger. *Correspondence* 1, pp. 71–75.

28. *CO* 8, col. 230–233.

29. 27 Nov. 1551. *CO* 14, col. 208, 210. For the treatment in the *Consensus*, see *CO* 7, col. 740. Bullinger's reference was to the sermon on predestination (*Decades*, IV:iv). On the Bolsec correspondence, see also Hollweg, *Hausbuch*, pp. 295ff; and Walser, *Prädestination*, pp. 168ff.

30. 1 Dec. 1551. *CO* 14, col. 214–215. For Zwingli's *De providentia*, see *S* 4, pp. 79–144; English translation in *ZLW* 2, pp. 128–234.

31. 8 Dec. 1551. *CO* 14, col. 218–219.

32. *CO* 14, col. 251–253.

33. 20 Feb. 1552. *CO* 14, col. 289–290. See Walser *Prädestination*, pp. 168–181, for his discussion of this Bullinger-Calvin correspondence.

    On 13 March 1552 (*CO* 14, col. 304), Calvin again briefly brought up the controversy, indicating that he was sending a little book on the subject to Bullinger, probably his *De aeterna Dei praedestinatione* (*CO* 8, col. 249–366).

About a year later, Bullinger wrote to Calvin, pledging his friendship, if not his agreement on predestination (*CO* 14, col. 510–511). Calvin responded favorably, although he specifically exempted Bibliander from his favor because of his open hostility to Calvin's doctrine (*CO* 14, col. 513–514).

34. 10 Dec. 1552. *CO* 14, col. 359–360 (*OL* 1, pp. 324–326). The very fact that Traheron had to ask Bullinger indicates how much more important predestination had become by midcentury. Traheron had been in Zurich in 1536 and 1537. Christina Hollowell Garrett, *The Marian Exiles: A Study in the Origins of Elizabethan Puritanism* (Cambridge, 1938), p. 308. See also Hollweg, *Hausbuch*, pp. 300ff.

35. "Henrici Bullingeri epistola ad Bartholomaeum Trahernum Anglum de providentia Dei eiusdemque praedestinatione electione ac reprobatione, deque libero arbitrio et quod Deus non sit autor peccati 1553." 3 March 1553. *CO* 14, col. 480–490. Both Schweizer and the editors of *CO* (14, col. 480) have confused this treatise with one written by Vermigli. See Walser, *Prädestination*, p. 24, n. 2; and p. 200, n. 25, concerning this confusion, and pp. 96–104, 124–130 for his treatment of Bullinger's letter to Traheron.

36. *CO* 14, col. 480–481.

37. *CO* 14, col. 481–486.

38. *CO* 14, col. 487–488.

39. *CO* 14, col. 488–489.

40. *CO* 14, col. 489–490. Traheron was not convinced. He felt that Bullinger deprived God of His freedom to act. See *OL* 1, pp. 326–328 (*CO* 14, col. 550–551).

41. Schweizer seems to have been the first to ascribe their authorship to Bullinger, although he confuses them with the letter to Traheron (*Centraldogmen*, pp. 266, 275, 285, n.2); Walser, however, argues convincingly that the author was Vermigli and not Bullinger (*Prädestination*, pp. 200–210); and John Patrick Donnelly proves decisively that Vermigli wrote the treatises ("Three Disputed Vermigli Tracts," *Essays Presented to Myron P. Gilmore, vol. 1: History* [Florence, 1978], pp. 37–46).

42. There is, in fact, plenty of evidence that he did not. In his *De gratia Dei* (1554), he reaffirmed his earlier teachings: faith was the proof of election (fol. 6), and therefore one should ask for faith (fol. 6); the universal atonement (fol. 12b–13); none was excluded except for his own sin (fol. 28–28b). In his *Sermones* (1558), he emphasized the universal atonement (fol. 8–10) and warned against inquiring into the secret counsel of God (fol. 172).

43. Printed in *Historiae*, pp. 691ff; partially translated into German in Schweizer, *Centraldogmen*, pp. 278ff. On the Vermigli-Bibliander conflict, see John Patrick Donnelly, *Calvinism and Scholasticism in Vermigli's Doctrine of Grace* (Leiden, 1976), pp. 182–183.

44. *Historiae*, pp. 694, 696, 699.

45. *Historiae*, p. 677. Schweizer, *Centraldogmen*, p. 282.

46. *Historiae*, pp. 705–706. Partial translation in Schweizer, *Centraldogmen*, pp. 282–283.

47. *CO* 14, col. 514.

48. 22 May 1553. *CO* 14, col. 533.

49. See Christoph Zürcher, *Konrad Pellikans Wirken in Zürich 1526–1556* (Zurich, 1975). Zürcher does not discuss Pellikan on predestination. Pellikan did, however, have a covenant idea that sounds much like Bullinger's (pp. 124ff).

50. On Vermigli's "Calvinism," see Donnelly, *Calvinism and Scholasticism,* pp. 13–41, and "Italian Influences on Calvinist Scholasticism," p. 97. For Vermigli on predestination, see *Loci communes (Vermigli)*, pp. 813–874. He also had a section on the covenant (pp. 723–750), in which he referred to the conditions of piety and faith; both conditions, however, depended on God's election and grace (pp. 727–728). The elect were heirs of the testament (p. 743) in both the Old and New Testament. He strongly affirmed the unity of the testament (pp. 730, 744). The use of the terms old and new covenant (Jere. 31) referred to law and gospel. His was a theology of testament.

    Donnelly also presents Vermigli's doctrine of predestination as supralapsarian, based on a double decree (*Calvinism and Scholasticism*, pp. 118–119, 132, 137–138), thus displacing J. C. McClelland's argument that Vermigli's was not really a doctrine of double predestination ("The Reformed Doctrine of Predestination According to Peter Martyr," *Scottish Journal of Theology* 8 [1955], pp. 255–271).

51. See Zanchi's letter to Calvin (July 1556); "I know that he [Vermigli] has been called by divine providence to Zurich perhaps for this purpose, that, besides the other opportunities that the church may afford, he may unteach many in that church of that pestilential doctrine (I tell you this heart to heart) of free will against predestination and God's grace. You know what I am talking about." *CO* 14, col. 46. As translated by Joseph N. Tylenda, "Girolamo Zanchi and John Calvin," *Calvin Theological Journal* 10 (1975), p. 111.

52. See Vermigli's letter to Calvin (1 July 1557). *Historiae*, p. 829.

53. Staedtke, "Der Zürcher Prädestinationsstreit von 1560," p. 546; but cf. Hollweg, *Hausbuch*, p. 310.

54. *Diarium*, pp. 64, 76. Schweizer says that Bibliander was fortunate that "with this naive point of view" he was Bullinger's colleague and not Calvin's. *Centraldogmen*, p. 280. One tradition has been that Bibliander was pensioned in 1560 because he had become mentally unbalanced. See Staedtke, "Der Zürcher Prädestinationsstreit von 1560."

55. Schweizer concluded long ago that Bullinger finally accepted the logic of the *Centraldogma* and accepted Calvin's teaching on predestination. *Centraldogmen*, pp. 291, 459. Recently this conclusion has been restated by Donnelly, *Calvinism and Scholasticism*, p. 184; and by Jürgen Moltmann, *Prädestination und Perseveranz: Geschichte und Bedeutung der reformierten Lehre "de perseverantia sanctorum"* (Neukirchen, 1961), pp. 100–103.

56. For Zanchi's theology, see Otto Gründler, *Die Gotteslehre Girolamo Zanchis und ihre Bedeutung für seine Lehre von der Prädestination* (Neukirchen, 1965); Donnelly, "Italian Influences on Calvinist Scholasticism"; and Tylenda, "Girolamo Zanchi and John Calvin."

57. On the controversy in Strassburg, see James M. Kittelson, "Marbach vs.

Zanchi, the Resolution of Controversy in Late Reformation Strasbourg," *SCJ* 8:3 (1977), pp. 31–44. Kittelson argues that it was not only a controversy over theology but also a dispute between the two institutions of school and church. See also Moltmann, *Praëdestination und Perseveranz*, pp. 72–109.

58. *Historiae*, pp. 833–834. See also Schweizer, *Centraldogmen*, p. 452, for a partial translation.
59. *Historiae*, p. 846. Certus est apud Deum tum electorum ad vitam, tum reprobatorum adque interitum praedestinatorum numerus. . . . Certum esse quendam numerum apud Deum tam Praedestinatorum ad aeternam vitam; quam reproborum, citra controversiam est.
60. *Historiae*, p. 847. Sicut electi ad vitam periri non possunt, ideoque salvantur necessario; ita quoque qui ad vitam aeternam praedestinati non sunt, salvari non possunt, ideoque necessario damnantur.
61. *Historiae*, p. 834. Sano sensu proposita.
62. *Historiae*, p. 849.
63. *Historiae*, pp. 855–857. Vel haereticum vel absurdum. Imo eas amplectimur partim ut necessarias, partim ut probabiles.
64. It also fell quite a bit short of Vermigli's actual viewpoint. See Donnelly, *Calvinism and Scholasticism*, pp. 122–123, 125, n. 4, 137–138, 183.
65. Hollweg comes to a similar conclusion (*Hausbuch*, pp. 317–318), as does Walser (*Prädestination*, pp. 190–193).
66. *Diarium*, pp. 66:11; 83:21–24.
67. See Ernst Koch, "Die Textüberlieferung der Confessio Helvetica Posterior und ihre Vorgeschichte," in *Glauben und Bekennen*, pp. 13–40.
68. *Ibid.*, p. 39, and p. 40, n. 67, where Koch states: "Substantial ecclesiastical-political necessities and intentions stand behind these changes."
69. Chapter 8. *Creeds* 3, pp. 247–248 (English, pp. 843–844).
70. *Creeds* 3, pp. 249–252 (English, pp. 844–847).
71. *Creeds* 3, pp. 252–254 (English, pp. 847–849). The covenant concept is subdued in the Confession, although it plays a prominent part in the section on baptism (chapter 20). Concerning the covenant in the Confession, Edward A. Dowey says, "Perhaps his caution about theological novelty held him back from using such a distinctive theological idea in a document meant for the entire church." "Die theologische Aufbau des Zweiten Helvetischen Bekenntnisses," in *Glauben und Bekennen*, p. 213. Koch, on the other hand, refers to "the theology of the Confession as an unfolding of the covenant idea." Ernst Koch, *Die Theologie der Confessio Helvetica Posterior* (Neukirchen, 1968), pp. 415ff.
72. *Fundamentum firmum*, fol. 32b–34b.
73. *Isaias*, fol. 8–8b, 10b–11, 36b, 60, 92b, 183, 250b–251, 266b, 275b, 327.
74. *Bekerung*, fol. 8–8b.
75. Walser sees Bullinger coming to use a double predestinarian formula in the *Decades*, the letter to Traheron and, to a lesser degree, in the Confession. But he concludes that he developed no firm doctrine of reprobation. *Prädestination*, pp. 130ff. Cf. Koch, *Die Theologie der Confessio Helvetica Posterior*, p. 94.
76. *Ursprung*, fol. 188b–190; cf. *Fraefel*, fol. 56, for a similar but shorter treatment.

See Koch's comment on this passage, *Die Theologie der Confessio Helvetica Posterior*, p. 96.

77. *Creeds* 3, p. 290 (English, pp. 889–890).
78. *Summa*, sig. ai(v)–aiv. The *Summa* was translated into Latin, also in 1556 (*HBBibl I*, no. 291); into French (published in Geneva) in 1556 (*HBBibl I*, no. 297); into Dutch in 1562 (*HBBibl I*, no. 310); and into English in 1572 (*HBBibl I*, no. 314).
79. *Summa*, fol. 3–4b, 23b–24, 29–31.
80. *Summa*, fol. 34–36b, 39–40.
81. *Summa*, fol. 48b–51, 71–73.
82. *Summa*, fol. 77–77b, 91–96.
83. *Summa*, fol. 104b–107b.
84. *Summa*, fol. 137b–142b, 146–147, 158–158b.
85. In *De testamento*, his great systematic work on the covenant, Bullinger did not discuss predestination at all.
86. Schaff says, "The doctrine of covenant belongs to a different scheme of theology from that of the divine decrees. It is biblical and historical rather than scholastic and predestinarian. It views man from the start as a free and responsible agent, not as a machine for the execution of absolute divine decrees." *Creeds 1*, p. 773. Although Schaff refers to seventeenth-century theological systems, the statement can as well be applied to Bullinger's approach in comparison with that of the sixteenth-century Calvinists.

Chapter Three

1. *Summa*, fol. 4, pundsbuecher . . . pundtsbuoch; *De testamento*, fol. 44b–45, tabulae testamenti . . . foederis tabulas. Cf. *Epitome*, fol. 4b; and *De omnibus scripturae libris*, sig. A4.
2. *De scriptura II*, fol. 7. Bullinger placed the birth of Christ in the year 3969 after creation. *Epitome*, fol. 97b. The B.C. dates given in parenthesis are calculated on this basis, for the reader's reference. No attempt has been made to correct Bullinger's dates, even when the error is flagrant.
3. Published in an English edition in 1624 with the title *Looke from Adam* (*HBBibl I*, no. 107). *Der alt gloub* was obviously inspired partially by Augustine's *City of God*. By no means, however, is it merely a pale imitation of that classic. It is much more succinct and unified, and it is organized not only around promise and fulfillment, or unilateral testament, but also around the concept of bilateral covenant. In it Bullinger emphasized the unity of the faith, the unity of the people, and the unity of the covenant. More significantly, Bullinger, because of the covenant, tended to equate the history of salvation and secular history among God's people and thus to be somewhat optimistic about the possibility of a true Christian political community. Augustine did not have such high expectations. The only true Christian society was the Heavenly City; the Christian was a sojourner in the earthly city. *The City of God*, XIX. 17, 20, 26, 27; *CSEL* 40, 2, pp. 402–405, 407, 420–423.

4. *Der alt gloub*, sig. Avi; cf. *Decades*, III:x, fol. 163b–164. Love and obedience were in fact the conditions of the covenant; but Bullinger never referred specifically to a covenant before the fall.

5. *Der alt gloub*, sig. Avii–Aviii(v), Bi(v); cf. *Isaias*, fol. 129b–130; *Apodixis*, p. 27; *Epitome*, fol. 4–4b.

6. *Der alt gloub*, sig. Biv–Bv, Bvi(v)–Bvii; cf. *Apodixis*, p. 27.

7. He first specifically mentioned the covenant in his treatment of Noah, where he referred its origins back to Adam. *Der alt gloub*, sig. Ciii(v).

8. "Von dem Touff," fol. 75v; *Summa*, fol. 2b, 31–31b; *De scriptura I*, fol. 5; *Nachtmal*, sig. Civ; *De origine erroris III*, fol. 19b; *Epitome*, fol. 4b, 12b; *Daniel*, fol. 108b; *Apodixis*, p. 28.

9. *Der alt gloub*, sig. Bvii(v)–Bviii(v), Cii; *Epitome*, fol. 5.

10. *De origine erroris III*, fol. 26b–27.

11. *Der alt gloub*, sig. Cii(v)–Ciii(v); *Epitome*, fol. 6b–7b.

12. *Der alt gloub*, sig. Civ(v)–Cv. See *Epitome*, fol. 7–10, for Bullinger's somewhat detailed reconstruction of the origins and progress of the pagan kingdoms up to the time of Abraham. See also *De origine erroris III*, fol. 32–46, where he discussed superstitions, idolatry, and polytheism among the ancient pagans. Since these errors had begun with Ham, polytheism had thus developed from the knowledge of the one true God.

13. *Der alt gloub*, sig. Cv–Cvi(v).

14. In *Der alt gloub*, except for references to Abraham's good works coming from his faith, Bullinger did not discuss the conditional nature of the covenant as renewed with Abraham. But he did discuss these conditions with reference to Abraham in many works, spanning his entire career. See *Summa*, fol. 31–31b; *Epitome*, fol. 12b; *Daniel*, fol. 108b; *De scriptura I*, fol. 6ff; *De testamento*, fol. 15b–16.

15. *De testamento*, fol. 41b–43; *Decades*, III:vi, fol. 121–123b; *Sermones*, p. 43.

16. *Der alt gloub*, sig. Cvii–Cviii; see also *Epitome*, fol. 16b.

17. *Epitome*, fol. 16b; *De scriptura I*, fol. 68b. Luther's first epoch of the history of the church, the age of the patriarchs, ended with Abraham. John M. Headley, *Luther's View of Church History* (New Haven, 1963), pp. 108–124.

18. *Der alt gloub*, sig. Cviii(v), Di(v).

19. See, for instance, "Von dem Touff," fol. 75v; and *Ieremias*, fol. 188.

20. *Epitome*, fol. 4b, 7b–8, 11–11b, 16b.

21. *De scriptura I*, fol. 5. Bullinger did not always insist that nothing had been written prior to Moses (especially when opposing the Roman position on tradition). Moses may have had some written sources for Genesis, particularly books extant from the patriarchs, and perhaps Egyptian books, in addition to the oral tradition. *De scriptura II*, fol. 7–7b; *Der alt gloub*, sig. Eii.

22. *Summa*, fol. 46–46b.

23. *De testamento*, fol. 17b.

24. *Epitome*, fol. 19. See also, *Summa*, fol. 50; *Der alt gloub*, sig. Dii; *De testamento*, fol. 23b–24.

25. *Der alt gloub*, sig. Diii(v).

26. Bullinger presents these three uses of the law in his *Decades*, III:viii, fol. 136–138

(*PSD* 2, pp. 237–245), and in his *Summa*, fol. 70–71. In the *Epitome*, the first is divided into two and the third becomes the second. See also *De testamento*, fol. 35b–37.

27. *Epitome*, fol. 20b–21; *Der alt gloub*, sigs. Diii(v)–Div.

28. Nor was it identical with Zwingli's. Zwingli posited a divine righteousness, summarized in the Love Commandment, which no man could fulfill. Human righteousness was based in the Decalogue and was enforced by the magistracy. *ZW* 2, pp. 482–486, 520–522.

29. See especially *Summa*, fol. 31–31b, 48–50, 72–72b, 158bff.

30. *Summa*, fol. 69b–70; *Der alt gloub*, sig. Ei(v).

31. *Der alt gloub*, sig. Dviii(v)–Ei. See also *De scriptura I*, fol. 67–68b.

32. *De testamento*, fol. 29b, 31. ascitia (fol. 31); *Summa*, fol. 69–69b.

33. *Epitome*, fol. 19–20.

34. *Der alt gloub*, sig. Dvii–Dviii(v). For an extended treatment of the ceremonial law, see *Decades*, III:v–vi, fol. 111b–132; see also *De origine erroris III*, fol. 188ff.

35. *Isaias*, fol. 158b–160, 281–283; *Ieremias*, fol. 187–188b. See Joachim Staedtke, "Die Juden im historischen und theologischen Urteil des Schweizer Reformators Heinrich Bullinger," *Judaica* 11 (1955), pp. 236–256. Staedtke's basic point, that Bullinger's covenant thought preserved him from anti-Semitism, may be well founded (pp. 250ff). But Bullinger's idea of an interregnum and the resulting ambivalence toward the Jews is not at all clear in Staedtke's presentation (see pp. 245ff).

36. *De testamento*, fol. 31b; cf. *Von dem Testament*, sig. Cvii(v). Although Luther also spoke of the age of the patriarchs as a golden age, he did not think that the gospel was clear then. It was a golden age of faith because the patriarchs' faith was based on very limited revelation. Headley, *Luther's View of Church History*, pp. 119ff.

37. *Decades*, III:v, fol. 112b–115 (*PSD* 2, pp. 130–142); *De scriptura I*, fol. 66–71b, 76; *De prophetae officio*, sig. Aii(v)–Av.

38. *Decades*, II:vi, fol. 59b–60, 61 (*PSD* 1, pp. 312–314, 319); see also *Sermones*, pp. 196–199. Some of Bullinger's arguments on the necessity of a magistrate because of human sin are so similar to Luther's that they may be based on Luther's *Von weltlicher Obrigkeit*. Calvin alluded to Exodus 18 only twice in the *Institutes*. Both allusions were brief and only one was in reference to the matter of government (IV,xi,8 and xx,8. *CO 2*, col. 898, 1098).

39. *Decades*, II:vi, fol. 61–61b (*PSD* 1, pp. 319–322); cf. "Loci communes," Zurich ZB, Ms. Car I 153, Articulus 18, "De magistratu," pp. 363–367. That the "Loci communes" was a preliminary sketch of what later became the *Decades* seems likely when one compares the sections on the magistrate (pp. 349–426 of "Loci communes" with *Decades*, II:vi–ix).

40. *Der alt gloub*, sig. Ei(v); *Summa*, fol. 69b–70, 71b; *Decades*, III:vii, viii, fol. 132b, 138 (*PSD* 2, pp. 220, 244–245); *Epitome*, fol. 20b.

41. *De testamento*, fol. 18–19.

42. *De scriptura I*, fol. 26b–28b.

43. *Decades*, II:vii, fol. 62–63b (*PSD* 1, pp. 323–330).

44. *Epitome*, fol. 23–23b; see also *Der alt gloub*, sig. Eiii(v)–Eiv.

45. *Epitome*, fol. 24. sed rempublicam, democratiam inquam temperatam aristocratia. Cf. Hans Baron, "Calvinist Republicanism and its Historical Roots," *CH* 8 (1939), pp. 30–42.

46. *Epitome*, fol. 24b–30, 31b.

47. *Epitome*, fol. 33–34b, 36.

48. *Epitome*, fol. 35b.

49. *Epitome*, fol. 36–39.

50. *Epitome*, fol. 39, 40, 42–43.

51. *Epitome*, fol. 43b–44, 45b. See also *Der alt gloub*, sig. Ev(v)–Fi(v).

52. *Epitome*, fol. 45b–48.

53. *Epitome*, fol. 48.

54. *Epitome*, fol. 48b–49, 51b–52, 55b–58. See also *Bericht*, p. 42; *Der alt gloub*, sig. Fiii(v); and *De origine erroris III*, fol. 51–53.

55. *Epitome*, fol. 60b–62b. Ioiada pepigit adeoque renovavit foedus inter Deum regem et populum . . . (fol. 62b).

56. *Epitome*, fol. 67b–68; *Isaias*, fol. 89 (see also fol. 126b, 168).

57. *Epitome*, fol. 70–72b. deinde foedere sancto & se & universum populum cum Deo quam arctissime constrinxit (fol. 70).

58. *Isaias*, fol. 158b–159b.

59. *Isaias*, fol. 12, 41b–42, 51b, 81b–82b, 129b–130, 310–310b.

60. *Isaias*, fol. 226b. Et quidem religio a religando dicitur. Religione enim Deo devincti sumus. Vinculum est, communio spiritus & vera fides. . . . Religio nostra etiam foedus in scripturis nuncupatur. . . . Hae sunt compedes gratae piis, ipsum inquam dei foedus & religio Christiana.

   Interestingly, Zwingli (and Calvin) felt that *religio* derived from *relegere* rather than from *religare*. See J. Samuel Preus, "Zwingli, Calvin and the Origin of Religion," *CH* 46 (1977), p. 192.

61. *Isaias*, fol. 281–282b. For other passages treating the covenant, see fol. 112–113b, 168–169b, 182b, 195–195b, 210–211, 244b–245, 271b, 277b, 310, 319b.

62. *Ieremias*, fol. 9b–14, 22–23b, 46b–47b.

63. *Ieremias*, fol. 84–86. See also *Epitome*, fol. 70b. In *Ieremias* (fol. 117), Bullinger also made his point about *religio* stemming from *religare* and thus referring to a binding together as in *foedus, pactum, pundt*, or *verbindung*.

64. *Epitome*, fol. 79–80, 84–85b. For Bullinger's summary of the history of the Greeks, the Romans, the Assyrians, and the Babylonians, see *Epitome*, fol. 72b–75b, and 80–81 for the years (according to his chronology) 3194 (775 B.C.) to 3354 (615 B.C.), and fol. 64b–66b for the accompanying chronological table.

65. *Epitome*, fol. 82, 85b–86, 87, 108; *Daniel*, fol. 102–102b; *De hebdomadis*, fol. 13–19b. The source for Bullinger's interpretation here is uncertain. No one else seems to have begun the 490 years in the seventh year of Artaxerxes Longimanus, although several chose the twentieth year. On the other hand, dating the middle of the last week with the baptism of Christ had some

238 *Heinrich Bullinger and the Covenant*

precedent, although apparently no earlier than Bede. See Franz Fraidl, *Die Exegese der siebzig Wochen Daniels in der alten und mittleren Zeit* (Graz, 1883).
66. *Daniel*, fol. 108b–109. Duo vel plures certis se obstringunt vel religant conditionibus.
67. *Epitome*, fol. 91b–95b (in this section Bullinger briefly discussed the rulers of Greece, Egypt, Syria, Macedonia, and Rome from 3641 [328 B.C.] through 3795 [174 B.C.]); 98b–99. See fol. 99b–107b for Bullinger's discussion of the kings of Egypt, the Maccabees, Herod the Great, and the Roman Republic and Empire.
68. *Der alt gloub*, sig. Fv–Fv(v).
69. *Ieremias*, fol. 187–188b.
70. *De testamento*, fol. 30–35.
71. *Epitome*, fol. 108, 110; *Der alt gloub*, sig. Gvi(v).

Chapter Four

1. *In omnes apostolicas epistolas* 2, pp. 10–11 (on 1 Pet. 1:10–11); *Der alt gloub*, sig. Giv–Gv. Als wenig als die auslegung one den text. Der text ist das gesatzt und die propheten/ die auslegung die Evangelisten und Apostlen (sig. Gv).
2. *Matthaeus*, fol. 54b, 200–201, 55b–56. See also *De testamento*, fol. 23b–24; and *Der alt gloub*, sig. Gvii(v).
3. *In omnes apostolicas epistolas* 1, pp. 59, 62–63, 67–70; *Summa*, fol. 31, 48b, 70–73, 167b; *Matthaeus*, fol. 57.
4. *In omnes apostolicas epistolas* 1, pp. 358–377 (see also pp. 37–48, on Romans 4). Compare this with Luther's comments on the same passage (Gal. 3:15–25), where he emphasized that the testament is equivalent to promise and made no reference to covenant (see esp. *WA* 40, 1, p. 463: 13ff; *LW* 26, p. 298). In the same section, Luther made his famous dichotomy between law and gospel (in this case, promise or testament) (*WA* 40, 1, pp. 473–501; *LW* 26, pp. 304–323).
5. *Matthaeus*, fol. 55, 224b, 225b, 227b, 231, 232b, 237b. See also *In omnes apostolicas epistolas* 1, pp. 188–212 (on 1 Cor. 11); *Nachtmal*, sig. bviii(v); *De coena*, fol. 15, 18; *Die rechten opfer*, sig. aiii(v)–avi(v).
6. *In omnes apostolicas epistolas* 1, pp. 687–693.
7. *In omnes apostolicas epistolas* 1, pp. 693–695. Luther, commenting on Hebrews 7:12, said that the gospel completely replaced the law, whether ceremonial, judicial, or moral. See *WA* 57, 3, p. 192: 16–25; *LW* 29, p. 193. Cf. Hagen, *A Theology of Testament in the Young Luther*, pp. 59–60.
8. *Ioannes*, fol. 205b; *Matthaeus*, fol. 261–261b.
9. *Matthaeus*, fol. 25–29b, 35, 112b, 167b; *De testamento*, fol. 43b–44; *Decades*, V:vii, fol. 337–337b; V:viii, fol. 349–349b, 352–352b, 355–355b, 359–359b (*PSD* 4, pp. 298–299, 353–355, 366–368, 382–384, 399–400); *Ioannes*, fol. 16b, 32b–34.
10. *Matthaeus*, fol. 36–38b. HIC EST ILLE FILIUS MEUS DILECTUS IN QUO PLACATUS SUM (fol. 37b). The Greek term εὐδόκησα (εὐδοκέω) does not permit the *placatus* rendering. Bullinger used this sentence, or a variation of

it, on the title page or the last page of all his books, always using *placatus*, or the German equivalent *versoenen* rather than *placitus*. The Vulgate rendering is *complacui mihi*.

11. *Sermones*, pp. 40–44. Is non dedignatur nobiscum confoederari cum deo, symbolumque foederis palam recipere in carnem suam (p. 44).

12. *Summa*, fol. 146–147; *Fundamentum firmum*, fol. 42–42b. Baptisatos quoque receptos & inscriptos esse in album filiorum Dei, obstrictosque esse ad veram vitam profitendam atque sancte vel innocenter vivendum (fol. 42). See also *Bekerung*, fol. 83b–89, and *De origine erroris III*, fol. 188b–190b.

13. *In omnes apostolicas epistolas* 1, pp. 188–190, 485.

14. *Matthaeus*, fol. 33–36, 266–267; *Marcus*, fol. 43b–44.

15. *Isaias*, fol. 65b (11:10), 95b–96 (19:22–25), 125 (27:13), 204–204b (42:1–7), 244b–245b (49:6); *Ieremias*, fol. 24bff(3:11–18); *De testamento*, fol. 31b–34.

16. *Vervolgung*, fol. 25–28b; *Series*, fol. 5b–8, 11–12b; *Epitome*, fol. 111b. Bullinger considered the destruction of the temple in A.D. 70 as further testimony of the abolition of the ceremonial law (*Epitome*, fol. 115b).

17. *De scriptura I*, fol. 76b–80; *In omnes apostolicas epistolas*, 2, pp. 49–51 (on 1 Pet. 5:1–3).

18. "Tractatus de excommunicatione," fol. 35r–36r. See also *Matthaeus*, fol. 158–160b; "Loci communes," fol. 313–321.

19. Bullinger to Dathenus, 1 June 1570. Printed in *Explicatio*, p. 362.

20. "Tractatus de excommunicatione," fol. 8r–11v, 13v–14r. Excommunicationem quae ob inhonestam vitam excludit, peccatores, non divinum esse preceptum, nec habere exemplum, sed humanum esse remedium (fol. 13v–14r).

21. "Tractatus de excommunicatione," fol. 12r. See also Bullinger to Friedrich III, 28 Oct. 1568. Zurich StA, E II 341 (Autograph), fol. 3616r–3616v; *Decades*, V:ix, fol. 376b–377 (*PSD* 4, pp. 473–477).

22. Bullinger to Berchtold Haller, 6 July 1531. *HBBW I*, pp. 207–209; "Tractatus de excommunicatione," fol. 3v–4r; Bullinger to Leo Jud, 15 March 1532. Printed in Fast, *Bullinger und die Täufer*, pp. 188–193.

    Police power is used here to mean the discipline or control of the community through the enforcement of its laws. The word was not used in this sense until the eighteenth century, and there was, of course, no police force in sixteenth-century Zurich. The magistracy did possess and exercise this power of enforcement, however.

23. "Tractatus de excommunicatione," fol. 21r–22v, 27r, 48r–49r; *Matthaeus*, fol. 175–175b; *In omnes apostolicas epistolas* 1, pp. 149–152 (on 1 Cor. 5:5); *HBBW I*, p. 210.

24. *De testamento*, fol. 18–19b.

25. "Tractatus de excommunicatione," fol. 6r, 25r–29r; *Refutatio*, fol. 56b–57.

26. *Isaias*, fol. 244b, 248b–249; *Sermones*, p. 197; *Refutatio*, fol. 44–46b; *Vermanung*, fol. 37–37b; *De scriptura I*, fol. 17b; *Ieremias*, fol. 162b; "Loci communes," fol. 384–385; *Decades*, II:vii, fol. 63–64 (*PSD* 1, pp. 327–333). For Bullinger's extended treatment of the persecutions of the early church, see *Vervolgung*, fol. 25–107b. The *Vervolgung* also covers the period before Christ,

beginning with the protoevangelium (Gen. 3:15), emphasizing the unity of the faith in the Old and New Testament.

27. "Tractatus de excommunicatione," fol. 5r–6v, 15v, 42r–43r. Nullum habuit vel praeceptum Dei vel exemplum. Longe aliter cum rege Davide egit Nathan propheta (fol. 42r). Ut nephas prompte antiquitatem existimaretur, illa non uti ad mode veteris, ecclesiae, et Ambrosius auderet sanctum Imp. Theodosium excommunicare (fol. 6v).

28. *Matthaeus*, fol. 31–32; *Epitome*, fol. 50; *Bericht*, p. 42.

29. *Daniel*, fol. 77–80b.

30. *Vervolgung*, fol. 73–76b; see also *Refutatio*, fol. 28–34; *Bericht*, pp. 176–183; *De scriptura I*, fol. 129b–135, 167–171b.

31. *De origine erroris III*, fol. 112–122; *De origine erroris II*, sig. B7–C4v; *Ieremias*, fol. 15–15b, 188; *Perfectio christianorum*, pp. 49–50; *Bericht*, pp. 89–107.

    For a history of the entire controversy, see Edward James Martin, *History of the Iconoclastic Controversy* (London, n.d. [1930]). He supports Bullinger's contention that Leo III's crowning of Charlemagne partially resulted from the controversy but emphasizes more the importance of territorial questions in Italy in the minds of both Charlemagne and Leo III (pp. 222ff).

32. *De origine erroris III*, fol. 123–139, 167–172; *Daniel*, fol. 26–26b; *Ieremias*, fol. 77b–78; *Apodixis*, pp. 28–30.

33. Actually, the three men were contemporaries. Ratramn, perhaps in 844, wrote a treatise in reply to Radbert. For the text of Ratramn's treatise, as translated into German by Leo Jud, see Bullinger's *Ein sendbrief*, sig. Biiiff.

    It should be noted that the early teaching on the eucharist was much more ambiguous than Bullinger would have it. See Bethune-Baker, *An Introduction to the Early History of Christian Doctrine*, pp. 393–418.

34. *De origine erroris III*, fol. 205–216b, 228–236; *Apologetica expositio*, pp. 95–98.

35. *Bericht*, pp. 135–141.

36. *Sermones*, pp. 67–70, 76; *De origine erroris III*, fol. 180–191b; *De gratia Dei*, fol. 18b–20b.

37. *De origine erroris I*, sig. e–e(v).

38. *De origine erroris III*, fol. 235b–236; *Vervolgung*, fol. 83–86. In his Daniel commentary Bullinger applied the prophecy to Antiochus Epiphanes and said only that Antiochus was a type of Antichrist, without specifically mentioning the papacy. *Daniel*, fol. 91b–93b.

39. *De scriptura I*, fol. 173b–175; *Vervolgung*, fol. 77–78.

40. *Vervolgung*, fol. 78–81b; *De scriptura I*, fol. 176–176b.

41. *Refutatio*, fol. 7–19b; *De scriptura I*, fol. 127–129, 163b; *De origine erroris I*, sig. evi–evi (v). See also Robert C. Walton, "Bullinger's Answer to John Jewel's Call for Help: Bullinger's Exposition of Matt. 16:18–19 (1571)," *HBGesA II*, pp. 243–256.

42. *Refutatio*, fol. 5, 39–39b (cf. *Defensor pacis*, Dictio 2, ch. 4; ch. 23, sec. 13; ch. 25, sec. 17 and 19. Gewirth 2, pp. 113–126, 320, 341–344). For further uses of Marsilius by Bullinger see *De scriptura I*, fol. 16b, 162b–163, 177 (cf. *Defensor pacis*, Dictio 2, ch. 19; ch. 24, sec. 5, 11, 15, 16; ch. 25, sec. 15. Gewirth 2, pp.

274–279, 323, 325–326, 328–329, 341). For another reference to Marsilius, see Bullinger to Ludwig von Sayn-Wittgenstein. 22 Feb. 1573. Zurich StA, E II 348, fol. 68r. Original copy with marginalia in Bullinger's hand.

43. *De origine erroris II*, sig. E5v.
44. *De origine erroris III*, fol. 244b–245. Quomodo cum Christo coniungamus (fol. 244b); cf. foedere coniungamur cum deo (fol. 19).
45. *Responsio*, fol. 33–36.
46. *Ieremias*, fol. 1–1b, 20, 23–23b; *Isaias*, fol. 9b–11, 112b–113b. Unde nunc quoque ebulliunt multiplicia nostri seculi mala, quae non tollentur, nisi per iustam poenitentiam, diligentemque aeterni foederis observationem (fol. 113b).
47. *Bericht*, pp. 41–45; *De scriptura I*, fol. 55–55b; *Kaetzeryen, passim*.
48. *Brevis Responsio*, fol. 37b–38.
49. *Sermones*, p. 79; *Responsio*, fol. 40; *Ein sendbrief*, sig. Aiiff.
50. *Apodixis*, p. 27.
51. *De testamento*, fol. 47b–48.
52. *Apodixis*, pp. 27–29, 67–69, 77–79, 85–92. Nos autem propter veram in Christum fidem esse verum semen Abrahae (p. 92). For the same argument that the evangelical (i.e., Reformed) faith had existed since Adam, see *Der alt gloub*, sig. Hvii(v)–Hviii; *De testamento*, fol. 46b–52; and *Bericht*, pp. 209–210.
53. *De origine erroris III*, fol. *3b–*4. Ad salutem ecclesiae ac reipublicae attinent (fol. *3b).
54. *Refutatio*, fol. 48b, 56b; *Vermanung*, fol. 36b–37; *De gratia Dei*, sig. Bb4v–Cci; *Bericht*, pp. 207–208; *Epitome*, fol. 61–61b.
55. *Anklag*, sig. Aii–Aiii. Published without date, publisher, place of publication, or author; but Bullinger refers in his *Diarium* (p. 12:8–9) to its publication in April 1528.
56. *Anklag*, sig. Aiii–Avii(v).
57. *Anklag*, sig. Aviii–Cii(v).
58. *Anklag*, sig. Cii(v)–Civ.
59. *Anklag*, sig. Cv(v)–Di.
60. *De prophetae officio*, sig. Ei–Eiv(v). This section of *De prophetae officio* has been recently printed: Fritz Büsser, "De prophetae officio: Eine Gedenkrede Bullingers auf Zwingli," in *Festgabe Leonhard von Muralt zum siebzigsten Geburtstag 17. Mai 1970, überreicht von Freunden und Schülern* (Zurich, 1970), pp. 254–257.
61. See also *Uff siben Klagartickel*, fol. 6b–12.

Chapter Five

1. For Bullinger on the distinctions between the visible and invisible church, see *Decades*, IV:vii, fol. 236–238 (*PSD* 3, pp. 275–281); and V:i, fol. 271b–274 (*PSD* 4, pp. 5–17). The distinction, hardly unique with Bullinger, neatly served his conception of the covenanted community.
2. *De prophetae officio, passim*. Since this treatise was published in 1532, it is likely

that these three points reflected his initial disagreements with the council, especially the attempt to impose the Meilener Articles on the new Antistes (see above, prologue). Although the freedom of the pulpit had already been decided in Bullinger's favor, the controversy over ecclesiastical income had just begun in early 1532.

3. *De prophetae officio*, sig. Aiii.

4. *De prophetae officio*, sig. Aiv(v)–Bvi.

5. *De prophetae officio*, sig. Bviii–Cvii. See also *Ieremias*, fol. 136b, and *De testamento*, fol. 21.

6. *De prophetae officio*, sig. Cviii–Di(v).

7. *De prophetae officio*, sig. Div–Dvii(v).

8. *Decades*, II:vii, fol. 63–63b (*PSD* 1, p. 329); V:i, fol. 279b–281 (*PSD* 4, pp. 38–46); *Summa*, fol. 112b–114; *De scriptura I*, fol. 130–135, 143b–145.

9. *De scriptura I*, fol. 110b.

10. *De prophetae officio*, sig. Dii–Div. See also *Decades*, III:i, fol. 94b (*PSD* 2, pp. 44–45); *Matthaeus*, fol. 229.

11. *Decades*, V:x, fol. 378–379b (*PSD* 4, pp. 479–486); *De scriptura I*, fol. 102–105b, 153–156b; *Daniel*, fol. 8–9b; *Isaias*, fol. 94–94b.

12. *Decades*, V:x, fol. 379b–383b (*PSD* 4, pp. 486–503).

13. *Decades*, II:vi, fol. 61–61b (*PSD* 1, pp. 319–322); *Sermones*, pp. 196–197; *Bericht*, p. 207.

14. *Früntliche ermanung*, sig. Sii–Sii(v).

15. *Sermones*, pp. 196–197; *Bericht*, pp. 203–208; *Vermanung*, fol. 36b–37; *Refutatio*, fol. 44b–46; *De scriptura I*, fol. 100, 143b–145; *Decades*, II:vii, fol. 62–64b (*PSD* 1, pp. 323–334); IV:vii, fol. 237–238 (*PSD* 3, pp. 277–282).

This is in contrast with Luther's view of the ruler as merely another Christian, who had no special authority over the church except in periods of crisis when he might serve as *Notbischof*.

16. *De testamento*, fol. 18–20; *Isaias*, fol. 158b–159b, 168–169b, 182b, 281–281b; *Ieremias*, fol. 22–23b; *Epitome*, fol. 60b–62b.

17. *Decades*, II:vii, fol. 62 (*PSD* 1, p. 323).

18. *Decades*, II:i, fol. 36–38 (*PSD* 1, pp. 193–206). See also *In omnes apostolicas epistolas* 1, p. 25 (on Rom 2:14–16). Prior to 1528, Bullinger, in opposition to Luther and Melanchthon, did not give a natural law interpretation to Romans 2. See Staedtke, *Theologie*, pp. 131–133; and Hausammann, *Römerbriefauslegung*, pp. 245–255.

19. *Decades*, II:ii, fol. 39–40 (*PSD* 1, pp. 209–215); see also *Summa*, fol. 46–50b.

20. *Decades*, II:i, fol. 36 (*PSD* 1, p. 193). This sentence referred back to the previous sermon on the Love Commandment (I:x), which Bullinger meant to be the introduction to the section on the law.

Bullinger's argument was not Thomistic. His approach was purely theological, not philosophical. Thus he did not emphasize the common rationality of man, nor did he make the Thomistic distinction between primary principles and secondary precepts. In fact, Bullinger did not really develop a very clear or systematic theory of natural law, as did Zwingli.

Zwingli's theory of natural law was much more fully developed. He equated natural law with divine law, and both with the Love Commandment. But then he distinguished this divine norm from what was possible for man. Because of man's sinful nature, God added other commandments, such as the Decalogue, to guide man in his social existence. The magistrate based his laws on these more specific commandments. This differentiation between the law of divine righteousness and the law of human righteousness was not present in Bullinger's thought. Instead, he equated the Decalogue with the divine norm. For Zwingli's treatment, see "Von göttlicher und menschlicher Gerechtigkeit." *ZW* 2, pp. 482–487. See also Otto Dreske, *Zwingli und das Naturrecht* (Halle, 1911), pp. 40–42; cf. Walton, *Zwingli's Theocracy*, pp. 165–166.

21. *Decades*, II:vii, fol. 64–66 (*PSD* 1, pp. 333–343); *Summa*, fol. 111–112. Cf. Calvin, "Institutio," 4.xx.14–16. *CO* 2, col. 1104–1107.

22. *Decades*, II:vii, fol. 66–66b (*PSD* 1, pp. 343–344); see also *Sermones*, pp. 197–200; and *De scriptura I*, fol. 40b–41b.

23. See *Summa*, fol. 31b–32, 69–69b, 73, 167–169; *Decades*, III:vii, fol. 132b (*PSD* 2, p. 220); III:viii, fol. 138 (*PSD* 2, pp. 244–245).

24. *Früntliche ermanung*, sig. Aiii(v), Bii–Biv. See also *Decades*, II:viii, fol. 66b–68 (*PSD* 1, pp. 345–351); *Isaias*, fol. 63b–64.

25. *Decades*, II:viii, fol. 68–68b (*PSD* 1, pp. 351–353).

26. *Bericht*, pp. 181–183; *Refutatio*, fol. 46–48; *De testamento*, fol. 19–19b; *Früntliche ermanung*, sig. Aiv(v); Bullinger to Berchtold Haller, 6 July 1531. *HBBW I*, pp. 207–214; Bullinger to Jud, 15 March 1532 (printed in Fast, *Bullinger und die Täufer*, pp. 188–193); "Tractatus de excommunicatione," *passim*; see also Baker, "In Defense of Magisterial Discipline."

27. *Decades*, II:viii, fol. 69–69b (*PSD* 1, pp. 357–360). At one point Bullinger even exhorted the magistrate to control the printing press. God had given printing to spread the gospel and to increase human learning. The magistrate must not allow it to be used against God and the truth. *Vermanung*, fol. 37b–38.

28. *Decades*, II:viii, fol. 70 (*PSD* 1, pp. 360–362); see also *Summa*, fol. 41ff.

29. *Decades*, II:viii, fol. 70b (*PSD* 1, p. 363); cf. "Loci communes," p. 414. Discriminandum est ergo inter Fidem ut est animi donum, et Fidem, ut est religio.

30. *Von rechter*, sig. aviii(v)–bi.

31. *Isaias*, fol. 152b–153, 17–19, 54, 168–169b; *Ieremias*, fol. 7b.

32. Zurich ZB, Ms. S34/190. Autograph.

33. *De testamento*, fol. 18–20. See *Lucas*, fol. 61, where Bullinger connected the function of the magistrate with the Love Commandment and "the duties of piety" (Luke 6:27–29).

34. Luther lists fourteen impediments that were grounds for declaring a marriage invalid in his day ("Vom ehelichen Leben." *WA* 10, 2, pp. 280–287; *LW* 45, pp. 22–30). Most of this background material can be found in the following: G. LeBras, "La Doctrine du mariage chez les théologiens et les canonistes depuis l'an mille," *Dictionnaire de théologie catholique*, vol. 9, pp. 2120–2190; A. Villien, "Divorce," *Dictionnaire de théologie catholique*, vol. 4, pp. 1455–1478;

Aug. Lehmkuhl, "Divorce," *The Catholic Encyclopedia*, vol. 5, pp. 54–69; W. M. Foley, "Marriage (Christian)," *Encyclopaedia of Religion and Ethics*, vol. 8, pp. 433–443; Joseph Selinger, "Moral and Canonical Aspect of Marriage," *The Catholic Encyclopedia*, vol. 9, pp. 699–703.

35. *ZW* 4, pp. 182–186; see also *Actensammlung*, no. 711. Walther Köhler points out that the church ceremony was the basis for marriage in the eyes of the people. For this reason, an ordinance of 1534 made the *Kirchgang* obligatory before the consummation of the marriage, for the protection of morals. *Zürcher Ehegericht und Genfer Konsistorium, vol. 1: Das Zürcher Ehegericht und seine Auswirkung in der deutschen Schweiz zur Zeit Zwinglis* (Leipzig, 1932), p. 104.

36. *ZW* 4, pp. 186–187. Köhler cites decisions of the *Ehegericht* that granted divorce for extreme incompatibility, desertion, illness such as leprosy, extreme mental illness, and fraud. *Zürcher Ehegericht und Genfer Konsistorium*, vol. 1, pp. 119–129.

37. "Satzung in Ehesachen," *Actensammlung*, no. 944.

38. "Ordnung und satzung von eim ersamen Radt der stadt Zürich von wegen der straf des ebruchs und unehlicher biwonung," *Actensammlung*, no. 1087. See also Köhler, *Zürcher Ehegericht und Genfer Konsistorium*, vol. 1, pp. 109–112, 142. Ley sees this statute as a decisive turning point: "The church is no longer capable of independent action. The state determines . . . concerning the worthiness or unworthiness of the communicant." Roger Ley, *Kirchenzucht bei Zwingli* (Zurich, 1948), p. 55.

39. Köhler, *Zürcher Ehegericht und Genfer Konsistorium*, vol. 1, pp. 162–163, 188–195.

40. *Eestand*, sig. Aiiii–Avii(v), Dvii(v)–Eiii.

41. *Eestand*, sig. Avii(v)–Aviii. In his Jeremiah commentary, he illustrated the covenant with marriage. *Ieremias*, fol. 22.

42. *Eestand*, sig. Bii.

43. *Eestand*, sig. Di(v)–Dii(v).

44. *Eestand*, sig. Di(v)–Div(v). The 1525 marriage ordinance in Zurich used Leviticus 18 as a norm and prohibited marriage to the second degree only. *ZW* 4, p. 185. Bullinger was not opposed to official policy on this point.

45. *Eestand*, sig. Hvii(v)–Ji(v).

46. *Eestand*, sig. Hviii(v)–Jiv(v).

47. *Eestand*, sig. Fii–Fvii.

48. *Eestand*, sig. Fvii–Gii(v), Gv–Gvi(v). In the preface of the *Eestand*, he complained that sexual offenses were common and harmful to the entire commonwealth, obscuring the true nature of marriage. This was the reason he gave for writing the *Eestand* (sig. Aii–Aiii[v]).

49. Köhler, *Zürcher Ehegericht und Genfer Konsistorium*, vol. 1, pp. 109–112.

50. *ZW* 4, pp. 186–187; Köhler, *Zürcher Ehegericht und Genfer Konsistorium*, vol. 1, pp. 119–129.

51. *Eestand*, sig. Ov(v)–Oviii. For a brief but similar argument on divorce, see Bullinger's comments on Matt. 19:9. *Matthaeus*, fol. 178b–179b.

52. Luther, on the other hand, based his case for divorce directly on the reason for

marriage. God's command to Adam and Eve to be fruitful and multiply was not a matter of choice but a necessary thing for all men and women, like eating or sleeping. If it was resisted, fornication would result. All three of Luther's grounds for absolute divorce follow logically from this view that marriage was instituted to fulfill physical needs. The first ground was a physical deficiency on the part of either party that made sexual relations impossible. The second cause was adultery. Here Luther's argument was so close to Bullinger's that Luther may have been Bullinger's source. The adulterer should be put to death, and if he was not, the other party could remarry just as though he had died. The third ground was deprivation of the conjugal duty by one party. Luther also insisted that the divorce must be public and be granted by the civil magistrate. *WA*, 10, 1, pp. 276, 287–291; *LW* 45, pp. 18, 30–34.

Bucer's argument for divorce, based in a similar manner on the nature of marriage itself, was much more complex. According to the divine institution of marriage in Genesis, there should be a union of both body and spirit. So his grounds for divorce were manifold: adultery, witchcraft, sacrilege, disobedience on the wife's part, treason, wife beating, impotence, leprosy, and insanity. *De regno Christi*, II,xxxiii, xxxvi–xxxvii, xli. *MBOL*, pp. 180–181, 201–204, 215–217.

53. John T. Noonan, Jr., *The Scholastic Analysis of Usury* (Cambridge, Massachusetts, 1957), pp. 38–39, 52–57.
54. Other biblical prohibitions included Lev. 25:35–37; Ps. 15:5; Ezek. 18:8; and Luke 6:35. Benjamin Nelson in his brilliant but tendentious study sees the Deuteronomy text as crucial in the development of the medieval economic ethic. *The Idea of Usury: From Tribal Brotherhood to Universal Otherhood*, 2d ed. (Chicago, 1969), pp. xix–xxv, 3–4, 14–15.
55. There is general agreement, for instance, that Luther's economic thought persisted within the medieval tradition. See Ernst Troeltsch, *The Social Teachings of the Christian Churches (New York, 1960), 2, pp. 554–556*; Karl Holl, *The Cultural Significance of the Reformation* (New York, 1959), pp. 77–81; Paul Althaus, *The Ethics of Martin Luther* (Philadelphia, 1972), pp. 105–111; and Nelson, *The Idea of Usury*, pp. 31–54. For a short treatment of Luther's position in the early 1520s, see J. Wayne Baker, "Heinrich Bullinger and the Idea of Usury," *SCJ* 5:1 (1974), pp. 51–52. During and after 1525, Luther retreated some from his earlier positions in the face of radical demands. For an excellent chronological statement of Luther's attitude toward usury, see Nelson, *The Idea of Usury*, pp. 30–56.
56. Troeltsch claims that Calvinism was the only form of Christianity that fully accepted the basis of the modern economic system. This acceptance resulted from Calvin's repudiation of the medieval ethic and his support of a theory of money, credit, and usury nearer to the modern point of view. *The Social Teachings of the Christian Churches*, vol. 2, pp. 643, 647. André Bielér also asserts that except for Calvin the reformers retained the medieval tradition on usury. *La pensée economique et sociale de Calvin* (Geneva, 1959), pp. 474–475; Nelson makes similar claims. *The Idea of Usury*, pp. 73–82.

57. See also Bullinger's "De ratione censuum," Zurich ZB, Ms. G 441, fol. 165r–172v, which is a set of rough notes from 1530 against Anabaptist positions on economic matters. Part of it was used in the "Bericht" (fol. 165r–167r; 172v). The rest of it was used in the body of the text of the *Fraefel* (fol. 168r–172r).

58. The German word *Zins*, in its modern usage, means interest, rent, or tax. But in Middle and Early New High German the term *Zins* in its different forms had several variations in meaning for which there is no single translation. Thus it will not be translated here. By the sixteenth century, the most common investment practice having to do with *Zins* was the *Zinskauf*. The term found its origins in the medieval feudal rent contract (*Rentenkauf*). The feudal landlord received in return for the land an annual, specified return or rent in the form of produce or livestock. In the later Middle Ages, when money became almost the sole means of exchange in such transactions, the term *Zinskauf* came into use. The *Zins* contract also became in essence a loan contract to avoid the ban on usury, but it was seen as the sale of the right to a regular income and not as a loan. Although the *Zins* contracts varied greatly, *Zins* was often, in effect, interest on a money loan. *LW* 45, pp. 253–273. The *Zinskauf* was commonly considered by both medieval canonists and theologians as the purchase of the right to money and not as a loan. For the various distinctions and different opinions on the *Zinskauf*, see Noonan, *The Scholastic Analysis of Usury*, pp. 154–164.

   In Middle High German, *Wucher* began to refer to interest on a money loan, and because of the medieval prohibitions, the word carried a deprecatory meaning. But *Wucher* lost its pejorative sense in the course of the sixteenth and early seventeenth centuries as governments imposed legal rates of interest. This led to such phrases as *redlicher Wucher*. In Early New High German, then, *Wucher* referred to interest from a loan and often was used interchangeably with *Zins*. If an author intended a pejorative meaning, he used such phrases as *juden Wucher* or *von Wucher wuchern* (cf. *Zinseszinsen*), thus clearly referring to exorbitant interest rates. *Deutsches Wörterbuch von Jacob Grimm und Wilhelm Grimm* (Leipzig), vol. 14, pt. 2 (1958), col. 1693–1695 (*Wucher*); vol. 15 (1956), col. 1485–1488 (*Zins*).

59. *Fraefel*, fol. 144b–149. See also "De ratione censuum," fol. 165r, where essentially the same argument is outlined.

60. *Fraefel*, fol. 149b–150.

61. *Fraefel*, fol. 151.

62. *Fraefel*, fol. 151b. For Calvin's somewhat different treatment of the Deuteronomy passage, see "De usuris," *CO*, 50, i, col. 247; and Baker, "Heinrich Bullinger and the Idea of Usury," p. 57.

63. *Fraefel*, fol. 151b–153b. In passing Bullinger considered Acts 2 and the apostolic common property. He defended private property and the right to temporal wealth. See also "De ratione censuum," fol. 166r, 172v.

64. Although he did not use the term, his argument pertained to the use of the *Zinskauf* as a credit instrument.

65. *Fraefel*, fol. 155b–156.

66. *Fraefel*, fol. 156. Der nervus, die kraft, enderung und die fertigung. Wilhelm Schulze thinks that Bullinger did not refer to Aristotle because of the nature of his audience: the followers of the Anabaptists, common people. "Die Lehre Bullingers vom Zins," *ARG* 48 (1959), p. 225. But the "Epistel" of the *Fraefel* addressed the work to the pastors of the area, not to the Anabaptists and their followers. Furthermore, his reference to the *Institutes* of Justinian would have been equally incomprehensible to the uneducated. Bullinger referred to the *Institutes* because the Roman law codes were being revived, adapted, and adopted throughout Europe at the time. The reference to Roman law made more sense than an appeal either to Aristotle or Aquinas would have.

67. *Fraefel*, fol. 156–156b. Schulze is impressed: "Bullinger, although he is only a pastor in a small village, has a vivid comprehension of the capital demands of the guilds." "Die Lehre Bullingers vom Zins," p. 228. But Bullinger was no stranger to the world of money and interest. His family, in Bremgarten, had income from lands, and he also had lived in Cologne and was familiar with Zurich. Schulze's article is generally well done but quite brief. His main interest is Bullinger's repudiation of Aristotle.

   For Calvin's discussion of the sterility of money, see "De usuris," *CO*, 50, i, col. 248; cf. Baker, "Heinrich Bullinger and the Idea of Usury," p. 58.

68. *Fraefel*, fol. 157–157b. Bullinger did not alter his opinion on usury even during the inflationary crisis in Zurich in the midcentury. In 1546, he gave a similar interpretation to Luke 6 (*Lucas*, fol. 61b) and then reiterated his argument in his *Decades* (III:i, fol. 94–95 [*PSD* 2, pp. 40–44]).

   Zwingli never justified the accepting of *Zins*; the good Christian would not engage in the practice. However, according to human righteousness, all legal *Zins* and *Wucher* must be paid. If it had been possible, Zwingli would have abolished *Zins*. See *ZW* 2, 519: 25–26; 520: 1–11. This point is made by each of the major interpreters of Zwingli's ethic. Ernst Ramp says, "According to Zwingli, it is the task of the magistrate to make use of the measures necessary to abolish the *Zins* and *Wucher*. . . . What Zwingli wants to attain is the most complete possible removal of the *Zins* in a legal manner." *Das Zinsproblem: Eine historische Untersuchung* (Zurich, 1949), p. 68. Heinrich Schmid agrees that there was no warranted *Zins* according to Zwingli, that Zwingli was willing to permit the practice only to prevent greater evil. *Zwinglis Lehre von der göttlichen und menschlichen Gerechtigkeit* (Zurich, 1959), p. 183. (See also note 24, pp. 183–184, where Schmid takes Emil Brunner to task for interpreting Zwingli as an advocate of a five percent *Zins*). Paul Meyer puts it even more strongly: "To abolish the *Zinsen* completely is Zwingli's goal." *Zwinglis Sociallehren* (Linz a. D., 1921), p. 62.

69. *Fraefel*, fol. 159–162b. See also "De ratione censuum," fol. 165v for a similar but much briefer argument. Later in the *Fraefel*, Bullinger noted in passing that a just *Zins* would be five percent (fol. 164b). The question of serfdom had been raised in Zurich during the peasant revolts of 1525. The peasants demanded that serfdom be abolished. On request of the council, Zwingli and the other pastors

gave their opinion, in favor of the peasants. But the council rejected their advice. Alfred Farner, *Die Lehre von Kirche und Staat bei Zwingli* (Tubingen, 1930), p. 9. Bullinger's argument for *Zins* on land did not break new ground since the scholastics also permitted *Zins* on land, treating this as a lease rather than a loan. Thus the *Zins* was rent rather than usury. Noonan, *The Scholastic Analysis of Usury*, pp. 41, 46.

70. *Fraefel*, fol. 164–168b. See also "De ratione censuum," fol. 166r.

71. *Fraefel*, fol. 169b–171b. The nature of Bullinger's advice to the poor suggests that the Puritan work ethic was not purely Calvinistic in origin.

72. In fact, Heinold Fast claims that Bullinger's views were not at all unique but that the "Bericht," so rashly praised by Zwingli (in his *Jeremiaserklärung* of March 1531, as cited by Ramp, *Das Zinsproblem*, p. 65), "is nothing but a popularization of the writing 'Von göttlicher und menschlicher Gerechtigkeit.' The practical goal, the defense of the magisterial legislation on *Zins*, as well as the theological argument, are the same in both treatises" (*Bullinger und die Täufer*, p. 161). If by "the practical goal" Fast means the goal of eliciting obedience to the laws in terms of the payment of *Zins*, certainly Bullinger and Zwingli were in agreement on that point. But Zwingli did not go on to make any distinction between honorable and dishonorable *Wucher*; nor did he discuss the productive loan in an approbative way. Finally, Zwingli cited the Old Testament prohibitions in the traditional fashion against *Zins* and *Wucher*.

Zwingli never affirmed the right to take *Zins*. This difference between Zwingli and Bullinger is attributable to a theological dissimilarity between the two men. Although Bullinger's treatment of the degrees of God's law appears at first glance to be identical to Zwingli's, there is one significant variation. Zwingli said that the Love Commandment was the summary of the divine righteousness and was thus unfulfillable for men. Bullinger, however, saw it as the summary of the second degree of the law, the covenant condition of piety; it was fulfillable for man. For Zwingli, then, *Zins* (human righteousness) violated the Love Commandment (divine righteousness). For Bullinger the *Zins* was honorable if it did not violate the commandment to love one's neighbor, if it was equitable. Fast notes this distinction between Bullinger and Zwingli concerning the Love Commandment but does not see its implications in the case of *Zins* (*Bullinger und die Täufer*, pp. 161–162). For an analysis of Zwingli's position on *Zins*, see Baker, "Heinrich Bullinger and the Idea of Usury," pp. 52–57, 61, 65–66.

73. Schulze seems to be the only scholar who has noticed this. "Die Lehre Bullingers vom Zins," pp. 225, 228. There is no evidence that Bullinger influenced Calvin on the subject of usury, but Calvin may have had access to Leo Jud's Latin translation of the *Fraefel*, which included the "Bericht." Leo Jud, *Adversus omnia catabaptistarum prava dogmata Heinrichi Bullingeri lib. IIII.* (Zurich, 1535), fol. 163–191 (*HBBibl I*, no. 29).

74. *De testamento*, fol. 18–19.

75. Nelson *The Idea of Usury*, p. 81.

76. For striking sermon treatments of the covenant, see *Von dem Heil*, sig. aii(v)–cvii, where Bullinger first treated the history of salvation from Adam to

Christ in conventional terms, then repeated the entire matter in covenant terms; and *Bekerung*, fol. 79b–89b, a sermon on baptism based on Acts 8:36–38, in which he also heavily emphasized the covenant and its conditions. See also *Sermones*, pp. 40–44; *Nachtmal*, sig. ci–civ; *Von rechter*, sig. dvi(v)–ei.

77. *Catechesis*, fol. 1–7.
78. *Catechesis*, fol. 7–8b.
79. *Catechesis*, fol. 8b–28.
80. *Catechesis*, fol. 28b–29b, 52b–53.
81. *Catechesis*, fol. 60b–65b.
82. *Catechesis*, fol. 66–69.
83. *De origine erroris III*, fol. 19–25; see also *De scriptura I*, fol. 35b–37.
84. *Ieremias*, fol. 187b.

Chapter Six

1. As, for instance, in *De scriptura I*, fol. 3–8; *De origine erroris III*, fol. 21–31b, 244b–245; *Apodixis*, esp. fol. 27ff.
2. *Brevis responsio*, fol. 37b–38, 40; *Sermones*, p. 79; *Apologetica expositio*, pp. 31ff.
3. See Baker, "In Defense of Magisterial Discipline"; see also *De testamento*, fol. 18–19b.
4. For this approach, see Fast, *Bullinger und die Täufer*, pp. 31, 66f, 90f, 132.
5. As cogently argued by Franklin H. Littel, *The Origins of Sectarian Protestantism* (New York, 1964), pp. 12–18.
6. It should be emphasized that Bullinger saw the New Testament as the authority in defining the faith itself. On the issue of the Anabaptists and the Old Testament, see John H. Yoder, "The Hermeneutics of the Anabaptists," *MQR* 41 (1967), pp. 306–307. Elsewhere Yoder makes the point that Zwingli's concept of covenant unity was ontological rather than historical and that it robbed the Christ event of its historical centrality. *Täufertum und Reformation im Gespräch:Dogmengeschichtliche Untersuchung der frühen Gespräche zwischen Schweizerischen Täufern und Reformatoren* (Zurich, 1968), pp. 32–42. It is clear that such was not the case with Bullinger. For a defense of Zwingli on this point, see Cottrell, "Covenant and Baptism," pp. 278–287.
7. Haller to Bullinger, 3 June 1532. Zurich StA, Ms. EII 343, fol. 6r. The Zofingen disputation took place from July 1 to July 9.
8. Fast and Yoder, pp. 85, 87. Fast and Yoder include both Bullinger's text and a translation. The translations here are mine.
9. Fast and Yoder, pp. 89, 91; cf. *Ursprung*, fol. 101–103b; see also "Contra anabaptistas consignata quaedam" (1542). Zurich ZB, Ms. G441, fol. 13r. My thanks to Dr. Heinold Fast for allowing me to xerox his handwritten copy.
10. *Ursprung*, fol. 103. Fast and Yoder (p. 91, note 27) have argued that Bullinger meant that Haller should use the context except when that would favor the Anabaptists. Then he should employ the principles of faith and love. In fact, he

argued that if a text was unclear, the context should be used along with faith and love.

11. See, for instance, *Apodixis*, pp. 17–18; *Isaias*, sig. aa5; *Summa*, fol. 17; *Decades*, I:iii, fol. 10–10b (*PSD* 1, pp. 75–79).

Fast claims that Bullinger first suggested the Love Commandment as an interpretive principle in this letter to Haller in 1532. *Bullinger und die Täufer*, p. 159. As a matter of fact, he used the exact same principle in a treatise directed against the Catholics in 1526. "Scripture must be interpreted from itself and through itself in faith and love." ("Gschrifft muoss uss ir selbs/ und durch sich selbs/ in glouben und liebe ussgeleit werden.") *Kaetzeryen*, sig. bi. Fast's discussion of the Love Commandment as the basis of Bullinger's ethic (*Bullinger und die Täufer*, pp. 159ff) shows only a partial understanding—the application of the Love Commandment, as the conditions of the covenant seems not to have occurred to Fast.

12. See *De testamento*, fol. 23–23b, 46–46b.

13. "De Scripturae negotio," fol. 45r–50r.

14. *Ursprung*, fol. 114–116b; "Contra anabaptistas consignata quaedam," fol. 18r–22v; *Daniel*, fol. 1b; *Isaias*, fol. 94. See also *Isaias*, fol. 48–48b, 164b–165; *Ieremias*, fol. 208b–209; *Apodixis*, pp. 14–17; *De scriptura I*, fol. 11–16, 62b; *De testamento*, fol. 28–41b.

15. *Ursprung*, fol. 114–116b.

16. *Ursprung*, fol. 193b–201. See also *Sermones*, pp. 172–173; *Von rechter*, sig. dvi(v)–ei; *Bericht*, pp. 130–134.

17. "Contra anabaptistas consignata quaedam," fol. 30r. Nam baptismus est signum populi dei et obsignatio foederis. (See also fol. 29r–39r.)

18. *Ursprung*, fol. 69b–74b. No attempt will be made here either to corroborate or to criticize Bullinger's perceptions of Anabaptist teachings. For the text of one contemporary (1527) statement of faith from the Anabaptists, the Schleitheim Confession, see *Quellen zur Geschichte der Täufer in der Schweiz, vol. 2: Ostschweiz*. Edited by Heinold Fast (Zurich, 1973), no. 26.

19. *Ursprung*, fol. 74–76b.

20. "Tractatus de excommunication."

21. *Ursprung*, fol. 205–212b; "Contra anabaptistas consignata quaedam," fol. 44r–44v. At one point Bullinger referred to Anabaptism as "the new monasticism" ("novus . . . monachismus"). *De prophetae officio*, sig. Cii(v).

22. As suggested by Fast, *Bullinger und die Täufer*, p. 142.

23. Fast refers to Bullinger's letter to Beza of 4 Dec. 1571 (printed in André Bouvier, *Henri Bullinger réformateur et conseiller oecuménique le successeur de Zwingli* [Neuchatel, 1940], p. 159). *Bullinger und die Täufer*, p. 156, note 729. He could just as well have pointed to Bullinger's letter to Dathenus of 1 June 1570, in which he said that the Zurich church never had forced its point of view on foreign churches. *Explicatio*, p. 366. See also Bullinger to Friedrich III, 28 Oct. 1568. Zurich StA, EII 341, fol. 3618v.

24. Baker, "In Defense of Magisterial Discipline," pp. 141, 146, 157–158.

25. *Ursprung*, fol. 138–140b.

26. *Ursprung*, fol. 140b–142.

27. *Ursprung*, fol. 143–144.
28. *Ursprung*, fol. 144–145. For the Anabaptist idea of the fall of the church, see Littell, *The Origins of Sectarian Protestantism*, esp. pp. 46–78.
29. *Ursprung*, fol. 145–146.
30. *Ursprung*, fol. 146–146b, 148. For similar treatments of the Anabaptists and the Christian magistrate, see "Contra anabaptistas consignata quaedam," fol. 51r–58r; *Fraefel*, fol. 97b–111b; *Decades*, II: ix, fol. 74b–75b (*PSD* 1, pp. 385–388).
31. From his *Früntliche ermanung* of 1526 through his *Vervolgung* of 1573, neither of which concerned the Anabaptists.
32. *Ursprung*, fol. 149–150b.
33. *Ursprung*, fol. 151b–152b.
34. *Ursprung*, fol. 152b–156.
35. *Ursprung*, fol. 156–158.
36. *Ursprung*, fol. 158b–159b.
37. *Ursprung*, fol. 160b–161.
38. *Ursprung*, fol. 173–174.
39. *Ursprung*, fol. 174–176.
40. *Ursprung*, fol. 176–177b.
41. See Harold S. Bender, "The Pacifism of the Sixteenth Century Anabaptists," *MQR* 30 (1956), pp. 5–18; and especially James M. Stayer, *Anabaptism and the Sword* (Lawrence, Kansas, 1972), pp. 93–131, for a thorough and careful discussion of the teaching of the Swiss Anabaptists on nonresistance.
42. See the discussion by Potter, *Zwingli*, p. 175. For Bullinger's extended treatment on war, see *Decades*, II: xi, fol. 71b–74b (*PSD* 1, pp. 370–385).
43. A point made by Potter, *Zwingli*, p. 174.
44. *Ursprung*, fol. 177b–180. See also *Fraefel*, fol. 112–116; and *Decades*, II: iii, fol. 45–48 (*PSD* 1, pp. 238–253).
45. *Ursprung*, fol. 180–181b. Der eyd bewaret und behalt uns in einer religion (181b). "Contra anabaptistas consignata quaedam," fol. 76r; *Decades*, II: iii, fol. 46b–47b (*PSD* 1, pp. 246–250).
46. *Sermones*, p. 214. Obligamur item iuramento in unum corpus cum ecclesiasticum tum politicum, conservamurque in tranquillitate & pace. . . . Breviter, vinculum est ecclesiasticae & politicae gubernationis, nexus foederum & contractuum.
47. *Fraefel*, fol. 118.
48. *Ursprung*, fol. 181b.
49. On the reality of the threat, see Claus-Peter Clasen, *Anabaptism, a Social History, 1525–1618* (Ithaca, 1972), pp. 208–209; and Lowell H. Zuck, "Anabaptist Revolution through the Covenant in Sixteenth Century Continental Protestantism," Ph.D. dissertation, Yale University, 1955.
50. See Fast, *Bullinger und die Täufer*, pp. 153–155.
51. *Refutatio*, fol. 53b–60b. For a similar argument, see *Decades*, II: viii, fol. 69b–71b (*PSD* 1, pp. 357–368). For a summary of the *Refutatio*, see David J. Keep, "Bullinger's Defense of Queen Elizabeth," *HBGesA II*, pp. 231–241.
52. Schiess 3, pp. 215–218.

53. Printed in Fuesslin 3, pp. 190–201. Most effective in terms of executions. During the sixteenth century there were ten executions of Anabaptists in Zurich, six of them during Bullinger's tenure as Antistes, four in 1536, the year following his opinion to the council. In Bern, between 1529 and 1571, there were thirty executions. See Claus-Peter Clasen, "Executions of Anabaptists, 1525–1618: A Research Report," *MQR* 47 (1973), pp. 120–121.
54. *Ursprung*, fol. 161–161b.
55. *Ursprung*, fol. 162–163.
56. *Ursprung*, fol. 164–165.
57. *Ursprung*, fol. 165b–166.
58. *Ursprung*, fol. 166b–167; see also *De testamento*, fol. 19–19b. On the matter of the reformers' interpretation of the parable of the tares, see Roland H. Bainton, "The Parable of the Tares as a Proof Text for Religious Liberty in the Sixteenth Century," *CH* 1 (1932), pp. 67–89; Willem Balke, "Calvijn en de gelijkenis van het onkruid in de tarwe," *Theologia Reformata* 20 (1977), pp. 38–54; Yoder, *Täufertum und Reformation im Gespräch*, p. 162, n. 13.
59. Fuesslin 3, p. 200.
60. *Ursprung*, fol. 169–170b. In the 1535 *Gutachten* Bullinger also advised that the offender should be given a chance to repent; but if he was recalcitrant he must be treated "like other evildoers, according to the circumstances, and according to divine, civil and imperial law." Fuesslin 3, p. 201.
61. *Ursprung*, fol. 170b–171. On the matter of Bullinger's opposition to the radicals, see Nikolaus Paulus, *Protestantismus und Toleranz im 16. Jahrhundert* (Freiburg im Breisgau, 1911), pp. 210–228. Paulus takes Bullinger severely to task for his intolerance and advocacy of the death penalty for heretics. He totally ignores Bullinger's plea that such executions were for civil disobedience and for spreading false faith, not for lack of faith in the heart. Nor does he once refer to Bullinger's social-political theory or the actual circumstances of the sixteenth century that made such intolerance seem necessary and desirable to most. That Bullinger, along with the vast majority of his contemporaries, was intolerant in the face of heterodoxy goes without saying. To understand him within the context of his own time and thought world is quite another matter.
62. *Epitome*, fol. 24, 31b, 35b. Et refutantur illi, qui statum regnorum & reipub. reducere volunt ad normam evangelicam (fol. 31b).

Epilogue

1. See appendix C for the fortunes of the ideas of covenant and testament in the sixteenth century.
2. Armstrong, *Calvinism and the Amyraut Heresy*, p. 48, note 139.
3. *Ibid.*, pp. 143ff. Jürgen Moltmann includes Bullinger, along with Melanchthon and Bucer, as an influence on the Academy at Saumur and thus on Amyraut. "Prädestination und Heilsgeschichte bei Moyse Amyraut. Ein Beitrag zur

Geschichte der reformierten Theologie zwischen Orthodoxie and Aufklärung," *Zeitschrift für Kirchengeschichte* 65 (1954), p. 302.

4. Schrenk says that Cocceius himself named Bullinger and Olevianus as his forerunners. He also suggests the indirect influence of Snecanus and Wiggertsz. (See appendix C). *Gottesreich und Bund*, p. 127. See also McCoy, "The Covenant Theology of Johannes Cocceius," p. 66.

5. Greaves, "John Bunyan and Covenant Thought in the Seventeenth Century," esp. pp. 152, 158, 160; and "The Origins and Early Development of English Covenant Thought," pp. 32–33. For Perkins, see appendix C.

6. Miller, "The Marrow of Puritan Divinity," pp. 58–60.

7. Miller, *The New England Mind: The Seventeenth Century*, pp. 414–416; and "The Marrow of Puritan Divinity," pp. 89–91. Staedtke says, "The fact that Bullinger made the doctrine of the covenant the chief point of his theology later had important consequences for the origin and development of the New England states in America. For to a much greater degree perhaps than the intensification of the doctrine of predestination by Beza, the covenant thought formed in Zurich awakened and animated the astonishing responsibility of the reformed people for the things of public life. Here one of the great strengths of the American people was born." "Bullingers Bedeutung für die protestantische Welt," p. 380.

8. As argued by Robert C. Walton, "The Institutionalization of the Reformation at Zurich," *Zwingliana* 13 (1972), pp. 497–508. For the structure of the Zurich government on the eve of the Reformation, see Hans Morf, *Zunftverfassung und Obrigkeit in Zürich von Waldman bis Zwingli* (Zurich, 1969).

9. *ZW* 9, pp. 451–467. For an English translation, see G. R. Potter, "Church and State, 1528: A Letter from Zwingli to Ambrosius Blarer (4 May 1528)," *Occasional Papers of the American Society for Reformation Research* 1 (Dec. 1977), pp. 110–122. See also Fritz Blanke, "Zwingli mit Ambrosius Blarer im Gespräch," in *Der Konstanzer Reformator Ambrosius Blarer 1492–1564* (Konstanz, 1964), pp. 81–86.

10. *ZW* 9, p. 452. Blarer's own letter to Zwingli is not extant.

11. *ZW* 9, pp. 455: 33–456: 29; 459: 5–21; 464: 1–467: 12.

12. Ego enim virum Christianum id arbitror esse ecclesiae, quod bonum civem urbi. *ZW* 9, p. 466: 10–11. Christianum hominem nihil aliud esse quam fidelem ac bonum civem, urbem Christianam nihil quam ecclesiam Christianam esse. *ZW* 14, p. 424: 20–22. Cf. Walton, "The Institutionalization of the Reformation at Zurich," p. 501.

13. See the introduction to Zwingli's Jeremiah commentary: *ZW* 14, pp. 417–425. See also Bernd Moeller, *Reichsstadt und Reformation* (Gütersloh, 1962), pp. 38–43; and Ley, *Kirchenzucht bei Zwingli*, esp. pp. 99–105.

14. In his introduction to his Isaiah and Jeremiah commentaries, Zwingli made no use of the covenant idea, even though the theme in each case was political theory and the Christian commonwealth. *ZW* 14, pp. 5–14, 417–425.

15. Headley, *Luther's View of Church History*, pp. 5–17. For a dissenting point of

view on the differences between Luther and Zwingli, see Steven E. Ozment, *The Reformation in the Cities: The Appeal of Protestantism to Sixteenth-Century Germany and Switzerland* (New Haven, Connecticut, and London, 1975), esp. pp. 131–138. Luther's view of the relationship between the church and the civil government has been the subject of much controversy. See especially Karl Holl, "Luther und das landescherrliche Kirchenregiment" (1911), in *Gesammelte Aufsätze zur Kirchengeschichte, Vol. 1: Luther* (Tubingen, 1948), pp. 326–379; Ernst Rietschel, *Das Problem der unsichtbar-sichtbaren Kirche bei Luther* (Leipzig, 1932); Franz Lau, *Luthers Lehre von den beiden Reichen* (Berlin, 1953); and Heinrich Bornkamm, *Luthers Lehre von den zwei Reichen im Zusammenhang seiner Theologie.* 3d ed. (Gutersloh, 1969).

16. Moeller, *Reichsstadt und Reformation*, pp. 43–47. For a short summary of Bucer's views, see Wilhelm Pauck, "Martin Bucer's Conception of a Christian State," *Princeton Theological Review* 26 (1928), pp. 80–88. For a thorough study of Bucer's view of the church and his influence on Calvin, see Jacques Courvoisier, *La Notion d'Eglise chez Bucer dans son Développement Historique* (Paris, 1933).

17. "Institutionis," IV, i–xiii, xx, 1–2. *CO* 2, col. 905–914, 1092–1094.

18. Walton points out that Köhler incorrectly sees the Genevan Consistory in the same light as the earlier Zurich *Ehegericht*. Köhler misses the point that the two courts were the result of opposite theories on the relationship between the church and the magistracy. "The Institutionalization of the Reformation at Zurich," pp. 505–506; but cf. Walther Köhler, *Zürcher Ehegericht und Genfer Konsistorium Vol. 2: Das Ehe- und Sittengericht in den Süddeutschen Reichsstädten, dem Herzogtum Würtemberg und in Genf* (Leipzig, 1942).

19. See Moeller, *Reichsstadt und Reformation*, pp. 35–38, on Luther's thought as contrary to the idea of a Christian community that identified the church and the civil community, and pp. 55–67, on the differences between a Lutheran and Reformed city. One basic difference was that the Reformed cities sought a community discipline and that Lutheran thought moved at cross-purposes to the late medieval trend toward the unity of the church and the civil community, with the corresponding, increasing role of the civil government in ecclesiastical affairs. But cf. James M. Estes, "Church Order and the Christian Magistrate according to Johannes Brenz," *ARG* 59 (1968), pp. 5–24; "Johannes Brenz and the Problem of Ecclesiastical Discipline," *CH* 41 (1972), pp. 464–479; and Ozment, *The Reformation in the Cities*, pp. 121 ff.

20. "Zwingli erörtert systematisch, während Bullinger heilsgeschichtliche begründet." Staedtke, *Theologie*, p. 228, note 4.

21. *Reichsstadt und Reformation*, pp. 13, 15.

22. *Ibid.*, pp. 12–15.

23. See especially Hans Morf, "Obrigkeit und Kirche in Zürich bis zu Beginn der Reformation," *Zwingliana* 13 (1970), pp. 164–205.

24. Pestalozzi, *Heinrich Bullinger*, pp. 620–621. Eine fromme Gemeinde als Väter des Volkes. . . . Ihr meine Herren, die Räthe und Zunftmeister von der Constaffel und den Zünften sammt den Bürgern, seid ein einiges Haupt des

einigen Leibes, der Gemeinde. The term "Bürger" referred only to members of the Great Council. For a concise description of the form and organization of the Zürich government, see Potter, *Zwingli*, pp. 48–53.

25. See above, chapter 4.
26. Alan Gewirth, *Marsilius of Padua: The Defender of Peace. Volume 1: Marsilius of Padua and Medieval Political Philosophy* (New York, 1951), pp. 291–302. See also Otto Gierke, *Political Theories in the Middle Ages* (Cambridge, 1958), pp. 191–192, note 326.
27. Gewirth, *Marsilius of Padua*, vol. 1, pp. 256–258.
28. "Tractatus de excommunicatione," fol. 50v; cf. *Explicatio*, pp. 160, 162.
29. See Baker, "In Defense of Magisterial Discipline," pp. 141–159.
30. As argued by Ruth Wesel-Roth, *Thomas Erastus* (Lahr/Baden, 1954), pp. 123–124.
31. Significantly, Bodin admits to a familiarity with at least Bullinger's historical writings, mentioning him as a foremost chronicler in the introduction to chapter 10; then under "Writers of Universal History," we find the entry, "Henry Bullinger, chronicle from the Creation to his own age," with the date 1545. Jean Bodin, *Method for the Easy Comprehension of History*, translated by Beatrice Reynolds (New York, 1969 [1945]), pp. 365, 367. Most probably, Bodin's reference was to the Latin translation of Bullinger's *Der alt gloub: Antiquissima fides et vera religio* (1544) (*HBBibl I*, no. 103).
32. Julian H. Franklin, *Jean Bodin and the Rise of Absolutist Theory* (Cambridge, 1973), esp. pp. 23–40.
33. Franklin, *Jean Bodin and the Rise of Absolutist Theory*, pp. 41ff.
34. In 1554, John Knox sent a set of questions concerning resistance to Bullinger. Although Bullinger's reply was exceedingly cautious, he did not completely deny the right of resistance. See *CO* 15, col. 91–93; and *OL* 2, pp. 745–747. Knox later used the covenant idea within the context of political resistance. See Richard L. Greaves, "John Knox and the Covenant Tradition." See also Dan G. Danner, "Christopher Goodman and the English Protestant Tradition of Civil Disobedience," *SCJ* 8:3 (1977), pp. 61–73.
35. Generally, Bullinger denied the right of active resistance, allowing only passive disobedience. The Christian must submit to every human government—pagan rulers and tyrants as well as Christian governments. In the case of tyranny, God's people should repent, pray, and effect a reformation. Then God would either change the heart of the tyrant or destroy him. In the latter case, God would also select the instrument, as He had done with Moses, Gideon, and Samson. But, he warned, if a person did not have a calling as firm and certain as these men had been given, it would be evil to kill even a tyrant. Unless God himself raised up a Samson, the faithful must endure tyranny, only resisting passively. *In omnes apostolicas epistolas* 1, pp. 101–105; 2, pp. 30–31; *Sermones*, pp. 204–205; *Daniel*, fol. 34–35, 63b–64b; *Ieremias*, fol. 167; *Decades*, II: vi, fol. 61b–62 (*PSD* 1, pp. 316–318).
36. For the argument for Mornay's authorship, see Franklin, pp. 138–139, 208, and Laski, pp. 57–60. In the seventeenth century, Mornay founded the Academy at

Saumur, where Cameron and Amyraut taught. (Moltmann, "Prädestination und Heilsgeschichte bei Moyse Amyraut," p. 271.)

37. Franklin, p. 143.
38. Franklin, p. 144; cf. Laski, pp. 71–75.
39. Laski, pp. 80–85; cf. Franklin, p. 145.
40. Laski, pp. 87–116; Franklin, pp. 146–158.
41. Franklin, p. 157.
42. Franklin, p. 158.
43. Franklin, pp. 158–179; Laski, pp. 117–174.
44. Franklin, pp. 180–181.
45. Franklin, pp. 181–197; Laski, pp. 174–213.
46. The Latin was printed in 1581 and 1589. The English translation appeared in 1622 and was reprinted in 1631, 1648, 1660, and 1689. Laski, p. 60.
47. For a full-scale study of the impact of sixteenth-century French resistance thought, including Mornay, on seventeenth-century English political thought, see J. H. M. Salmon, *The French Religious Wars in English Political Thought* (Oxford, 1959).
48. Laski (p. 53) says that John Locke "did little, the theory of toleration apart, but adapt the teaching of the *Vindiciae* to an English atmosphere." See also the provocative essay of Gerhard Oestreich, "Die Idee des religiösen Bundes und die Lehre vom Staatsvertrag," in *Geist und Gestalt des frümodernen Staates: Ausgewählte Aufsätze* (Berlin, 1969), pp. 157–178. Trinterud ("The Origins of Puritanism," pp. 41–42) also discusses the probable connection between social contract theory and covenant theology.

Appendix A

1. "Wir sind pettler. Hoc est verum," pp. 242, 247–248.
2. Preus discusses this same material in terms of "promise" rather than "covenant." *From Shadow to Promise*, pp. 153–265.
3. *A Theology of Testament in the Young Luther*, esp. pp. 68–70. See also Hagen, "From Testament to Covenant," pp. 5–7.
4. Heinrich Bornkamm, *Luther and the Old Testament* (Philadelphia, 1969), pp. 254ff.
5. Hagen, "From Testament to Covenant," pp. 7–10.
6. Bornkamm, *Luther and the Old Testament*, pp. 255–257, 207–218. See also Hagen, "From Testament to Covenant," pp. 20–21.
7. Cottrell, "Covenant and Baptism," pp. 400–402.
8. Hagen, "From Testament to Covenant," p. 21, note 107. Hagen also discusses Erasmus and concludes that he relegated the Old Testament to an inferior position. Hagen thus dismisses Erasmus as an influence on the development of the sixteenth-century concepts of testament and covenant. *Ibid.*, pp. 6–7.
9. Schrenk, *Gottesreich und Bund*, pp. 48–49; and Hagen, "From Testament to Covenant," pp. 10–15.

10. Pauck, pp. 70–74, 84, 94, 99–104; *CR* 21, col. 139–143, 154–155, 164–165, 170–176.
11. Hagen, "From Testament to Covenant," p. 11.
12. Pauck, pp. 120, 123, 124, 126, 129–130; *CR* 21, col. 196, 199, 205–206.
13. Pauck, p. 133; *CR* 21, col. 208. See Hagen, "From Testament to Covenant," p. 14.
14. *CR* 21, col. 390–392, 398–399.
15. *CR* 22, col. 437. Manschreck, p. 199; cf. *CR* 21, col. 461.
16. *CR* 21, col. 453–456, 461.
17. *CR* 13, col. 1013.
18. *CR* 23, col. 42–43. Melanchthon referred to 1 Pet. 3:21 in terms of this stipulation. The Greek term is ἐπερώτημα, "demand."
19. *CR* 13, col. 1013–1014.
20. Manschreck, pp. 51–52, 57, 60, 61; *CR* 22, col. 146–147, 154, 157–158.
21. Manschreck, pp. 53–57, 199; *CR* 22, col. 149–153, 437.
22. Manschreck, pp. 66–67; *CR* 22, col. 163–166.
23. Manschreck, pp. 188–190; *CR* 22, col. 419–422. Italics Melanchthon's.
24. "The Origins of Puritanism," p. 41.
25. *De testamento*, fol. 38–38b; *In Hieremiam (Oecolampadius)*, sig. Rii–Rii(v). The entire quotation has been given from Bullinger, but he deleted several lines from Oecolampadius, as indicated in the translation.
26. *In Hieremiam (Oecolampadius)*, sig. Ri–Rii.
27. *In Hieremiam (Oecolampadius)*, sig. Rii–Riii(v).
28. *In Hieremiam (Oecolampadius)*, sig. Riii(v). Quia dabo, inquit, legem meam, quae quidem in conditionibus foederis est, in medio eorum & super cor eorum scribam.
29. Ernst Staehelin, *Das theologische Lebenswerk Johannes Oekolampads* (Leipzig, 1939), pp. 407–408.
30. *Ibid.*, pp. 189–191.
31. "The Origins of Puritanism," p. 41; "Covenant and Baptism," p. 357.
32. *In Iesaiam (Oecolampadius)*, fol. 150. Partially translated by Cottrell, "Covenant and Baptism," p. 356.
    Unfortunately, Trinterud's *interpretive* statement, "To be blessed of God man must keep this covenant by obeying the law," has been quoted by Greaves as the words of Oecolampadius. Richard L. Greaves, "The Origins and Early Development of English Covenant Thought," *The Historian*, 31 (1968), p. 24.
33. *In Iesaiam (Oecolampadius)*, fol. 255b. Quoted by Cottrell, "Covenant and Baptism," p. 355.
34. *In Iesaiam (Oecolampadius)*, fol. 271. Quoted by Cottrell, "Covenant and Baptism," p. 355.
35. See Cottrell, "Covenant and Baptism," pp. 354, 357.
36. As cited in Cottrell, "Covenant and Baptism," p. 373. Oecolampadius began to lecture on Haggai in the summer of 1525, then on Zechariah, and finally on Malachi, finishing in the summer of 1526. Staehelin, *Oekolampadius*, p. 396. Cottrell sees an influence by Zwingli on Oecolampadius. "Covenant and Baptism," p. 374.

37. Schrenck, *Gottesreich und Bund*, p. 37; Trinterud, "Origins of Puritanism," p. 41.

38. *De operibus Dei* (1525), fol. 43b–44, 45b. My thanks to Prof. James M. Kittelson of Ohio State University for providing a copy of this treatise.

39. *De operibus Dei*, fol. 57b–58. Pacis foedere, reconciliari neque velit, neque possit . . . per ineluctabile damnationis ac reprobationis decretum.

40. "Origins of Puritanism," p. 41.

41. James M. Kittelson, *Wolfgang Capito from Humanist to Reformer* (Leiden, 1975), p. 181, note 21, and p. 185. Capito wrote: "Baptismus et Eucharistia non successerunt in locum illorum, sed Christus, ceu corpus umbris praelucentibus successit, qui has novas ceremonias instituit, ceu umbras earum rerum, quas ipse conpleturus esset, nobisque elementa mundi non sunt, qui exaltatum Christum intelligimus." *In Hoseam (Capito)*, fol. 155. The entire section (fol. 150–155) is a discussion of how the internal covenant of grace differed from the external covenant presented to Abraham. The external covenant was a figure of the spiritual promises of the internal covenant.

42. Kittelson, *Capito*, pp. 230–237.

43. "Origins of Puritanism," p. 41; cf. p. 56, note 27.

44. "From Testament to Covenant," pp. 22–23, and note 111.

45. *Gottesreich und Bund*, p. 37. Schrenk says that Cellarius used the covenant idea *against* infant baptism. As Kittelson points out, however, Cellarius said that infant baptism should not be prohibited, because the law of charity regulated all external things. He did not defend it; neither did he take an Anabaptist stance. Nor is there any evidence that he was rebaptized or that he rebaptized others. *Capito*, p. 178.

46. A. Lang, *Der Evangelienkommentar Martin Bucers* (Leipzig, 1900), p. 258, note 4.

47. Karl Koch, *Studium Pietatis: Martin Bucer als Ethiker* (Neukirchen, 1962), p. 62.

48. *Ibid.*, p. 215, note 176.

49. *MBDS* 1, p. 217: 4–5; p. 251: 10–13.

50. *MBDS* 1, p. 220: 29; p. 234: 31– p. 235: 35.

51. *MBDS* 1, p. 272: 31–37; p. 277: 26–29.

52. *MBDS* 2, p. 62: 4–5; p. 121: 5–8; p. 122: 13–16; p. 167: 17.

53. In covering much of the same material, Cottrell comes to essentially the same conclusion. "Covenant and Baptism," pp. 326–336.

54. *MBDS* 2, p. 219: 13–14.

55. *Enarrationum I (Bucer)*, fol. 150b–157b.

Appendix B

1. Perry Miller, "The Marrow of Puritan Divinity," *Errand into the Wilderness* (New York, 1964), pp. 48–98; see also Miller, *The New England Mind: The Seventeenth Century* (New York, 1939); for a critique of Miller's treatment of

Calvin, see Marsden, "Perry Miller's Rehabilitation of the Puritans: A Critique."

2. "Origins of Puritanism," pp. 45, 56 (note 27).
3. Torrance, "Covenant or Contract?" pp. 54–56.
4. Wolf, *Die Einheit des Bundes*, esp. pp. 19–21, note 12.
5. *Gottesreich und Bund*, pp. 36, 47–48.
6. See especially, Josef Bohatec, *Budé und Calvin. Studien zur Gedankenwelt des französischen Frühhumanismus* (Graz, 1950), pp. 246–248. Other recent studies which take this point of view include Peter Y. DeJong, *The Covenant Idea in New England Thought, 1620–1847* (Grand Rapids, Michigan, 1945), pp. 18–23; Anthony A. Hoekema, "The Covenant of Grace in Calvin's Teaching," *Calvin Theological Journal* 2 (1967), pp. 113–161; and Marsden, "Perry Miller's Rehabilitation of the Puritans."
7. "Institutio Christianae Religionis" (1559), II, vi, 4. CO 2, col. 251. Battles, p. 346. Translations are Battles' unless otherwise indicated.
8. "Institutio" (1559), II, vii, 2; xi, 2; II, ii, 22; xvii, 6, 15; xviii, 7; xxi, 1, 5. CO 2, col. 254, 330–331, 416, 594–595, 602–603, 609–610, 678–680, 682–684.
9. See especially, "Institutio" (1559), III, xxi, 1, 6, 7. CO 2, col. 678–679, 684–686; Battles, pp. 920–921, 929–931.
10. "Institutio" (1559), III, xxi, 6. CO 2, col. 684; Battles, p. 929.
11. "The Covenant of Grace in Calvin's Teaching," p. 148.
12. "Institutio" (1559), III, xxi, 5. CO 2, col. 684; Battles, p. 928. Italics added.
13. "Institutio" (1559), II, xi, 10. Ad novum testamentum. CO 2, col. 336–337. Cf. Battles, p. 459, where the translation is "New Covenant."
14. "Institutio" (1559), II, x, 7, 15, 19. Spirituale foedus . . . spiritualis foederis; carnale . . . foedus. CO 2, col. 317, 323, 326; Battles, pp. 434, 441, 446.
15. "Institutio" (1559), II, xi, 4. Foedus legale cum foedere evangelico. CO 2, col. 323; Battles, p. 454.
16. "Institutio" (1559), II, xi, 2; IV, i, 24. CO 2, col. 330, 764; Battles, pp. 451, 1037.
17. "Institutio" (1559), II, x, 4, 20, 23. CO 2, col. 314–315, 326–329; Battles, pp. 429–431, 446–449.
18. "The Covenant of Grace in Calvin's Teaching," pp. 155–159.
19. "Institutio" (1559), III, xxi, 6; xxii, 11; CO 2, col. 685, 697–698; Battles, pp. 929, 946–947.
20. "Institutio" (1559), II, vii, 12. CO 2, col. 261–262; Battles, pp. 360–361.
21. "Institutio" (1559), III, xvii, 5. CO 2, col. 594; Battles, p. 808.
22. "Institutio" (1559), II, x, 2–23. CO 2, col. 313–329; Battles, pp. 429–449.
23. "Institutio" (1559), II, xi, 2–3. CO 2, col. 330–331; Battles, pp. 451–453.
24. "Institutio" (1539), XL, 1–39. CO 1, col. 801–827; cf. 1559 edition, II, x–xi. CO 2, col. 313–340.
25. "Institutio" (1539), XIV, 1–22. CO 1, col. 861–877.
26. "Institutio" (1559), II, vi; III, xxi, 5–7; xxii, 4–6. CO 2, col. 247–252, 682–687, 690–694.
27. Reid, p. 91. Nec vero aliter stare potest inviolabile illud Dei pactum . . . nisi Dominus arbitrio suo discernat, quibus gratiam largiatur, vel quos aeternae

morti velit manere addictos. *CO* 8, col. 289. *De aeterna Dei praedestinatione* was actually written against Pighius, but it was also, in effect, a reply to Bolsec. Recent scholarship, such as François Wendel, *Calvin: The Origins and Development of His Religious Thought* (London, 1963), esp. pp. 263ff, 357–360, tends to deemphasize the importance of predestination in Calvin's thought. This subordination of his testament-covenant concept to predestination in his theology demonstrates, however, that predestination was a particularly powerful motif in his thought, if not the most important idea.

28. "Origins of Puritanism," p. 45, 56 (note 27).
29. "The Marrow of Puritan Divinity," p. 60.
30. "The Covenant of Grace in Calvin's Teaching," pp. 155–158.
31. "Perry Miller's Rehabilitation of the Puritans," pp. 91–105.
32. "The Marrow of Puritan Divinity," pp. 93ff.
33. *Ibid.*, pp. 58ff. See appendix C for Perkins.

Appendix C

1. Alexander Schweizer, *Centraldogmen*, esp. chapter 1, pp. 1–19.
2. Lindsay, "The Covenant Theology," pp. 523–527, 533–538.
3. McCoy, "The Covenant Theology of Johannes Cocceius," pp. 136–137.
4. I. A. Dorner, *History of Protestant Theology* (Edinburgh, 1870), vol. 2, pp. 41–42.
5. Heinrich Heppe, *Reformed Dogmatics Set Out and Illustrated from the Sources* (New York, 1950), p. 371.
6. Miller, "The Marrow of Puritan Divinity," pp. 93ff.
7. A study comparing Bullinger's covenant idea with that of Cocceius or Witsius could be very fruitful. At the least it would determine how closely their thought was connected with the early Reformation.

     De testamento was not republished in the seventeenth century. However, Bullinger's *Der alt gloub* was published in Dutch in 1599 (*HBBibl I*, no. 109), his *Summa*, which heavily emphasizes the covenant, in Dutch, in 1608 (*HBBibl I*, no. 313), and his *Decades*, also in Dutch, in 1601, 1607, 1612, and 1622 (*HBBibl I*, nos. 204, 205, 206, and 210).
8. *Loci communes (Musculus)*, pp. 142–146. For Musculus, see Schrenk, *Gottesreich und Bund*, pp. 50–51; and Ritschl, *Dogmengeschichte*, vol. 3, pp. 415–416.
9. *Loci communes (Musculus)*, pp. 20–24, 237–239, 248–251, 253–254.
10. For Ursinus, see Karl Sudhoff, *C. Olevianus und Z. Ursinus* (Elberfeld, 1857); Bard Thompson et al., *Essays on the Heidelberg Catechism* (Philadelphia and Boston, 1963); J. W. Nevin, "Zacharius Ursinus," *Mercersburg Review* 3 (1851), pp. 490–512; E. Sturm, *Der junge Zacharias Ursin* (Neukirchen, 1972).
11. Hendrikus Berkhof says that Bullinger had a great influence on Ursinus' idea of the covenant. "The Catechism in Historical Context," *Essays on the Heidelberg*

Catechism, pp. 77, 86–90; see also Schrenk, *Gottesreich und Bund*, pp. 57–59; and Ritschl, *Dogmengeschichte*, vol. 3, pp. 416–417.

12. *Doctrinae Christianae compendium*, pp. 3, 7.

13. *Doctrinae Christianae compendium*, pp. 225–226. Foedus, quod hominibus per Mediatorem Deus pepigit, est promissio et pactio mutua, qua Deus per et propter Mediatorem se obligat ad remittenda credentibus peccata, et dandam iis vitam aeternam: qua vicissim sese homines obligant ad recipiendum vera fide tantum hoc beneficium, et ad praestandam Deo veram obedientiam, hoc est, ad vivendum secundum ipsius voluntatem. Pactio haec mutua signis sacramentalibus confirmatur.

14. *Doctrinae Christianae compendium*, p. 227.

15. *CR* 13, col. 1013. Novum testamentum est novae et aeternae iusticiae et vitae promissio propter Filium morientem, in qua Deus se obligat nobis ad dandam remissionem peccatorum et reconciliationem, iusticiam et vitam aeternam, et vicissim nos obligat ad credendum promissioni quae gratuita est. . . .

16. *Doctrinae Christianae compendium*, pp. 682ff. Ritschl points out that Ursinus spoke once of a *foedus naturale* but dropped the idea in his later thought. Both Ritschl and Schrenk see Melanchthon influencing the development of the idea of a covenant of works with his concept of the natural law (*lex naturale*), the knowledge of the divine or moral law with which every person is born. Ritschl, *Dogmengeschichte*, vol. 3, pp. 416–417; Schrenk, *Gottesreich und Bund*, pp. 48–49, 59.

17. *Doctrinae Christianae compendium*, pp. 688–689.

18. Sept. 2, 1573. Printed in German translation in Sudhoff, *Olevianus und Ursinus*, pp. 614–633 (see pp. 614–618, 623–633).

19. John Patrick Donnelly, "Italian Influences on the Development of Calvinist Scholasticism," pp. 82–83.

20. Sudhoff, *Olevianus und Ursinus*, p. 614.

21. John S. Bray, *Theodore Beza's Doctrine of Predestination* (Nieuwkoop, 1975), esp. pp. 119–143; Donnelly, "Italian Influences on the Development of Calvinist Scholasticism," *passim*; and Donnelly, *Calvinism and Scholasticism in Vermigli's Doctrine of Grace*.

22. *De substantia foederis gratuiti* (1585), pp. 1–2. For other descriptions of Olevianus on the covenant, see Ritschl, *Dogmengeschichte*, vol. 3, pp. 418–420; and Schrenk, *Gottesreich und Bund*, pp. 59–62.

23. *De substantia foederis gratuiti*: "foedus creationis" (p. 9); "foedus legale" (pp. 13, 252); and "naturale foedus" (p. 251).

24. *De substantia foederis gratuiti*, pp. 9–12, 212, 251–255.

25. *De substantia foederis gratuiti*, p. 16. Atque ita totum hoc foederis mere esse gratuitum & nulla conditione virium nostrarum, sed gratuita Dei misericordia in Christo per fidem, quam ipse donat apprehensa constare, certum est.

26. *Romanos (Olevianus)*, p. 430 (cf. p. 432), 452. Vasa irae sunt (ut Pharao & similes) quae Deus paravit ad damnationem.

27. *De substantia foederis gratuiti*, pp. 28–30; cf. *Romanos (Olevianus)*, p. 443.

28. *De substantia foederis gratuiti*, pp. 56–58, 86, 253–255.
29. Supralapsarianism holds that God decreed election and reprobation, then decreed or permitted the fall as a means of carrying out these decrees. Infralapsarianism teaches that God foresaw and permitted the fall, then decreed election. The supralapsarian position assumed a double decree; infralapsarianism could be squared with either single or double predestination. On the Remonstrance of the Arminians and the Canons of Dort, see Schaff, *Creeds* 1, pp. 509–523; 3, p. 545 ff.
30. "Oratio, de foedere Dei" (1594). This short three page discourse is at the very beginning of part 1 of Gomarus' *Opera Theologica Omnia* (Amstelodami, 1654). It is unpaginated. Cf. Schrenk, *Gottesreich und Bund*, pp. 63–65; and Ritschl, who discusses not only Gomarus but also Franz Junius, who presented a similar covenant doctrine in 1582 (*Dogmengeschichte*, vol. 3, pp. 420–424).
31. *A Golden Chaine*, sig. B4, B7(v), D2. Perkins knew and seems to have been influenced by Olevianus' *De substantia foederis gratuiti*. Møller, "The Beginnings of Puritan Covenant Theology," p. 58.
32. *A Golden Chaine*, sig. E6. Patrick Collinson uses this very quotation to argue that Perkins held to a contractual covenant, ignoring the distinction, which Perkins goes on to make, between testament and covenant, and the fact that Perkins himself attaches the conditions to the covenant of works. *The Elizabethan Puritan Movement* (London, 1967), pp. 434–435.
33. *A Golden Chaine*, sig. E6–E6(v).
34. *A Golden Chaine*, sig. O3–O3(v).
35. *A Golden Chaine*, sig. A2–A2(v).
36. *A Golden Chaine*, sig. T6–V1(v). See Møller, "The Beginnings of Puritan Covenant Theology," pp. 59–64, for his summary of the argument of *A Golden Chaine*. He makes the significant point that Perkins placed the establishment of the covenant of works after the fall, not before, as his contemporary Dudley Fenner and later figures theorized. See also I. Breward, "The Life and Theology of William Perkins, 1558–1602," Ph.D. dissertation: University of Manchester, 1963, for Perkins on the covenant (pp. 58–65) and on predestination (pp. 194–220).
37. Greaves sees a continuing Zurich influence in terms of a conditional covenant in late-century figures such as Dudley Fenner and Thomas Cartwright, and even to some extent in Perkins. "The Origins and Early Development of English Covenant Thought," pp. 29–30. Møller, however, after discussing Perkins, Cartwright, Fenner, and the anonymous *Sacred Doctrine*, says, "Apart from their teaching on the sacraments, there can be no doubt about the Calvinist origin of the covenant theology in these early puritan systematic theologians." "The Beginnings of Puritan Covenant Theology," p. 63.
38. *The newe Testament*, "W. T. to the Reader," sig. *.iii–*.iiii. For other descriptions of Tyndale's covenant idea, see William A. Clebsch, *England's Earliest Protestants, 1520–1535* (New Haven and London, 1964), pp. 181–204; and Møller, "The Beginnings of Puritan Covenant Theology," pp. 50–54.
39. "Origins of Puritanism," p. 40.

40. *The newe Testament*, fol. 215b–216.

41. "Origins of Puritanism," pp. 40, 42–43; *England's Earliest Protestants*, p. 199.

42. "The Beginnings of Puritan Covenant Theology," p. 54.

43. *Fraefel*, fol. 55ff.

44. G. E. Duffield, *The Work of William Tyndale* (Philadelphia, 1965), p. xxiv.

45. The first German edition carried a slightly different title. See *HBBibl I*, no. 99; cf. nos. 100–102. Coverdale's translation was first entitled *The olde fayth* (*HBBibl I*, nos. 104–106); a seventeenth-century edition was entitled *Looke from Adam* (*HBBibl I*, no. 107).

46. Clebsch, *England's Earliest Protestants*, p. 193. However, cf. Trinterud, "The Origins of Puritanism," p. 44: "Coverdale's editions of the Bible are all wholly indifferent to the covenant notion."

47. The Pollard and Redgrave citation (S.T.C. No. 2063) reads, "Biblia the bible that is the holy scrypture. Tr. out of the Douche and Latyn [M. Coverdale] 6 pt. fol. [Zurich?] 1535."

Both A. G. Dickens, *The English Reformation* (New York, 1964), p. 130; and C. H. Williams, *William Tyndale* (London, 1969), p. 168, indicate that it was published in Zurich by Froschauer. Probably, however, they have simply followed Alfred W. Pollard (ed.), *Records of the English Bible* (London, 1911), pp. 12–13, who presents some evidence of the Zurich printing. J. F. Mozley opts for a Cologne printing, based on an argument involving the capital letters, which were used by the printers Cervicorn and Soter in Cologne. He also rejects the assertion that Cologne was too unfriendly a location. *Coverdale and His Bibles* (London, 1953), pp. 74–77.

48. For this section on Hooper, I am indebted to W. M. S. West, *John Hooper and the Origins of Puritanism*, Th.D. dissertation, Universität Zürich, 1955.

49. "Unto the Christian Reader," in *Early Writings*, pp. 255–257. Møller charges West with exaggeration in calling the covenant the framework of Hooper's thought, insisting that "Unto the Christian Reader" contains "the only explicit covenant teaching in Hooper." West's presentation is "unscientific and misleading." "The Beginnings of Puritan Covenant Theology," pp. 55–56, note 3. Such a harsh indictment is unfair. First, although West does see the covenant as the framework for Hooper's theology, he does so hesitantly and with qualification. It was "something of a framework," for a man who was neither original nor very systematic (*John Hooper*, p. 15). Secondly, although Hooper did not often use the terms covenant, peace, or league, it is reasonable to expect that he would follow through with the themes established in "Unto the Christian Reader" in his actual exposition of the law, to which it was a preface. And he did, at times not using the covenant terms (*Early Writings*, pp. 271–272, 282–283) and elsewhere referring explicitly to covenant (*Early Writings*, p. 415).

50. *Early Writings*, pp. 259, 264–265. See also his "Sermons on Jonah," where he says, "That God repenteth on the evil he purposed to do unto the Ninivites, we learn that all the threatenings of God be conditionally, that is to say, to fall upon us if we repent not of our evil deeds." *Early Writings*, p. 547.

51. West, *John Hooper*, p. 65, note 57.

52. Møller, "The Beginnings of Puritan Covenant Theology," pp. 57–59.
53. See Van t'Hooft, *De Theologie van Heinrich Bullinger*, esp. pp. 162–163, 184–185; and Korff, *Die Anfänge der Foederaltheologie*, pp. 30 ff.
54. Printed in *BRN* 4, pp. 123–376.
55. Carl Bangs, *Arminius, a Study in the Dutch Reformation* (Nashville, Tennessee, 1971), pp. 21–22.
56. *Vom Nachtmal Christi* (1557) (*BRN* 4, pp. 389–451) and *Von dem waren leib Christi* (1561) (*BRN* 4, pp. 461–486).
57. *BRN* 4, pp. 140, 164, 190–191. German translation in Korff, *Die Anfänge der Foederaltheologie*, p. 34.
58. *BRN* 4, p. 415.
59. *BRN* 4, pp. 473–474. See also Schrenk, *Gottesreich und Bund*, pp. 51–52, for a short summary of Veluanus' covenant idea.
60. *BRN* 4, pp. 153–156, 317. Partial German translation in Korff, *Die Anfänge der Foederaltheologie*, p. 33.
61. *BRN* 4, p. 418. Bangs says that Veluanus' ideas on predestination were the same as Arminius' later teaching. *Arminius*, p. 22.
62. *BRN* 4, pp. 220, 267, 361, 363, 397, 415. Cf. *HBBibl II*, nos. 1376, 1390, 1439. See Korff, *Die Anfänge der Foederaltheologie*, p. 30; Schrenk, *Gottesreich und Bund*, p. 51.
63. This summary of Snecanus' covenant ideas is based on Korff, *Die Anfänge der Foederaltheologie*, pp. 36–43; and on Schrenk, *Gottesreich und Bund*, pp. 53–54.
64. Quoted by Korff, *Die Anfänge der Foederaltheologie*, p. 41, note 52.
65. Bangs, *Arminius*, pp. 194–195. Ritschl also includes Snecanus, along with Veluanus, among the Arminian group. *Dogmengeschichte*, vol. 3, p. 427.
66. This summary is based on Korff, *Die Anfänge der Foederaltheologie*, pp. 44–52.
67. Quoted by Korff. *Ibid.*, pp. 48–49.
68. See Edward A. Dowey, *The Knowledge of God in Calvin's Theology* (New York and London, 1965), pp. 211–220; and Bray, *Theodore Beza's Doctrine of Predestination*, esp. pp. 63–66.
69. See Donnelly, "Italian Influences on Calvinist Scholasticism," pp. 96–100.
70. Barth asserts that election for Calvin was the "final (and therefore a first) word on the whole reality of the Christian life. . . ." *Church Dogmatics by Karl Barth*, vol. 2: *The Doctrine of God*, 2d half-vol. (Edinburgh, , 1957), p. 86.
71. *The New England Mind: The Seventeenth Century*, pp. 385–397; "The Marrow of Puritan Divinity," *passim*.
72. *Calvinism and the Amyraut Heresy* (Madison, Wisconsin, 1969), esp. pp. 42 ff, 141–152, 183 ff, 195 ff, 263–267.
73. McCoy, "The Covenant Theology of Johannes Cocceius," esp. pp. 276–319.

Bibliography

I. Abbreviations:
   A. *Journals:*

ARG	*Archiv für Reformationsgeschichte*
CH	*Church History*
JEH	*Journal of Ecclesiastical History*
MQR	*Mennonite Quarterly Review*
SCJ	*Sixteenth Century Journal*
TZ	*Theologische Zeitschrift*

   B. *Others:*

BRN — *Bibliotheca Reformatoria Neerlandica.* S'Gravenhage: Martinus Nijhoff, 1906.

HBBibl I — *Heinrich Bullinger Werke, pt. 1: Bibliographie, vol. 1: Beschreibendes Verzeichnis der Gedruckten Werke von Heinrich Bullinger.* Edited by Joachim Staedtke. Zurich: Theologischer Verlag, 1972.

HBBibl II — *Heinrich Bullinger Werke, pt. 1: Bibliographie, vol. 2: Beschreibendes Verzeichnis der Literatur über Heinrich Bullinger.* Edited by Erland Herkenrath. Zurich: Theologischer Verlag, 1977.

HBGesA I — *Heinrich Bullinger 1504–1575. Gesammelte Aufsätze zum 400. Todestag, vol. 1: Leben und Werk.* Edited by Ulrich Gäbler and

	Erland Herkenrath. Zürcher Beiträge zur Reformationsgeschichte, vol. 7. Zurich: Theologischer Verlag, 1975.
HBGesA II	*Heinrich Bullinger 1504-1575: Gesammelte Aufsätze zum 400. Todestag, vol. 2: Beziehungen und Wirkungen.* Edited by Ulrich Gäbler and Erland Herkenrath. Zürcher Beiträge zur Reformationsgeschichte, vol. 8. Zürich: Theologischer Verlag, 1975.
B-T 1975	*Bullinger—Tagung 1975. Vorträge, gehalten aus Anlass von Heinrich Bullingers 400. Todestag.* Im Auftrag des Instituts für Schweizerische Reformationsgeschichte. Edited by Ulrich Gäbler and Endre Zsindely. Zurich, 1977.
RTK	*Realenzyclopädie für protestantische Theologie und Kirche.* 3d ed. (1879).

II. Sources:
    A. *Bullinger's Works* (in chronological order):
        1. *Manuscript Collections:*

Zurich StA	Zürich Staatsarchiv (correspondence from E II 341; E II 343; E II 348).
Zurich ZB	Zürich Zentralbibliothek (see below for specific manuscripts).

        2. *Manuscripts:*

"De Scripturae negotio"	"Epistola ad Rudolphum Asper de Scripturae negotio." 30 Nov. 1523. Zurich ZB, Ms. A 82, fol. 45r–50r. Original copy.
"Von dem Touff"	"H. Bullinger an Heinrich Simler von dem Touff." Undated (late Nov.–early Dec. 1525). Zurich ZB, Ms. A 82, fol. 75r–81r. Original copy.
"De institutione eucharistiae"	"De institutione et genuino eucharistiae usu epistola." Heinrich Bullinger to Werner Steiner and Bartholomäus Stocker. 10 Dec. 1525. Zurich ZB, Ms. A 82, fol. 81r–89r. Original copy.
"Antwort an Burchard"	"Uff D. Iohansen Burckardi predigers ze Bremgartten gespraechbuechlin, antwort Heilrychen Bullingers die Geschrifft und Mess betraeffende." Undated (1527–early 1528). Zurich ZB, Ms. A 82, fol. 56v–73v. Original copy.
	"De ratio censuum." (1530?). Zurich ZB, Ms.

Car I 152, 153. Autograph.
"Quod in ecclesia Christi MAGISTRATUS SIT, Qui iure illam adversus haereticorum seditiones, et tyrannorum incursiones defendat." 1534. Zurich ZB, Ms. S 34/190. Autograph.

"Tractatus de excommunicatione"   "Tractatus de excommunicatione seu Sylva. HB." 1568. Zurich ZB, Ms. Car I 195, 52 fol. Autograph.

3. *Sixteenth-Century Imprints* (in chronological order):

Kaetzeryen   *Verglichung der uralten und unser zyten kaetzeryen. zuo warnen die einfaltigen Christen/ durch Octavium Florentem beschriben.* Zurich, 1526. (*HBBibl I*, no. 1)

Früntliche ermanung   *Früntliche ermanung zur Grechtigheit wider alles verfelschen rychtigen gerychts/ beschriben durch Heylrychen Bullinger.* Zurich, 1526. (*HBBibl I*, no. 2)

Anklag   *Anklag und ernstliches ermanen Gottes Allmaechtigen/ zuo eyner gemeynenn Eydgnoschafft/ das sy sich vonn jren Sünden zuo jmm keere.* [Zurich, 1528]. (*HBBibl I*, no. 3)

De origine erroris I   *De origine erroris, in negocio eucharistiae, ac missae, per Heinrychum Bullingerum.* Basel, 1528. (*HBBibl I*, no. 10)

De origine erroris II   *De origine erroris, in divorum ac simulachrorum cultu. Per Heinrychum Bullingerum.* Basel, 1529. (*HBBibl I*, no. 11)

De hebdomadis   *De hebdomadis, quae apud Danielem sunt, opusculum.* Zurich, 1530. (*HBBibl I*, no. 27)

Fraefel   *Von dem unverschampten fraefel ergerlichem verwyrren/ unnd unwarhafftem leeren/ der selbsgesandten Widertoeuffern/ vier gespraech Buecher/ zuo verwarnenn den einfalten/ Durch Heinrychen Bullinger geschribenn.* Zurich, 1531. (*HBBibl I*, no. 28)

De prophetae officio   *De prophetae officio, et quomodo digne administrari possit, oratio Heinrycho Bullingero Authore.* Zurich, 1532. (*HBBibl I*, no. 33)

Ein sendbrief   *An den Durchlüchtigen Hochgebornen Fürsten und herren/ Herrn Allbrechten Marggrauen zuo Brandenburg/ in Prüssen etc. Hertzogen etc. Ein sendbrieff und vorred der dieneren des wort Gottes zuo Zürich. Item ein buechlin Bertrami des Priesters von dem lyb und bluot Christi an Keyser Karle/ vertütscht durch Leonem Jud/ diener der kilchen Zürich.* Zurich, 1532. (*HBBibl I,* no. 34)

De testemento *De testemento sev foedere dei unico & aeterno Heinrichi Bullingeri brevis expositio.* Zurich, 1534. (*HBBibl I,* no. 54)

Von dem Testament *Von dem einigen unnd ewigen Testament oder Pundt Gottes/ Heinrychen Bullingers kurtzer bericht.* [Zurich, 1534]. (*HBBibl I,* no. 60)

In omnes apostolicas epistolas *In omnes apostolicas epistolas, divi videlicet Pauli XIIII., et VII. canonicas, commentarii Heinrychi Bullingeri, ab ipso iam recogniti, & nonnullis in locis aucti.* 2 vols. Zurich, 1537. (*HBBibl I,* no. 84)

Der alt gloub *Der alt gloub. Das der Christen gloub von anfang der waelt gewaert habe/ der recht waar alt unnd ungezwyflet gloub sye/ klare bewysung Heinrychen Bullingers.* Zurich, 1539 (1537). (*HBBibl I,* no. 100 [no. 99])

De scriptura I De scripturae sanctae authoritate, certitudine, *firmitate et absoluta perfectione, deque Episcoporum, qui verbi dei ministri sunt, institutione & functione, contra superstitionis tyrannidisque Romanae antistes, ad Sereniss. Angliae Regem Heinrychum VIII. Heinrychi Bullingeri Libri duo.* Zurich, 1538. (*HBBibl I,* no. 111)

De origine erroris III *De origine erroris libri duo, Heinrychi Bullingeri. In priore agitur de Dei veri iusta invocatione & cultu vero, de Deorum item falssorum religionibus & simulachrorum cultu erroneo. In posteriore disseritur de Institutione & vi sacrae Coenae domini, & de origine ac progressu Missae Papisticae, contra varias superstitiones pro religione vera antiqua & orthodoxa.* Zurich, 1539. (*HBBibl I,* no. 12)

De omnibus scripturae libris *De omnibus sanctae scripturae libris, eorumque praestantia & dignitate, Heinychi Bullingeri Expositio, ad Lectorem Christianum.* Zurich, 1539. (*HBBibl I,* no. 114)

Eestand — *Der Christlich Eestand. Von der heiligen Ee harkummen/ wenn/ wo/ wie/ unnd von waem sy ufgesetzt/ und was sy sye/ wie sy recht bezogen werde/ was jro ursachen frucht und eer: dargegen wie uneerlich die huory und d' Eebruch sye. Ouch wie man ein kommlichen Eegmahel erkiesen/ eeliche liebe trüw und pflicht halten und meeren/ und die kinder wol und recht ufziehen soelle/ durch Heinrychen Bullingern beschriben.* Zurich, 1540. (*HBBibl I*, no. 129)

Matthaeus — *In sacrosanctum Iesu Christi Domini nostri Evangelium secundum Matthaeum, Commentariorum libri XII. per Heinrychum Bullingerum.* Zurich, 1542. (*HBBibl I*, no. 144)

Ioannes — *In divinum Iesu Christi Domini nostri Evangelium secundum Ioannem, Commentariorum libri X. per Heinrychum Bullingerum.* Zurich, 1543. (*HBBibl I*, no. 153)

Brevis responsio — *Brevis ANTIBOAH sive responsio secunda Heinrychi Bullingeri ad maledicam implicatamque Ioannis Cocclei de Scripturae & ecclesiae authoritate Replicam, una cum Expositione De sancta Christi catholica ecclesia, ad illustrissimum principem & dominum D. Ottonem Heinrychum Palatinum Rheni, & utriusque Bavariae Ducem & c.* Zurich, 1544. (*HBBibl I*, no. 160)

Marcus — *In sacrosanctum Evangelium Domini nostri Iesu Christi secundum Marcum, Commentariorum lib. VI. per Heinrychum Bullingerum.* Zurich, 1545. (*HBBibl I*, no. 170)

Lucas — *In Luculentum et sacrosanctum Evangelium domini nostri Iesu Christi secundum Lucam, Commentariorum lib. IX. per H. Bullingerum.* Zurich, 1546. (*HHBibl I*, no. 173)

Series — *Series et digestio temporum et rerum descriptarum a beato Luca in Actis Apostolorum, authore Heinrycho Bullingero.* Zurich, 1548. (*HBBibl I*, no. 176)

Decades — *Sermonum Decades quinque, de potissimis Christianae religionis capitibus, in tres tomos digestae, authore Heinrycho Bullingero, ecclesiae Tigurinae ministro.* Zurich, 1552. (*HBBibl I*, no. 184)

Die rechten opfer	*Die rechten opffer der Christenheit. Ein predig uss dem XIII. Cap. S. Pauli zuo den Hebreern/ Zürych/ dess XIIII. Augusti/ gethon/ durch Heinrychen Bullinger.* Zurich, 1551. (*HBBibl I*, no. 246)
Perfectio Christianorum	*Perfectio Christianorum. Iesum Christum Dominum nostrum a patre coelesti datum esse mundo salvatorem, in quo fideles veluti in compendium recollecta habeant omnia quae ad veram pietatem discendam, vitamque vere beatam consequendam, & retinendam pertinent, ita ut nihil opus sit ea aliunde colligere, ad Christianissimum, eundemque potentissimum Francorum regem Heinrychum eius nominis II. Heinrychi Bullingeri demonstratio.* Zurich, 1551. (*HBBibl I*, no. 249)
Apodixis	*Ecclesias evangelicas neque haereticas neque schismaticas, sed plane orthodoxas & catholicas esse Iesu Christi ecclesias, Apodixis, ad illustrissimum principem & dominum D. Georgium Comitem Vuirtenbergen. & Montis Bellgardi, & c. authore Heinrycho Bullingero.* Zurich, 1552. (*HBBibl I*, no. 258)
Verklaerung	*Von der Verklaerung Jesu Christi/ Unsers Herren: ouch von unserer verklaerung/ unseren stand und waesen in ewiger froeud und saeligkeit. Das ouch unser Herr Jesus Christus der waar Messias/ der raecht frid unnd der einig aller waelt leerer sye: uss dem 17. cap. Matthei/ zwo Predginen Heinrychen Bullingers/ gethon zuo Zürych im October. 1552.* Zurich, 1552. (*HBBibl I*, no. 265)
Von rechter	*Von rechter buoss oder besserung dess sündigen menschens: Ouch von der grossen Gottes Barmhertzigkeit/ die er gnaedigklich allen armen sünderen bewysen wil/ dry Predginen Heinrychen Bullingers über die zwey letsten capitel des heiligen propheten Jone/ Zürych im October des 1552. jars gethon.* Zurich, 1553. (*HBBibl I*, no. 267)
Nachtmal	*Von dem heiligen Nachtmal Unsers Herrenn Jesu Christi/ wie oder welcher form unnd gstalt/ unnd warumb er das yngesetzt habe:*

ouch wie der mensch sich zuo soemlichem hochwirdigen mal rüsten unnd schicken soelle/ zwo Predginen Heinrychen Bullingers zuo Zürych gethon. Zurich, 1553. (*HBBibl I*, no. 268)

De gratia Dei — *De gratia Dei iustificante nos propter Christum, per solam fidem absque operibus bonis, fide interim exuberante in opera bona, Libri IIII. ad Sereniss. Daniae Regem Christianum, & c. Heinrycho Bullingero authore.* Zurich, 1554. (*HBBibl I*, no. 276)

Von dem Heil — *Von dem Heil der Gloeubigen. Wie es alle zyt/ von anfang der waelt glych/ durch das wort Gotts und die heiligen Sacramenta/ den menschen verkündt und fürtragen worden sye/ ein Predig Heinrychen Bullingers/ zuo Zürych des 26. Maij gethon/ im jar 1555.* Zurich, 1555. (*HBBibl I*, no. 278)

Summa — *Summa Christenlicher Religion. Darinn uss dem wort Gottes/ one alles zancken und schaelten/ richtig und kurtz/ anzeigt wirt/ was einem yetlichen Christen notwendig sye zuo wüssen/ zuo glouben/ zuo thuon und zuo lassen/ ouch zuo lyden/ und saeligklich abzuosterben: in X. Artickel gestelt/ durch Heinrychen Bullingern.* Zurich, 1556. (*HBBibl I*, no. 283)

Apologetica expositio — *Apologetica expositio, qua ostenditur Tigurinae ecclesiae ministros nullum sequi dogma haereticum in Coena domini libellis quorundam acerbis opposita, & ad omnes synceram veritatem & sanctam pacem amantes Christi fideles placide scripta, per Heinrychum Bullingerum, Tigurinae ecclesiae ministrum.* Zurich, 1556. (*HBBibl I*, no. 315)

De fine seculi — *De fine seculi & iudicio venturo Domini nostri Iesu Christi, deque periculis nostri huius seculi corruptissimi gravissimis, & quo ratione fiant innoxia pijs, Oratione duae, Habitae in coetu cleri, per Heinrychum Bullingerum.* Basel, 1557. (*HBBibl I*, no. 320)

Ieremias — *Ieremias fidelissimus et laboriosissimus Dei*

propheta, expositus per Heinrychum Bullingerum, ministrum Ecclesiae Tigurinae, Concionibus CLXX. Zurich, 1575 (1557–1561). (*HBBibl I*, no. 361 [no. 357–360])

De coena   *De coena Domini sermo. In quo paucissimis, & tamen dilucide satis, totum Coenae dominicae negotium, ceu spectandum oculis subijcitur, Heinrycho Bullingero authore, recitatus in Concione sacra Tiguri 19. Decemb. 1557.* Zurich, 1558, (*HBBibl I*, no. 363)

Sermones   *Festorum dierum Domini et servatoris nostri Iesu Christi Sermones ecclesiastici, Heinrycho Bullingero authore.* Zurich, 1558. (*HBBibl I*, no. 369)

Catechesis   *Catechesis pro adultioribus scripta, de his potissimum capitibus. De Principijs religionis Christianae, scriptura sancta. De Deo vero, vivo et aeterno. De Foedere dei & vero dei cultu. De Lege dei & Decalogo mandatorum domini. De Fide Christiana, & Symbolo apostolico. De Invocatione dei & Oratione dominica, & De Sacramentis ecclesiae Christi, authore Heinrycho Bullingero.* Zurich, 1559. (*HBBibl I*, no. 377)

Bericht   *Bericht Wie die so von waegen unsers Herren Jesu Christi und sines heiligen Evangeliums/ jres glaubens ersuocht/ unnd mit allerley fragen versuocht werdend/ antworten und sich halten moegind: beschriben durch Heinrychen Bullingern.* Zurich, 1559. (*HBBibl I*, no. 386)

Ursprung   *Der Widertoeufferen ursprung/ fürgang/ Secten/ waesen/ fürnemen und gemeine jrer leer Artickel/ ouch jre gründ/ und warumb sy sich absünderind/ unnd ein eigne kirchen anrichtind/ mit widerlegung und antwort uff alle und yede jre gründ und artickel/ sampt Christenlichem bericht und vermanen dass sy jres irrthumbs und absünderens abstandind/ und sich mit der kirchen Christi vereinigind/ abgeteilt in VI. Buecher/ und beschriben durch Heinrychen Bullingern/ dienern der kirchen zuo Zürych.* Zurich, 1561 (1560). (*HBBibl I*, no. 395 [no. 394])

Lamentationum explicatio	*Threnorum seu Lamentationum beati Ieremiae Prophetae, brevis explicatio, authore Heinrycho Bullingero, Tigurinae Ecclesiae ministro.* Zurich, 1575 (1561). (*HBBibl I*, no. 420 [no. 419])
Fundamentum firmum	*Fundamentum firmum, cui tuto fidelis quivis inniti potest, hoc praesertim difficili seculo, quo dissidijs doctorumque adversarijs scriptis omnia conturbata sunt, positum ad institutionem & consolationem simplicium, per Heinrychum Bullingerum Tigurinae Ecclesiae ministrum.* Zurich, 1563. (*H B Bibl I*, no. 425)
Daniel	*Daniel sapientissimus Dei propheta, qui a vetustis polyhistor, id est, multiscius est dictus, expositus Homilijs LXVI, quibus non tam sensus Prophetae redditur, quam usus & fructus prophetiae ostenditur, adeoque omnibus in Ecclesia docentibus commonstratur, quomode perspicue, iusto ordine, & cum utilitate, populo Dei, hic Propheta praedicari possit, authore Heinrycho Bullingero Tigurinae Ecclesiae ministro.* Zurich, 1565. (*HBBibl I*, no. 428)
Epitome	*Epitome temporum et rerum ab orbe condito, ad primum usque annum Iothan regis Iudae: in qua praecipue attinguntur, quae pertinent ad sacras literas illustrandas, & ad veram antiquamque religionem & eius certudinem, progressum item, & mutationem, cognoscendam. Una cum VI. tabulis Chronicis, a temporibus Iothan usque ad excidium urbis Hierosolymorum deductis, potissimum pertinentibus ad Expositionem Danielis Prophetae, authore Heinrycho Bullingero Tigurinae ecclesiae ministro.* Zurich, 1565. (*HBBibl I*, no. 430)
Isaias	*Isaias excellentissimus Dei propheta, cuius testimoniis Christus ipse Dominus et eius apostoli creberrime usi leguntur, expositus Homilijs CXC. quibus non tam sensus Prophetae redditur, quam usus & fructus eius in Ecclesia Christi, ostenditur, authore Heinrycho Bullingero, Tigurinae Ecclesia ministro.* Zurich, 1567. (*HBBibl I*, no. 558)

Bekerung	*Von der Bekerung dess menschen zuo Gott und dem waaren Glouben/ VI. predigen/ gethon von Heinrychen Bullingeren/ dieneren der kyrchen Zürychüber das 8. Capitel der Geschichten der heiligen Apostlen/ von der Bekeerung dess Herren uss Morenland/ durch den heiligen Philippum.* Zurich, 1569/1570. (*H B Bibl I*, no. 561)
Refutatio	*Bullae Papisticae ante biennium contra Sereniss. Angliae, Franciae & Hyberniae Reginam Elizabetham, & contra inclytum Angliae regnum promulgatae, refutatio, Orthodoxaeque Reginae, & universi Regni Angliae defensio, Henrychi Bullingeri. S.* London, 1571. (*HBBibl I*, no. 562)
De scriptura II	*De scripturae sanctae praestantia, dignitate, excellentissimaque authoritate, perfectione, vel sufficientia, claritate item, facilitate, perspicuitateque, & vero earum usu, pijssima doctissimaque dissertatio.* Zurich, 1571. (*HBBibl I*, no. 565)
Vermanung	*Vermanung An alle Diener des worts Gottes und der kyrchen Jesu Christi/ dass sy jre spaenn/ die sy gegen andern habend und uebend/ hinlegen/ und in disen letsten verderbten gefaarlichen zyten/ der waelt einhaellig allein unnd einfaltig den waaren glouben in Jesum Christum/ und die besserung des laebens/ predigen woellind/ geschriben durch Heinrychen Bullingeren Dienern der kyrchen Christi zuo Zürych.* Zurich, 1572. (*HBBibl I*, no. 572)
Vervolgung	*Vervolgung. Von der schweren langwirigen vervolgung der Heiligen Christlichen Kirchen: ouch von den ursachen der vervolgung: und vermanung zur gedult/ und bestand/ sampt erzellung der raach unnd straaff Gottes/ wider die vervolger/ Verzeichnet durch Heinrychen Bullingern/ Dienern der Kirchen zuo Zürych.* Zurich, 1578 (1573). (*HBBibl I*, no. 576 [no. 575])
Uff siben Klagartickel	*Uff siben Klagartickel/ so diser zyt mit grosser ungestueme/ unwarheit und unbescheidenheit/ von etlichen unruewigen Scribenten/ geklagt werdend/ wider die Chris-*

tenlichen diener und Kyrchen/ die sy Zwinglisch schaeltend/ Heinrychen Bullingers/ der Kyrchen Zürych dieners/ kurtze/ waarhaffte/ nodtwendige und bescheidne verantwortung. Zurich, 1574. (*HBBibl I*, no. 584)

Responsio   *Heinrychi Bullingeri ad D. Iacobi Andreae suggestionem, responsio.* Zurich, 1575. (*HBBibl I*, no. 589)

4.   *Edited Works and Translations:*

Bromiley   Bromiley, G. W. (ed.). *Zwingli and Bullinger.* The Library of Christian Classics, vol. 24. Philadelphia: Westminster Press, 1953.

Diarium   Egli, Emil (ed.). *Heinrich Bullingers DIARIUM (Annales vitae) der Jahre 1504–1574. Zum 400. Geburtstag Bullingers am 18. Juli 1904.* Quellen zur Schweizerischen Reformationsgeschichte, vol. 2. Basel: Basler Buch- und Antiquariatshandlung vormals Adolf Geering, 1904.

Fast and Yoder   Fast, Heinold and John H. Yoder (ed. and trans.). "How to Deal with Anabaptists: An Unpublished Letter of Heinrich Bullinger." *MQR* 33 (1959), pp. 83–95.

Fuesslin   Fuesslin, Johann Conrad. *Beiträge zur Erläuterung der Kirchen- Reformationsgeschichte des Schweitzerlandes.* Volume 3. Zurich: Conrad Orell und Comp., 1747.

HBBW I   Gäbler, Ulrich and Endre Zsindely (eds.). *Heinrich Bullinger Werke, pt. 2: Briefwechsel, vol. 1.* Zurich: Theologischer Verlag, 1973.

PSD   Harding, Thomas (ed.). *The Decades of Henry Bullinger, Minister of the Church of Zurich.* 4 vols. Cambridge: Parker Society, 1849–1852.

Reformations-geschichte   Hottinger, J. J. and H. H. Vögeli (eds.). *Heinrich Bullingers Reformationsgeschichte nach dem Autographon.* 3 vols. Frauenfeld: Ch. Beyel, 1838–1840.

Schiess   Schiess, Traugott (ed.). *Bullingers Korrespondenz mit den Graubündnern.* 3 vols. Quellen zur Schweizer Geschichte, vols. 23–25. Basel: Basler Buch- und Antiquariat-

| | shandlung vormals Adolf Geering, 1904– 1906. |
| Simler | Simler, Johann Jacob. *Sammlung alter und neuer Urkunden zur Beleuchtung der Kirchengeschichte vornemlich der Schweizer-Landes.* Vol. 2. Zurich: J. K. Ziegler, 1763. |

B. *Other Sources:*

  1. *Sixteenth-Century Imprints:*

Ennarationum I (Bucer)	Bucer, Martin. *Ennarrationum in evangelia Matthaei, Marci, et Lucae, libri duo.* Vol. 1. Argentorati, 1527.
In Hoseam (Capito)	Capito, Wolfgang. *In Hoseam prophetam V. F. Capitonis commentarius.* Argentorati, 1528.
	Cellarius, Martin. *De operibus Dei.* Argentorati, 1525.
	Coverdale, Miles. *Biblia. The Bible, that is, the holy Scripture of the Olde and New Testament, faithfully and truly translated out of the Douche and Latyn into English.* 1535.
Explicatio	Erastus, Thomas. *Explicatio Gravissimae Questionis utrum Excommunicatio, quatenus Religionem intelligentes & amplexantes, a Sacramentorum usu, propter admissum facinus arcet; mandato nitatur Divino, an excogitata sit ab hominibus.* Pesclavii, 1589.
	Gomarus, Franciscus. *Opera theologica omnia.* Amstelodam, 1654.
Loci communes (Musculus)	Musculus, Wolfgang. *Loci communes theologiciae sacrae, ut sunt postremo recogniti & emendati.* Basel, 1599 (1559).
In Hieremiam (Oecolampadius)	Oecolampadius, Johannes. *In Hieremiam prophetam commentariorum libri tres Ioannis Oecolampadii.* Edited by Wolfgang Capito. Argentinae, 1533.
In Iesaiam (Oecolampadius)	Oecolampadius, Johannes. *In Iesaiam Prophetam Hypomnematon, hoc est, Commentariorium, Ioannis Oecolampadii. Libri VI.* Basel, 1525.
De substantia foederis gratuiti	Olevianus, Gaspar. *De substantia foederis gratuiti inter Deum et electos, itemque de mediis quibus ea ipsa substantia nobis com-*

municatur, libri duo praelectionibus Gasparis Oleviani excerpti. Geneva, 1585.

Romanos
(Olevianus)
Olevianus, Gaspar. *In epistolam D. Pauli apostoli ad Romanos notae, ex Gasparis Oleviani, concionibus excerptae, & a Theodoro Beza editae: cum praetatione eiusdem Bezae. Editio secunda ab ipso Authore recognita.* Geneva, 1584.

A Golden Chaine
Perkins, William. *A Golden Chaine, Or The Description of Theology, containing the order of the causes of Salvation and Damnation, according to Gods woord. A view of the order wherof, is to be seene in the Table annexed.* Written in Latin by William Perkins, and Translated by another. London, 1591.

Perkins, William. *De praedestinationis modo et ordine.* Cantabrigiae, 1598.

The newe
testament
Tyndale, William. *The newe Testament/ dylygently corrected and compared with the Greke by William Tyndale.* 1534.

Doctrinae
Christianae
Compendium
Ursinus, Zacharius. *Doctrinae Christianae Compendium: seu, Commentarii Catechetici, ex oro D. Zachariae Ursini, vere Theologe (qui Heydelbergae Catecheseos explicationem continuare solebat & iterare) diverso tempore ab ipsius discipulis excepti.* Cantabrigiensis, 1585.

Loci communes
(Vermigli)
Vermigli, Peter Martyr. *Petri Martyris Vermilii Locorum Communium Theologicorum exipsius scriptis sincere decerptorum, tomus primus in quatuor classes distinctus.* Basel, 1580.

2. *Edited Works and Translations:*

CO
Baum, Guilielmus, *et al.* (eds.). *Ioannes Calvini opera quae supersunt omnia.* 59 vols. Corpus Reformatorum, vols. 29–87. BrunsvigaeBerolini: C. A. Schwetschke et Filium: 1863–1900.

Correspondance
Bèze, Théodore de. *Correspondance.* Recueillie par Hippolyte Aubert, publiée par Fernand Aubert, Henri Meylan, Alain Dufour, Arnaud Tripet, Alexandre de Henseler, Claire Chimelli, Mario Turchetti. Vol. 1–9. Travaux d'Humanisme et Renais-

sance, vols. 40, 49, 61, 74, 96, 113, 136, 146, 164. Geneva: Librairie Droz S. A., 1960–1978.

CR   Bretschneider, C. G. and H. E. Bindseil (eds.). *Philippi Melanthonis opera quae supersunt omnia.* 28 vols. Brunsvigae: C. A. Schwetschke et filium, 1834–1860. Corpus Reformatorum, vols. 1–28.

Reid   Calvin, John. *Concerning the Eternal Pre-destination of God.* Trans. by J. K. S. Reid. London: James Clark & Co., 1961

Early Writings   Carr, Samuel (ed.). *Early Writings of John Hooper, D.D. Lord Bishop of Gloucester and Worcester, Martyr, 1555.* Cambridge: Parker Society, 1858.

CSEL   *Corpus scriptorum ecclesiasticorum latinorum.* Vindobonae: C. Geroldi filium, etc., 1866–

            Duffield, G. E. (ed.). *The Work of William Tyndale.* Philadelphia: Fortress Press, 1965.

Actensammlung   Egli, Emil (ed.). *Actensammlung zur Geschichte der Zürcher Reformation in den Jahren 1519–1533.* Zürich: J. Schabelitz, 1879.

ZW   Egli, Emil, *et al.* (eds.). *Huldreich Zwinglis sämtliche Werke.* 14 volumes. Berlin/ Leipzig/ Zürich: C. A. Schwetschke und Sohn, etc., 1905– CR, vols. 88–101.

Katechismen   Farner, Oskar (ed.). *Leo Jud. Katechismen.* Zürich: Max Neihans Verlag A G, 1955

            Fast, Heinold (ed.). *Quellen zur Geschichte der Täufer in der Schweiz. Zweiter Band: Ostschweiz.* Zürich: Theologischer Verlag, 1973.

Franklin   Franklin, Julian H. (trans. and ed.). *Constitutionalism and Resistance in the Sixteenth Century. Three Treatises by Hotman, Beza, and Mornay.* New York: Pegasus, 1969.

Gewirth II   Gewirth, Alan (trans.). *Marsilius of Padua: The Defender of Peace. Volume II: The Defensor pacis.* New York: Columbia University Press, 1956.

ZLW   Hinke, William John (ed.). *The Latin Works*

of Huldreich Zwingli: vol. 2. Philadelphia: Heidelberg Press, 1922.

UZSW   Jackson, Samuel Macauley (ed.). *Ulrich Zwingli (1484–1531): Selected Works.* Philadelphia: University of Pennsylvania Press, 1972 (1901).

Laski   Laski, Harold J. (ed.). *A Defense of Liberty against Tyrants. A Translation of the Vindiciae Contra Tyrannos by Junius Brutus.* New York: Burt Franklin, 1972 (1924).

WA   *D. Martin Luthers Werke. Kritische Gesamtausgabe.* 99 volumes. Weimar: Herman Böhlaus, 1883–

LW   *Luther's Works.* 50 volumes. St. Louis: Concordia Publishing House, 1955.

Manschreck   Manschreck, Clyde L. (ed. and trans.). *Melanchthon and Christian Doctrine. Loci Communes, 1555.* New York: Oxford University Press, 1965.

Battles   McNeill, John T. (ed.). *John Calvin: Institutes of the Christian Religion.* Translated by Ford Lewis Battles. The Library of Christian Classics, vols. 20 and 21. Philadelphia: The Westminster Press, 1960.

PL   Migne, J. P. (ed.). *Patrologiae cursus completus, Series Latina.* 221 vols. Paris: Migne, 1844–1864.

PG   Migne, J. P. (ed.). *Patrologiae cursus completus, Series Graeca.* 161 vols. Paris: Migne, 1857–1887

Pauck   Pauck, Wilhelm (ed.). *Melanchthon and Bucer.* The Library of Christian Classics, vol. 19. Philadelphia: The Westminster Press, 1969.

ANF   Roberts, Alexander and James Donaldson (eds.). *The Ante-Nicene Fathers. Translations of the Writings of the Fathers Down to A.D. 325. American Reprint of the Edinburgh Edition. Revised and Chronologically Arranged, with Brief Prefaces and Occasional Notes by Cleveland Coxe.* 10 vols. Buffalo: The Christian Literature Publishing Co., 1885–1926.

OL   Robinson, Hastings (ed.). *Original Letters*

	Relative to the English Reformation Written during the Reigns of King Henry VIII., King Edward VI., and Queen Mary: Chiefly from the Archives of Zurich. 2 vols. Cambridge: Parker Society, 1856, 1857.
Creeds	Schaff, Philip (ed.). *Bibliotheca Symbolica Ecclesiae Universalis: The Creeds of Christendom, with a History and Critical Notes.* 3 vols. 4th Edition. New York: Harper and Brothers, 1905.
PNF	Schaff, Philip (ed.). *A Select Library of the Nicene and Post Nicene Fathers of the Christian Church. First Series.* 14 vols. New York: The Christian Literature Publishing Co., 1886–1889.
PNF2	Schaff, Philip and Henry Wace (eds.). *A Select Library of Nicene and Post-Nicene Fathers of the Christian Church. Second Series.* 14 vols. New York, The Christian Literature Publishing Co., 1890–1900.
S	Schuler, M. and J. Schulthess. *Huldreich Zwinglis Werke.* 8 vols. Zurich, 1828–1842.
MBDS	Stupperich, Robert (ed.). *Martin Bucers Deutsche Schriften.* 4 vols. Gütersloh: Gerd Mohn, 1960ff.
	Veluanus, Ioannes Anastasius. *Der Leken Wechwyser* (1554). *BRN* 4, pp. 123–376.
	Veluanus, Ioannes Anastasius. *Vom Nachtmal Christi* (1557). *BRN* 4, pp. 389–451.
	Veluanus, Ioannes Anastasius. *Von dem waren leib Christi* (1561). *BRN* 4, pp. 461–486.
MBOL	Wendel, Francois (ed.). *Martini Buceri Opera Latina,* vol. 15: *De Regno Christi Libri Duo 1550.* Gütersloh: C. Bertelsmann Verlag, 1955.

III.   Secondary Works:

    A. *Articles:*

Bächtold, Hans Ulrich. "Bullinger und die Obrigkeit." *H-B 1975*, pp. 77–86.

Bainton, Roland H. "The Parable of the Tares as a Proof Text for Religious Liberty to the End of the Sixteenth Century." *CH* 1 (1932), pp. 67–89.

Baker, J. Wayne. "Das Datum von Bullingers 'Antwort an Johannes Burchard.' " *Zwingliana* 14 (1976), pp. 274–275.

Baker, J. Wayne. "Heinrich Bullinger and the Idea of Usury." *SCJ* 5:1 (1974), pp. 49–70.

Baker, J. Wayne. "In Defense of Magisterial Discipline: Bullinger's 'Tractatus de Excommunicatione' of 1568." *HBGesA I*, pp. 141–159.

Balke, Willem. "Calvijn en de gelijkenis van het onkruid in de tarwe." *Theologia Reformata* 20 (1977), pp. 38–54.

Baron, Hans. "Calvinist Republicanism and Its Historical Roots." *CH* 8 (1939), pp. 30–42.

Bender, Harold S. "The Pacifism of the Sixteenth Century Anabaptists." *MQR* 30 (1956), pp. 5–18.

Berg, Hans Georg vom. "Die 'Brüder vom gemeinsamen Leben' und die Stiftschule von St. Martin zu Emmerich: Zur Frage des Einflusses der devotio moderna auf den jungen Bullinger." *HBGesA I*, pp. 1–12.

Berg, Hans Georg vom. "Noch Einmal: Zur Datierung von Heinrich Bullingers 'Antwort an Johannes Burchard.' " *Zwingliana* 10 (1978), pp. 581–589.

Blanke, Fritz. "Zwingli mit Ambrosius Blarer im Gespräch." In *Der Konstanzer Reformator Ambrosius Blarer 1492–1564*, ed. B Moeller, pp. 81–86. Konstanz: Jan Thorbecke, 1964.

Burrell, S. A. "The Covenant Idea as a Revolutionary Symbol: Scotland, 1596–1637." *CH* 18 (1958), pp. 338–350.

Büsser, Fritz. "De prophetae officio: Eine Gedenkrede Bullingers auf Zwingli." In *Festgabe Leonhard von Muralt zum siebzigsten Geburtstag 17. Mai 1970, überreich von Freunden und Schülern*, pp. 245–257. Zurich: Verlag Berichthaus, 1970.

Clasen, Claus-Peter. "Executions of Anabaptists, 1525–1618: A Research Report." *MQR* 47 (1973), pp. 115–152.

Cottrell, Jack Warren. "Is Bullinger the Source for Zwingli's Doctrine of the Covenant?" *HBGesA I*, pp. 75–83.

Danner, Dan G. "Christopher Goodman and the English Protestant Tradition of Civil Disobedience." *SCJ* 8:3 (1977), pp. 61–73.

Diestel, Ludwig. "Studien zur Föderaltheologie." *Jahrbuch für Deutsche Theologie* 10 (1865), pp. 209–276.

Donnelly, John Patrick. "Italian Influences on the Development of Calvinist Scholasticism." *SCJ* 7:1 (1976), pp. 81–101.

Donnelly, John Patrick. "Three Disputed Vermigli Tracts." In *Essays Presented to Myron P. Gilmore, vol. 1: History*, ed. Sergio Bertelli and Gloria Ramakus, pp. 37–46. Florence: La Nuova Italia, 1978.

Dowey, Edward A. "Der theologische Aufbau des Zweiten Helvetischen Bekenntnisses." In *Glauben und Bekennen: Vierhundert Jahre Confessio Helvetica Posterior: Beiträge zu ihrer Geschichte und Theologie*, ed. Joachim Staedtke, pp. 205–234. Zurich: Zwingli Verlag, 1966.

Egli, Emil. "Zur Errinerung an Zwinglis Nachfolger Heinrich Bullinger geboren 1504: Akademischer Rathausvortrag am 7. Januar 1904." *Zwingliana* 1 (1904), pp. 419–437.

Emerson, Everett H. "Calvin and Covenant Theology." *CH* 25 (1956), pp. 136–144.

Estes, James. "Church Order and the Christian Magistrate according to Johannes Brenz." *ARG* 59 (1968), pp. 5–24.

Estes, James. "Johannes Brenz and the Problem of Ecclesiastical Discipline." *CH* 41 (1972), pp. 464–479.

Fast, Heinold. "On the Beginnings of Bernese Anabaptism." *MQR* 31 (1957), pp. 292–293.

Fischer, Joseph. "Die Einheit der beiden Testamente bei Laktanz, Viktorin von Pettau und deren Quellen." *Münchener Theologische Zeitschrift* 1 (1950), pp. 96–101.

Foley, W. M. "Marriage (Christian)." In *Encyclopaedia of Religion and Ethics* 8, pp. 433–443.

Gäbler, Ulrich. "Bullingers Vorlesung über das Johannesevangelium aus dem Jahre 1523." *HBGesA I*, pp. 13–27.

Gäbler, Ulrich. "Der junge Bullinger und Luther: Zum Erscheinen des ersten Bandes von Bullingers Briefwechsel." *Lutherjahrbuch* 42 (1975), pp. 131–140.

Gelzer, M. "Antistes." In *Die Religion in Geschichte und Gegenwart* 1, p. 459.

Goebel, Max. "Dr. Caspar Olevianus." *Mercersburg Review* 7 (1855), pp. 294–306.

Greaves, Richard L. "John Bunyan and Covenant Thought in the Seventeenth Century." *CH* 36 (1967), pp. 151–169.

Greaves, Richard L. "John Knox and the Covenant Tradition." *JEH* 24 (1973), pp. 23–32.

Greaves, Richard L. "The Origins and Early Development of English Covenant Thought." *The Historian* 31 (1968), pp. 21–35.

Greschat, Martin. "Der Bundesgedanke in der Theologie des späten Mittelalters." *Zeitschrift für Kirchengeschichte* 81 (1970), pp. 44–63.

Hagen, Kenneth. "From Testament to Covenant in the Early Sixteenth Century." *SCJ* 3:1 (1972), pp. 1–24.

Hausammann, Susi. "Anfragen zum Schriftverständnis des jungen Bullinger in Zusammenhang einer Interpretation von 'De scripturae negotio.' " *HBGesA I*, pp. 29–48.

Heer, Justuis [Emil Egli]. "H. Bullinger." *RTK* 3, pp. 536–549.

Henderson, G. D. "The Idea of the Covenant in Scotland." *Evangelical Quarterly* 27 (1955), pp. 2–14.

Herkenrath, Erland. "Bullingers Beziehungen zur politischen Führungsschicht Zürichs." *B-T 1975*, pp. 63–67.

Hoekema, Anthony A. "The Covenant of Grace in Calvin's Teaching." *Calvin Theological Journal* 2 (1967), pp. 133–161.

Hüssy, Hans. "Aus der Finanzgeschichte Zürichs in der Reformationszeit." *Zwingliana* 8 (1948), pp. 341–365.

Jacob, P. "Bund. IV. Föderaltheologie, dogmengeschichtlich." In *Die Religion in Geschichte und Gegenwart* 1, pp. 1518–1520.

Keep, David J. "Bullingers Defence of Queen Elizabeth." *HBGesA II*, pp. 231–241.

Keep, David J. "Heinrich Bullinger, 1504–1575: A Sketch of His Life and Work, with Special Reference to Recent Literature." *London Quarterly and Holborn Review* 191 (6th ser.): 35 (1966), pp. 135–146.

Kittelson, James M. "Marbach vs. Zanchi, The Resolution of Controversy in Late Reformation Strasbourg." *SCJ* 8:3 (1977), pp. 31–44.

Koch, Ernst. "Die Textüberlieferung der Confessio Helvetica Posterior und ihre Vorgeschichte." In *Glauben und Bekennen: Vierhundert Jahre Confessio Helvetica Posterior: Beiträge zu ihrer Geschichte und Theologie*, ed. Joachim Staedtke, pp. 13–40. Zurich: Zwingli Verlag, 1966.

Künzli, Edwin. "Zwingli als Ausleger des Alten Testamentes." *ZW* 14, pp. 871–899.

Le Bras, G. "La Doctrine du mariage chez les théologiens et les canonistes depuis l'an mille." In *Dictionnaire de théologie catholique* 9, pp. 2123–2317.

Lehmkuhl, Aug. "Divorce." In *The Catholic Encyclopedia* 5, pp. 54–69.

Lindsay, T. M. "The Covenant Theology." *The British and Foreign Evangelical Review* 28 (1879), pp. 521–538.

Locher, Gottfried W. "Die Prädestinationslehre Huldrych Zwinglis: Zum 70. Geburtstag Karl Barths." *TZ* 5 (1956), pp. 526–548.

Locher, Gottfried W. "The Shape of Zwingli's Theology: A Comparison with Luther and Calvin." *Pittsburgh Perspective* 8 (June 1967), pp. 5–26.

McClelland, Joseph C. "Covenant Theology: a Re-evaluation." *Canadian Journal of Theology* 3 (1957), pp. 182–187.

McClelland, Joseph C. "The Reformed Doctrine of Predestination according to Peter Martyr." *Scottish Journal of Theology* 8 (1955), pp. 255–274.

Maeder, Kurt. "Bullinger und die Synode." *B-T 1975*, pp. 69–76.

Marsden, George M. "Perry Miller's Rehabilitation of the Puritans: A Critique." *CH* 39 (1970), pp. 91–105.

Møller, Jens G. "The Beginnings of Puritan Covenant Theology." *JEH* 14 (1963), pp. 46–67.

Moltmann, Jürgen. "Föderaltheologie." In *Lexikon für Theologie und Kirche* 4, pp. 190–192.

Moltmann, Jürgen. "Prädestination und Heilsgeschichte bei Moyse Amyraut: Ein Beitrag zur Geschichte der reformierten Theologie zwischen Orthodoxie und Aufklärung." *Zeitschrift für Kirchengeschichte* 65 (1954), pp. 270–303.

Morf, Hans. "Obrigkeit und Kirche in Zürich bis zu Beginn der Reformation." *Zwingliana* 13 (1970), pp. 164–205.

Muralt, Leonhard von. "Zwingli als Socialpolitiker." *Zwingliana* 5 (1930), pp. 276–296.

Nevin, J. W. "Zacharius Ursinus." *Mercersburg Review* 3 (1851), pp. 490–512.

Oberman, Heiko A. "Facientibus quod in se est Deus non denegat gratiam: Robert Holcott O. P. and the Beginnings of Luther's Theology." *Harvard Theological Review* 55 (1962), pp. 317–342.

Oberman, Heiko A. "Wir sein pettler: Hoc est verum: Bund und Gnade in der Theologie des Mittelalters und der Reformation." *Zeitschrift für Kirchengeschichte* 78 (1967), pp. 232–252.

Oestreich, Gerhard. "Die Idee des religiösen Bundes und die Lehre vom Staatsvertrag." In *Geist und Gestalt des frühmodernen Staates: Ausgewählte Aufsätze*, pp. 157–178. Berlin: Dunker & Humblot, 1969.

Pauck, Wilhelm. "Martin Bucer's Conception of a Christian State." *The Princeton Theological Review* 26 (1928), pp. 80–88.

Potter, G. R. "Zurich and the Reformation in Switzerland." *History Today* 15 (1965), pp. 12–19.

Preus, J. Samuel. "Zwingli, Calvin and the Origin of Religion." *CH* 46 (1977), pp. 186–202.

Schulze, Wilhelm A. "Die Lehre Bullingers vom Zins." *ARG* 48 (1957), pp. 225–229.

Schweizer, P. "Die Behandlung der zürcherischen Klostergüter in der Reformationszeit." *Theologische Zeitschrift aus der Schweiz* 2 (1885), pp. 161–188.

Selinger, Joseph. "Moral and Canonical Aspect of Marriage." In *The Catholic Encyclopedia* 9, pp. 699–703.

Staedtke, Joachim. "Die Anfänge der Täufertums in Bern." *TZ* 11 (1955), pp. 75–78.

Staedtke, Joachim. "Bullingers Bedeutung für die protestantische Welt." *Zwingliana* 11 (1961), pp. 372–388.

Staedtke, Joachim. "Heinrich Bullingers Bemühungen um eine Reformation im Kanton Zug." *Zwingliana* 10 (1954), pp. 36–39.

Staedtke, Joachim. "Die Juden im historischen und theologischen Urteil des Schweizer Reformators Heinrich Bullinger." *Judaica* 11 (1955), pp. 236–256.

Staedtke, Joachim. "Der Zürcher Prädestinationsstreit von 1560." *Zwingliana* 9 (1953), pp. 536–546.

Torrance, James B. "Covenant or Contract? A Study of the Theological Background of Worship in Seventeenth-Century Scotland." *Scottish Journal of Theology* 23 (1970), pp. 51–76.

Trinterud, Leonard J. "The Origins of Puritanism." *CH* 20 (1951), pp. 37–57.

Tylenda, Joseph N. "Girolamo Zanchi and John Calvin." *Calvin Theological Journal* 10 (1975), pp. 101–141.

Usteri, Johann Martin. "Vertiefung der Zwinglischen Sakraments- und Tauflehre bei Bullinger." *Theologische Studien und Kritiken* 1 (Gotha 1883), pp. 730–758.

Villien, A. "Divorce." In *Dictionnaire de théologie catholique* 4, pp. 1455–1478.

Walton, Robert C. "Bullinger's Answer to John Jewel's Call for Help: Bullinger's Exposition of Matt. 16:18–19 (1571)." *HBGesA II*, pp. 243–256.

Walton, Robert C. "The Institutionalization of the Reformation at Zürich." *Zwingliana* 13 (1972), pp. 497–515.

Yoder, John H. "The Hermeneutics of the Anabaptists." *MQR* 41 (1967), pp. 291–308.

Zsindely, Endre. "Aus der Arbeit an der Bullinger-Edition: Zum Abendmahlsstreit zwischen Heinrich Bullinger und Johannes Burchard, 1525/1526." *Zwingliana* 13 (1972), pp. 473–480.

Zsindely, Endre. "Heinrich Bullingers Berufungen im Jahre 1531." *Zwingliana* 12 (1968), pp. 668–676.

B. *Books:*

Adam, Gottfried. *Der Streit um Prädestination im ausgehenden 16. Jahrhundert: Eine Untersuchung zu den Entwürfen von Samuel Huber und Aegidius Hunnius.* Beiträge zur Geschichte und Lehre der Reformierten Kirche, vol. 30. Neukirchen: Neukirchen Verlag des Erziehungsvereins, 1970.

Althaus, Paul. *The Ethics of Martin Luther.* Philadelphia: Fortress Press, 1972.

Armstrong, Brian G. *Calvinism and the Amyraut Heresy: Protestant Scholasticism and Humanism in Seventeenth-Century France.* Madison: University of Wisconsin Press, 1969.

Bangs, Carl. *Arminius, a Study in the Dutch Reformation.* Nashville, Tennessee: Abingdon Press, 1971.

Barth, Karl. *Church Dogmatics by Karl Barth, vol. 2: The Doctrine of God. 2d half-vol.* Edited by G. W. Bromiley and T. F. Torrance. Edinburgh: T. & T. Clark, 1957.

Bethune-Baker, J. F. *An Introduction to the Early History of Christian Doctrine to the Time of the Council of Chalcedon.* 2d ed. London: Methuen, 1920.

Bielér, André. *La penseé economique et sociale de Calvin.* Geneva: Librairie de l'Université, 1959.

Bizer, Ernst. *Studien zur Geschichte des Abendsmahlsstreits im 16. Jahrhundert.* Darmstadt: Wissenchaftliche Buchgesellschaft, 1972 (1940).

Blanke, Fritz. *Der junge Bullinger 1504–1531.* Zurich: Zwingli Verlag, 1942.

Bohatec, Joseph. *Budé und Calvin: Studien zur Gedankenwelt des französischen Frühhumanismus.* Graz: Verlag Hermann Böhlaus, 1950.

Bornkamm, Heinrich. *Luther and the Old Testament.* Translated by Eric W. and Ruth C. Gritsch, edited by Victor I. Gruhn. Philadelphia: Fortress Press, 1969.

Bouvier; André. *Henri Bullinger réformateur et conseiller oecuménique, le successeur de Zwingli, d'après sa correspondance avec les réformés et les humanistes de langue française.* Neuchatel: Delachaux & Niestlé, 1940.

Bray, John S. *Theodore Beza's Doctrine of Predestination.* Bibliotheca Humanistica & Reformatorica, vol. 12. Nieuwkoop: B. de Graaf, 1975.

Christoffel, R. H. *Bullinger und seine Gattin.* Zurich: Friederich Schulthess, 1875.

Clasen, Claus-Peter. *Anabaptism, a Social History, 1525–1618: Switzerland, Austria, Moravia, South and Central Germany.* Ithaca, New York: Cornell University Press, 1972.

Clebsch, William A. *England's Earliest Protestants 1520–1535.* New Haven, Connecticut: Yale University Press, 1964.

Collinson, Patrick. *The Elizabethan Puritan Movement.* London: Jonathan Cape, 1967.

Courvoisier, Jacques. *La Notion d'Eglise chez Bucer dans son développement historique.* Paris: Librairie Félix Alcan, 1933.

De Jong, Peter Y. *The Covenant Idea in New England Theology, 1620–1847.* Grand Rapids, Michigan: Wm. B. Eerdmans, 1945.

Dickens, A. G. *The English Reformation.* New York: Schocken Books, 1964.

Diestel, Ludwig. *Geschichte des Alten Testamentes in der christlichen Kirche.* Jena: Mauke's Verlag, 1869.

Donnelly, John Patrick. *Calvinism and Scholasticism in Vermigli's Doctrine of Grace.* Studies in Medieval and Reformation Thought, vol. 18. Leiden: E. J. Brill, 1976.

Dorner, I.A. History of Protestant Theology, vol. 2. Edinburgh: T & T Clark, 1870.

Dowey, Edward A., Jr. *The Knowledge of God in Calvin's Theology.* New York: Columbia University Press, 1965 (1952).

Dreske, Otto. *Zwingli und das Naturrecht.* Halle a.S.: A. Kaemmerer, 1911.

Farner, Alfred. *Die Lehre von Kirche und Staat bei Zwingli.* Tubingen: J.C.B. Mohr, 1930.

Fast, Heinold. *Heinrich Bullinger und die Täufer: Ein Beitrag zur Historiographie und Theologie im 16. Jahrhundert.* Schriftenreihe des Mennonitischen Geschichtsverein, no. 7. Weierhof (Pfalz): Mennonitischen Geschichtsverein, 1959.

Fraidl, Franz. *Die Exegese der siebzig Wochen Daniels in der alten und mittleren Zeit.* Graz: Verlag von Leuschner & Lubensky, 1883.

Franklin, Julian H. *Jean Bodin and the Rise of Absolutist Theory.* Cambridge: At the University Press, 1973.

Garrett, Christina Hollowell. *The Marian Exiles: A Study in the Origins of Elizabethan Puritanism.* Cambridge: At the University Press, 1938.

Gewirth, Alan. *Marsilius of Padua: The Defender of Peace, Vol. 1: Marsilius of Padua and Medieval Political Philosophy.* New York: Columbia University Press, 1951.

Gierke, Otto. *Political Theories of the Middle Age.* Translated by Frederic William Maitland. Cambridge: At the University Press, 1958.

Gooszen, M. A. *Heinrich Bullinger en de strijd over de Praedestinatie.* Rotterdam: D.J.P. Storm Lotz (H. van Tricht), 1909.

Gründler, Otto. *Die Gotteslehre Girolami Zanchis und ihre Bedeutung für seine Lehre von der Prädestination.* Neukirchen: Neukirchen Verlag des Erziehungsvereins, 1965.

Hagen, Kenneth. *A Theology of Testament in the Young Luther: The Lectures on Hebrews.* Studies in Medieval and Reformation Thought, vol. 12. Leiden: E. J. Brill, 1974.

Harkness, Georgia. *John Calvin: The Man and His Ethics.* New York/Nashville, Tennessee: Abingdon Press, 1958.

Harnack, Adolph. *History of Dogma.* Translated by Neil Buchanan. 7 vols. Boston: Little, Brown & Company, 1901.

Hausammann, Susi. *Römerbriefauslegung zwischen Humanismus und Reformation: Eine Studie zu Heinrich Bullingers Römerbriefvorlesung von 1525.* Studien zur Dogmengeschichte und Systematischen Theologie, vol. 27. Zurich/Stuttgart: Zwingli Verlag, 1970.

Headley, John M. *Luther's View of Church History.* New Haven, Connecticut: Yale University Press, 1963.

Heppe, Heinrich. *Geschichte des Pietismus und der Mystik in der reformirten Kirche, namentlich der Niederlande.* Leiden: E. J. Brill, 1879.

Heppe, Heinrich. *Reformed Dogmatics Set Out and Illustrated from the Sources.* Translated by G. T. Thomson, revised and edited by Ernst Bizer (foreword by Karl Barth). London: George Allen & Unwin, 1950.

Holl, Karl. *The Cultural Significance of the Reformation.* New York: Meridian Books, 1959.

Holl, Karl. *Gesammelte Aufsätze zur Kirchengeschichte, vol. 1: Luther.* Tubingen: J.C.B. Mohr (Paul Siebeck), 1948.

Hollweg, Walter. *Heinrich Bullingers Hausbuch: Eine Untersuchung über die Anfänge der reformierten Predigtliteratur.* Beiträge zur Geschichte und Lehre der Reformierten Kirche, vol. 8. Neukirchen: Neukirchen Verlag der Buchhandlung des Erziehungsvereins, 1956.

Hundeshagen, C. B. *Die Conflicte des Zwinglianismus, Lutherthums und Calvinismus in der Bernischen Landeskirche von 1532–1558.* Bern: Verlag von C. A. Jenni, Sohn, 1842.

Kittelson, James M. *Wolfgang Capito from Humanist to Reformer.* Studies in Medieval and Reformation Thought, vol. 17. Leiden: E. J. Brill, 1975.

Koch, Ernst. *Die Theologie der Confessio Helvetica Posterior.* Beiträge zur Geschichte und Lehre der Reformierten Kirche, vol. 27. Neukirchen: Neukirchen Verlag des Erziehungsvereins, 1968.

Koch, Karl. *Studium Pietatis: Martin Bucer als Ethiker.* Beiträge zur Geschichte und Lehre der Reformierten Kirche, vol. 14. Neukirchen: Neukirchen Verlag der Buchhandlung des Erziehungsvereins, 1962.

Köhler, Walther. *Zürcher Ehegericht und Genfer Konsistorium, vol. 1: Das Zürcher Ehegericht und seine Auswirkung in der deutschen Schweiz zur*

Zeit Zwinglis. Quellen und Abhandlungen zur Schweizerischen Reformationsgeschichte, vol. 7. Leipzig: M. Heinsius, 1932.

Köhler, Walther. *Zürcher Ehegericht und Genfer Konsistorium, vol. 2: Das
Ehe- und Sittengericht in den Süddeutschen Reichsstädten, dem Herzogtum Würtemberg und in Genf.* Quellen und Abhandlungen zur
Schweizerischen Reformationsgeschichte, vol. 10. Leipzig: M. Heinsius,
1942.

Korff, Emanuel Graf von. *Die Anfänge der Foederaltheologie und ihre
Ausgestaltung in Zürich und Holland.* Bonn: Emil Eisele, 1908.

Lang, A. *Der Evangelienkommentar Martin Butzers und die Grundzüge
seiner Theologie.* Studien zur Geschichte der Theologie und der Kirche,
vol. 2, pt. 2. Leipzig: Dieterich'sche Verlags-Buchhandlung, 1900.

Lau, Franz. *Luthers Lehre von den beiden Reichen.* Berlin: Lutherisches
Verlagshaus, 1953.

Ley, Roger. *Kirchenzucht bei Zwingli.* Quellen und Abhandlungen zur
Geschichte des schweizerischen Protestantismus, vol. 2. Zurich: Zwingli
Verlag, 1948.

Littell, Franklin Hamlin. *The Origins of Sectarian Protestantism: A Study
of the Anabaptist View of the Church.* New York: Macmillan, 1964.

Locher, Gottfried W. *Huldrych Zwingli in neuer Sicht: Zehn Beiträge zur
Theologie der Zürcher Reformation.* Zurich/Stuttgart: Zwingli Verlag,
1969.

Locher, Gottfried W. *Die Theologie Huldrych Zwinglis im Lichte seiner
Christologie, pt. 1: Die Gotteslehre.* Zurich: Zwingli Verlag, 1952.

McGiffert, Arthur Cushman. *A History of Christian Thought.* 2 vols. New
York: Charles Scribner's Sons, 1933.

Martin, Edward James. *A History of the Iconoclastic Controversy.*
London: Society for Promoting Christian Knowledge, n.d. (1930).

Maurer, Wilhelm. *Das Verhältnis des Staates zur Kirche nach humanis-
tischer Anschauung, vornehmlich bei Erasmus.* Giessen: Alfred Töpel-
mann, 1930

Meyer, Paul. *Zwinglis Sociallehren.* Linz a.D.: Oberösterreichisches
Verlags-Gesellschraft, 1921.

Miller, Perry. *Errand into the Wilderness.* New York: Harper & Row, 1964.

Miller, Perry. *The New England Mind: The Seventeenth Century.* New
York: Macmillan, 1939.

Moeller, Bernd. *Reichsstadt und Reformation.* Shriften des Vereins für
Reformationsgeschichte, vol. 18. Gütersloh: Gütersloher Verlagshaus
Gerd Mohn, 1962.

Moltmann, Jürgen. *Prädestination und Perseveranz: Geschichte und
Bedeutung der reformierten Lehre "de perseverantia sanctorum."*
Beiträge zur Geschichte und Lehre der Reformierten Kirche, vol. 12.
Neukirchen: Verlag der Buchhandlung des Erziehungsvereins, 1961.

Morf, Hans. *Zunftverfassung und Obrigkeit in Zürich von Waldman bis
Zwingli.* Zurich: Leeman, 1969.

Mörikofer, J. C. *J. J. Breitinger und Zürich: Ein Kulturbild aus der Zeit des dreizigjahrigen Krieges*. Leipzig: C. Hirzel, 1873.

Mozley, J. F. *Coverdale and His Bibles*. London: Lutterworth Press, 1953.

Murray, John. *The Covenant of Grace: A Biblico-Theological Study*. London: Tyndale Press, 1954.

Nelson, Benjamin N. *The Idea of Usury: From Tribal Brotherhood to Universal Otherhood*. 2d ed. Chicago: University of Chicago Press, 1969.

Noonan, John T., Jr. *The Scholastic Analysis of Usury*. Cambridge, Massachusetts: Harvard University Press, 1957.

Oberman, Heiko A. *Forerunners of the Reformation. The Shape of Late Medieval Thought. Illustrated by Key Documents*. New York: Holt, Rinehart & Winston, 1966.

Oberman, Heiko A. *The Harvest of Medieval Theology: Gabriel Biel and Late Medieval Nominalism*. Grand Rapids, Michigan: Wm. B. Eerdmans, 1967.

Ozment, Steven E. *Homo Spiritualis: A Comparative Study of the Anthropology of Johannes Tauler, Jean Gerson and Martin Luther (1509–16) in the Context of their Theological Thought*. Studies in Medieval and Reformation Thought, vol. 6. Leiden: E. J. Brill, 1969.

Ozment, Steven E. *The Reformation in the Cities: The Appeal of Protestantism to Sixteenth-Century Germany and Switzerland*. New Haven, Connecticut: Yale University Press, 1975.

Paulus, Nikolaus. *Protestantismus und Toleranz im 16. Jahrhundert*. Freiburg im Breisgau: Herdersche Verlagshandlung, 1911.

Pestalozzi, Carl. *Heinrich Bullinger: Leben und ausgewählte Schriften. Nach handschriftlichen und gleichzeitigen Quellen*. Leben und ausgewählte Schriften der Väter und Begründer der reformirten Kirche, vol. 5. Elberfeld: R. L. Friderichs, 1858.

Pestalozzi, Carl. *Das zürcherische Kirchengut in seiner Entwicklung zum Staatsgut*. Zurich: Buchdruckerei Berichthaus, 1903.

Pfister, Rudolf. *Kirchengeschichte der Schweiz, vol. 2: Von der Reformation bis zum Zweiten Villmerger Krieg*. Zurich: Theologischer Verlag, 1974.

Pollard, Alfred W. (ed.). *Records of the English Bible: The Documents Relating to the Translation and Publication of the Bible in English, 1525–1611*. Oxford: Oxford University Press, 1911.

Potter, G. R. *Zwingli*. Cambridge: At the University Press, 1976.

Preus, James Samuel. *From Shadow to Promise: Old Testament Interpretation from Augustine to Luther*. Cambridge, Massachusetts: The Belknap Press of Harvard University Press, 1969.

Ramp, Ernst. *Das Zinsproblem: Eine historische Untersuchung*. Zurich: Zwingli Verlag, 1949.

Rietschel, Ernst. *Das Problem der unsichtbar-sichtbaren Kirche bei Luther*, Leipzig: M. Heinsius, 1932.

Ritschl, Otto. *Dogmengeschichte des Protestantismus.* Göttingen: Vandenhoeck & Ruprecht, 1926.

Salmon, J. H. M. *The French Religious Wars in English Political Thought.* Oxford: The Clarendon Press of Oxford University Press, 1959.

Schmid, Heinrich. *Zwinglis Lehre von der göttlichen und menschlichen Gerechtigkeit.* Studien zur Dogmengeschichte und systematischen Theologie, vol. 12. Zurich: Zwingli Verlag, 1959.

Schrenk, Gottlob. *Gottesreich und Bund im älteren Protestantismus vornehmlich bei Johannes Cocceius, zugleich ein Beitrag zur Geschichte des Pietismus und der heilsgeschichtlichen Theologie.* Darmstadt: Wissenschaftliche Buchgesellschaft, 1967 (1923).

Schulthess-Rechberg, Gustav von. *Heinrich Bullinger, der Nachfolger Zwinglis.* Schriften des Vereins für Reformationsgeschichte, vol. 22. Halle: Verein für Reformationsgeschichte, 1904.

Schweizer, Alexander. *Die protestantischen Centraldogmen in ihrer Entwicklung innerhalb der reformierten Kirche, 1st half: Das 16. Jahrhundert.* Zurich: Orell, Fuessli, 1854.

Staedtke, Joachim. *Die Theologie des jungen Bullinger.* Studien zur Dogmengeschichte und systematischen Theologie, vol 16. Zurich: Zwingli Verlag, 1962.

Staedtke, Joachim (ed.). *Glauben und Bekennen: Vierhundert Jahre Confessio Helvetica Posterior: Beiträge zu ihrer Geschichte und Theologie.* Zurich: Zwingli Verlag, 1966.

Staehelin, Ernst. *Das theologische Lebenswerk Johannes Oekolampads.* Quellen und Forschungen zur Reformationsgeschichte, vol. 21. Leipzig: M. Heinsius, 1939.

Stayer, James M. *Anabaptists and the Sword.* Lawrence, Kansas: Coronado Press, 1972.

Sturm, Erdmann K. *Der junge Zacharias Ursin: Sein Weg vom Philippismus zum Calvinismus (1534–1562).* Beiträge zur Geschichte und Lehre der Reformierten Kirche, vol. 33. Neukirchen: Neukirchen Verlag, 1972.

Sudhoff, Karl. *C. Olevianus und Z. Ursinus: Leben und ausgewählte Schriften.* Leben und ausgewählte Schriften der Väter und Begründer der reformirten Kirche, vol. 8. Elberfeld: R. L. Friderichs, 1857.

TeSelle, Eugene. *Augustine the Theologian.* New York: Herder and Herder, 1970.

Thompson, Bard, et al. *Essays on the Heidelberg Catechism.* Philadelphia and Boston: United Church Press, 1963.

Troeltsch, Ernst. *The Social Teachings of the Christian Churches.* Translated by Olive Wyon. 2 vols. New York: Harper Torchbooks, 1969.

Van t'Hooft, Antonius Johannes. *De Theologie van Heinrich Bullinger in betrekking tot de Nederlandsche Reformatie.* Amsterdam: Is. de Hoogh, 1888.

Walker, Williston. *A History of the Christian Church.* New York: Charles Scribner's Sons, 1926.

Walser, Peter. *Die Prädestination bei Heinrich Bullinger im Zusammenhang mit seiner Gotteslehre.* Studien zur Dogmengeschichte und systematischen Theologie, vol. 11. Zurich: Zwingli Verlag, 1957.

Walton, Robert C. *Zwingli's Theocracy.* Toronto: University of Toronto Press, 1967.

Weisz, Leo. *Leo Jud: Ulrich Zwinglis Kampfgenosse 1482–1542.* Zurich: Zwingli Verlag, 1942.

Wendel, François. *Calvin: The Origins and Development of His Religious Thought.* Translated by Philip Mairet. London: Collins, 1963.

Wesel-Roth, Ruth. *Thomas Erastus: Ein Beitrag zur Geschichte der reformierten Kirche und zur Lehre von der Staatssouveränität.* Veroffentlichungen des Vereins für Kirchengeschichte in der evangelische Landeskirche Badens, vol. 15. Lahr/Baden: Moritz Schauenburg, 1954.

Williams, C. H. *William Tyndale.* London: Thomas Nelson, 1969.

Wolf, Hans Heinrich. *Die Einheit des Bundes: Das Verhältnis von Altem und Neuem Testament bei Calvin.* Beiträge zur Geschichte und Lehre der Reformierten Kirche, vol. 10. Neukirchen: Neukirchen Verlag der Buchhandlung des Erzeihungsvereins, 1958.

Yoder, John H. *Täufertum und Reformation im Gespräch: Dogmengeschichtliche Untersuchung der frühen Gespräche zwischen Schweizerischen Täufern und Reformatoren.* Basler Studien zur historischen und systematischen Theologie, vol. 13. Zurich: EVZ-Verlag, 1968.

Zürcher, Christoph. *Konrad Pellikans Wirken in Zürich 1526–1556.* Zürcher Beiträge zur Reformationsgeschichte, vol. 4. Zurich: Theologischer Verlag, 1975.

C. *Dissertations:*

Breward, I. "The Life and Theology of William Perkins, 1558–1602." Ph.D. dissertation, University of Manchester, 1963.

Cottrell, Jack Warren. "Covenant and Baptism in the Theology of Huldreich Zwingli." Th.D. dissertation, Princeton Theological Seminary, 1971.

McCoy, Charles Sherwood. "The Covenant Theology of Johannes Cocceius." Ph.D. dissertation, Yale University, 1956.

West, W. M. S. "John Hooper and the Origins of Puritanism." Th. D. dissertation, Universität Zürich, 1955.

Zuck, Lowell H. "Anabaptist Revolution Through the Covenant in Sixteenth Century Continental Protestantism." Ph.D. dissertation, Yale University, 1955.

Index

Adlischwyler, Anna, xvi, 11, 18, 218
Agricola, xiii
Aistulf, King of the Lombards, 96
Ambrose, Bishop of Milan, xiv, 94, 101
Ames, William: on testament and covenant, 166, 198
Amyraut, Moïse, 252; and Bullinger, 165; and the covenant, 165, 214; and Reformed scholasticism, 214
Anabaptists, xv-xvi, xvii, xxi, 5, 22, 48, 224; and baptism, 144-145; and the church, 145-146, 154; and the covenant, 1, 141-142, 162-163, 221; and the oath, 156-158; and discipline, 146-163 *passim*; and the magistracy, 146-163 *passim*; and pacifism, 154-156; and Scripture, 142-144, 162; subversive nature of, 154-158; and usury, 130, 132, 136
Antinomianism, 195, 214
Antistes, xvii, 219
Aquinas, Thomas, 5, 129, 242
Aristotle, xiii, and usury, 129
Arminianism, 29, 47, 200, 205, 207, 213, 214
Arminius, James, 205, 212-213
Armstrong, Brian G.: on Amyraut and the covenant, 214; on Cameron and the covenant, 214
Athanasius, xiv
Augustine, 5, 22, 23, 38, 44, 50, 101, 227; Bullinger and, 19-20, 234; on testament and covenant, 19-20

Bainton, Roland, 252
Barth, Karl, 264
Basel, xvii, 34, 147
Baxter, Richard: and Bullinger, 166; on the covenant, 166
Berengar of Tours, 97

Berg, Hans Georg vom, 218
Berkhof, Hendrikus, 260
Bern, xvii, 34
Beza, Theodore, xxiii; and Olevianus, 203; and Snecanus, 213; and Ursinus, 203
Bibliander, Theodore, 27; and Bullinger, 40; on predestination, 39-41; and Vermigli, 40-41
Biel, Gabriel, 23-24
Bielér, André, 245
Blanke, Fritz, 217, 218
Blarer, Ambrosius, xvi, 166
Bodin, Jean, 171; and Bullinger, 172-173, 255; theory of sovereignty, 172-173. Works: *Methodus ad facilem historiarum cognitionem*, 172; *Les six livres de la république*, 173
Bolsec, Jerome, 27, 35, 49, 196-198, 260; and Bullinger, 34-35; on predestination, 34, 39
Boniface III, Pope, 95
Boniface VIII, Pope, 99
Bornkamm, Heinrich: on Luther on law and gospel, 182
Breitinger, Johann Jacob, 29, 44, 48
Bremgarten, xii, xvi, xvii
Brenz, Johannes, xxi, 44
Bromiley, G. W., 218
Bucer, Martin, xvi, xxv, 25, 44, 252, 254; and Bullinger, 190-191; on covenant and testament, 181, 189-191; on discipline, 168; on divorce, 128, 245; on magistracy and church, 168; and Oecolampadius, 191; and Zwingli, 190-191. Works: *De regno Christi*, 168; *Grund und Ursach*, 190
Bullinger, Anna. *See* Anna Adlischwyler
Bullinger, Heinrich: advice to magistrates at Zurich, 170-171; and the Anabap-

293